IRISH
COUNTRY
FURNITURE
1700–1950

IRISH COUNTRY FURNITURE 1700–1950

Claudia Kinmonth

1993
Yale University Press
New Haven & London

Dedicated to Michael,
and in memory of my father

Endpapers: The pierced facia board of a county Tipperary dresser with hearts, shamrocks and flying wheel motifs. Mid nineteenth century. (Courtesy of Victor Mitchell.)

Frontispiece: Built-in kitchen dresser, from a farmhouse near Ballydehob, county Cork. Late nineteenth century.

Set in Linotron Caledonia by Best-set Typesetter Ltd, Hong Kong
Printed and bound by CS Graphics PTE Ltd, Singapore.

ISBN 0 300 05574 9
Library of Congress Catalog Card Number 93 60784

Contents

Preface

This book evolved from work which I began on the Royal College of Art/Victoria and Albert Museum joint postgraduate course. My approach to the objects under discussion has inevitably been coloured by my practical woodworking background and a firm belief that furniture forms are fundamentally influenced by materials and techniques. My use of paintings to illustrate Irish furniture, influenced by the work of Peter Thornton, would have been more extensive, but paintings of the less affluent Irish rural interiors, with which we are concerned, are comparatively rare.

Ireland is an extraordinary place for an historian to work. Not only do many ancient traditions live on, especially amongst the most senior members of the population, but there is an enthusiastic interest in history combined with a unique sense of hospitality. The rate of change in rural Ireland during the last half of the twentieth century is now accelerating. It was with a sense of urgency that I first embarked on fieldwork, knocking on farmhouse doors and enquiring about old furniture. Most pieces that survive are owned by an admirably stubborn breed of people who have resisted persistant offers of cash from tenacious dealers. Recently such dealers have begun to appear complete with suites of modern upholstered furniture with which to barter. Much of the most elaborate examples of Irish furniture have already been stripped of their paintwork and exported, via this network, since the 1960s. My familiarity with the boldly painted farmhouse interiors has made stripped pine appear uncomfortably naked in comparison.

Furniture collections from Irish museums have on the whole only been thoroughly documented in recent decades, which is why my fieldwork was first undertaken. Research in some counties produced richer results than in others. Consequently the material is unevenly spread across the four provinces. There are many fundamental regional differences between furniture traditions, but for ease of reference the book has been laid out typologically, explaining furniture by particular types and their evolution, rather than by area. The introductory sections examine some of the fundamental influences on Irish furniture; vernacular architecture, timber, types of furniture makers and the way in which it was painted. Terms for furniture vary greatly throughout Ireland, but I have rejected the many fictitious labels invented by the antique trade for their own convenience. As with any pioneering work, new systems of categorisation have had to be worked out which may not suit everybody.

The dates outlined in the title, 1700–1950, are guidelines. Most of the underlying furniture traditions (and some actual examples), can now be seen to date from long before 1700. Although the majority of surviving examples of furniture date from the nineteenth century, the myth that none survives from before the famine of the 1840s, can now be dispelled. Precise dating of such painted furniture, on grounds of condition or style, is unreliable and therefore has been deliberately avoided, except where there is firm provenance. The mid twentieth-century cut-off point marks an approximate period at which traditional furniture making was becoming increasingly influenced by modernisation. This was apparent not only in terms of materials and techniques, but as rural houses became equipped with electricity and running water, the traditional layout and purpose of the rural home began to change. The widespread move from the traditional house into the modern bungalow brought with it a shifting away from the focal point of the hearth and towards the television, with inevitable changes of attitude. Likewise the widespread rejection of the working horse in favour of tractors and cars, literally widened peoples horizons and changed their outlook and sense of time. Grants for improvements both on the farm and in the home have accelerated such inevitable changes, and made life easier, but they have been provided with scant regard for aesthetics and the preservation of tradition, let alone traditional furniture. For some, the rejection of their old furniture has been a necessary part of the banishment of hard times.

Furniture historians have traditionally concentrated on the designer as a hero; upon attribution, precise dating of 'fine' (yet often anonymous) craftmanship, of furniture belonging to a fortunate elite. In contrast, this study focuses on the various customs and behaviour surrounding the objects which belonged to the majority of the Irish population. Where some were too impoverished to own furniture, it looks at how they managed without it, as well as the interaction of people with their environment and their means of survival. The emphasis is placed upon materials, techniques and makers; within this framework there emerges a functionalism and purity which has no heroes.

ACKNOWLEDGEMENTS

Public collections in Ireland contain relatively little properly documented country made or vernacular furniture. Where it is on public display, it is usually as part of a reconstructed traditional house, with the notable exception of the Irish Agricultural Museum, Wexford, which houses a study collection of over eighty pieces of furniture, arranged according to region. I am particularly grateful for the enthusiastic assistance of that collection's curator, Dr Austin O'Sullivan, as well to Countess Bernstorff, the chair of the Irish Country Furniture Society, which has gathered a fine display of furniture which would otherwise have been lost through exportation.

I am also indebted to Professor Christopher Frayling, whose sketch of a *súgán* chair first sparked my interest in Irish vernacular furniture as my thesis subject for the Royal College of Art/Victoria and Albert Museum M.A. course. Financial assistance, was generously provided through the Royal College by the Basil Taylor Award and by Fleur Cowles (via her 'Award for Excellence'), also by the Irish Agricultural Museum and the Allied Irish Bank, who together, made it possible to continue the research.

The lack of documented furniture in Irish museums led to research into private houses throughout Ireland, not only into furniture, but also into paintings and manuscripts. Therefore, this book depended more than most on the goodwill and hospitality of countless individuals throughout rural Ireland, who allowed their furniture to be studied and photographed. Many of these people also provided oral history, the value of which is too often overlooked as it breathes life into the study of objects and documents. Most owners understandably prefer to remain anonymous, therefore the captions to my photographs mention no names. They are too numerous to mention individually but I am indebted to them all. The following is a list of only a few people to whom I am particularly grateful; Dominic Berridge, the late Danny Burke, the Burns family, Sally and Colin Barnes, Philomena Callinan, Michael Casey ('The Seanachie'). John Clancy (The Derragarra Inn), Eric Connor, James Conway, Diarmuid Donovan, Mike and Jo Dwyer, Glyn Ewing Evans, Nicholas Furlong (who published my appeals for rare furniture), Dr Muriel Gahan and Julia Galvin. The Knight of Glin has been particularly helpful in the search for suitable paintings, as well as furniture. More invaluable help was provided by John and Annie Gallagher, Maura Harkin, the Hawkins family, The Revd Brendan Haythornthwaite, Kitty and Patrick Hennessy, Séamus Kirwan, Nell and Ned Leahy, John Lowday, Nicholas Loughnan, the McDermott family (who kindly took me on their milk delivery round, while in county Donegal), Harry McDowell, Victor Mee, Victor Mitchell, Elizabeth Mosse, Meriel Murdoch, Frank Murphy, Dr Harman Murtagh, Al O'Dea, Mary and Ted O'Driscoll, Barry O'Reilly, John O'Sullivan, the O'Sullivan family, Matt O'Sullivan, Hanna and Bertie Plant, Ellen Prendergast, Patrick Purcell, the Richardson family, Charles, Michael and Tom Robinson, Patrick Scott, David Shaw-Smith, Jo Sheehy, Nathalie Stutchbury and the members of the Union Hall Ladies Club, Christie and Noirin Sullivan, John Surlis, Peter Thornton, Father Walsh, Eileen Wilson, Eddie Whitty, Bill Wolfe and Ian and Linney Wright.

I am indebted to Aengus O'Carroll (Cuala Press) and Anne Yeats for generously allowing me to reproduce the drawings by Jack B. Yeats. Rosemary ffolliott's devotion to the publication of many rare Irish inventories in *The Irish Ancestor*, and her enthusiastic correspondence on the subject, have been of immeasurable assistance. Thanks are due also to my Irish relatives: especially Dorothy Cross and the Kearney family, for their endless hospitality during research in Dublin.

Staff from the following Irish organisations have generously assisted my work in their collections, provided information and illustrative material and entered into correspondence. I am grateful to those in charge for permitting the reproduction of illustrations and the quotation from manuscripts. Catherine McCullough, Roger Weatherup (Armagh County Museum), Belfast Central Library, Ralph Keely (Borde Fáilte), Tom Sheedy and Dermot Hurley (Bunratty Folk Park, Shannon Heritage Ltd), County Carlow Museum, Therese O'Mahony (Ceim Hill Museum), Peter Murray (Crawford Municipal Art Gallery). Professor Bo Almqvist, Dr Patricia Lysaght (for help with the Glossary), Áine O'Neill and Míceál Ross (all from the Department of Irish Folklore, University College Dublin), Father Brendan Kellegher (Edmund Rice Museum), Fintan Murphy (Enniscorthy County Museum), Peter Walsh (Guinnness Hop Store), Professor R.H. Buchanan and Angélique Day (Institute of Irish Studies, Queen's University), The Irish Agricultural Museum, The Irish Architectural Archive, Nicholas Carolan (Irish Traditional Music Archive), John Gallagher (Knock Folk Museum), Elaine Flanagan (Lisburn Museum), Patrick Long (Monaghan County Museum), The National Gallery of Ireland, Dr Patricia Donlon and Elizabeth Kirwan who was particularly helpful with illustrations (both from the National Library) of Ireland), Dr Anne O'Dowd, Valerie Dowling and Raghnall O'Floinn (National Museum of Ireland), Mrs Faris (The Pighouse Collection), Dr A.P.W. Malcomson (Public Records Office of Northern Ireland), Roscrea Heritage Centre, the J.M. Synge Trustees and The Board of Trinity College Dublin, Dr Frederick Aalen, Professor Louis M. Cullen, Professor Anne Crookshank, Dr Edward McParland, Dr William Vaughan (all of Trinity College, Dublin), Dr P. Mowat (The Ulster American Folk Park), Timothy O'Neill (University College, Dublin), the University of Ulster Library (for reference to the late P.D. Conlan's thesis). The enthusiastic support of the staff of the Ulster Folk and Transport Museum made my work there pure pleasure; Dr Jonathan Bell, especially Fionnuala Carragher, Dr William Crawford, Dr Alan Gailey (Director, who edited the section on architecture), Dr Caroline Macafee (who provided expert advice on the Glossary), Megan MacManus and Sally Skillings all responded swiftly and uncomplainingly to my flow of enquiries. Dr Vivienne Pollock of The Ulster Museum, was also particularly helpful with the locating and dating of early photographs by R.J. Welch.

I would also like to thank some of the many organisations and individuals beyond Ireland who gave their time and expertise during the preparation of the book;

James Ayres (Director of the John Judkin Memorial), Olivia Elton Barratt, Patrick Cappelli, Leslie Charteris, Mrs Sarah (née Flaherty) Connor, Dr Caroline Earwood (who advised on wooden vessels), Christopher Gilbert, Judy Goldhill (back flap photo), Marianna Kennedy, Margie Kinmonth, John Lowday, the Library of the National Maritime Museum, Sarah Medlam (Victoria and Albert Museum, formerly of the Bowes Museum), John Morley, Gabriel Olive, Walter Peddle, the Pyms Gallery, R. Ross Noble (The Highland Folk Museum, Kingussie) and the staff of the Welsh Folk Museum.

Thanks are also due to Paula Cox, who helped with the printing of my black-and-white photographs, and the choice of illustrations. Some of the early illustrations came from The British Library and Newspaper Library, Tim Imrie-Tait, The London Library, Ian MacKenzie of Sotheby's, London and the National Gallery of Art, Washington D.C. and The Witt Library (Courtauld Institute of Art).

Many thanks are due to Kathleen Kinmonth Warren, who meticulously weeded out solecisms from the text. Dr William Crawford (Keeper of the Department of Material Culture, the Ulster Folk and Transport Museum) and Dr Kevin Whelan (Newman Scholar, University College, Dublin), both suggested sources and provided expert historical criticism and comments on parts of the text, although any shortcomings are entirely my own.

I am also grateful to John Nicoll and Mary Carruthers of Yale University Press for their expert guidance and careful editing of the text.

I am indebted to my late father (from county Clare) for my Irish upbringing and for instilling a deep appreciation of Irish culture. Above all I am grateful to my husband Michael Duerden, who accompanied me on innumerable expeditions throughout Ireland and has been unfailingly supportive.

All photographs and line drawings are the author's except where stated otherwise. The following abbreviations have been used in the captions: D.I.F. (Department of Irish Folklore, University College, Dublin); N.L.I. (National Library of Ireland); N.M.I. (National Museum of Ireland); and U.F.T.M. (Ulster Folk and Transport Museum). Dimensions of furniture are given where possible, in inches.

Introduction

The range of furniture illustrated and described in this volume, is loosely entitled 'country', in order to emphasise its essentially rural origins. Irish country or alternatively vernacular furniture is primarily local, indigenous and often idiomatic. Other authors describing similar furniture elsewhere have used headings such as 'common', 'regional', or 'provincial', none of which do justice to the variety under discussion here. The following range of furniture was made or owned primarily by the less affluent sections of the rural Irish community, who made up the great majority of the population. They comprised people such as tradesmen, farmers, fishermen, weavers and spinners, labourers, cottiers and itinerants; from those struggling in conditions of extreme hardship, up to the manufacturing classes and so called 'strong farmers' who could afford to employ servants. Distinction has been made in the text, where possible, between these different strata of society but any research encompassing the study of surviving objects as part of its evidence, is unlikely to be able to pinpoint the status of each original owner.

This rurally made furniture, from all over Ireland, is not the product of any organised centre of mass production, but rather represents mainly individual and 'one-off' examples, often built within the home to satisfy a range of basic needs. It was made not only by a huge range of woodworkers but frequently by the householders themselves, and it was they who were accustomed to twisting the rope for new seats for their 'súgán chairs' and repainting their furniture. The range encompasses examples as diverse as chairs made entirely out of straw, furniture fashioned from driftwood or recycled from butter boxes, to formidable four-poster beds.

The majority of examples illustrated date from the nineteenth to the mid twentieth century, with a few notable exceptions from the eighteenth century. The centuries of turmoil and upheaval which have characterised Irish history have contributed to the destruction of what would undoubtedly have been a fascinating array of seventeenth- and eighteenth-century furniture. During this final quarter of the twentieth century rises in living standards, modernisation and even in many households marriage, aided by the relentless activities of the antique trade, have resulted in vernacular furniture becoming a rarity in the houses for which it was built. Research into a rich mixture of early sources, however, including paintings and engravings, government reports, poetry, diaries and inevitably inventories, has helped to assemble the missing pieces of the furniture jigsaw of the eighteenth century. It can be seen from that evidence that much of what existed then went on being made without radical change during the nineteenth century, and has survived to be examined now.

The dramatic rise in population which preceded the great famine of the 1840s, made its effects even more devastating. Although there had been many periods of famine throughout the eighteenth and nineteenth centuries due to crop failure, this one was especially devastating because it endured for several successive years. It affected every county of Ireland to some extent, but the west and south-west suffered particularly badly. The reason for the famine was a fungal growth which caused the potatoes, the staple diet of the majority of the population, to rot in the ground. Starvation and disease on an unprecedented scale resulted; over two million people either emigrated or died. In the face of such hardship it is hardly surprising that material possessions lost their significance, except as fuel for the fire or as currency to gain food.

The gradual consolidation of the many previously subdivided landholdings following the great famine, contributed to the emergence of a new class of comparatively wealthy farmers. Short leases and high rents were still a common problem for those who worked the land under these 'strong farmers'. Evictions of tenants who were unable to pay the rent, which had occurred even during the great famine, continued throughout the nineteenth century. The activities of the Land League, which helped establish tenants' rights and fair rents, included putting pressure on unfair land agents like the infamous Captain Boycott, whose name consequently passed into the English language. By 1891, the formation of the Congested Districts Board began to alleviate the misery of the poorest sectors of the population in the west. A series of government acts secured the rights of tenants to buy their farms, resulting in the gradual emergence of a new class of owner-occupiers.

The dawn of the twentieth century saw the introduction of many new materials such as plywood and glass into the woodworkers' repertoire. The products of factories which were strategically located close to centres of communication began to compete with locally made vernacular furniture. By the 1950s, sweeping changes were infringing upon the rural majority's traditional way of life. The replacement of horses by cars and tractors had already forced tradesmen such as the wheelwright and blacksmith to adapt their workshops to garages and their traditional skills to those of a mechanic. The new supply of electricity and the provision of mains water began to alter the appearance and priorities of the farm kitchen dramatically. Improvements in transport and communication, such as the introduction of television, combined with social pressure, led to the abandonment for many of the old ways. Rates of change varied enormously between regions and households and can be measured visibly by the number of new bungalows in the Irish landscape. By listening to the traditional woodworkers themselves, now in old age, much can still be learnt. To survive, they had to be able to make everything that people needed, from the cradle to the grave. Periods of economic depression between the First and Second World Wars meant that many woodworkers were spending more time mending than making, keeping old things going rather than building new. In order to put such twentieth-century information into perspective, it helps to examine the evidence concerning furniture from the years preceding the great famine.

Some quite poor people liked to dress smartly, and were often accused by outsiders of dressing 'above their station'.[1] Parlour furniture, including imported clocks, *chaises longues*, mass-produced mahogany chairs and tables, was comparable to smart clothing as a display of wealth. It was a luxury that only a minority could afford; it was seldom used, but like fine clothing, gave a grand impression. However, amongst the 'lowest classes' of county Tyrone in the 1820s, the Ordnance Survey reporters noticed that 'more money is expended on their backs than on their dwellings' and personal appearance was given a higher priority than domestic comforts.[2] Even if the working classes chose not to spend money on stylish furniture, they evidently took care of what they had. When the reporters explored the interiors of farmhouses in Island Magee, county Antrim, they noted that 'Presses, armchairs and chests of massive oak, bearing dates of the 17th century, some as old as 1659, are numerous. They are proud of them as having been handed down from their forefathers.'[3] In the absence of surviving examples of such 'black oak' carved chairs and 'curiously carved chests', it seems likely that such seventeenth-century furniture was copied by subsequent makers. This would help explain the persistence of such medieval features as pegged joints, through-wedged tenons and the 'sledge foot' which supported the bases of dressers and settles from the northern counties of Ireland and was made well into the twentieth century.

The prototypes for vernacular furniture have also come to light from the tower houses and mansions of the gentry from the seventeenth and eighteenth centuries. The strongest links between common furniture and that of the servants' quarters and kitchens of these so-called 'big houses' can be traced through inventories from the 1600s. In 1640, a wealthy Waterford merchant had a 'Settle bedd or bench bedd' amongst his furniture.[4] Subsequently settle beds and coops for confining fowl were mentioned regularly amongst other inventories. It is no coincidence that the local carpenters who would have been employed to build the functional furniture for the big house, adapted some of these most ingenious designs for their own homes.

The widespread use of four-poster (or tester) beds cannot simply be attributed to vanity. Their presence in some of the poorest Irish 'cabins' in the nineteenth century stemmed from their original medieval function of excluding draughts and cold while providing privacy, rather than from fashionable caprice. Instead of being hung with expensive textiles the posts had curtains of plaited straw, and were built into corners or against walls to save materials. Other examples of 'canopy' beds with their distinctive arched pine covers, could be compared to the shapes of the fashionable upholstered 'tent' beds of the early 1800s. The vernacular canopy bed may well have been fashionable within its own level of rural society. However, its primary function was to compensate for the shortcomings of the thatched house: to keep the sleepers warm while its paper-lined interior excluded draughts, drips, dust and insects liable to fall from a leaky thatched roof. At the same time, a great many people up to the nineteenth century suffered from absolute poverty, and families, having little or no furniture slept communally 'in stradogue': huddled on straw before the fire (fig. 240).

In terms of furniture style, the rate of change in rural Ireland was much slower (due to poverty) than in England.[5] Even the words used to describe such things as 'tester' beds and 'presses' (rather than cupboards) demonstrate the persistance of ancient vernacular forms. In parts of Munster carpenters continued to build peculiar hooked mantelpieces called 'clevies', which had been copied faithfully from earlier wooden spit racks, long after the spits themselves had been lost to memory. The dug-out chair, laboriously gouged and hewn from a tree trunk, is often cited as one of the first steps in the evolution of chairmaking, yet at least one example survives which was made as recently as the first half of this century (fig. 79). The singularly Irish 'mether', a square-topped wooden drinking vessel, is another example of an object whose design and use endured from early historic times into the nineteenth century (fig. 319).

Idiosyncracies in furniture, like variations in patterns of speech, differed greatly and distinctively between one region, or maker and the next. Fieldwork has also highlighted variations in furniture design between different classes of householders as well as between areas and trades of makers. One maker's work looks quite different from the next, even where they have produced the same typically local design. This is partly due to their different tool kits: rural woodworkers often made their own, sometimes with some help from the blacksmith. The individually shaped moulding planes cut a familiar yet anonymous signature along a cornice, leaving a unique profile. Such differences can also be explained by the wide range of skills encompassed by rural woodworkers. Specialists in furniture making were exceptional until this century because few rural communities could generate enough demand to make such specialisation worthwhile. Instead, local vernacular furniture was made by a range of people whenever the opportunity arose, from the hedge carpenter, to the boatbuilder, wheelwright or thatcher.

Surviving examples of furniture with purposefully placed signatures are very rare in Ireland (fig. 62). This is partly due to the fact that if they did exist, they have been invariably engulfed with layer upon layer of paint. Occasionally when an example is stripped in a tank of caustic soda, pencil marks are revealed (which remain unaffected) made by someone about to paint, or a name and date, but by this time the object has usually been transported far from its place of origin. Straw and basketwork furniture is even more difficult to attribute: it is not only unsigned but its makers were frequently itinerant.

Rural isolation also contributed to distinct regional variation. Travelling writers such as Dr Pococke complained of impassable boggy roads in the north-west, inaccurate maps in county Louth and filthy narrow streets in Cork city in 1752.[6] The poet Keats was scornful about the 'sadan' chair carried by two 'ragged tattered Girls' near Belfast in 1818, but they were also for hire in Dublin, Cork and Waterford well into the nineteenth century.[7] Some woodworkers travelled considerable distances to markets in order to sell the furniture they made. Makers of straw, wickerwork and new furniture, gathered at Lisburn market, county Antrim, and travelled from up to 18 miles away. There was considerable trade done in secondhand furniture too. 'Bent bottomed' chairs were transported some 12 miles from coastal county Down and straw mattresses came from Lurgan, county Armagh, some 13 miles, to the same market.[8] These things must have been carried by horses and carts since it was before the advent of the railway in that area.

There are many connections between distinct designs found in Ireland and in other countries. Some were undoubtedly introduced during the seventeenth century by planted settlers from England and from Scotland. The relatively recent interest in vernacular furniture in Britain has yet to provide us with any English examples of settle beds or hen coops. However, a few isolated examples of settle tables from Somerset, Devon and Cornwall (where they were known as chair tables), have recently been located, providing a possible link with those found in fieldstudies in southern Leinster.[9] Links between Scotland and parts of Ulster are also strong, because of plantation and close proximity. The unique chairs of Sutherland and Caithness are almost identical to examples found in county Derry.[10] Box beds and outshot beds used to be common in both regions too.[11]

The settle bed may well have evolved within Ireland, as there is still no evidence for its existence in England, Wales or Scotland. Its design has migrated with Irish emigrants however, and numerous examples have been recorded in areas of known Irish settlement in America and Upper Canada.[12] There are links between crafts such as the straw lip-work of Wales and England and that found in Ireland, but the actual term 'lip-work' was not apparently used in Ireland and so it has been avoided here when describing Irish examples. Chairs and dressers with distinctly Irish features, some even with sledge feet, have been discovered in Australia as a result of Irish settlement there.[13] Folding press beds, widely used throughout Ireland in cramped rural dwellings, were less common in England. In California, where examples are still used, their Irish origins have resulted in the label 'Murphy beds', while in New York they are well suited to Manhatten's lack of space. The list of cross-cultural connections is almost endless. Further comparisons can easily be made by examining furniture in museums and publications pertaining to other countries.

In contrast to other books on vernacular furniture, this volume deals chiefly with furniture from domestic settings, touching only briefly on examples from institutions such as schools, workhouses, workshops etc. Instead it examines various social and cultural conditions, using surviving examples of furniture as social documents. There is still much work to be done on the subject of Irish institutional and mass-produced furniture, and compared with the study of English material culture, many fields await exploration. For a variety of reasons, historical research in Ireland has not suffered the same bias towards the study of the aristocracy that has traditionally dominated historians of English furniture.

Much remains to be learnt from interdisciplinary research and cross-cultural communication, and it is hoped that this work will encourage others to break new ground. Through the study of Irish furniture and the traditions which surround it, it has been possible to link and illuminate the complex social history, culture and religion of the Irish people. John Millington Synge aptly observed that 'they [the objects] seem to exist as a natural link between the people and the world that is about them'.[14]

There's a low house, a thatched house,
At the foot of Bantown lane,
With a half-door and a hearth fire,
And a pot linked on a crane.

. . . And they all have a share of the soda
   bread,
And the strong tea in the bowls,
And maybe the night is a wild night,
And the sleet spits on the coals.

W.F. Marshall, n.d.[1]

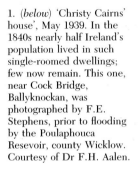

1. (*below*) 'Christy Cairns' house', May 1939. In the 1840s nearly half Ireland's population lived in such single-roomed dwellings; few now remain. This one, near Cock Bridge, Ballyknockan, was photographed by F.E. Stephens, prior to flooding by the Poulaphouca Resevoir, county Wicklow. Courtesy of Dr F.H. Aalen.

2. 'Hovel near the foot of the Reek', Croagh Patrick, county Mayo, 'built of stones, loosely heaped together, with no window, the roof miserably thatched'. From J. Barrow's *A Tour Round Ireland, Through the sea-coast counties, in the autumn of 1835* (1836).

The nature of the rural Irish houses occupied by the majority of the population within the period considered here, had a greater impact on furniture design than perhaps any other factor. Much has already been published on the history of vernacular housing in Ireland.[2] By the nineteenth century in Ireland, the term cottage was used disparagingly, mainly by visiting English observers, to describe a landless dwelling. The term is not used in this text as it was considered derogatory by country people, who called their homes houses, regardless of size and status.[3] The traditional long, low house, typically one room deep (from front to rear), has attracted more scholarly attention than most other aspects of Ireland's material folk culture. This section therefore concentrates on those architectural features with the strongest bearings on vernacular furniture.[4]

The fact that much furniture was built within the home, often literally into the wall of the kitchen or bedroom, whenever a dresser, press or bed was required, has contributed to its survival as it cannot be extracted without difficulty.[5]

The Census of Ireland, taken in 1841, not only recorded the population, but also their houses, which were divided into four grades for convenience. The fourth and lowest grade 'comprised all mud cabins having only one room'. The commissioners results showed that 'nearly half the families of the rural population' were living in these single-roomed 'cabins'. This appalling percentage rose even higher in the poorest parts of the west of Ireland. However, the number of better graded houses rose proportionately and considerably towards the close of the nineteenth century and by the twentieth century the single-roomed cabin was becoming a rarity (figs. 1–2).[6] The statistics demonstrate the widespread rural poverty of the early 1800s, and help emphasise the underlying constraints on furniture makers of lack of space, poor conditions and lack of materials.

Although house types did vary considerably from one area to the next, it is nevertheless possible to group distinct layouts (of the dwellings with several rooms) broadly according to region. In the north-west there are still many houses whose kitchen floor-plan incorporates a hearthside 'outshot' or wall niche, usually let into the rear wall of the house, in which a raised and curtained

3. Rear view of a house showing a bed outshot, placed traditionally alongside the hearth. *Loch na Fuaidhe*, county Galway, c.1935. Photograph by K. Danaher, courtesy of the Head of the D.I.F., U.C.D.

4. (*below*) Traditional clay walled, wheat thatched house of the lobby entrance type: its front door adjacent to the kitchen hearth. The windows to the left and right typically served a parlour and a bedroom, leading off the central kitchen. Built before 1837, Gaulstown, Dunshaughlin, county Meath.

5. (*right*) 'Better sort of Connaught Cabin', from J. Barrow's *A Tour Round Ireland. Through the sea-coast counties, in the autumn of 1835.*

bed was once located near the warmth of the fire (fig. 3) (see chapter 5). In the south-east, houses with walls of clay or mud predominated (fig. 4), whereas in parts of the west, locally abundant stone was the most common wall-building material (figs. 2 and 5).[7] All but the rich favoured locally abundant materials, resulting in houses which blended beautifully with their surroundings. Roofs were thatched with straw, reeds, flax, heather or even potato stalks according to ones means. The appearance of thatched roofs varied greatly from one district to the next. The roped and rounded tops of the low dwellings of the western seaboard were well protected against relentless Atlantic winds (fig. 296). Slated roofs cost more and were therefore something of

a status symbol for those who could afford them.[8] Slate lasted longer than thatch, but lacked the insulating properties which kept the house cool in summer and warm in winter.

The widespread use of thatch, which was frequently unlined inside, was an influential factor on the design of the common 'canopy' beds. The wooden canopy or tester with its draught excluding curtains, prevented drips, dust and insects from falling on the sleepers, as well as retaining body heat. Such covered beds required less timber than a ceiling. In county Donegal and elsewhere in Ulster, people re-used flour bags to line the underside of the thatch, whitewashing them to maximise reflected light.

6. 'Cabin built with Turf, Magilligan, county Derry', as photographed by R. Welch, c.1900. The British Government Poor Reports of the 1830s often mentioned houses built like this, or excavated from peat bogs. Furniture was also made from turf, but none survives. Outside is a composite seated chair (see fig. 39). Photo courtesy of the Ulster Museum.

Dr Alan Gailey has published extensively on Irish vernacular housing, and distinguishes two different categories of traditional dwelling according to the relationship between the main entrance and the hearth. In the north and west, he describes how most traditional houses have a front door which is at the opposite end of the kitchen to the hearth. In contrast, in the south and east, most houses have a front entrance which is adjacent to the hearth (figs. 4).[9] This latter type generally has a 'jamb wall' screening the hearth from the front door, forming a small corridor/lobby, with doors leading into 'the room' (parlour) and the kitchen (figs. 103, 105). It is often fitted with a small window or spy hole to allow a preview of approaching visitors. These two categories of house both arise from a common west European house type, which includes many of the features described above, combined with the floor-level hearth being placed somewhere along the central axis of a rectangluar floor plan.[10] Doors and windows were most often positioned in the long front and rear walls.[11]

Knowledge of these two main house types and where they commonly occurred can be invaluable in identifying the locations of paintings and illustrations. The typical arrangements of furniture in both house types correspondingly varies. The southern and eastern house type, with its 'jamb wall' screening the fire, often provided the opportunity for a built-in settle or bench beside

the hearth, thereby saving the timber otherwise required for a wooden back. The 'kitchen' served as the main living/activities room and it has frequently been said that the kitchen hearth (rather than the table) was the focal point of work and relaxation in the home. The huge hooded smoke canopies above these hearths were sometimes made with mud-covered wicker or straw rope, or locally fired brick (figs. 97, 101, 105, 218) supported on a massive beam, running across the width of the house. The following description comes from nineteenth-century county Wicklow: 'the great fireplace is still there where you can sit on benches beside the hearth fire right under the chimney and see the sky above you . . . the whole life of the house has its centre in the kitchen.'[12] The hearth area was often emphasised and delineated by flagstones or by patterned arrangements of pebbles, which were sunk into the earth floor.[13] One house in north county Antrim had a heart shape of inset white stones set into the floor before the fire.[14]

Furniture was commonly devised as an integral part of the house from the day it was built. Common features were the stone fireside seats built into the hearth wall, the recessed 'keeping holes' which were left in the back wall of the hearth and much larger recesses fitted with slate shelves and wooden doors which sometimes flanked the hearth. Draughts and the cold dampness of the walls may account for the popularity of the ubiquitous high backed settles and settle beds. Even the earthen floor provided the opportunity to create hollows from which the cats could drink their milk.[15] Few things were made to serve only a single purpose. Many accounts tell how the door was taken off its hinges to be used as a surface for a tailor to work on, or as a resonating board for dancing on. Half doors were common, allowing light into the kitchen while also serving as a barrier against animals.

Floors of beaten earth (figs. 97, 152) were usual in rural dwellings until the early twentieth century, when many were covered over with concrete.[16] These probably gave rise to the medieval feature of the renewable 'sledge foot', which was a common feature of dressers and some settles from parts of Ulster and Connaught (figs. 128,

178–80). Earth floors of puddled clay, mixed on occasions with lime, cowdung, ashes or oathulls, were said to raise little dust. In Armagh, such floors were set by digging the ground and then holding a dance to compress it. William Carleton, the early nineteenth-century novelist from county Tyrone, tells us how in anticipation of visitors, 'Several concave inequalities, which constant attrition had worn in the earthen floor of the kitchen, were filled up with blue clay, brought on a car from the bank of a neighbouring river, for the purpose.'[17]

Floors composed of earth, solid rock or flagstones in areas of local stone, were generally uneven (fig. 105). This probably contributed to the popularity of three-legged stools ('creepies') and of the three-legged 'Sligo chair' which could stand on rugged terrain quite firmly, unlike their four-legged counterparts. The comparatively flexible structures of many súgán chairs as well as the lack of stretchers used on hedge chairs, also resulted from a need for survival on rough flooring. Floors often sloped slightly upwards towards the fireplace, and in Donegal this gave rise to chairs which had shorter front legs than back legs, upon which one could only sit comfortably when facing the fire. In county Cork one still occasionally finds settles which have slightly shorter legs at the hearth end, to balance this floor slope (fig. 114).

Another architectural feature which had an important effect upon seating was the general lack of chimneys in the poorer dwellings (fig. 6). This was commented upon constantly during the eighteenth and nineteenth centuries, particularly by the many foreign visitors to the island, who were deterred from entering such 'cabins' by palls of turf smoke. As a result, seats were often made remarkably low to enable people to sit close to the floor level fire with their heads beneath the wreaths of smoke.[18]

Conditions of housing varied enormously from one period and region to the next. A county Kildare landlord in the 1830s coolly described his 'bog colony' of tenants who lived in dwellings made from turf; 'some attempt walls, with large blocks or squares of turf, which they commonly raise two or three feet: the common breadth of these tenements is about six feet . . . Some of these

huts are mere excavations of the dry bog . . . Their clothes and furniture are of a piece with the buildings.' (fig. 6).[19] He goes on to explain that 'the dearness of glass in consequence of the Excise [tax] operates greatly against the improvement of cottage architecture.' In many places the Government Poor Inquiry reporters explained that tenants were expected to build and furnish their own dwellings. A decline in living standards is indicated by a reporter from county Meath, who explained that 'formerly there were dressers [in the kitchens], at present these are seldom seen'.[20]

The so called 'byre dwelling' which was built to accommodate people and their animals beneath the same roof, was well known in parts of north-west Europe and in parts of western Ireland, up until the close of the nineteenth century (figs. 240–1).[21] Descriptions of such dwellings vary, but the 'upper end' of the house accommodated the family, perhaps with a hearthside bed outshot and meal bin close to the warmth of the fire, with cows tethered at the 'lower end' of the house, separated by an open drain.[22] A visitor to Achill Island at the turn of the last century described a typical island dwelling; 'The old man and his wife slept in a sort of box-bed inserted in the wall on the right hand side of the fireplace in the large living room, at the end of which the live stock, cattle, etc., were housed . . . In the room behind the fireplace the younger members of the family slept.'[23] This arrangement was normal for those of the population who had no outhouses. It ensured the safety of the animals, their body heat helped to keep the house warm and dairy cows benefitted particularly from being kept in.[24]

Martin Doyle, whose *Hints to Small-holders* came out in 1832, wrote that whereas in cold weather the gentry had no eggs from their poultry (which were kept outside) the poor had eggs throughout the winter, because their fowl were kept indoors.[25] The hen coop, coop dresser and various strawwork or basketwork hens' nests doubtless arose from this tradition, providing a convenient and warm indoor place which benefited hatching poultry.

In poor areas lacking timber, a room was sometimes divided off with 'a long straw mat that hung from the ceiling'[26] or even a 'wall made of pieces of branches of trees . . . and briars or twigs woven between them . . . The door going down into the room . . . was also made of twigs.'[27] For the more fortunate, a partition was often formed by placing a dresser and/or a press across the room as a divider (fig. 171).[28] This type of division was an easy way to create two rooms from one.[29] Some conversions left a space above the dividing furniture right up to the rafters (fig. 186).[30] Later ones incorporated these pieces into a cross wall which was often made of timber sheeting (figs. 143, 148, 166, 170, 173).[31]

The presence of a partition sometimes provided the opportunity for a loft area, which was used for children to sleep on or simply for storage (figs. 155, 186).[32] Such sleeping lofts could be reached by a ladder or by steep steps and in many houses they were built above the warmth of the fireplace (figs. 120, 197, 282).[33]

The extra room created by a partition or built onto the end of an existing house was commonly known as 'the room', *an seomra*, the chamber, the room *par excellence*'.[34] It served the purpose of a parlour in which strangers or special visitors could be welcomed, while at night some of them could be doubled up as a bedroom. This dual purpose 'room' explains the popularity of paired beds which could be hidden by day with curtains. Or instead there might be a press bed which conveniently folded up to be cunningly disguised as a chiffonier or wardrobe (figs. 265, 269). The paired beds,[35] sometimes filled the entire length of the back wall, appearing by day as a continous length of curtain (fig. 246). This positioning must initially have governed the size of 'the room' and saved timber, as three sides of these beds were actually walls. Sometimes such a curtained bed was created simply by hanging a pair of curtains and a valance from the ceiling (fig. 259). 'The room' also housed any items of mahogany or oak furniture that the family might possess and was often adorned with religious and political prints. Its importance is emphasised by the fact that it was often the only ground floor area with a boarded floor.[36]

Synge, who spent some time in the Aran Islands, wrote of the kitchen 'full of beauty and distinction . . . the walls have been toned by the turf-smoke to a soft brown that blends with the grey earth-colour of the floor'.[37] On the Great Blasket Island, also in the early 1900s, their walls were 'lime-washed, in some cases yellow, or yellow with a broad pink border below, from the floor to about half the height of a man, in others a peculiarly unhealthy and gloomy shade of red.'[38] In county Fermanagh kitchen walls were traditionally painted darkly along the lower sections, with whitewash above. Old photographs show that walls were sometimes decorated with pale spots, made by dabbing with a round brush onto a contrasting background.[39] Throughout the nineteenth century, whitewashing was encouraged inside and out and sometimes it was even provided free by landlords concerned about appearance and cleanliness.[40] Wallpaper became an increasingly popular substitute for painted kitchen walls by the beginning of the twentieth century.

By the final quarter of the nineteenth century, governing bodies and legislation at last combined to improve the living conditions of the poor. The Congested Districts Board was set up in 1891 to tackle many problems, including that of substandard housing, particularly in the west of Ireland, and rehousing the poor and over-crowded homes.[41] Many of the resulting new buildings followed broadly traditional lines. Recent fieldwork has shown that the most easily portable, freestanding furniture was often moved by its owners into homes which were built well into the twentieth century.

The confined space, earth floors and thatched roofs of the old long, low houses were of fundamental influence upon the form of most common furniture. The general move of recent decades away from such houses into more comfortable modern bungalows is understandable;[42] but the rejection of the old houses has also inadvertantly contributed to the wholesale destruction or exportation of the furnishings they once contained.

Tis cause enough for grieving,
Our shelter felled around us . . .
What shall we do for timber?
The last of the woods is down . . .
There's no holly nor hazel nor ash there,
The pasture's rock and stone,
The crown of the forest has withered,
And the last of the game is gone.

Anon, 'Lament for the Woodlands'[1]

The final disappearance of Ireland's ancient forests accompanied the downfall and departure of the old Gaelic nobility, whose decline was often lamented by the many poets of the seventeenth and eighteenth centuries.[2] The anonymous poem quoted above was translated from Irish and is one of many that mourned the deforestation.

Ireland was exploited as a resource for England's timber consumption long before the Great Fire of London when considerable amounts of Irish oak was used for rebuilding.[3] The effects of such deforestation were exacerbated by the huge rise in population, especially in the late eighteenth century, accompanied by a growing intensity of farming. Greater immediate profit could be gained from letting land for farming than from planting young trees. The grazing of cattle was detrimental to tree growth and where there once had been timber, there was a 'nationwide lack of interest in replacing it'.[4] Much Irish vernacular furniture design has consequently been influenced by a fundamental and crucial shortage of timber, which inevitably affected the rural poor above all. It was as a result of this general absence of wood that people resorted to a variety of alternatives such as rush, straw, willow and even turf to furnish their homes. Such constraints also resulted in a wide range of highly ingenious dual-purpose furniture, which not only saved timber but was also economical with space and labour. This section will discuss the background and consequences of this dire shortage of timber in a country which had one-eighth of its land forested in 1600. By 1800 that figure had been reduced to a mere fiftieth.[5]

In the early seventeenth century Ireland's great woodlands, which had long been a dominant feature of her landscape, were in the least accessible areas, yet still abundant with native oak trees. These forests however, provided cover for wolves and for the many dispossessed and wandering Irish landowners, who consequently became known as Wood-kernes. This had long been a reason put forward for programmes of forest clearance. Many of the newly planted landowners, feeling nervous about the security of their recently acquired estates, felled and exported their stands of timber for quick returns. Much of this was sent to England to build ships and houses. Charcoal burning ironworks also added to the deforestation, along with felling to supply a variety of other needs such as pipe staves, and barrel staves for wine casks. Dr Pococke commented on such ironworks in county Waterford during his tour of 1752, but almost a century later Mrs Hall remarked how that county was 'for the most part barren of trees'.[6]

By the close of the eighteenth century timber was in such short supply in Ireland that acts were passed in parliament to penalise people for owning wood unless they could account for it.[7] The travelling Arthur Young described how 'the greatest part of the kingdom presents a naked bleak and dreary view for want of wood, which has been destroyed for a century past, with the most thoughtless prodigality, and still continues to be cut and wasted as if it was not worth the preservation.[18] By the 1840s, William Makepeace Thackeray, who had made a special journey through Limerick to view 'an ancient forest' which was described in his guide book, noted sarcastically that 'the monarchs of the woods which I saw around about would scarcely have afforded timber for a bed post'.[9]

The eighteenth century saw a marked change in the movement of timber. Instead of being a source of supply, Ireland's imports of timber from abroad began to outweigh her exports. Cheap wood was being imported into Ireland from the Baltic, Spain, Britain and its American colonies, explaining why some Irish landlords could sell timber for as little as sixpence per tree. A huge range of hardwoods were imported from the American colonies, some of which was probably used for making the mahogany furniture so popular in the farmers' parlours. Vernacular furniture makers, however, would have utilised the softwoods which by that time were being imported cheaply from the Baltic.[10] Dr Pococke, describing the port of Wexford in 1752, mentioned that 'The chief trade is an export of corn, and an import of deal boards and some wine'.[11] 'Deals' (mainly Norwegian Spruce and Scots pine of particular dimensions, but also fir) formed the largest percentage of timber types imported from the Baltic.[12] Timber was needed for the barrels, casks and hoops used by the Irish brewers, distillers and the provisions trades: hardwoods for wet-coopering containers for liquids, and softwoods for dry-coopering to hold flaxseed and objects packed in straw or sawdust. Exotic hardwoods such as walnut, mahogany, ebony and cocoa wood, which were imported during the eighteenth century, were used by the top urban cabinetmakers. Wainscot, balk (for beams) and clapboard were used in the building trade and would have helped to supply the requirements of those building Dublin's many Georgian houses. More timber was used for shipbuilding: 'knee' timber of naturally bent shape was useful for this purpose but awkward to pack and therefore the cost of its transportation was higher. Transportation costs from abroad and within Ireland raised the home price of timber considerably, putting supplies beyond the reach of the poorest 'hedge carpenters' who often gleaned their timber from hedgerows or sufficed with off-cuts from the sawmills.[13]

Until the battle of Waterloo in 1815, timber was imported into Ireland from parts of northern Europe such as Spain, Portugal, France and Holland, but during the eighteenth century, softwoods such as pine in particular, were being brought in from Norway and Russia. Subsequently higher taxes were imposed and a new import trade from British North America began to flourish.

By the eighteen-forties, the trade, which had barely existed thirty years previously, had grown to an annual importation of over 925,321 loads of timber and planks, and the 100 ships or fewer which sailed for British North America in 1800 had increased, by 1845 to 2,000 ships, totalling over 1,000,000 tons.[14]

Huge quantities of flaxseed were imported into Ireland, with short stave timber packed in between the barrels. Much of this imported timber was used for housebuilding, but a significant amount found its way into the hands of furniture makers. The owners of such ships found it uneconomic to sail them empty on the return route and their solution was to carry emigrant passengers for low fares to ports on the coast of North America and Canada.[15]

For much of the rural population in Ireland, timber for furniture came from the cheapest imported softwood. There was however, a range of alternatives to buying new timber, and depending on location it included such materials as bog oak, bog yew and bog fir (semi-fossilised timber dug from peat bogs). This was skilfully extracted from peat bogs; people located it by the absence of morning dew on the bog surface, and then probed around with spears before digging the timber out. Massive trunks of bog fir used to be dug from bogs in county Clare in the early 1800s: none was wasted as the smaller roots and branches were often processed into twisted ropes for bed cords (fig. 66). The author has examined both bog fir and bog oak large enough for furniture making in bogs in county Cavan. In some areas (especially county Donegal) bog fir is still used for fuel. In county Tyrone it provided woodworkers with their chief timber supply and was 'looked upon to be full as good for roofing and lofting stables, etc. as foreign fir or pine' in 1801.[16] Bog fir was widely resorted to for rural furniture making (it was easier to work than bog oak and therefore preferred), but it can prove difficult to distinguish from ordinary fir and pine, particularly once it has aged and been covered with layers of paint. Bog oak is much denser than bog fir, and because of its distinctive black sheen and similar properties to ebony, was widely sought after and highly valued by cabinetmakers, carvers and even jewellers.[17] It is perhaps because of its decorative value (as well as its extreme hardness) that so few examples of vernacular furniture exist that incorporate bog oak (fig. 222).

For the majority of the working population, the importance of recycling timber previously used for other purposes and the renewing of worn parts of existing furniture cannot be overestimated. In coastal districts the gathering of driftwood and 'wreck timber' from the sea was an important source of wood for furniture making as well as for provisions. The use of a range of alternative materials to timber was widespread amongst the poor and is discussed in the sections dealing with straw seating and basketry (pp. 63–8, 202–3). Small dimension timber was gleaned from hedgerows: naturally bent 'knees' (like smaller versions of those used in shipbuilding) were sought out by householders or by the appropriately named 'hedge carpenters' to make curved chair backs. However, the widespread practice of building stone and earth banks rather than planting hedges prevented the growth of vigorous hedgerow trees. Small dimensions of whitethorn, with its smooth, pale, close grain, was often used in chairmaking as it was commonly grown along these 'ditches' or banks. Many of the trees introduced into Ireland in the sixteenth and seventeenth centuries, such as beech and sycamore, were used for woodworking jobs around the farm and also in furniture making. Ash was also a favourite timber for farm use, especially for 'wheel-cars and ploughs' and was sought out because of its strength for making chair legs. Around 1800, in county Tyrone, ash was said to be scarce and was sold by the cubic foot for as much as 3s. 3d.[18] It is clear from surviving examples that elm, when obtainable, was favoured for chair seats.

In terms of timber use throughout Ireland, wood from shipwrecks and drift amounted to only a tiny percentage of the overall supply. But for coastal and island dwellers in windswept regions without trees it was nevertheless important. Material from wrecked ships could be consumed, sold or bartered, thereby providing a rare and welcome source of wealth. There are many accounts of people risking their lives and even fighting over the spoils of wrecks. Ireland's rocky and storm-ravaged coastline was the scene of numerous marine catastrophies, making the notorious activities of the wreckers in Cornwall an unnecessary occurrence in Ireland. However, wreckers, or wreckmongers as they were known in seventeenth-century Ireland, were not entirely unknown.[19] Some of the best accounts of salvaging wreckage were written by the many literary island dwellers from Ireland's west coast, who describe them as notably exciting aspects of their everyday life.[20]

Tomás Ó Criomhthain (1856–1937) of the Great Blasket, describes a boat journey to draw lobster pots which turned into a timber salvaging operation:

The driftwood was coming in masses round a point where there was a swirl of tide. There were white planks, absolutely new, afloat. We had to untie a rope from a pot and bind together a dozen planks with it and tow them in our wake . . . Later on in the day we saw first one boat and then another, gathering driftwood like ourselves on this side and that . . . Often enough we'd be a long way from the shore by the time I had a dozen planks tied up . . . if there had been a puff of wind against us, we should never have made it . . . I believe we made a dozen pounds out of it.[21]

The new white planks, presumably of pine, must have come from a ship with a cargo of timber. This was sometimes jettisoned during stormy weather. On such occasions there was great debate about the exact size of the pieces of driftwood gathered by the men in their currachs, some saying they had spars of driftwood, others that it was just scantlings, 'bits of timber the ships throw overboard when they are finished with them'. 'Wreckage' was evidently considered of greater worth (and dimension) than mere 'timber'.[22]

New wood washed in from timber carrying ships was obviously ideal for furniture making, but in the case of a major shipwreck, pieces of the ship itself were also turned into furniture.[23] Fieldwork in coastal districts has shown that woodworkers frequently used driftwood and wreck timber, its origins have often been revealed by discussions with the owners as well as by examination of surviving examples. Wrecks were, after all, particularly memorable events. Sometimes the unexpected use of an exotic timber, such as a remarkably large dimension of mahogany (usually beyond the purse of a country carpenter) to make a dug-out chair (fig. 78), can be traced back to a shipwreck. Another example is the three-legged winch cover stool from the wreck of the steamship *Asian*, which struck the Stag rocks off the coast of west Cork in 1924 (fig. 320).[24]

The First World War was another provider of shipwrecks for the poor coastal communities. Ó Criomhthain wrote of one such marine disaster: 'she had in her cargo everything that feeds mankind except drink . . . The sea filled up with everything eye had ever seen and that we had never seen in this place. Hundreds of pounds worth was salvaged from the wreck, and the islanders made a great deal of money out of her.'[25]

The westerly islands are still mostly treeless. During the winter rough weather often isolates them from the mainland, but islanders sometimes benefited from their proximity to Atlantic shipping lanes. During the 1930s, a visitor to Tory island, off the county Donegal coast, observed how 'Everywhere one sees portions of iron ships – the hearths are "tiled" with iron plates, footbridges over drains outside cottages are composed of iron plates and I even saw a home-made harrow whose teeth were ships' bolts.' He spoke to an islander who remembered a wreck of fifteen months before, saying 'it was a grand wreck; it had carried a cargo of flour which lasted the islanders for more than a year . . .' tis time there was another wreck, there was no want in the island then.' For the islanders, such a marine disaster provided a rare opportunity for material gain, so the proceeds were eagerly gathered. The fact that such activities were actually illegal was offset by the islanders' frequent and daring rescues of passengers and crew.[26]

Furniture was also often made from driftwood, as opposed to wreck timber. The presence in woodwork of distinctive holes, up to an inch in diameter and lined with shiny shell, are an indication of the past presence of the marine Toredo or Shipworm. This mollusc tunnels its way only through timber that is submerged in sea water, so that when such holes are found in furniture it indicates that the timber from which it was made was once either part of a ship's hull, or driftwood. The holes can sometimes be found on the unpainted insides of drawers and cupboards, whereas they are usually filled and disguised on the outside.

Another common use for shipwreck timber was for housebuilding. The bressumers or beams over many Irish hearths commonly originated from wrecks, peculiar notches and holes revealing a former use. Off the coast of county Antrim, on Rathlin Island, roofs which incorporated wreckage were called 'jury-rigged'.[27]

What we know today as 'recycling' and material economy was a vital and integral part of rural life in eighteenth- and nineteenth-century Ireland. If a piece of furniture was no longer used, rather than putting it on the fire it was often remade into something new: for instance, a Wexford bed which was no longer used was rebuilt into a fireside settle and a form (fig. 97). In parts of Munster where buttermaking was a major part of the provisions trade, butter boxes were commonly inverted and turned into fireside stools (fig. 28); some even had their 'seats' upholstered, while others became toolboxes.[28]

However, during times of particular hardship or of famine, a shortage of fuel for cooking or keeping warm was often the cause of furniture being burnt.[29] Some authors have gone as far as to claim that virtually no vernacular furniture at all pre-dates the great famine, but in fact a considerable number of eighteenth-century examples are still in existence, as will be seen in the following chapters. More recently, furniture found to be badly infested with woodworm was quite often burnt by its owners.

It is perhaps ironic that restrictions such as the shortage of materials available to Irish country furniture makers have so often contributed positively to a range of ingenious designs, which might otherwise never have evolved.

What other could so well have
   counselled us
In all the lovely intricacies of a house
As he that practised or that understood
All work in metal or in wood,

               W.B. Yeats, c.1919.[1]

The rural population in Ireland during the period with which we are concerned, was on the whole too poor to support the services of specialist furniture makers. Instead, vernacular furniture was made by a wide variety of tradesmen, most often by the local carpenter or wheelwright, but also by masons, boatbuilders, woodturners, sawyers, basketmakers, coffinmakers or coopers, by those who combined these trades or simply by the resourceful householder.[2] This helps to explain why some tradesmen preferred to keep their skills undisclosed and why, for instance, some basketmakers always started and finished their baskets unobserved.[3] A county Cork wheelwright was remembered as being particularly covert about his techniques for graining on furniture.[4] Indeed this concealment was an important part of an apprentice's contract or indenture; hence, 'the said apprentice his said master shall faithfully serve, his secrets keep'.[5]

One account of Ireland during the seventeenth century states that as many as five or six men out of every hundred were carpenters and masons: 'these more handy and ready in building ordinary houses, and much more prudent in supplying the defects of instruments and materials, than the English artificers.'[6] By the nineteenth century this remarkably high percentage had dropped considerably,[7] although an extraordinary adaptability and resourcefulness in the face of shortage of suitable materials still prevailed.

Many of the rural carpenters undertook a wide range of woodworking jobs. They were also shopfitters whenever the need arose and it is perhaps with the many surviving decorative Irish shopfronts that their work with furniture is most obviously comparable.[8] This is true not only for the woodworking techniques involved, but also for the paint finishes and the use of classical pilasters and cornices, all of which were also used to adorn the most ornate dressers.

Patrick Purcell who was born at the close of the nineteenth century, and spent his working life as a carpenter in Carlow, made decorative ceilings and shopfronts as well as furniture. His work was typical of many rural woodworkers with a broad range of skills.[9] He fitted out 'The Phoenix' public house in Carlow and his grandmother French-polished the bar. (Both French-polishing and the preparation of feathers and down for upholsterers were traditionally the work of women.)[10] Purcell, like many other rural woodworkers, used a distinctive decorative motif to distinguish his work from others. His favoured incised saw-tooth mouldings can still be seen on a Carlow shopfront and doubtless appeared on his furniture too. He recalled how the twisted rope mouldings, which were frequently used to decorate furniture from east Munster and south Leinster (fig. 17), were a common form of decoration on coffins. Coffins were not always made of wood however, especially in counties Westmeath and Down, where woven hazel and willow coffins have been recorded, probably made in response to a shortage of timber. One of these 'rod' coffins, buried in a graveyard in Kilbride, is said to have sprouted, producing a sally tree from the grave.[11]

During the 1820s in Derry, cabinetmakers were paid roughly 10 per cent more than their carpenter counterparts.[12] However, these better trained cabinetmakers would have been producing comparatively expensive, fashionable mahogany furniture for the gentry, which rarely found its way into the majority of rural homes. By the late eighteenth century many towns in south-east Ireland could have supported such cabinetmakers, but they could not have made a living in county Donegal, for instance. They tried to keep up with new styles, using pattern books to keep abreast of the latest designs. As country carpenters were often employed to make kitchen furniture for the so-called 'big houses', they would have noticed and been influenced by the cabinetmakers' work; This helps to explain the many similarities between furniture of the average rural kitchen and that of the grander houses of the aristocracy. Many rural carpenters became adept at copying the cabinetmakers' more fashionable pieces, only they tended to use less expensive pine rather than mahogany, which they then grained to upgrade it.

A list of kitchen furniture ordered by a curate for his big house in northern county Roscommon in 1825, provides a rare insight into the range of furniture that a local carpenter was expected to make. Kilgeffin is a little parish about 90 miles from Dublin, which is where Reverend Armstrong bought most of his fine mahogany furniture. Other towns such as Sligo, Galway and Enniskillen which were about half that distance away, were presumably unable to compete with the Dublin suppliers' services. The list is part of an inventory written by Reverend Armstrong entitled 'Carpenter's work done by John Fox at Kilgeffin'. It includes forms, kitchen chairs, tables, a dresser and plate drainer and two servants beds (probably settle beds), but also a bookcase, hatstand, dressing tables and basin stands. All this would have been made from pine, or deal as it was then known. The fact that they were locally made, rather than bought in Dublin, may have been due to high transport costs. Finer fashionable furniture was bought from the upholsterers and cabinetmakers in Dublin, 'wrapped in straw inside deal crates' and transported via canal.[13]

It is interesting to compare the differences in pay between the hedge carpenter, carpenter and journeyman. The hedge carpenter, whose work was less refined than the fully trained carpenter, was paid the least. He often did such work around the farm as fence building and making pig troughs as well as undercutting the carpenter's prices with his hedge chairs (figs. 32–6). Wages varied considerably from one county to the next and although on the whole they rose with time, in periods of hardship there was less work and wages dropped.[14] In some remote areas skilled tradesmen were hard to procure. In Gweedore, county Donegal in the 1830s, the efforts of a well-meaning landlord to improve his tenants' poor conditions were hampered by an acute shortage of skilled masons and carpenters. 'So great was the difficulty of getting even a coffin made, that to secure the services of a carpenter ... many of the people gave him

annually by way of retaining fee, sheaves of oats, on the express condition of making their coffins when they died!' Tradesmen would desert the place as soon as they were paid their weekly wage, and the absence of local supplies of bread and meat, combined with the wildness of the countryside made it extremely difficult to persuade them to stay.[15]

A few years later, during the famines of the late 1840s, Cook Street in Cork city was so entirely devoted to coffinmaking that it became known as Coffin Street.[16] Woodworkers traditionally made their own coffins, which like the furniture were often of pine, painted and grained in imitation of oak or mahogany. These can still sometimes be seen standing in the corners of traditional workshops and they are the subject of many an apocryphal tale.

One of the earliest accounts of carpenter's wages comes from Galway. 'In 1526 a carpenter and man's pay was two pence a day with diet.'[17] Presumably the 'man' was a lesser paid assistant, but what is really significant about this is the inclusion of diet as part of the bargain. This practice of feeding the carpenter (as well as some other specific tradesmen) as he worked, continued right up until this century. In 1808 in county Clare, house-carpenters earned about 4s. per day; roughly twice as much as hedge carpenters, whose wages were supplemented by meals whereas the 'herdsman and shepherd [were paid] by agreement'.[18] These rates were comparable to county Derry in the first quarter of the nineteenth century.[19] The significance of meals as part payment for carpentry, well into the start of the twentieth century, cannot be overstressed. John Coakley, one of a family of county Cork carpenters, was forced to give up the trade because his acute shyness meant he could not bear to eat in other peoples homes, but could only eat at home.[20]

One of several Government Poor Inquiries carried out during the 1830s set out to ascertain which trades were most prosperous in particular areas and what these tradesmen and the 'labouring classes' ate.[21] It is perhaps easier to relate to the furniture makers' food than to their wages (unless the latter is comparative and viewed alongside current prices). The commissioners dis-

7. John Gallagher, a farmer from Glenties, county Donegal, with one of the plaited oat straw *saoisteógs* which he used to make, until hand-cut oat straw became difficult to obtain. Straw mattress making is another of his skills (see figs. 8, 248). Photo, 1992, kindly provided by A. Gallagher.

covered that in county Cork 'masons and carpenters [were the] most prosperous' trades,[22] whereas by contrast in county Leix, 'shoemaking is the most prosperous' and 'tradesmen eat milk and potatoes and butter and unlike labourers get meat twice a week'.[23]

In county Cork 'the carpenters' wages are £1. 1*s*.' per week, almost three times as much as the labourers could expect to earn. There, 'tradesmen having high wages, live generally on animal food [meat] and bread. They breakfast and sup on tea.'[24] The poor reporters go on to inform, somewhat disapprovingly, that in Passage West, Cork 'the diet is potatoes, milk, and fish. The house and ship carpenters use bread, tea, butter, and coffee: Sometimes meat and porter with whiskey *when unemployed*.'[25] The tradesmen in the 1830s enjoyed a considerably higher standard of living than the labouring classes and consumed a more substantial range of food and drink. Another Poor Inquiry into clothing in county Clare gives us a glimpse of the real poverty of those who worked the land: 'The clothing of the labourer is generally very bad; so bad that great numbers are prevented, from shame, from going to chapel on Sundays.'[26]

The number of references to child employment suggests that it was considered quite acceptable up to the first half of the nineteenth century.[27] In county Fermanagh the government commissioners inquired whether children found employment, and of what description; the answer was 'none except working straw plat', suggesting that some of the common straw plaited seats or mattresses could have been made by children (figs. 8, 86, 88, 93, 248).[28] However, strawwork was also an occupation for which adult makers became locally well known throughout Ireland (figs. 7–8).[29] The Poor Reports also tell us that in the 1830s in county Cork, children had no employment 'until they be bound to some trade, and masters are with difficulty procured'.[30]

By the close of the nineteenth century, we learn from the indenture papers of apprentice William Cunnane, that the sum of eight pounds had to be paid (in instalments) to James Sloyan, a 'general carpenter of Lecarrow, Knock' to learn his 'art and trade'. During the three years of training, the young apprentice had to agree to abide by the rules laid down in a formal contract, forbidding such things as marriage. Further constraints were detailed: 'he shall not play at cards, dice, tables or any unlawful games . . . Hurt to his master he shall not do', 'he shall not buy or sell without leave of said master' and basically he 'shall behave himself'. In exchange for the fee, the apprentice received board and lodgings ('befitting such an apprentice') teaching and instruction.[31]

At the beginning of the twentieth century a county Cork carpenter and furniture maker, Tim McCarthy (1915–42), began his five-year apprenticeship aged 17 in the town of Skibbereen, returning some 10 miles to his home at weekends.[32] Once qualified, he teamed up with local masons, fitting doors, windows, stairs and furniture where required. A local farm diary of the time shows how he was employed for about a month fitting partitions, putting up shelves, steps, glazing windows 'and doing odd jobs' with an assistant.[33] These visits by tradesmen to big farms to work on site were quite common. A contemporary account from county Down relates how one such carpenter made himself an improvised workbench 'of two long planks laid on three barrels set up in the straw shed, which had an open roof'.

16

8. Patrick Monks making a plaited mattress from oat straw, at Nevitt, Lusk, county Dublin, *c*.1967 (see figs. 93 and 248). Photo courtesy of the N.M.I.

9. The village carpenter, Dunboyne, county Meath, in 1953. He is assembling the frame of a double-stretchered table, with through-morticed joints, on a homemade bench. Photo courtesy of Bord Fáilte.

Like McCarthy, this carpenter also returned home every night, about a mile away.[34] Tim McCarthy's wages were '28 days at 7/– per day'. One Friday during this period in 1939, amongst the perfunctory notes relating to weather and crops, the diary reveals 'T. McCarthy putting glass in windows . . . War declared by Germany'. Although south-west Ireland was comparatively unaffected by the so-called 'Emergency' of the Second World War, it was nevertheless a catalyst for woodworking innovation. Like so many other rural carpenters before him, McCarthy had his own workshop in the village of Union Hall where he made kitchen tables, presses (cupboards) and dressers, many of which still survive (fig. 149). His style of furniture was characterised by particular idiomatic details, reflecting clearly the changing mood of the early twentieth century. It was an era of change and of new materials and techniques, of glass and plywood and gloss paints. Despite his short life (tragically, he died of tuberculosis aged 27) McCarthy's distinctive style and favoured forms of decoration still set his work aside from other contemporary local woodworkers.

Not all carpenters had formal apprenticeships. Many learnt their skills from their parents, frequently resulting in several generations of woodworkers.[35] This made good sense when the comparatively high cost of a kit of tools and a paid apprenticeship was taken into account. Journeymen were craftsmen who travelled the country, staying in one place for as long as there was work and moving on to the next whenever they felt like it.[36] They are known to have carried small, portable samples of their workmanship with them and to have hired themselves out by the day. The small-sized dressers and decorated panelsaw box may well have been such examples of their skill (figs. 10, 192, 195). In mid nineteenth-century county Down, a mason and a journeyman both earned 6*s*. 6*d*. per week, somewhat less than a head carpenter who earned 8*s*. 8*d*.[37]

The notes in a diary kept by a county Wicklow landlady during the 1840s, provide a rare insight into the way a carpenter and his family lived at that time.

James Ryan the carpenter, [who has] a good two story, slated house with four rooms, a closet, a dairy, workshop, shed, yard, three acres of land, one apprentice, one journeyman, a boy, a maid, wife and five children; one boy and two girls at school, two little girls are babies. All comfortable here, neater than is general.[38]

10. Hinged pine box, recessed to hold a panel-saw, painted pale blue over red. It is patterned with fans and circles in chip-carved decoration on its lid and sides. 'G.E' and the date '1907' are carved into the lid. It was probably an apprentice piece: an example of the maker's skill. Location unknown, but probably from Connaught, or county Clare. 28½ in. long by 7½ in. wide and 2 in. deep. Courtesy of the N.M.I.

The fact that they employed a maid may seem surprising, but such servants were quite commonly employed in the households of farmers and tradesmen.[39]

The survival of ancient techniques of craftsmanship well into the twentieth century in Ireland was quite remarkable, compared with other neighbouring countries. The use of the pole-lathe for turning and of two-man pitsaws to cut up whole trees into planks survived in counties such as Clare and Wicklow well into the first half of this century (figs. 11–12).[40]

James O'Keeffe is one of a few highly individual furniture makers in the south-east to have attracted scholarly attention.[41] His primary profession was as a builder, but he is now best known for his unique and distinctively carved oak furniture. Born in 1850, son of Edward and Ellen O'Keeffe, he died aged 73 in 1923. Family tradition recalls how he preferred to carve unobserved,

in an outhouse workshop beside his family home at Bridgetown, in county Wexford's Barony of Forth. Surviving examples of his carved furniture (none of which is signed or dated) include a round table (fig. 13), a tall oak sideboard with more than sixteen carved panels,[44] a carved and pierced overmantel, a large shrine, several low carved presses (fig. 14) and picture frames. His furniture is characterised by his favoured use of oak, usually busily adorned with bas relief female figures, bordered by intertwined flowers and foliage (figs. 13–14). Less typical, is his depiction of female angels, eclesiastically robed men holding flowers, or his serpents and scaly marine creatures. This prolific carving was evidently his prime concern, as the design of some of his furniture is otherwise unorthodox and almost incidental, simply providing a convenient saleable framework for his panels. Several shallow, low cupboards or presses survive

13. Extraordinary pedestal table of carved oak, made by James O'Keeffe (1850–1923), a builder, carpenter, woodcarver and sculptor of Mulrankin, county Wexford. The round top was once inlaid with pieces of timber; its central cross is partially painted white. The pedestal (5 in. square) is carved with his favoured motifs of women, flowers and leaves (see fig. 14). Top 23¼ in. diameter, 32¼ in. high. Courtesy of the N.M.I.

Facing page, below:
11. William O'Flynn, wheelwright, and son, beside his saw pit near Donard, county Wicklow. The longer, open pitsaw, for ripping down logs into planks, has a lower handle (or 'box') which can be removed to extract the blade from the kerf. The framed pitsaw (left) with its narrower blade, was for finer work. Photo, *c*.1948, courtesy of the N.M.I.

12. William O'Flynn (senior, top sawyer) and son (junior, bottom sawyer), using an open pitsaw to rip along the length of a board. Their saw pit combines characteristics of the raised continental structure, and the sunken pit which was usual in England. They used string dipped in a mixture of water and burnt straw, to 'snap' a guide line along each plank. Donard, county Wicklow, *c*.1950. Photo courtesy of the Head of D.I.F., U.C.D.

14. One of several low carved oak presses, made by James O'Keeffe. The thick front panels and door are deeply carved with religious figures, typically surrounded by flowers and leaves (see fig. 13). The front half of the top hinges upwards to reveal a shallow compartment. Late nineteenth century. 37 in. high, 16 in. deep, 34½ in. wide. Courtesy of the N.M.I.

(of a type not typical in rural houses), lavishly carved on the front and sides and usually with a shallow lidded compartment where one would otherwise expect to find a drawer. Some of these panels are between 2 and 3 inches thick, with figures set into recesses of such deep relief that the oak is reduced

in places to paper thinness. Little attention seems to have been paid to details such as knobs and catches.

His carved work was nearly always left unpainted, revealing how his eagerness to use wide boards of oak tempted him to include pale areas of soft sapwood, which have subsequently been attacked by woodworm. The top of a round pedestal table has partial paintwork, and seems originally to have been thickly inlaid with contrasting woods, which are now missing, probably due to exposure to damp (fig. 13). A shrine, (now exhibited in a room dedicated to his work, at the Irish Agricultural Museum), is also painted. Plasterwork panels in a similar style, for internal doors as well as for an imposing fire surround, may have been cast from wooden masters, and are typically painted white, black or green.

Perhaps his most appealing work is that depicting rural Irish women from the past, bearing pails or amongst young children. Little is known of what influenced his highly individual style, but his use of natural organic forms and romantic female figures was in keeping with the work of craftspeople involved in Ireland's 'Celtic revival'. Artists such as Daniel Maclise and Frederick Burton, who favoured rural and historical scenes (fig. 281), coincided with the literary and theatrical work of J.M. Synge and W.B. Yeats, and the cultural activities of the Gaelic League.

It was in a theatre designed and built by James O'Keeffe at the Moor of Mulrankin, that over 1,100 people gathered for one of the Gaelic League's many concerts. O'Keeffe was also a keen amateur painter of local and historical scenes, some of which were shown in his three-part exhibition. In the second part he exhibited '417 views on 5,000 yards of canvas of a tour of the world, starting with a picture of Dublin City'. He was almost certainly responsible for the 'curtains and drop scenes used on the stage' in the Mulrankin theatre, that had 'familiar places painted on them'.[42] A few of his naive oil paintings, which he framed himself with oak carved with flowers, still survive.

A final concert was held in the theatre shortly after his death; indicating that he was indeed the driving force behind the activity and entertainment which it provided

19

for the local community. Only a sketch now remains of the theatre, showing its extraordinary square gable ends surmounted by rows of women's heads.[43] These were perhaps sculpted in reinforced concrete, like another surviving bust, which appears to have been his self portrait. He was finally buried beneath the formidable family monument, which he built out of reinforced concrete, surmounted by a life-sized male figure, at Kilmannon, Cleerystown.

The prolific work of James O'Keeffe should not be confused with the lighter carved furniture of Edward Fitzhenry (dates unknown), with whom he worked periodically, and who was evidently greatly influenced by him. Fitzhenry also used oak. A surviving bureau bookcase, is less confidently carved than O'Keeffe's work, in shallower relief. Like some of O'Keeffe's pieces, the naive construction of the furniture itself suggests that it may have been inspired by pictures of grander furniture, rather than by examination of existing examples. It tends towards a geometric style and has been darkened by a finish of linseed oil.

Towards the end of the nineteenth and the beginning of the twentieth centuries, the distribution of mass-produced furniture made in Irish factories began to influence the appearance of many rural interiors. Although not strictly speaking vernacular, the products of these factories are now more common than their locally made predecessors and being notably Irish in their design deserve a mention. Wilson brothers of Manchester operated a steam sawmill in Athlone, county Westmeath, mainly for the manufacture of wooden bobbins for the textile industry. The factory operated between 1860 and 1894, at which point the business was transferred to England 'due to excessive railway freight [charges] lately established'.[45] The firm had between one and two hundred employees in 1890. Subsequently from 1897–8 to 1910 the Norfolk firm Hobbies Ltd had a sawmill on the premises which made 'Windsor chairs'.[46] Athlone's central location must have been advantageous for the distribution of their products throughout Ireland. From 1899, a technical school with a good reputation for its joinery, repaired, produced and sold furniture in Athlone. A type of so-called

'Windsor chair', which is quite English in style, with turned legs but two rather than one stretcher running from side-to-side beneath the seat (in the manner of Irish kitchen tables, fig. 234), was probably the product of the Wilsons' original sawmill. Identical examples of these chairs are widespread throughout Ireland, but are very rarely marked. During fieldwork near Buncrana in county Donegal, a set of four of these double-stretchered slat-backed chairs were all found to have been stamped 'WILSON ATHLONE' on the rear seat edge, indicating a date between 1860 and 1894.

By the first decade of the twentieth century, special training courses were being set up by the Department of Agriculture and Technical Instruction for Ireland, to train woodworkers between the ages of 21 and 30 to teach their craft. Itinerant teachers were already widespread, but the new instruction courses provided grants and included drawing, maths, class management and woodwork, and were concluded with formal written and practical exams.[47]

Most of the major towns throughout Ireland had established furniture factories by the twentieth century. Their establishment has benefited from locations close to lines of communications for distribution. The 'Ardee Chair Company' was set up in 1928 in Ardee, county Louth. By 1951 its founder claimed to be the sole producer of bentwood chairs in Britain and Ireland and employed nearly one hundred people. By then they were making their own plywood and supplying an appealing range of bentwood kitchen chairs with heart- or shamrock-shaped backrests as well as 'Eversafe' folding plywood chairs.[48]

Another factory called the 'Windsor Chair Works' was opened near Ardee in 1938. It began by manufacturing kitchen chairs and progressed to specialise in the production of an upholstered chair with a drop-in seat. Their manufacturing process began 'with the tree' and used traditional furniture making hardwoods such as beech, sycamore, oak, elm and ash. By 1951 one of the main obstacles to their expansion was said to be scarcity of timber, the same difficulty that vernacular furniture makers had struggled to overcome since the seventeenth century.[49]

The vast majority of Irish furniture was intended by its makers to be painted. The fashion since the sixties of stripped and waxed pine furniture therefore reveals it as it was never intended to be seen. Fieldwork has revealed a tiny percentage of furniture which has never been painted. Carleton's early nineteenth-century description of 'the white and well scoured dresser' or 'the white settle and chairs' from the more prosperous farmhouses of county Tyrone, are quite exceptional.[1] However, the tops of kitchen tables, the seats of settles and the work tops of dressers were usually scrubbed regularly. Cleanliness and the particular use of each piece of furniture, combined with the type of timber used, were considered important factors when deciding which areas to paint.

As has been pointed out earlier, poor timber and shortages of readily available or affordable timber commonly resulted in one piece of furniture being built from a variety of woods, or from driftwood and wreck timber, which could be visually unified and improved by painting. A non absorbent, painted surface is far easier to keep clean than a bare wooden one which requires laborious scrubbing.

Another reason for painting was that it protected the timber from the damp which was so prevalent in many nineteenth-century Irish houses. Painting amounted to a widespread tradition. An eighteenth-century settle bed, recently discovered in a manse on the Inishowen peninsula of county Donegal, showed absolutely no traces of paint. It had, however, never been stripped, and was said by its elderly owner to have been 'scrubbed every Saturday' (fig. 123). The grain stood out and it had the same smooth, undulating surface as an ancient piece of driftwood. Another unpainted example was a dresser, still used in a traditional county Cavan kitchen, and its elderly owner testified to decades of laborious scrubbing. It stood out in stark contrast to her other, painted furniture. In the Aran Islands small stools were scrubbed with sand in a nearby stream at the turn of this century (fig. 15).

Another factor which has had a marked effect on the number of times the furniture is repainted, is a Roman Catholic celebration of longstanding tradition,[2] known simply as the 'Stations' (abbreviated from 'Stations of confession'). The Station is the enduring practice of holding confessions and administering communion in peoples' homes, during a weekday (fig. 16). In rural Ireland, this practice was widespread by the eighteenth century; apparently it was 'solidly established in Munster by the 1780s'.[3] Indeed in some areas, such as Armagh in 1834, even though the practice was already customary, the holding of Stations was made obligatory.[4] The visiting priest was traditionally given breakfast or a substantial meal by the householder and since in some parishes the number of Stations held might exceed a hundred per year, this saved him considerable sums of money.[5] By the nineteenth century the Stations were well established and universally held. Despite various failed attempts from Rome to abolish the practice, it survived, enabling poor people in remote areas to attend confession.[6]

The following is from an account by a Roman Catholic visitor to Ireland in the seventeenth century. He suggests that one-third of the population at that time was Catholic, although the religion was heavily and relentlessly suppressed by the authorities;

there are . . . more than twenty houses where Mass is secretly said, and above

15. Young women on the Aran Islands scrubbing stools in a running stream. Many people used 'shelly sand' to scour seats and table tops. Photograph by F.E. Stephens, early twentieth century, courtesy of the N.M.I.

16. *Mass in a Connemara Cabin*, Exh. R.A., 1883, a drawing by Aloysius O'Kelly (b. 1850) from his original oil painting (both untraced). 'The Stations' as such Masses were called, provided a regular incentive for householders to upgrade their furniture by repainting. Photo courtesy of Pyms Gallery (London).

a thousand places, and subterraneous vaults and retired spots in the woods, where peasants assemble to hear Mass celebrated by some priests they secretly maintain . . . I was in [Drogheda] on a Sunday, and it was told that if I was desirous of hearing mass, one would be said at two miles distance from the town. It would be astonishing to relate the numbers of Catholics that I saw arrive from across the woods and mountains to assemble at this Mass, which was said in a little hamlet, and in a chamber poorly fitted up. Here I saw, before mass, above fifty persons confess . . . This priest informed me that . . . there were many in different parts of the kingdom who found great difficulty to perform freely the functions of their religion.[7]

Detailed accounts of the history of the Stations are rare, but it is probably a practice which has developed through centuries of Catholic repression, surviving as a tradition long after the reasons for secrecy have passed.

Dr Pococke, touring Donegal in the 1750s, noticed that 'the Papists being so few and so poor' gathered openly in the hills on Sundays with 'the priest celebrating Mass . . . on an altar made of loose stones'.[8] By 1830 Carleton described how the impending Station, to be held in the Lisnaskey farm kitchen caused a flurry of excitement: 'Every preparation was accordingly entered into . . . The dresser, chairs, tables, pots, and pans, all underwent a rigour of discipline, as if some remarkable event was about to occur; nothing less, it must be supposed, than a complete domestic revolution, and a new state of things.'[9] How the Stations came to affect the way furniture was repainted can be clearly seen from Alice Taylor's light-hearted account of 1930s Munster:

In our townland our turn for the Stations came around every six years and then it was like three Christmases rolled into one. The preparations might start as much as twelve months in advance as they provided an opportunity to get everything done in the house that needed to be done. The reason, of course, for this big clean-up was that Mass was going to be said in the house and all the neighbours for miles around were going to descend on us . . . Bags of rubbish were burned indiscriminately and many a family treasure was reduced to ashes. Rooms that were full of clutter before, now doubled in size . . . When the burning and washing had finished the painting began and nothing escaped the paint brush. Ceilings, walls, tables and chairs all took on a new, bright look. It was the era of slow drying paint and if you forgot to watch your step you could end up with a multi-coloured look yourself. The Stations only affected the downstairs rooms fully . . . After Mass . . . A volunteer was sought for the next Station, which posed no problem as every house took its turn and everybody knew who was next.[10]

The number of Catholic households per parish still dictates the frequency with which the Stations is held in any given house. Smaller parishes are likely to make this rotation more frequently than larger ones. Elderly members of the parish are not usually expected to go through the upheaval which such an event necessarily imposes upon the household. An old bachelor in west Cork, whose settle was particularly nicely grained, was able to say categorically that the graining had been done in 1944, because that was the date of the last Stations held in his home. Alice Taylor describes an elderly person's distinctly less elaborate preparations for Stations. Her childhood neighbour, a reclusive old woman, hatched hens in boxes beneath her kitchen table and refused to light her fire lest she should upset them:

Despite her lack of visitors, Nell decided that she would have the Stations when her turn came. She was not expected to have them but, contrary as she was, that was sufficient reason for Nell to do so. She sent word to all the neighbours . . . that she did not want them eating her out of house and home when they came, however. Undoubtedly they got the message, for there was none of her neighbours involved in Nell's Stations or the preparation apart from Tim Joe and me. And, compared with what went on in other houses, there were almost no preparations at all . . . The colour of Nell's altar cloths and the lack of anything for

the priest to eat caused my mother sleepless nights, but they did not cost Nell a thought . . . We whitewashed the inside walls and any parts of the outside not covered by ivy and, having washed out the floor and cleaned the windows, we thought the little place was a palace.[11]

Other events in the religious calendar also have their bearing on schemes of redecoration.

Tradition demanded that the dwelling house and all its appurtenances should be thoroughly cleaned and set in order in preparation for Easter, and this occupied much of the time of the housewife and her helpers during Holy Week. The house was everywhere swept and cleaned. The walls were whitewashed inside and outside. Woodwork was repainted, furniture scrubbed white, pots and containers scoured, delf and ornaments washed and polished.[12]

Carpentry (and therefore furniture making) was effectively ruled out on Good Friday when 'no wood should be worked or burned and no nail should be driven on the day which the Saviour was crucified.'[13]

Of course, it would be wrong to assume that religion was the sole impetus for housework and painting. Many people can remember the regular routine of scrubbing table tops and settle seats. According to Eric Cross repainting was undertaken biannually in some households:

Twice a year the settle and the dresser and the doors and the shutters of the windows are painted by Ansty until by now the accumulation of paint must be near to half an inch thick. The Tailor never gives a hand and views it all with cynical amusement. The only good that he can see in it is that it keeps the paint manufacturers busy and makes them rich . . . Ansty sees it in a very different light . . . The house must be clean in case she should die tomorrow and the place not be ready for her wake.[14]

Cross's reference to paint being half an inch thick is no exaggeration. Repeatedly one finds dressers which have been so thickly painted that any carved surface decoration has become barely discernible (figs. 17,

17. Detail of thickly painted rope mouldings and scroll decorating a four-door press (see fig. 221) from Ballynaclogh, county Limerick. At the Irish Agricultural Museum; courtesy of the N.M.I.

19. Thickly over-painted detail of the gouge-carved decoration on the front of a rare canopy bed, from county Waterford (fig. 256). Part of the Irish Country Furniture Society's collection; courtesy of the Irish Agricultural Museum.

18. (*below*) Detail of the craquelure of nineteenth-century paintwork, over many previous layers, on the panel of a food press made *c*.1750–75. Part of the Irish Country Furniture Society's collection; courtesy of the Irish Agricultural Museum.

20. (*below, right*) Carved decoration on the top of an open arcaded corner press (fig. 208), with a horizontal guilloche freize and incised circles nearly obscured beneath thick overpainting, finished with scumble.

20–1, 23). This is why many dealers of Irish furniture have since the 1960s persisted in stripping down painted items, rather than attempting the more skilled (and expensive) work of surface restoration. Ironically this destructive practice continues despite current demand for ancient looking distressed paintwork. Furniture dealers complain that decorative details are lost under countless layers of multi-coloured paint, rather than accepting it as a phenomenon of Ireland's unique material culture and giving the buying public a chance to see and appreciate it.

The desirable 'grained' finish which was customary up until the early part of the twentieth century is usually concealed beneath many other subsequent layers of paint (fig. 22). By studying cross sections of samples of this paint under the microscope, as many as two dozen separate layers of paint can sometimes be detected. Skilled restorers can now remove specific layers of paint discerningly to reveal subsequent older finishes. The most popular finish during the eighteenth and nineteenth centuries was in imitation of expensive figured hardwoods such as mahogany (fig. 24), oak or sometimes even satinwood (fig. 235). Graining was carried out using special graining combs or equivalent improvised

21. Close-up of decades of layers of accumulated overpainting from the back of a Gibson chair (fig. 37) recently stripped by hand. It is not uncommon to find over twenty layers of different coloured paint on Irish vernacular furniture.

tools (feathers, rags, sticks or even a piece of cork).

Techniques amongst furniture makers were sometimes closely guarded secrets. A wheelwright and furniture maker named Con Coakley from west Cork, made a point of graining the furniture that he built, late at night when no one was around to watch. Presumably this was in order to keep his technique – and therefore his livelihood – to himself. Coakley was frequently employed to make furniture, and also to redecorate all the painted furniture and woodwork before the Stations came around. He had a habit of working slowly, which made his employers anxious in case the job should not be ready for the service.[15] Another west county Cork wheelwright and furniture maker, Johnny Brien, used to prepare and seal the bare wood before graining it with a thinned animal glue 'size' which he

made up himself using cows' horns and hooves. He was renowned for his skill at 'marbling' and is said to have been capable of marbling a wooden fire surround so convincingly that one could not tell the difference without touching it. The 92-year-old furniture maker from county Carlow, Patrick Purcell, related how he stained the furniture that he made with 'Turkey Umber Powder' and when he could not get that he would make a nutbrown stain using strong tea. His grandmother used to mix her own French polish with ingredients such as allum, shellac, methylated spirits, vandyke brown crystals, raw sienna pigment (both to give darker tones) and linseed oil.

Graining is still an enduringly traditional finish for shopfronts, doors and furniture throughout Ireland.[16] The technique requires a base coat, usually of a light colour, which is allowed to dry thoroughly

before the application of a contrasting, darker glaze coat of 'scumble'.[17] The scumble coat has the characteristic grained effect drawn through it before it dries by means of the graining combs (fig. 22). These used to be made of metal and more recently have been replaced by rubber patterned graining rollers. The appearance of grained finishes varies on Irish furniture enormously, from that of a convincing imitation of curl mahogany or quarter sawn oak (the best and most expensive cuts) to naive patterned finishes with the same tools, but bearing little resemblance to wood.

The majority of pieces of furniture which have not been over painted recently, display a variety of shades of deep red or brown colours (fig. 18). Without any attempt at grained surface finishes, they nevertheless provided the general dark appearance of more fashionable 'parlour' furniture of the nineteenth century. A sample of matt dark red paint which was analysed from a dresser found in a long derelict house in county Cork, was shown to contain organic pigment, probably blood from a pig. When repainting was carried out for an event such as the Stations, not only the furniture but also all the other woodwork in the house (doors, window frames, stairs etc.) was usually painted to match. Sometimes the colour scheme would vary from one room to the next (fig. 203).

As commercially available paints gradually came onto the market during the nineteenth century, fashions in colour schemes moved away from traditional graining. Householders began to favour the use of two contrasting colours for their larger items of furniture, rather than just one. Indeed the colours themselves changed. The use of brightly coloured 'two-tone' combinations was widely adopted. These colours varied enormously, presumably ranging from whatever was available, to blends and mixtures of commercial gloss paints (figs. 17, 19–21, 23). In poorly lit rooms, with only a few small windows, decoration and ornamentation was often limited to a few religious or political pictures. The use of contrasting coloured paints accentuated the role of the dresser as an important aesthetic focal point, with its display of 'ware'. The backing boards of the dresser were generally painted the lighter

24. Detail of the back of an oak and pine 'carpenters' chair', which has been painted in imitation of mahogany and inlaid with stringing (see fig. 58). *c.*1840. Early paint finishes are rare because vernacular furniture was usually regularly repainted. Courtesy of the N.M.I.

Facing page:
22. Detail of woodgraining: dark scumble applied over a pale base coat, then removed while wet, with graining combs. From the upper section of a dowry chest (fig. 236) *c.*1800, from Carrigbeg, Doon, county Limerick. Shown at the Irish Agricultural Museum; courtesy of the N.M.I.

23. Detail of the back of an intricately carved settle bed, from Woodstown, county Waterford (see fig. 132). The heart, a favourite Irish motif, surmounts one of several different fielded panels, held in place originally by integral mouldings. The layered cornice has saw-tooth mouldings and complex dentil friezes which have become rounded beneath numerous coats of paint. Courtesy of the Irish Agricultural Museum, Wexford.

cupboards, meal chests and canopy beds) were occasionally painted but more often they were lined with newspaper or wallpaper (figs. 203, 244, 256, 257). This not only served to draw in light and decorate the interiors, but also prevented the accumulation of dust through gaps in the boards. This was an especially important practice for the so-called canopy beds, as it would exclude draughts as well as dust (fig. 256). In some households beds were traditionally relined with new wallpaper every Christmas.[18] Like the paintwork, the multiple layers of coloured papers bear testimony to this tradition. A large meal chest in a farm kitchen in the Wicklow mountains is lined with wallpaper, originally this would have prevented flour from escaping through cracks. Every year when the owner repaints throughout the house, she uses a spare piece of last year's wallpaper to decorate the inside of the meal chest (fig. 203).

Patterned and coloured oilcloth, where available, has been used to colour and decorate kitchen table tops, shelves and worksurfaces since at least the early nineteenth century. This material is also sometimes overlaid, and can be seen in paintings hung over the fronts of dresser shelves, with a carefully cut-out edge (fig. 171). Formica or 'beauty board' as it is sometimes known, has become a popular new labour saving worksurface for the old previously scrubbed kitchen tables (fig. 297).

The latest systems of hygiene and of saving labour have now become a high priority in all the but the most traditional Irish houses. This has changed the appearance of many 'unconverted' homes. Bright contrasting two-tone paintwork is now the hallmark of older houses containing traditional furniture forms. The fashion for stripped pine has ironically recently been the reason for young householders to keep (rather than burn or sell) their traditional furniture. Increasingly one finds a kitchen which still has its old dresser, but it has been stripped and wax polished rather than being sold, or even burnt. Recent trends towards the 'worn paintwork' look, with new furniture being offered for sale with a painted and distressed finish, may well further influence the retention of traditional furniture finishes in Irish homes.

of the two colours, helping to accentuate the shapes of the rows of 'ware' on display. Panels of doors and settle backs were made to stand out in contrast. During the latter part of this century, ceilings were also sometimes painted in contrasting colours, open joists contrasting with the undersides of the floorboards, which helped to reflect light into the otherwise dark kitchen (fig. 148).

Favourite colour combinations which I have noted repeatedly include: pale blue, with yellow, grey, cream, pink or white, or white contrasting with various shades of green, yellow or brown, and blue with red etc. Two-tone dressers usually have the lighter of the colours for the backing boards and cupboard door panels, while with settles the panels or backing boards might be picked out in a contrasting hue. Furniture painted since the 1970s has shown a marked tendency towards one rather than two colours. When it is simply painted one colour (often white, mushroom or pale grey), the result is notably less dramatic than either the two-tone or grained finishes.

The insides of furniture (dressers, presses,

Chapter 1
STOOLS & CHAIRS

An Introduction to Seating, Low Stools,
The Effect of Flooring upon Seat Design, Improvised and Recycled Stools,
Stool Terminology, Hedge Chairs, Interlocking Arm Chairs,
Gibson Chairs, Hedge Chairs with Composite Seats,
Sutherland Chairs and their Derry Relatives, Comb Back Chairs, Carpenters' Chairs,
The 'Sligo Chair', Súgán Chairs, Súgán Chair Construction,
Other Unusual Chairs and Dug-out Chairs, Chairs made of Straw, Children's Chairs

AN INTRODUCTION TO SEATING

'The Memorial of Patrick McKye' of 1837, takes the form of a horrifyingly meagre list of the possessions of the 9,000 or so inhabitants of a parish in western county Donegal. For these almost destitute members of the Catholic population of West Tullaghobegly, stools were evidently more common than any other item of furniture. McKye, teacher at the only National School in the district, wrote his list or memorial as a plea for assistance to the Lord Lieutenant of Ireland. The pitiful list includes only the following household items; 'Seven table-forks, Ninety-three chairs. Two hundred and forty three stools . . . Two feather beds, Eight chaff beds . . . No clock, Three watches, Eight brass candlesticks, No looking glasses above 3*d*. in price.'[1] Due to poverty, no settles, dressers or meal chests and very few beds are listed in the McKye Memorial, so the high number of stools and chairs listed highlights their functional importance: they enabled people to keep away from the dampness of earthen floors and to sit around the fire.

Stools not only varied in size, from as little as 4 to 18 inches high, but also in the range of functions they were required to fulfill. This is demonstrated by Andrew M'Kenzie's poetic inventory of 1807, 'The Poor Man's Petition';

Three stools, one larger than the rest
Our table when we have a guest.[2]

The fact that stools were commonly used as small improvised tables is discussed in

some detail in the chapter about tables (figs. 262, 286). It is perhaps significant that the many emigrants who left Ireland took with them, as well as supplies of food for their long voyage, 'quite often a stool or a chair as no sitting accommodation was to be had on the "coffin" ships'.[3]

There are occasionally clues as to whether certain seats or positions close to the fire had a special importance. The Ordnance Survey memoirs for county Antrim in the 1830s inform us: 'The chairs and a couple of very low stools called "Creepies" are kept near the fire. If a stranger comes in he is invariably handed a chair, as being the highest seat.'[4] Carleton describes the head of a household being seated amongst his friends on one of the two (built in) hobs, the 'seat of honour'.[5] Also during the 1830s, the Government Poor Inquiry stated that in county Meath people usually had 'some stools, [and] a chair "for any of the quality who may come in"'.[6] Synge, writing of the Aran Islands at the start of the twentieth century mentions how visitors were given 'a chair, or stool, according to age'.[7] The limited amount of space close to the warmth of the hearth meant that large chairs were rare and that the most important seat would have been determined by position rather than by size.[8] Early accounts vary, but the nineteenth-century diary of a farmer's son from county Wicklow, reveals some interesting details about seating arrangements;

the big deal table where the serving men eat; they sit on long four-legged deal

25. Four hedge chairs made in the late nineteenth century by a wheelwright, Thomas Murphy (1839–1937), of Stratford on Slaney, county Wicklow. The group illustrates a remarkable diversity of design, and incorporates elm, ash, maple, beech, whitethorn, pine and sycamore. The mixed woods are unified by blue, mulberry red and black paint (see figs. 29, 31).

stools, scrubbed like the table white with river sand. The master's large wooden armchair stands in front of the hearth: It was my father's seat in the later years. There are wooden chairs for others, and the whole life of the house has its centre in the kitchen.[9]

The wooden chairs 'for others' that he writes of, might well have been something like those illustrated (fig. 25), which originate from precisely the same area of county Wicklow. However, the special seat was not necessarily the largest or most comfortable one. In 'The Tailor and Ansty,' an amusing and controversial tale of a Cork couple in 1942,

> it was a chair, but age and usage have worn down the legs unevenly till the seat of it is only a stool's height from the floor . . . The Tailor always bows the most favoured guest to it as if it were a throne . . . If a guest should already be installed in the chair of honour and a guest of higher rank arrives, Ansty will simply and directly command, 'Get up, 'oo, and give the chair to So-and-so.'[10]

LOW STOOLS

> For sitting low, on rushes spread,
> The smoak still hover'd over head;
> And did more good than real harm,
> Because it kept the long house warm,
> And never made their heads to ake;
> Therefore no chimney would he make.
>
> W. Moffat, 1724[11]

Seating was very often extraordinarily low, some surviving stools being a mere 3 or 4 inches from the floor. Visitors to Ireland consistently observed that such diminutive seats made it easy for people to keep their heads low beneath the pall of smoke that inevitably gathered in the many chimneyless dwellings (fig. 6).[12] As we have seen, these smoky conditions prevailed in rural houses from the seventeenth century, which was when John Stevens noted in his *Journal*: 'They say it is of late years that chimneys are used, yet the house is never free from smoke.'[13] Another of the many travelling authors, Dr Pococke, wrote about this as

he toured western county Mayo in the mid-eighteenth century. Upon entering a 'Cabbin' and being troubled by the smoke, his host made him 'a low seat near the fire . . . it was not so inconvenient, the smoak rising up and condensing above'. He also noticed how 'their stools are long and narrow like a stilion' (a stand for casks or buckets).[14] About a century later, conditions had changed little, as Caesar Otway, travelling through the same district described 'a great fire on the hearth, from which smoke floated in volumes around, and if you didn't keep your head down near the floor, you will be suffocated'.[15] These and many more similar descriptions of smoky, floor-level fires, plus the use of the central hearth, resulted in a widespread adoption of such low seats. The total lack of chimneys meant that the poor made more efficient use of their fuel. Indeed Hely Dutton wrote of county Clare in his survey of the area in 1808:

> Formerly there was scarcely a cottage, that had a chimney, and where the landlord has built them, he has frequently found a flag or sod on top of the chimney to keep in the smoke, which, they say, keeps them warm . . . the lower part of the cottage has three or four feet from the ground but little smoke, they seem not to feel it, when they sit down.[16]

THE EFFECT OF FLOORING UPON SEAT DESIGN

Floors made of beaten earth known as 'daub'[17] or of compacted river clay were widespread in the smaller traditional homes throughout Ireland since the seventeenth century.[18]

Those who could obtain the material had the hearth area or the whole floor stone flagged (figs. 105, 155, 198), perhaps with a suspended wooden floor in 'the room' or parlour (fig. 211).[19] A small number of traditional houses still have such earthen floors in use (figs. 97, 152), although the great majority have now been covered over with concrete. In county Derry 'clabber' (earth or mud) from the surface of rough roads was gathered and scattered with oathulls and

26. Detail from *News of The Land League* by Howard Helmick (1845–1907), an American artist who worked in Ireland after 1872. Oil on canvas. It shows a table and seats supported by 'earth fast' posts outside an inn. Furniture made like this, by driving timber directly into the ground, is described from the homes of the poor, although its lifespan was limited and none seems to have survived. Courtesy of the N.G.I.

27. Small creepie stool with beech seat and ash legs, dating from the early nineteenth century. Many stools, or 'creepies' as they were called in northern counties, were made from thick or irregularly shaped pieces of timber. This example came from Larne, on the east coast of county Antrim. Photo courtesy of the U.F.T.M.

then a dance might be held to help compress the resulting mixture.[20] Alternatively a herd of sheep was driven into the house and encouraged to keep moving to consolidate it. Inevitably the results were somewhat uneven and frequently rather damp, generally with a slight slope upwards towards the hearth.[21]

This type of flooring had a number of important effects on the way stools and chairs were built.[22] Folklorists in the 1930s, collecting information before the flooding of part of county Wicklow for the Poulaphouca Resevoir, entered a house that was 'built on the bog, and was dark and damp within. Beside the fire in the kitchen was a stool, the supports of which were two round sticks driven through the bog floor.'[23] These 'earth fast' legs used less valuable timber than a freestanding three-legged stool, and the seat was probably fixed to the two legs by through-wedging (like the majority of surviving examples of other seats, fig. 35). The same system was used for 'The Tailor's Table, standing on four logs, set in the floor (fig. 298)'.[24] Carleton also describes 'a potato-bin, made up of stakes driven into the floor, and wrought with strong wickerwork'.[25] Although such descriptions are

rare, and no actual examples have come to light other than as illustrations (fig. 26) or descriptions, furniture made in this way may well have been quite common.[26] If such pieces were made from bog fir or bog oak, then they would probably have been able to survive the damp conditions without rotting.

Uneven floors have a bad effect upon seats with legs rigidly joined by stretchers. Except for mass-produced chairs, the majority of locally made stools and chairs had independent unlinked legs, which could be individually removed and replaced by the householder whenever they become worn or loose (figs. 27, 34). This lack of stretchers combined with the common use of the through-wedged tenon (fig. 35) to attach legs into seats, meant that chairs could survive inclement conditions for long periods.

Many surviving seats have had legs renewed from time to time, which can be hard to detect as quite often contrasting types of wood were originally used for different legs. Sometimes a newer leg shows up because of a different method of fixing, like the front leg replacement of a chair made by William O'Neill, from county Wicklow. It is easily detected as it lacks the octagonal section of the originals and has been replaced with a piece of cloth rather than a wedge to hold it firmly in place (fig. 34). Similarly, another hedge chair from county Wicklow has a replaced front leg which tapers abruptly as it meets the seat, whereas whoever originally made the chair took care

to taper the other legs gradually and more elegantly (fig. 36; see also fig. 32). The examination of paint samples can help determine the replaced parts; sometimes a new set of holes has been drilled to accept new legs, leaving the old sawn-off ones clearly visible.[27] Through-wedged joints were used to unite every part of the typical hedge chair, the wedges were aligned carefully so that their length ran across the grain direction of the seat (and never with it), to avoid splitting (fig. 35). Their use facilitated renewability, as the following singular account from county Tipperary in the 1930s explains; 'He knocked the knee out of the chair. He was after putting a new knee in the chair.'[28]

The characteristic interplay between renewability of parts, economy of materials and function, gives rise to a surprisingly wide variation in design. Stools seats in particular were rarely machined in any way and often assumed a wild, organic looking form, hardly different from their original growing state. Traces of bark have sometimes been left on legs and seat edges (fig. 34). Stools with individual legs (three, four or even only two when 'earth fast', fig. 26) used less material than those using boards. The board-ended type of stool, rather like a small version of a form, was also commonly used (figs. 15, 100, 207).

IMPROVISED AND RECYCLED STOOLS

Opposite the door a wooden stair with a rail runs up into the bedrooms. This is a great addition to the seating resources of the house, and on the night of assembly, a dance, or other occasion, an ascending line of boys and girls sits from stair to stair, till at last the final couple are visible only as four legs showing below the level of the ceiling.

Robin Flower, *The Western Island*, 1944[29]

The use of the stairs or loft ladder to accommodate an overflow of visitors is perhaps an obvious resource and is one that is often mentioned in nineteenth-century texts.

Improvised stools and low seats were frequently made of stone, turf or any other common material. The Government Poor Reports of 1836 noted repeatedly that poor householders had little more than a pot and one or two stools for furniture. One of these entries for county Roscommon mentioned how people, rather than sitting on the damp floor, used 'a block of wood or peat for a stool'.[30] According to the same reports from county Cork 'one or two [bog] fir seats' were the norm,[31] while in county Meath the most destitute usually had 'two stools or stones to sit on'.[32]

As we have seen, recycling of materials has always been an important part of the vernacular furniture maker's resourcefulness. This meant both putting an old object (or parts of it) to a new use or utilising materials lost or discarded by others. The resulting forms were sometimes influenced by the materials from which they originated (fig. 97). For those living along the coast or on the islands, the rocks and beaches were regularly checked for driftwood, wreck timber and anything that could be of use or value. The sun dried vertebrae of a stranded whale made a serviceable fireside seat. Baulks of exotic mahogany jettisoned in storms became the rafters for a new barn,[33] or their immense size inspired the carving of a one-piece medieval-style 'dug-out' chair (fig. 78). Stories of wrecks still abound in coastal districts, living on vividly in peoples' memories. Accounts of brave rescues are intermingled with the risks taken to salvage valuable materials.

Several stories, told by many different members of the same west Cork parish, related to the wreck of the large steamer *Asian*, on 17 September 1924. She struck the west side of the notorious Stag Rocks and quickly broke up and sank within the next few days. All but one of her passengers and crew were rescued, but according to the wireless operator's reports 'a few hatches and small deck fittings were picked up' along with '60 bales cotton, 220 barrels wax, 10 barrels oil, [a] small quantity of oak boards, [and] stores. Local motor fishing boats on look out for cargo washing out.'[34] The manager of the local creamery, Denis O'Mahony, was one of many who flocked to the scene. He came home with some of the 'small deck fittings' in the form of a pair of turned winch covers. He drilled holes in them, added wedged legs and put them to new use as three-legged stools. One of them

28. A pair of recycled, inverted and painted butter boxes being used as fireside stools, in a house at Moycullen, county Galway, c.1948. A by-product of the Irish Creamery during the first half of the twentieth century, these tapered pine boxes held 56lb. of butter and were put to many uses in the south and west. Photo courtesy of Bord Fáilte.

the Tailor does periodically fall into it. He estimates that a butter box lasts him about three years and then collapses beneath him. But it is never changed until it fails. He enjoys the element of danger and surprise.[36]

Many surviving examples have been upholstered and are still used, mouth downward.

Similarly, barrels were kept and evidence from old paintings shows them used as flour bins, seats or tables (figs. 218, 282).

STOOL TERMINOLOGY

The term 'creepie' or occasionally 'creepy' was until recently often applied to a three-, or sometimes four-legged stool, especially in the most northerly counties of Ireland (fig. 27).[37] The name was already a familiar one during the first half of the nineteenth century, as *The Dublin Penny Journal* confidently proclaimed to its reading public: 'our own three legged stool, or *creepy* . . . is evidently the most primitive and ancient form [of seating] in the world, and which retains its appropriate place in the mud cabin'.[39] Both the object and its name seem to imply the scuttling movements of some small creature, inconspicuous in its dark red or brown paint on an earthen floor. The origins of its name vary, but a four-legged one from county Fermanagh is described as being 'So small that it moves across the floor with you as your body shifts, it gains the name "creepie".'[39] The term was also used in Scotland in the eighteenth century for a church stool of repentence, and may have migrated along with the planted Scottish settlers since the seventeenth century.

In county Leitrim in 1955

the three legged stool of course was always and still is a very vital part of furniture. Its three legs meant that it would always be firmly placed on the ground, even if its angle was not so preeminently conducive to comfort . . . It could be made by any man. Of course it was used very much, and still is, for milking.[40]

The stool used for milking was sometimes called '"the block", maybe because it con-

is amongst other furniture made by him in Ceim Hill Museum, county Cork (fig. 320).

Locally, other stories relating to that same wreck are still told. Skill was required to salvage such materials in the face of local competition and rough weather, but also to avoid the inevitable seizures by customs officers, used to the usual frantic gathering of 'wreck'. They simply waited for a few days before making house to house searches. One woman was delighted to have got hold of the captain's table cloth, and upon seeing the uniformed men approaching her farm, quickly threw it into the bottom of a bath full of washing, covering it up with clothes. They searched her house so thoroughly that the table cloth was found and confiscated.

An object which was commonly recycled into a container or seat, and which is still common in homes in Munster, is the simple four-sided, tapered butter box. At least one found new life as a toolbox, it was made of 'fine timber with a yellow waxen sheen. Many found their way into local farmers' houses where they were put to good use.'[35] Inverted it became a solid looking seat, tapering gently inwards towards the top (fig. 28). Such a box was a favourite fireside seat, placed sideways

so that its opening is between his legs, and here he sits, never upon a chair . . .

33

sisted of a 2 inch block of solid timber with three legs broadening out at the base to give balance'.[41] However, the common assumption that three-legged stools were called milking stools is more appropriate to England than Ireland. An early eighteenth-century reporter's description of a farmer who had 'two blocks for stools' may have been referring to solid blocks of wood rather than the type with legs.[42]

Four-legged stools were also common and both types were usually made by inserting a wedge of hard wood into a saw cut made in the top of each leg, once the legs had been pushed into angled holes in the slab seat. This method of through-wedging created a tight socketed joint requiring no glue. In Scotland, holes for chair legs were known to have been burned through the seat with a red hot poker rather than drilled.[43] It is likely that such an ingenious system was resorted to by Irish householders as well.

In the light of so many literary references to three-legged stools and creepies, it is sad that so few have survived (although four-legged examples are still quite common). They have disappeared along with their original *raison d'être*; the smoky, chimney-less cabins. In time such a smoky atmosphere made everything dark brown and grimy. All kinds of seats were left unpainted and instead were taken occasionally to a nearby stream to be scrubbed clean (fig. 15).[44]

Stools are mentioned repeatedly amongst the descriptions given by the government commissioners for the Poor Reports in the 1830s. These inform us that the poor in county Mayo for instance, possessed 'a pot and a few seats, called stools' but also that much of this meagre furniture was home made.[45]

Few documents have come to light which provide useful evidence of furniture prices for the period under consideration here. However, we do know that 'Kitchen stools' were in abundant supply in Lisburn market, county Antrim in 1837 and were being sold for 3*d*. each. As we have seen, a stool is a very variable object, so the price is only useful when compared with that of *súgán* chairs at 1*s*. each, kitchen chairs at 1*s*. 8*d*. each and timber chairs at 1*s*. 10*d*. each, at the same market that year.[46]

HEDGE CHAIRS

In the broadest context of furniture history it has often been said that the chair evolved from the stool. The term 'back stool' occurred in many English seventeenth-century inventories as a result. The close association between stool and chair is more obvious with the slab-seated hedge chairs of rural Ireland than perhaps anywhere else (fig. 25).[47]

The term 'hedge chair' stems from the fact that such chairs were often made by so called 'hedge carpenters'. The hedge carpenter did not serve the same long apprenticeship as the carpenter, but he 'could choose part of a tree for the job to be done. Or "go to a tree and carry home a plough" – a wooden plough – used everywhere.'[48] This skill of finding timber which saved him labour explains his choice of naturally bent 'knees' of timber for chair parts, which achieved a desired shape with minimum cutting. At the beginning of the nineteenth century, the wages of a county Clare 'House Carpenter, [were] from 3*s*. 9½*d*. to 4*s*. 4*d*. per day', whereas those of the 'hedge carpenter, [were] 2*s*. 2*d*. and diet per day'.[49] Such comparisons explain his low status amongst woodworkers and his use of inexpensive timber. Timber for hedge chairs was often simply gleaned from hedgerows. This is evident from the broad variety of contrasting wood types with which each chair is commonly made. Thus, the name hedge chair reflects both the rural makers and the varied arboreal origins of the chairs themselves.

The term 'kitchen chair' was also used as a label for this distinctive seat, perhaps in order to distinguish it from the more stylish parlour chairs.[50] However, for the purposes of this study it is helpful to differentiate between the several distinct types of chair which were commonly found in kitchens throughout rural Ireland between the eighteenth and the mid twentieth centuries. Antique dealers seem to have been responsible for the label 'famine chair', applied for their own convenience, but fieldstudies have never discovered this evocative term applied by householders themselves; neither is there any documentary evidence to support its use as a household term. It seems to have resulted from a common misconception that these chairs date from the period of the worst famines of the 1840s, with their minimal and undecorated appearance perhaps another factor suggestive of famine. Dealers often tend to date objects earlier than they really are in order to increase their value. These chairs have even been seen for sale in London with the label 'primitive', implying that they are centuries old. Hard wear in a smoky atmosphere tends to build up an ancient looking patina comparatively quickly, thus adding weight to such claims.

The misnomer 'Irish Windsor' has occasionally been attached to such chairs, but since there is little or no evidence to support the theory that the makers of hedge chairs were influenced by the English chairmaking tradition, it seems wholly inappropriate.[51] 'Windsor' has become a common generic name for chairs of stick construction, where the legs and upper frame are fixed independently of each other into the seat.[52] English Windsors are characterised by the use of the lathe to turn the spindles and legs, which are joined by stretchers. In contrast, Irish hedge chairs rarely exhibit these characterstics; lathe work is highly exceptional and the legs are rarely linked by stretchers. In the absence of previous publications on Irish hedge chairs, almost identical chairs made by Irish settlers in Australia, have (understandably) been wrongly assumed to have had English origins.[53]

The Robinson brothers, fine cabinetmakers of Milltown, county Cavan, recalled such chairs and stools being made by their neighbour, whom they knew as the hedge carpenter, during the first half of the twentieth century. As fellow woodworkers, their heightened awareness of such activities makes their account especially noteworthy. He always had a stack of offcuts from the local sawmill behind his house; waney-edged boards (complete with bark) and the curved outermost slices from trunks he put aside for a year or so to season. These could be riven (split) along the grain and quickly shaped up with a drawknife to make legs, while the widest pieces became the seats for chairs. Stools were made from the smaller sections. When he had completed enough chairs he would load up his donkey and cart

and take a batch to sell at the local market.

The work of the hedge carpenter was looked down upon by other finer woodworkers whose use of the term was somewhat derogatory. Some people, however, appreciated their artistry, as 'they had never become enslaved to line and level; their minds had not been trained to revolt if their work deviated from the square, or if it was slightly on the twist and the faces of their joints not absolutely flush'.[54] When the limited range of timber, tools and equipment available to the average maker of these chairs is considered, the result is even more admirable. Hedge carpentry was in England primarily involved with the building of fences, gates, pig troughs and wooden objects around the farm. In Ireland such a term embraced a much wider assortment of talents; in poor areas tradesmen's skills had to be diverse as an economic necessity. The hedge carpenter of Milltown was also a small farmer, growing his own food to feed his family.

Hedge chairs varied from the crudest or most simple slab-seated stool with a backrest usually attached by means of cigarshaped spindles, through-wedged at both ends, to more complex varieties with arms (figs. 32, 34–7). The strength of the chair depended upon obtaining a broad piece of timber for the seat, which in some examples is over 2 inches thick. It mattered little if the seat was not completely seasoned, as any shrinkage would result in a positive tightening of the mortices around the legs and back sticks. The vertical back sticks or spindles were riven or cleft to take advantage of the strength of the grain, then shaped into a subtle cigar shape with a two-handled drawknife, spokeshave or even an axe. Some chairmakers dried the ends of the spindles before the fire, to shrink them slightly before assembly. The tapered shape of the legs meant that the joints tightened when sat upon. The naturally bent 'knees' of hedgerow timber provided the backrest with a curve that was strong and comfortable. It used far less timber than cutting a curved piece from a board and needed fewer tools. Some of these naturally bent backrests have been persuaded into a more acute shape using heat and steam;

29. (*right*) Hedge chair with curved backrest and 'D' shaped seat with bevelled edges. One of a variety of designs made at the end of the nineteenth century by Thomas Murphy. The cigar-shaped side spindles have been carefully inclined forwards to add strength. Made of mixed timbers, painted mulberry red (fig. 25).

30. (*below*) Low hedge chair with its backrest made out of an extraordinarily curved, natural 'knee' of ash. The thickly painted wine red seat, over 2 in. thick, is probably elm. The ash spindles taper slightly at each end. Late eighteenth century, from the same house as fig. 46, at Greatdown, county Westmeath. Seat 22½ in. wide (at front), 13½ in. deep, 13 in. high; back 25 in. high. Courtesy of the N.M.I.

others have obviously grown that way (figs. 30–1). Steam bending of timber to make curved chair backs is a difficult technique to accomplish successfully, requiring fuel to heat the water and often resulting in wasted timber. The use of 'natural knees' eliminated this time consuming and sometimes risky process which is doubtless why it was preferred in rural Ireland.[55] This emphasis on economy of timber, wasting nothing and using everything, can be seen in the many examples of chair seats which retain their uncut waney edges and even bark, in order to provide the maximum size of seat (figs. 31, 33–4).

Not all hedge chairs were made by hedge carpenters. Farmers in the habit of making and mending as part of their routine often made their own chairs too. Tradesmen skilled in other country crafts such as coffin building, house carpentry, coopering, boatbuilding, blacksmithing and even shoemaking were also known to have turned their hands to stool and chairmaking when the need arose. Wheelwrights, who also liked to seek out naturally curved pieces of timber to incorporate into wheels and carts, were responsible for some of the most accomplished of these chairs (figs. 25, 29, 31,

31. (*facing page, top right*) An unusual wedge backed hedge chair, made by Thomas Murphy, with beech legs braced economically by crossed stretchers of ash. The elm seat was made from the outer cut of a trunk, hence its waney edge. The backrest is a natural 'knee' of maple. Traces of original black paint remain. Height 17½ in./27½ in. Seat 17½ by 13½ in. wide (see fig. 25).

32. Hedge chair from Drumcoo, Scotstown, county Monaghan, early twentieth century. The underside of the elm seat has marks from a circular saw. Such chairs were built to last: its ash legs are through-wedged and one sycamore leg has been replaced. Two of the back spindles are also renewed. Traces remain of its original brown paintwork. Seat 17 in. wide, 13½ in. deep and 16½ in. high; back 31 in. high. Courtesy of Monaghan County Museum.

33. (*top, right*) Hedge chair made by the shoemaker Patrick Lyttle, from Dernawilt, Roslea, county Fermanagh. He was probably unfamiliar with chairmaking, because he has used square tenons to fix the back spindles into the seat and backrest, rather than round ones. The slab seat, of sycamore, has been left as large as possible, as evidenced by the waney edge (where the bark was attached) along the front. Seat 21½ in. wide, 13½ in. deep, 13 in. high. Ash back rest 24 in. wide and 25 in. high. Courtesy of Monaghan County Museum.

34). An example of a hedge chair from Drumcoo, county Monaghan, is perhaps even closer to its natural roots, incorporating some barely worked twig-like timber in the back (fig. 32). The mixture of different woods such as ash, elm, sycamore and whitethorn is typical, and was once unified by brown paint of which only traces now remain. Chairs made by tradesmen unused to furniture making, sometimes exhibit unusual and interesting characteristics. An example of a hedge chair made in about 1910 by a shoemaker called Patrick Lyttle, of county Fermanagh, has back spindles which are fitted into square, rather than round mortices in the seat (fig. 33).

At least two remarkable chairs survive which were made by the wheelwright and furniture maker William O'Neill. He worked not far from Donard in county Wicklow, in the second half of the nineteenth century and although his chairs have generous seats, their upper frameworks are characterised by extreme minimalism. One example has only five uprights supporting the back and arms (fig. 34), while another has six (fig. 160). The lack of stretchers on the majority of

these chairs saved valuable timber, but perhaps more importantly, enabled the chair to survive rough treatment on uneven floors and made the periodical replacement of worn legs easier. It is a distinctly Irish feature. English vernacular chairs usually have stretchers linking the legs, except for some examples from areas such as the West Country. Scottish and Welsh stick chairs also often share this lack of stretchers, perhaps due to their proximity to parts of Ireland, but also because of similarities in economic and architectural conditions.

INTERLOCKING ARM CHAIRS

The type of chairs made at the close of the nineteenth century by William O'Neill were strong and simple, requiring little or no glue for their construction. Their strength lay in the interlocking of the corner spindles (or sticks) through holes in the rear of each armrest (figs. 34, 35). Thomas Murphy, who shared the same combined trades of wheelwright and furniture maker, lived in a nearby parish and produced at least two more of these chairs. He was more generous with his use of back spindles, and his examples have a more substantial look, but with the

34. Hedge chair with interlocking arms and back spindles, made by William O'Neill, a wheelwright near Donard, county Wicklow. Like his other chairs (fig. 160) it is made of ash with an elm seat. Rather than trim and reduce the size of the seat, he has left waney edges and strips of bark at the front and back. All joints are through-wedged except where the spindles meet the backrest. The spindles were shaped with a drawknife, as were the hexagonal legs, (one is renewed and secured with the help of sackcloth). Traces of original brown paintwork. Late nineteenth century. Seat 26½ in. wide, 19½ in. deep; height of back 39 in.

same clever and essential device of interlocking the rear of the armrest with the outer back spindle (fig. 25, 35). Other woodworkers in the Wicklow mountains also favoured this design, which must have been considered successful. However, it would be wrong to assume that this type of construction is typical only of this area, as more have been found originating in areas as far apart as west county Cork and county Leitrim. Versions of this type of stretcherless hedge chair have turned up repeatedly throughout Ireland, and as such they amount to an original indigenous design.

Small versions have also been found which were made for children (figs. 94, 96). Their

system of construction enabled the backrest to be raised to a far more comfortable and supportive position than the level of the arms, while at the same time the back was reinforced considerably by its junction with the armrests. This functional solution, allowing for a gently raked rather than an upright back, was at the same time an ergonomic improvement on the more fragile, simple hedge chair without arms (compare fig. 33).

The success of this design can be measured by the fact that its production continued up until the early 1980s. A family of chairmakers, who originally came from county Leitrim, is survived by John Surlis, now retired, – the latest in a line of seven generations of chairmakers to have continued making this and various other designs of slab-seated chairs. In 1951, he was chosen to give demonstrations of his traditional craft at the Royal Dublin Show.[56] His methods, were traditional and barely mechanised. He shaped the riven ash legs with a spokeshave, seated on a special bench-like vice called a 'cooper's mare'. Long handled 'T' shaped augers were used to drill the holes

for legs and spindles. The shapes of the chair seats were cut out on his home made bandsaw. One of his chairs was known as the 'Leitrim chair' because it was a design made by his grandfather who moved from that county to Sligo, where he now lives.[57]

The movement and settlement of Irish emigrants can often be traced through their particular furniture designs, which they carried on making upon arrival in the 'New World'. The distinctly Irish form of armchair, with its interlocked armrest and corner spindle, and its lack of stretchers, identifies the work of Irish settlers in parts of Australia and Upper Canada.[58]

GIBSON CHAIRS

Another interesting variation of the stretcherless hedge chair with the interlocking arm and corner spindle, has been referred to as the 'Gibson chair', although the origin of the name, which may be associated with Oldcastle, county Meath, is unclear (fig. 37).[59] This design is distinguished from others by the distinctive 'W' (or less often

35. (*facing page, top*) Detail of the curved ash backrest of a hedge chair, showing how the through-wedges are carefully aligned at right angles to the grain direction, to avoid splitting.

36. (*above*) Hedge chair with interlocked armrests and rear spindles, made in the early nineteenth century, from near Rathdangan in the Wicklow Mountains. Some spindles and legs have been renewed over the years, and it has been overpainted repeatedly, most recently with brown gloss (compare with figs. 25, 34).

37. (*right*) A so-called 'Gibson chair', characterised by its interlocked arms and rear spindles, which describe a 'W'. This design was once common in northeastern Leinster, especially in counties Monaghan, Cavan, Louth and Meath, where it was still made in the 1940s. Its legs and spindles are ash, and the seat, arms and backrest are sycamore. Originally, it was painted repeatedly with at least eight layers in contrasting colours (fig. 21). The front left leg is a replacement. Seat 24½ in. wide, 15 in. deep, 13 in. high; overall height 33½ in.

39

an 'M') shaped arrangement of back spindles or sticks, the generously broad 'D' shaped seats, substantial backrests and broadly curved armrests (fig. 37). These were once common in county Cavan, although more generally they can be seen as indigenous to north-east Leinster. They were made especially in counties Louth, Monaghan, Meath and Westmeath. The Irish Country Furniture Society has a pair on display as part of its furniture study collection at The Irish Agricultural Museum, county Wexford. Like most other examples they are made from a combination of elm, ash and sycamore.[60] The diagonal arrangement of the back spindles is not only striking to

look at but is also a structural improvement on parallel spindles: they brace the high back rigidly against lateral movement. This successful combination of durability and aesthetics (form following function) is a recurrent characteristic of Irish vernacular furniture, undoubtedly contributing to the survival of so many fine examples of this chair.

HEDGE CHAIRS WITH COMPOSITE SEATS

Most surviving hedge chairs have seats made of a single slab of relatively thick timber, often elm or some other suitably close-grained hardwood. In Ulster, especially in county Antrim many chairs of a similar pattern have seats made up from a variety of composite pieces.[61] Whether this amounts to a local tradition or, as seems more likely, is the result of a shortage of substantial sized timber, is unclear. However, the durabilty of these chairs depends on an adequate thickness of seat (in the absence of stretchers), to withstand the strain of legs fixed in with a slight outward slant. The same applies to the backrest of the chair,

40

39. (*facing page, right*) Ash and pine hedge chair, with a composite seat, made up from four thick pieces, joined with exposed mortice and tenons, to support the thin pine seat. Its turned ash legs and spindles are through-wedged into the thickest parts of the seat, and splayed for strength. This labour intensive construction was widely resorted to in county Antrim, presumably to overcome a lack of large dimension timber. Compare figs. 6, and 45. From Carnmoon, Dervock, county Antrim. Photo courtesy of the U.F.T.M.

40. Low, late nineteenth-century chair, strikingly made from a pair of natural knees of timber, linked by riven (split) back and seatrails, pegged in place and made of ash. Traces of red paint remain on the seatrails. The turned legs are through-morticed into the 'knees'. This distinctive type of chair is related to examples made in the north of Scotland, called Sutherland chairs. Natural knees and forks of timber were chosen for their strength and were also used in boatbuilding and to make ploughs. Seat, 11½ in. wide, 12 in. high; overall height 26½ in. Photo courtesy of the U.F.T.M.

which needs to take considerable strain and weight; too thin a seat would tend to split along the grain where the back sticks are attached. The composite seated chairs achieved this thickness in layers, sometimes with additional boards running from front to back beneath the seat to form a simple lamination (fig. 39). This sandwich of timber need not necessarily have been glued (gluing boards at right angles can create problems with shrinkage), but could have been securely anchored by all the through-wedged joints of the attached legs and spindles which pierced them. Some of these seats are made up by interlocking and morticing the pieces at right angles to each other. Sometimes the front of the seat can be fixed by a bridle joint to the side pieces.[62] This system enabled chairmakers to create seats from five or six relatively narrow (and easily obtained) boards. The results are perhaps less aesthetically satisfying than the single slab-seated hedge chairs found elsewhere, but the number that have survived is proof of the success of this method of construction.

A lot of hedge chairs share common characteristics; many more are unique and individual. Chairs made by householders frequently include eccentric or peculiar characteristics symptomatic of rural isolation. Others echo the primary skills of a practised woodworker so clearly it is possible to attribute them positively to a wheelwright, a boatbuilder, or someone accustomed to making coffins by the marks left by their favourite tools and techniques. A good example is the 'rib back' chair from the Ulster Folk and Transport Museum (fig. 38). An accomplished woodworker must have been responsible for this, influenced by the through-wedged method of fixing the legs, like other local hedge chairs. The legs, one of which is replaced, are (unusually) lathe turned and splayed, with a low 1½ inch thick slab seat, like so many others. The spine-like back, although elegant looking, is so uncomfortable that whoever made it cannot have been used to chairmaking. Yet, the method of over-lapping and pegging the slender curved laths into carefully cut mortices to form the back and armrests is indicative of well practised woodworking, and is possibly the work of a boatbuilder.

'SUTHERLAND' CHAIRS AND THEIR DERRY RELATIVES

So called 'Sutherland chairs' originated from the area of the same name in the extreme north of mainland Scotland, with further related types from neighbouring Caithness.[63] The dozen or so surviving examples from northern Scotland are linked by their unique and extraordinary method of construction to some found in northern Ireland, especially in county Derry. Their main structure is composed of a pair of acutely bent, naturally grown 'knees' of timber, which in some examples have been cleaved from a single piece, or are otherwise closely matched (fig. 40). These paired knees are united by a series of through-wedged horizontal rails, and upheld by four similarly jointed legs, with or without stretchers. The rails and legs are either wittled, or in later examples turned on a lathe.

The use of natural knees and natural forks of timber both in Scotland and Ireland, was common in rural areas in housebuilding,

41

domestic implements and agricultural tools such as ploughs.[64] Some of the Scottish hawthorn and blackthorn chairs were made around 1900 by Samuel Clark, a shepherd. An interesting feature of some of these chairs is the front seatrail, which it is suggested was spaced forwards from the rest of the seat in order to accommodate wet socks, which could be hung there to dry before the fire. The examples from Caithness, the Wester Ross and the Hebrides are by contrast more refined: the main structural elements being a pair of back legs which follow through to form the back support, the two side seatrails are then joined to the back. These so-called 'Caithness chairs' also have their counterparts in northern Ireland (fig. 41).

Four chairs of the same peculiarly unique construction to the Scottish ones are known to have originated from county Derry, and two of the main contrasting types are illustrated here (figs. 40–1).[65] The port of Derry's history of maritime links with the north of Scotland probably explains the close similarities between the chairs from both areas. Other closely similar examples are also known from Australia and Romania.[66]

These designs of chair may have initially evolved through the makers' resourcefulness in response to a lack of substantial sawn timber. The fact that they were copied and made by other people elsewhere is a measure of their success as designs suited to poor conditions. As such they can be allied to the hedge chairs from county Antrim with their composite seats (fig. 39).

COMB BACK CHAIRS

Still in the tradition of hedge chairs, is a rare design, surviving examples of which originated predominantly from eastern counties. It is no coincidence that the only intact examples of these comparatively fragile, tall backed chairs survive in museums (figs. 42–6). A badly broken example from county Roscommon could only be reassembled by the author's drawing (fig. 42). If they were ever common in the poorer rural houses, only one, from county Wexford, has come to light, and this unfortunately had its upper section sawn off by its owners. Definite conclusions cannot be drawn regarding regional variation, with a mere half-dozen or so examples surviving. Outside Ireland this type of chair has been referred to as the comb back Windsor. The regional distribution, style and common use of the lathe in their construction indicates possible links with Wales and parts of England, where such designs were popular since the eighteenth century.[67] However, these Irish examples do not all have stretchers uniting their legs and one pair in the collection of the National Museum seems more closely allied to the hedge chairs than to their Welsh and English comb backed counterparts (fig. 46). This pair, painted red and brown, have such diminutive upper combs as to render them mere decoration, rather than forming a heightened extension of the chair backs to make useful headrests.

The most elaborate of these examples (fig. 43) is from the collection of Armagh County Museum. It was donated to the

41. Late nineteenth-century pine chair from Gortinney, Eglinton, county Derry, of a type also known in Caithness, in northern Scotland. The way the seatrails attach to a pair of continuous back uprights is the same as its Scottish counterparts, except this one has a more refined and comfortable set of slightly curved backrails, held fast by pegs. Traces of a reddish brown stain are visible in unworn areas. The legs have worn down several inches, so the stretchers which once linked all the legs, have now gone. Seat 14½ in. wide, 11 in. high; overall height 33 in. Photo courtesy of the U.F.T.M.

42

42. (*left*) Reconstruction of a badly broken comb back chair, with plain turned spindles and curved back legs, painted black. *c*.1800, from Derrycahill, Dysart, Athlone South, county Roscommon. Drawn from the collection of the N.M.I.

43. (*bottom, left*) Comb backed chair ash arms supported on eighteen finely turned and through-wedged spindles, and turned pine front legs. Each back spindle pierces the bow in one long piece. This design shows English Windsor influence, born out by the predominantly east coast location of the few surviving chairs of this type. Family tradition relates that John Wesley sat in it when he preached at Drummond in 1789. Painted black. Seat 24 in. wide, 18 in. deep; overall height 37 in. Courtesy of Armagh County Museum (57.66).

44. (*top, right*) Turned comb back chair, incorporating elm, its back spindles interlocked through the shaped armrests and held with horizontal wedges. One leg has been renewed. It was a wedding present from a cottier to an estate owner, along with a spinning wheel, in 1904. From Tullynally, county Westmeath. Seat; 23½ in. wide, 12 in. deep, 15½ in. high; overall height 34½ in. Photo courtesy of The Bowes Museum (county Durham U.K.).

45. (*bottom, right*) Comb back chair from Ballywettick, Ballymoney, county Antrim. Its lack of stretchers, and the unaligned, separate upper comb, indicate that its maker was more accustomed to making hedge chairs. The spindles and legs are lathe-turned and the elm backrest shows traces of its original paintwork. Such composite seats are a common feature of county Antrim hedge chairs (fig. 39). Photo courtesy of the U.F.T.M.

46. A pair of comb back hedge chairs to use beside a kitchen fire, at Greatdown, county Westmeath. Instead of using steam-bent timber for the backs, the maker has found naturally curved 'knees'. Their small upper combs, supported by spindles which follow through from the seat, are less fragile than their taller counterparts (fig. 43). The left-hand one, overpainted in dark reddish brown, has had its two ash back legs replaced in new holes. The right-hand one, with wine red paintwork, has had its seat secured with bolts. Both are late eighteenth century, and have 2 in. thick elm seats and are of closely similar dimensions; Seats 23½ in. wide, 13½ in. deep, 14½ in. high; backrest 26½ in. wide and 27½ in. high. Courtesy of the N.M.I.

museum by Mrs J.H. Hutton, whose family tradition relates that it 'formerly belonged to Simon Reilly [her great-great-grandfather, of] Drummond, Grange Parish . . . this is the chair in which John Wesley [b.1703— dd.1791] sat when he preached in the kitchen at Drummond [in 1789].' Indeed, Wesley's journal of that time does mention 'Simon Reilly, who for half a century received the preachers in his house at Drummond'.[69] Made by a skilled chairmaker, it still has its original black paint and the irregularly parallel marks of the pitsaw struck across the underside of the thin seat. Unusually light in weight, its construction incorporates decorative turned spindles and many of the joints are concealed. These refinements all indicate the work of an accomplished chairmaker, rather than a woodworker from an allied trade. Elegant examples such as this doubtless inspired local woodworkers to produce their more

straightforward and functional versions (figs. 45–6).

Another example of a comb back chair incorporating spindles turned on a lathe shows signs of being derivative and imitative, setting it apart from the other examples illustrated (fig. 45). Here the maker has perhaps heard of or seen a comb back chair and then copied it from memory, using an entirely different (but easier) and less elegant method of construction. Instead of the centre back spindles passing right through the central backrest, the upper comb has been added separately, giving the impression of an afterthought. This somewhat uncomfortable arrangement is heightened by the maker's choice of contrasting pattern for the upper spindles. The seat of this chair is made up of several pine boards, joined by dowels, a typical feature of so many of the other hedge chairs from county Antrim.

47. A pair of 'Carpenters' chairs', their style typical of many from west county Cork. Made in the second half of the nineteenth century, of pine, repeatedly painted brown. The distinct curve on their front leg stems from the early nineteenth-century fashion for 'sabre legged' chairs, and went on being copied well into the twentieth century. The originals would not have had stretchers linking the legs, which in this pair have been decorated with lines, from a scratch stock. Cupid's bows decorate the backrests. All the joints have been secured by pegs. From a farmhouse near Glandore, west county Cork.

CARPENTERS' CHAIRS

Here is another name which reflects the occupation of the maker. Characterised by the single piece of timber which forms the back leg and backrest, such chairs usually have a thin boarded seat nailed onto a framework of tenoned and pegged rails (figs. 47–51). They have been made since the early nineteenth century, when the fashionable English Regency curves of 'sabre legs' were adopted and varied as an unusual and (in Irish terms) extravagent concession to style. Extravagent, because such a curve requires more timber than a straight version, but often adapted to rough flooring by the addition of a series of bracing stretchers, notably absent in the originals (fig. 47). The use of sawn timber from the mill contrasted with the gleanings of the hedge carpenters, enabling more substantial and stronger joints to be made. Despite the fact that they sometimes have fashionably curved legs, it is interesting to see the same unconcealed, through-wedged tenons being used for the frame, rather than the more fragile stopped (concealed) mortices of finer chairs.

They can still be found all over Ireland, particularly in areas prosperous enough to

48. Parlour chair with turned legs, which are somewhat awkwardly linked by substantial stretchers. The board seat has a neatly moulded edge. Made of mixed timbers, painted brown, c.1850–70. From near Baltinglass, county Wicklow.

support the work of carpenters. A small percentage of these chairs have turned front legs, indicating the use of a lathe, although the favoured use of limewood for turned legs has often contributed to their deterioration, because it is soft and prone to woodworm.

These chairs, in contrast to the hedge chairs, were not commonly made by householders. Their production differs from other furniture described here, because it often consisted of small batches of half a dozen or so, which could be sold in sets or singly. Their design is indicative of small-scale production in rural workshops, which did not depend on machinery but nevertheless used 'patterns' (flat wooden jigs or templates) to draw around and repeat a chosen shape, typically for the curved back leg (fig. 47). John O'Sullivan, a traditional carpenter from Skibbereen, county Cork, still recently had such a chair pattern hung from a nail on his workshop door, which he used to make such carpenters' chairs. He was born in 1915, and had his own oak-grained coffin propped up and ready for himself in his earthen floored workshop. He recalled how 'Everything we made, we made a pattern first and they were kept, they'd be hanging at one end of the workshop.'[69] His workshop was unusual because it had amongst its machinery a hand operated mortice-cutter, with a long lever-action handle. This dispensed with the time consuming hard labour of chopping out countless mortices for these sets of carpenters' chairs. Other woodworkers depended on the use of sets of 'T' shaped hand augers with which to do this work, completing the corners of each mortice laboriously with chisel and mallet.

Much is known about the methods of construction of this comparatively sophisticated type of Irish chair, because it was still being made well into the twentieth century and is therefore easily remembered by those involved. In county Cavan, the three Robinson brothers, Charles, Michael and Tom Joe (cabinetmakers) helped their father (a cooper) make sets of these chairs. They remembered carefully painting all the mortices with protective white lead paint to prevent woodworm before assembling them. Six could be made in a day if activities were carefully coordinated: all the gluing and

assembly was done using hot animal glue, in the evening. The many pairs and matching groups of these chairs left in derelict houses throughout the country, bear witness to the activity of making them in sets.[70]

They are known to have been made by carriagemakers and wheelwrights, as well as house carpenters, from whom they get their name. It is a name which was used by some owners and makers alike. There is a great contrast between the functional, yet simple jointing techniques employed for the making of hedge chairs, and the more complex and sophisticated joints of the carpenters' chairs, which are obviously made by experienced woodworkers. On some examples, the broad backrest is attached to the uprights by means of a slot dovetail, whereas others are more solidly slotted and pegged (figs. 47, 49). These backrests vary from being completely flat (and economical with timber), like fig. 49, to being more comfortably curved: they were cut from the solid, rather than made from naturally grown 'knees'.

Carpenters' chairs demanded many more specialist woodworking tools in their construction than hedge chairs. Some of them

50. A carpenters' chair in the Regency style, without stretchers and with an unusually wide backrest. Made between 1830 and 1840, more care has been taken to round and taper the legs, and decorate the back, than with other later examples (figs. 47, 58). Original ochre paintwork, from a farmhouse in the vicinity of Glandore, west county Cork.

have patterns of lathe work on their turned front legs which are refreshingly original (fig. 51). Many examples display naive idio-syncracies characteristic of isolation from the fashions and styles which inspired them. This is evident in the extraordinary shapes that were cut out for the horizontal back-rests. Often they were plain, or exhibited the favourite curve of the cupid's bow (figs. 47, 50–1), but just as frequently they were original (fig. 49). A few are exag-geratedly wide, reminiscent of some of the Egyptian chairs which were the inspir-ation for Regency designers (fig. 50). Per-haps more conventionally, earlier examples occasionally have baluster-shaped splats, more reminiscent of the early eighteenth rather than the early nineteenth century (fig. 52). Where suitable hardwoods were available, decorative pierced splats were made, as in the example from county Cavan (fig. 55). These characteristics are unreliable reflections of their true date, as with rural furniture, there is frequently a considerable timelag between the urban fashion and the subsequent provincial style.

Several examples have had upholstery as

51. An early carpenters' chair with an extraordinary pattern of turning on the front legs. Made primarily of pine, with square pegged or through-wedged tenons securing the frame, c.1830–40. The lack of stretchers sets this chair apart from other examples, but many versions of the cupid's bow curves cut along the backrails occur from furniture in this area. From a farmhouse in the Glandore vicinity, west county Cork.

52. Rare mid to late eighteenth-century low oak chair, with a flat, Queen Anne style, baluster splat. It would originally have had an upholstered 'drop-in seat', rather than this plywood one. Access to the nearby Coolatin estate woods may account for this uncommon use of oak. Its sturdy construction, with stretchers anchored by square pegs, helps explain its survival. Painted brown, from a small farmhouse near Coolatin, south county Wicklow.

53. *The Irish Matchmaker*, oil on canvas, signed by Charles H. Cook (1830–1906), exhibited at the R.H.A. in 1864, approx. 34 in. × 44 in. An intriguing St Patrick's Day celebration in a county Cork inn, showing a round, three-legged table with turned legs, and people seated on stools and carpenters' chairs (one has a decorated backrest). A reflective metal candle sconce and sets of shelves are hung on the wall. Photo courtesy of the N.L.I.

54. E. Fitzpatrick's *Drowning the Shamrock on St Patrick's Night*. The scene is the interior of a public house, showing people seated on carpenters' chairs, the one on the right with a nicely decorated back. The barrel of Smithwicks porter, Kilkenny, suggests a location in the south-east. A bird in a cage, a wall clock and candles in sconces, as depicted by many other artists, are hung on the wall. Substantial forms with solid boarded ends provide extra seats. *Illustrated London News* (March 1853). Photo courtesy of the Irish Traditional Music Archive.

a later addition tacked on top of the board seat. Others were intentionally made to accept an upholstered drop-in seat, often recovered repeatedly with leatherette (fig. 56). The latter type are more stylish, resembling more closely their grander Regency counterparts. They would have been intended for use in the parlour: the Ordnance Survey Memoirs for county Antrim in the 1830s reported that there was 'a boarded floor, which is general[ly] supplied with excellent modern furniture of mahogany, sometimes though not always chosen with good taste'.[71] The painting and graining of some furniture to resemble mahogany was often so convincing, that it is tempting to suggest that the surveyors may have been fooled by it. Although mahogany furniture was undoubtedly used in the parlours of those who could afford it, it was comparatively expensive and was usually the product of the urban factories rather than of local vernacular makers. Occasionally a chair is found which demonstrates how valuable mahogany was. The parlour chair from a small single-storey farmhouse in county Wexford (fig. 56) incorporates a mixture of timbers, with its mahogany back, oak frame

55. (*top, left*) A late eighteenth-century oak side chair with a fashionably pierced back splat, boarded seat and square pegged joints. Courtesy of the Pighouse Museum, Cornafean, county Cavan.

56. (*bottom, left*) Parlour chair made of mahogany on an oak frame, and with turned pearwood front legs stained to match. The drop-in seat has been re-upholstered with leatherette. Its rounded backrail (fixed by slot dovetails) and curved back legs are examples of a range of vernacular interpretations of fashionable Regency style chairs. Upholstered chairs were comparatively expensive, seldom used, and something of a status symbol for those who could afford them. This mid nineteenth-century example came from a single-storey farmhouse at Ballylibernagh, Mayglass, county Wexford. Maximum width 20 in., seat height 17½ in.; overall height 35 in.

57. (*top, right*) A matching pair of parlour chairs with board seats and turned front legs, mid nineteenth century. Notable for their absence of stretchers, they are of mixed timbers which have been painted to imitate mahogany. From a farmhouse at Clandrole, Clones, county Monaghan.

58. (*bottom, right*) A carpenters' chair, unusual for its oak construction, which nonetheless has been painted in imitation of mahogany with lines of inlaid stringing (see fig. 24). The board seat is of pine, *c*.1840. Courtesy of the N.M.I.

and pearwood front legs, stained to match the mahogany. However, ordinary carpenters' chairs were also widely used in parlours in place of mahogany ones (fig. 47). Some examples survive without the repeated over-painting of the twentieth century and from these it can be seen that even the expensive inlaid lines of contrasting stringing which decorated the originals, were imitated by paintwork in the vernacular versions (figs. 24, 58).

ANCIENT IRISH CHAIR.

Inevitably there is confusion regarding this distinctive design of chair, which is now rarely found outside museum collections.[72] Examples of these striking looking chairs have survived since the early nineteenth century in Ireland and there is every indication that they were used much earlier than that (figs. 59, 60), particularly if the following passage from an 1832 edition of *The Dublin Penny Journal* is to be believed;

> It is an ancient oak chair, which we saw a few years since, in the little decayed village of Drumcliffe in the county of Sligo . . . Four legs he deemed a superfluity, and we are of the opinion that he was right, for we have sat in this chair and found it steady and pleasant. We are sorry to have to add . . . that this interesting vestige of the greatness of Drumcliffe no longer exists; it has been used for firing during a severe winter, being deemed by its owner as a useless and inappropriate article of luxury.[73]

The illustration accompanying this article (entitled 'The Ancient Irish Chair', fig. 59), shows the chair described with arms, although examples of them both with and without arms survive. The location of this chair (from county Sligo), plus the fact that it depends on a single substantial board for the back section, helps explain why it has come to be referred to either as the 'Sligo chair' or the 'board chair' by the Irish Country Furniture Society. The simple 'T' shaped seat is more minimal (and uncomfortable looking) than other examples, although possibly, being drawn from memory, it is incomplete.

The writer and traveller Mrs Hall, toured Ireland in 1840 and provides us with another illustration which more closely resembles surviving examples of these Sligo chairs (fig. 60). Upon entering a single-storey, three-roomed house, she wrote;

> This cottage contained, indeed, nearly every article of furniture in use in such dwellings of the humbler classes. Each of them we had often seen, but very seldom had been enabled to notice all together.

The first object that attracted our attention was a singularly primitive chair, which is very commonly used throughout Connaught. It is roughly made of elm, the pieces being nailed together . . . There is evidence that this piece of furniture has undergone little change during the last eight or ten centuries.[74]

Mrs Hall saw her example in a house in Erive [now Erriff], at the head of Killery bay, county Galway.

Her comment that it was made of elm nailed together, is interesting, because by the 1930s, a maker of these chairs, *Tomas MacDhuarcain* [T. Durkan], insisted to the contrary that in the making of such chairs 'No nails or screws are used and no glue'.[75] Durkan used his English name for his maker's mark which he stamped into the endgrain of the chair seat illustrated (figs. 61–3). It is interesting that he lived barely a few miles east of the house where Mrs Hall noticed her chair, on the shores of Lough Mask, near Tourmakeady, county Mayo. Durkan was apparently 'a very well known *seanchaidhe* [storyteller], joiner and cooper . . . He asserted that [in the old time] there were no other kinds of chairs and that there should be seven different woods in it – the seven woods of the cross; ash, alder etc.'[76] Although Durkan's chair appears to be made primarily of oak, his claim that it could be made without glue may well be true. The wedging or dowelling of all the joints would make glue technically un-

59. Sketch of an 'ancient' armchair from Drumcliff, near Sligo, published in 1832, which was subsequently burnt as a 'useless and inappropriate article of luxury' by its owner. The basic structure of a single board for a back, joined to a 'T' shaped seat, is essentially the same as that of surviving examples. The curious headrest is not repeated on other known examples, nor does it appear on sixteenth-century Scottish and English prototypes. By 'P' of *The Dublin Penny Journal* (August 1832).

60. An early sketch of a so-called 'Sligo Chair', from county Galway, described by Mrs Hall as 'a singularly primitive chair . . . very commonly used throughout Connaught . . . roughly made of elm'. (Compare to figs. 59, 61). From Mrs S.C. Hall, *Hall's Ireland* (1841). Photo courtesy of the N.M.I.

that the majority of the National Museum's collection of these chairs originate from the area around the county Galway town of Tuam, probably accounts for the recent name 'Tuam chair'. Also, reproductions of the design began to be made there in 1969.[77] Comparatively elaborate, oak examples, may be traced back to the sixteenth century, when such *Caquetoire* types

61. Two oak 'Sligo chairs', by different makers. The lighter, left-hand example from near Tuam, county Galway has a greater curve cut along its back leg, with a rebated hand-hole at the top, for lifting. Their 'T' shaped seats each have a protruding tenon, which is held firmly by a large wedge, reminiscent of sixteenth-century methods of construction. Their three legs, joined by 'T' shaped stretchers, made them stable on uneven floors (compare to figs. 62–3). Left-hand chair: mid nineteenth century, seat width at front 21 in., depth 16 in., height 16 in., width of back 5 in.; overall height 32 in. Right-hand: (marked T. Durkan, late nineteenth century), seat width at front 21 in., depth 19 in., height 17 1/2 in., width of back 6 1/2 in.; overall height 35 in. Courtesy of the N.M.I.

62. A rare example of a maker's mark: of Tomas Durkan, a chairmaker, joiner and cooper from Tormakeady east, county Mayo. It was stamped on the right-hand edge of the seat of one of his chairs (see right-hand example in fig. 61). Courtesy of the N.M.I.

necessary. His chair, along with the other eleven stored by the National Museum of Ireland, has a 'T' shaped stretcher joining the legs and providing stability.

Comparing Durkan's chair with the others in the same collection, it can be seen that his has more monumental dimensions. The whole chair weighs considerably more than the others, with its front seat board a full 2 inches thick and 8 1/4 inches across, compared with the smaller, lighter version illustrated alongside it (fig. 61) which is 5 5/8 inches wide. Weight is an important consideration in these chairs, for despite the fact that they are three legged (ensuring, as we have noted, stability on uneven floors) they have often had a hand-hole carved out of the back to lift them by. The amount of timber required for the back leg and rest depends on how generous a curve the maker wanted to achieve. This curve, cut from the solid, determines the stability and comfort of the chair, which sometimes has a tendency to tip over. The more accomplished chairmaker could achieve a strong yet lightweight chair, with a back that is not too severely upright.

Reproductions of these chairs were first made for Yeats's tower house at Thoor Ballylee, where they can still, be seen. Made of pine rather than a local hardwood, their backs are disappointingly straight. The fact

were known in France, England and Scotland. The Sligo chair probably arrived in Connaught with planted settlers who were originally from Scotland during the seventeenth and eighteenth centuries.[78]

SÚGÁN CHAIRS

The Irish word *Súgán* translates as rope (made of hay or straw). The use of such twisted rope in rural Ireland (figs. 64–5) to create inexpensive and comfortable chair seats has lent its name to the variety of *súgán* seated chairs which are to be found in all four provinces of Ireland. The fact that a large number of these chair frames have simple horizontal backrails has mislead some

63. (*facing page*) Detail of a typical triangular open-work seat of a 'Sligo chair', made by Tomas Durkan of Tormakeady East, county Mayo (see fig. 62). The tops of the legs are secured with through-wedged tenons, and the seat itself is joined by a mortice and tenon joint held in place by square pegs. Of mixed hardwoods including oak.

64. (*below*) Photograph by John Millington Synge (1871–1909) of 'Ropemaking on Aran'. This shows the second stage, after the rope has been twisted, of gathering it back into a ball, to stop it untwisting. On the right is a boy ('to prevent their being taken by the fairies young boys of the south and west were dressed as girls'); he walks towards the man who winds the rope into a ball, which might be used for tying down thatch, as on the roof above his head (see also figs. 5, 6). Photo and quotes from J.M. Synge's *My Wallet of Photographs* (Oxford, 1971). Photo courtesy of The Board of Trinity College Dublin and the J.M. Synge Trustees.

65. (*right*) W.M. Thackeray's depiction of straw rope making (*súgán*), in the 1840s. The man is feeding loose straw, evenly into a single strand rope, which is twisted by the woman with an old style twister or 'thraw hook' who walks backwards to keep it taught; see fig. 64 for the next stage. In the foreground are the coiled up bundles of finished rope, ready for chair seating etc. The twister is the braced hook type, made from bent sally (willow), which had various local designs and names. It was later widely replaced by a cranked wire twister which looked similar to a 'brace and bit'. From Thackeray's *The Irish Sketchbook* (London, 1843).

authors into calling them ladder backs rather than *súgán* chairs. Other materials (rather than hay or straw) were also used to seat or to 'bottom' chairs, providing a few other more specific names which were either in household use or are mentioned in early eighteenth- and nineteenth-century documents, such as 'bent [marram grass] bottomed chairs',[79] 'rush bottomed chaiers'[80] or even 'bullrush chaiers'.[81] In parts of Ulster they were also sometimes known as rope bottomed chairs.[82]

Unlike in England, few inventories of furniture from Irish houses have survived the ravages of time, and those which list the contents of cottiers' and farmers' homes form only a tiny percentage of the total. When such inventories can be found, the descriptions provided of the contents are frequently abrupt and uninformative. Chairs are generally listed simply as 'chairs', so that most of these inventories cannot provide a pattern of the distribution and age of the *súgán* chair. However, one entry from a poor farmer's will of 1732, does list 'Some old Sugane Chairs. [and] Wan borded chair'; the only seating listed amongst his possessions.[83] This list, from north Munster, was so meagre that it did not even include a dresser, for the display of his 'putor dishes [and] trenchors'.

We gain a further impression of *súgán* chairs as seating for the poor majority of the population, with the reports from the British Government's Poor Inquiry of the 1830s. They describe cabins furnished with 'two or three chair-frames with hay-rope bottoms' [county Limerick] or simply 'chairs with

53

66. Twisting a bog deal rope, which as it is formed, is wrapped around the back of a chair to prevent it untwisting. Bog deal ropes were made for a variety of uses including bed cords and chair seating. During the 1830s, some people in the vicinity of bogs made their living from this work. Photographed by K. Danaher at Kenmore, county Kerry, c.1951. Reproduced courtesy of the Head of the D.I.F., U.C.D.

67. The traditional Irish weave of twisted oat straw rope, which lent its name to the *súgán* chair. Unlike English rush chairs, with their seats woven into four triangles (fig. 73), the Irish method was finished with this front to back weaving, broadening slightly towards the wider front. The ash framework was constructed in a way well suited to this thick weaving, with its high front legs (figs. 68, 71). Such *súgán* seats settled and became matted and shiny with use. This example, from a child's chair, was made by Christopher Sullivan of Lauragh, county Kerry in 1991.

68. Two ash *súgán* chairs of essentially the same design, from county Cork. Both have recent twine seats, but are woven in the traditional way. The one on the left, made in the mid nineteenth century, has cigar-shaped stretchers and through-wedged joints: it was built to last. The one on the right, with its higher seat, lathe-turned straight stretchers and stopped mortices, involved less skill and more machinery in its making. The later, more angular version is one of many which were semi mass-produced along traditional lines, during the first half of the twentieth century.

hay-rope bottoms' [county Tipperary]. In county Clare, people were 'very often without bedsteads' and had 'only a few ill-made chairs, bottomed with hay'.[84]

It would be wrong to assume from these reports that such chairs were confined solely to the west of Ireland. They were very commonly used in north Munster but in fact they were also used and known all over the country.[85] The Ordnance Survey Memoirs for county Antrim inform us that in the 1837 fair at Lisburn; 'Chairs, bent bottomed, [were being sold at] 1s. each. These brought from Castle Wellin, county Down, chiefly, distance 12 miles and upwards.'[86] The reference to bent evidently means chairs with twisted grass seats, this could have been Bent-grass, Marram grass or Sea-bent in coastal areas.[87] Their prices varied, but generally they undercut the prices for 'timber chairs' considerably, which helps to explain their widespread use. At the same fair in mid summer, the prices were higher and the impression is of a large number of stalls selling such chairs; 'timber chairs, stalls 6, each 1s. 10d.; bint [bent] bottomed chairs, stalls 5, each 1s. 3d.; household furniture, stalls 4, various prices.'[88] These prices are about twice as much as those given in inventories of the same district in the first half of the eighteenth century.[89]

In counties Galway and Kerry during the nineteenth century, instead of using straw rope, many people made their chair seats using twisted bog deal (fig. 66).[90] As we have seen, bog timber such as deal and oak was also used for a wide variety of other purposes, including bed cords and clothes drying lines 'as they do not cause any stain from the application of wet'.[91] The method

in which such ropes were made is explained fully in the section entitled 'Bed Cords and Bedding' (pp. 157–8).

Súgán chairs were a common sight in the old farmer's and cottier's houses until well into the mid twentieth century (fig. 308). By 1936), the Irish Homespun Society's first spring show (in the Royal Dublin Society's Hall), included a *súgán* chairmaker by the name of Mr Tatton, from Ennis, amongst their ten demonstrators of traditional crafts.[92] As far as the author is aware, the only areas where *súgán* chairs are still made in the 1990s are counties Kerry and Galway.[93] Perhaps because these chairs were once so widespread, many examples still survive in their original settings, although their twisted straw or *súgán* seats (fig. 67), have nearly all been replaced by various types of modern cord, woven in the traditional Irish way (figs. 68, 71–2).

The emphasis on function and durability with the *súgán* chair frame is typical of a broad range of Irish vernacular furniture. Shortage of timber encouraged the use of *súgán* for a seat, which when compared to the hedge chair, required completely different construction. The *súgán* chair has a backrest which is a continuation of the back legs (figs. 68–74). The legs are all linked by a series of cigar-shaped stretchers which are pushed through round mortices and secured by through-wedges, and sometimes by pegs as well. Most nineteenth-century examples have stretchers which have been roughly rounded and tapered with a spokeshave or drawknife. Early twentieth-century ones are often evenly turned on a lathe, producing a sharper, less comfortable look (fig. 68). The legs are roughly square in section, the back ones curving as they meet the backrest, according to the amount of timber available. Some examples are nearly straight, or the backrest tapers from a square to a feather edge where such a thickness of timber is no longer required for large mortices at the top (fig. 71). This device uses less timber and lowers the chair's centre of gravity, reducing the possibility of it tipping over backwards. The backrests are generally held by pegs into stopped mortices.

The majority of surviving examples are of ash, or a combination of locally available hardwoods and sometimes bog deal.[94] In the Mourne mountains of county Down, holly was locally abundant and therefore relied upon for a variety of uses – for fishermen's net needles and bobbins as well as the frames of 'rope-seated chairs'.[95] Identification of timbers can be difficult when so many examples are heavily overpainted. Traditionally ash was used for many jobs around the farm, such as fences and gates; its resistance to splitting also made it particularly suitable for chairmaking.[96] The upper siderails are always placed an inch or two higher than the front and back seatrails, for comfort and in order to accommodate the through-wedged joints and to facilitate the weaving of the uniquely Irish pattern of seat (figs. 68, 71).

69. A rare eighteenth-century stipple engraving, showing spinners seated on *súgán* chairs in a house in county Down in 1783. The low, narrow backs were well suited for this work. Beside the fire, a small boy is seated on a plaited straw mat of a type which was also commonly used as a chair cushion (fig. 84). Above him hangs a salt box with its distinctively sloped lid. The shelf on the right, with its noggin and trenchers, is simply supported on pegs driven into the wall. From William Hincks' series on the Irish Linen Industry, *Plate VI. Representing Spinning, Reeling with the Clock Reel, and Boiling the Yarn.* Photo courtesy of Lisburn Musem.

70. *An Irish Wake*, drawn by N.A. Woods, Smart and Sutherland, an aquatint; 1 February 1819 (12½ × 17 in.). Although Woods has juggled with the layout of the traditional house, the depiction of carousing people seated on splay legged stools is accurate. In the centre sits a man on a stretcherless *súgán* chair. Beside him a man holds a jug emblazoned with the symbol of the female Irish harp. Candles light the corpse, which is laid out in white on a bed apparently lengthened with a board.

71. Ash *súgán* chair from the province of Munster, probably county Kerry, dating from the first half of the nineteenth century. The cigar-shaped stretchers are held in place by pegs rather than wedges. The backrests have been riven and their edges decorated with lines using a scratch stock. The replacement seat is traditionally woven using faded green fisherman's twine. The low seat, which narrows towards the back, is ergonomically ideal for spinning. Seat width at front 20$^{1/2}$ in., width at rear 14 in., depth, 15 in., height 14 in., overall height 32$^{1/2}$ in.

72. A *súgán* armchair, its
seat rewoven in the traditional Irish pattern, but with
string. *Súgán* armchairs are
uncommon; this one has
front legs which curve
outwards to meet the arm-
rests. The backrest is also
comfortably curved, with a
cupid's bow shape decorating the centre rail. Unlike
others, it has no stretchers
between the front legs.
Made around 1850, of ash, it
has recent pink overpainting. From Clarewilliam, the
south riding of county
Tipperary. Outside width
26 in., seat width 21½ in.,
depth 19 in., height 14½
in.; overall depth 25 in.,
overall height 33½ in.
Courtesy of the N.M.I.

themselves once they wore out. The fact that
súgán was already commonly homemade
and used for a great variety of rural tasks
helped. In exposed coastal areas *súgán* was
used for tying down thatch, elsewhere for
making into smoke hoods by soaking the
rope in mud, for burden ropes, barbed wire
(interlaced with thorns), for circular carrying
pads,[97] tying down haycocks,[98] as stirrups,[99]
animal tethers[100] and even on at least one
occasion for suspending a pot over the fire.[101]
Rope twisting was therefore a familiar occupation. It required two people. Incidentally,
this important activity was celebrated in
W.B. Yeats's *Casadh an tSugain* or 'The
Twisting of the Rope', the first play performed in Irish, in Dublin.[102]

Many people can still remember twisting
súgán for chair bottoms, probably in the
autumn and winter months following the
harvest. Having gathered a heap of the hay
or straw, 'Usually an older person had a lot
of the material and let it out by hand,
to some young person, usually a child on
school holidays, the child worked the twis-
ters, as I did many a time, the pay was
threepence per day and food.'[103] This description from county Down is typical, although another account from county Armagh
mentions that 'The ropes for the seats of
chairs were made thin and twisted until
they were quite hard'.[104] The fact that they
were comparatively thin led to other names
for the rope. The following description
comes from county Limerick and was recalled in the 1950s;

The seats of chairs [were] of twisted straw
and also of twisted hay . . . I used to have
to hold the lamp, a small decapitated
cone with a 'pipe' line of yarn as a wick,
while my father 'bottomed' the chairs.
He used *méarorgins* [thumbropes or
'golden fingers'] of oaten straw. They
were made during the day and the 'bottoming' was done in the kitchen at night.
I hated the task of holding the lamp.'[105]

These chair frames could be made with
unseasoned timber by drying the ends of
the tapered stretchers beside the fire to
shrink them. If the main posts into which the
stretchers slotted were unseasoned, this
mattered little as the joints would then
tighten up when the frame dried and shrank.
Surviving examples often have considerable
movement in their frames, the result of
years of use on uneven floors. The system of
through-wedging into round mortices accommodated this movement without damage, enabling them to survive far longer
than chairs with rigid frames.

The great advantage of these chairs was
that it was a relatively simple process for
householders to replace the *súgán* seats

The *súgán*, once twisted, was rolled up into
a ball which could then be passed around
the chair frame. The spaces between seat
and stretchers were left deliberately large
to facilitate this process.

The use of oat straw is often mentioned,
and Christopher Sullivan, who still makes

73. 'Súgán chair', with its original straw rope seat recently replaced in an English pattern by twine. This example, unusual because of its neatly turned ash elements, is similar to chairs made in north-west England. The concealed joints are another feature reminiscent of English rather than Irish chairs. Covered by many layers of nicely worn brown paint, its central back spindle is a replacement. c.1890–1910, from Derryhubbert, Dungannon, county Tyrone. Seat 16 in. high, 19 in. wide; overall height 32 in. Courtesy of Armagh County Museum (81–70).

74. An unusual *súgán* armchair with an ash frame, and inset panels with a double weave of thick string. The way the front legs rise to support the armrests is the usual arrangement with *súgán* armchairs (fig. 72), but the woven sides and back are exceptional. Most of the joints have been pegged in addition to their wedges. Part of the N.M.I.'s collection, from Ballynagally, Pallas Green, county Limerick. On show at the Irish Agricultural Museum, county Wexford.

grass rope, in south county Down, which presumably was manufactured on a large scale, accompanied the decline in use of straw and sun dried mountain grass (*Molinia*).[108] The fact that so few *súgán* chairs survive with straw rope seats bears testimony to their widespread replacement with mass-produced substitutes. Most examples still in use have seats of thick green fishing twine, already giving the impression that they have lasted several decades (figs. 68, 71). As early as the second quarter of the nineteenth century, 'foreign soogawn' was being blamed for a decline in trade of those who made a living from producing objects made from it in county Kilkenny.[109] Substitutes for *súgán* which were inexpensive and more durable have long competed with the straw rope. New straw *súgán* seats have a tendency to shed loose pieces of straw for a while, until they become matted with use. Contemporary makers are now resorting to the use of blue nylon rope, its novel permanence apparently being a positive selling point.

The lathe has been used in some areas (notably Ulster and county Waterford), to make *súgán* chairs which necessarily have no

súgán chairs at Lauragh, county Kerry, grows oats specially for the purpose because, he says, oat straw produces the most beautifully coloured golden seats (fig. 67). The most common Irish method of 'bottoming' is to start weaving from side to side, until the seat, which often narrows towards the back, is covered. Then another layer is woven, resulting in a simple pattern of parallel ropes running from front to back and widening gradually towards the front (figs. 67–8, 71).[106] This parallel weave was more common than the English method of rush seating, which divided the seat into four unequal triangles (fig. 73). There is evidence that another type of pattern was sometimes used, as in the seat of a *súgán* armchair in Yeats's Tower House, Thoor Ballylee. It is made up of a series of woven squares of rope, diminishing in size towards the centre.[107]

The introduction of cheap 'Hairy Ned'

75. Rare panelled back armchair, made of riven (cleaved) ash, with a board seat of pine and partially concealed jointing. Dating from the mid eighteenth century, its design first evolved around 1600. The early oak protoypes were often highly decorative, but this vernacular version retains the form without added carving. The cupid's bow which is cut out of the cresting rail, often graces rural Irish furniture. Typically, the pale colour of the ash has been hidden by layers of brown and red paint, which has gradually worn off on the backrest. Overall height 40in., bases of legs renewed. Courtesy of Armagh County Museum (126: 1966).

comfortable curve on the back uprights, but manage to incorporate some nicely turned decoration (fig. 73). Lathe-turned *súgán* chairs are comparatively scarce, perhaps because more timber was required to make them than when using a spokeshave or drawing knife. Similar designs are also found on the Continent, particularly in Spain and Portugal, linking them to a wider Atlantic European tradition.

OTHER UNUSUAL CHAIRS AND DUG-OUT CHAIRS

There are notably fewer examples of *súgán* chairs with arms (*súgán* armchairs) than without (figs. 72, 74). The few inventories that provide information about chairs in farmhouses also show that armchairs were in a minority and sometimes cost twice as much as chairs without arms.[110] The lack of arms may have saved space around the hearth, but ease of construction and shortage of materials also played their part. Since comparatively few armchairs survive, it is hard to determine what was typical.

Armagh County Museum has a panelled back armchair from Annasamry townland, county Armagh, which is reminiscent of some English early seventeenth-century joined chairs in style, but is of simplified form (fig. 75). Unlike many other Irish vernacular chairs, it may well have been influenced by chairs imported or remembered by planted English settlers. However, the generous cupid's bow profile of the back cresting is a favourite Irish motif and the unconcealed through-wedged or pegged joints exhibit a functionalism typical of rural craftsmen. This sturdy system of construction was built to last – which it has done since the eighteenth century. Other early features of the chair include the seat framework, made of riven (split) rather than sawn ash and supporting a pine seat. The bottoms of the legs have been restored where they were worn down. The whole was once unified by painting, initially in brown and subsequently in red. The backs of many sitters have worn away a patch of paint down to the wood and further wear from feet on the front rail bears witness to its age.

Other armchairs bear the stamp of the trade of a particular maker, being influenced more by the way they would build a cart, for instance, than by other styles of furniture. An armchair from west county Cork (fig. 76) is a good example of this interplay of woodworking skills. The arms sit in bridle joints, reminiscent of local settle arms, while the curved back supports are linked by a generously chamfered crossrail. Chamfering was an important yet simultaneously decorative technique which reduced the

76. Unusual pine armchair, stripped of its original paint; probably made by a wheelwright and decorated with chamfering. The construction of the arm-rests echoes that of local settles. Late nineteenth century, county Cork.

77. (*below*) An unusual armchair, dating from the close of the eighteenth century, from the vicinity of Union Hall, west county Cork. Made primarily of pine, the turned decoration is rare in this area, but the chamfering of the front legs is a typical adornment of furniture made by local wheelwrights. The frame has concealed mortice and tenon joints, which are secured by pegs. Originally painted black, except for the seat which was once regularly scrubbed.

weight of carts (refer to Glossary). It can often be seen looping its way around the panels of house or dresser doors, betraying the cartwright's work rather than that of the house carpenter. The lack of stretchers to link this chair's legs, which works well as a characteristic of hedge chairs, has here become a point of structural weakness. Unusually, for a chair, it is made of pine and was originally painted. Another chair which echoes even more faithfully the construction of the typical west county Cork settle, with its distinctive arms, retains its pale green paintwork, with the seat left unpainted for regular scrubbing (fig. 79).

In contrast, a far more sophisticated example of an armchair from the same area, dates from the close of the eighteenth century (fig. 77). Unusually for this region, it incorporates some finely turned spindles in the back, and the upper sections of the front legs are turned. Again the seat has been left unpainted (it is now always used with a cushion) while the frame was originally painted black. Lathe-turned chairs do not usually reappear until the beginning of the twentieth century in that

79. Armchair made in the style of a county Cork settle, indicating that its maker was more accustomed to making settles than chairs. Made of pine and painted pale green, its seat has been left unpainted, and its arms have rounded flat ends, like local settles (fig. 110). Mid nineteenth century, from the vicinity of Union Hall, west county Cork.

78. (*facing page, right*) Mahogany 'dug-out' chair from near Union Hall, west county Cork. Made by J. Sheehy, early twentieth century. The mahogany from which it is made was from a wrecked timber ship. It has pierced handles for carrying, is very heavy and has lost its wooden seat, which fitted on a projecting ledge on the inside. The front has split, due to years of being placed beside the fire. Approximately 20 in. square and 44 in. high.

area, and then only as a product of urban chair factories. It has been carefully made by an experienced chairmaker, rather than by an allied woodworker.

Ancient forms of so-called 'dug-out' chairs, hewn from tree trunks or large baulks of timber, are generally considered part of the tradition of medieval furniture in England. However an example from county Cork was made at the beginning of the twentieth century and is a fine example of how ancient crafts endured in Ireland, despite close proximity to mass production and industrialisation (fig. 78). Another example, thought

originally to have come from a hotel in Drogheda, county Louth, bears the crest of a crowned Irish harp gilded above a date of 1690.[111] This may well be the date of the chair's construction; alternatively, it could have been added posthumously, to commemorate the Battle of the Boyne (figs. 80–1). This Drogheda example is surprisingly small, its size being governed by the diameter of the tree trunk from which it was made. Only a child or a featherweight adult could sit in it comfortably. The inside has been roughly hollowed out, the thickest part being at ground level, tapering gradu-

ally towards the top. The original seat is missing but the replacement seat rests on a projecting ledge and is probably much like the old one. Solid bog deal chairs, not necessarily with their bases hollowed out yet also made from single pieces, were remembered in the 1930s in western county Donegal. They were recalled as being small, with a projecting piece attached as a backrest. Their name, *cnaiste*, apparently related to their usual position in the chimney corner, giving rise to the saying 'don't be a *cnaiste* in the chimney corner', or 'don't be a lazy lump'.[112] The general shortage of timber in Ireland helps account for the rarity of such chairs, which are comparatively wasteful and labour intensive in their method of construction.

The boarded 'tub chairs' of Ballydehob, county Cork, amount to a local tradition. Born of the twentieth century, when pine for house building had begun to be imported in quantity, these chairs are completely enclosed, excluding fireside draughts (fig. 82). In contrast to the fine jointwork normally associated with chairmaking, the construction of these 'tub chairs' depended instead upon careful cutting and nailing. Mobility was considered unimportant as

82. Nailed pine armchair with enclosed seat and base, *c.*1930: a type commonly made near Ballydehob, west county Cork, during the late nineteenth century. Originally it was painted.

Facing page:
80. Rare early , walnut dug-out chair, with traces of red paint. The replaced seat rests on an integral ledge and its edges taper from 2 in. thick at floor level, to 1 in. thick at the top. It is only 28 in. high and 15 in. diameter: the size of the tree trunk. Family tradition relates that it came from an old hotel in Drogheda, county Louth. The symbol of the female Irish harp, crowned, is gilded onto the back, above the date 1690 (see fig. 81). Its form, decoration and location are commensurate with the battle of the Boyne of 1690. Now loaned by the Murdoch family to Millmount Museum, Drogheda, county Louth.

81. Infra-red photograph of the symbol of the female Irish harp, crowned, applied with gold leaf onto a gesso ground (water gilt) onto the back of a dug-out chair, above the date 1690 (see fig. 80).

83. A rare and fragile coiled and bound straw armchair, with a rectangular seat plan, dating from the second half of the nineteenth century. The binding is typically made from split and stripped bramble bark. The seat is supported by a timber subframe, restored with additional wood and metal strips. By kind permission of Carlow County Museum.

the chair is unusually heavy and extravagent with timber compared to earlier Irish chairs. The design was once particularly common around the Ballydehob area (although another example was found near Dungarvan, county Waterford) and was probably made initially by one maker, who was later copied, as surviving examples exhibit contrasting methods of construction.

CHAIRS MADE OF STRAW

The County Carlow Museum is one of very few museums that display a type of coiled straw chair which was once a common sight in small farm-houses, but has now become extremely rare (fig. 83). Such chairs should not be confused with the ash-framed, straw rope seated *súgán* variety, but belong in a class of their own. They are however related to the extraordinarily wide variety of other coiled straw and brierwork objects such as bee skeps,[113] cradles, kidney-shaped seed baskets,[114] food baskets (kishauns[115]), carpenters' toolkit bags,[116] curtains,[117] hassocks and bosses (stools).[118] Many things were also made of plaited rather than coiled

straw. Plaited strawwork required no split bramble binding and a few plaited mattresses, cushions, mats and hens' nests[119] do still survive in museums. The Irish Agricultural Museum in county Wexford has a fine example of a plaited straw hens' nest.[120] Straw was such a widely used material that in the 1830s it was even fashioned into chimney pots, some of which were 'ornamented with thick, circular ropes of straw, sewed together like bees' skeps, with the peel of a brier'.[121]

In Wales and England, where the technique of coiling straw and binding it together with split bramble bark was known as 'lip-work', surviving examples of chairs are more common.[122] In Scotland, Orkney chairs were made with arched hoods of coiled straw attached to a substantial timber base, sometimes with a contrasting drop-in seat of rush or seagrass.[123] Unfortunately, in Ireland, although there is ample documentary evidence to prove that coiled straw chairs and stools have been widely used for centuries, only about a dozen examples are known to have survived intact. The fragile

84. Plaited straw seat in the form of a circular pad, from Shranagarvangh, Ballinaglera, county Leitrim. Such pads were used simply as low seats in the eighteenth century (fig. 69) and also as cushions for chairs. Made before 1957. Drawing courtesy of the N.M.I. by museum artist E. Johnstown.

nature of their construction has resulted in their disappearance. Straw deteriorates quickly when allowed to get damp, is inflammable and prone to attack by rats and other vermin. The extensive restoration of County Carlow Museum's example testifies to its perishability. It is ironic that the very fact that they were once so common has also contributed to their destruction: people have disgarded them as cheap and unimportant. Pat Purcell, who rescued the Carlow example for the museum, remembers that these armchairs were once commonplace in the smaller local houses of the county and popular among those who could not afford wood.

The British Government's Poor Reports for the 1830s, indicate that children in parts of county Fermanagh, found employment plaiting straw.[124] The popular novelist Charles Kickham mentioned that 'straw arm-chairs' were used in rural Tipperary in the 1800s, and the writer, Patrick Kennedy similarly described how a farmer 'was taking his rest in a straw chair' in a farmhouse in county Wexford.[125] In 'Legends of Mount Leinster', Kennedy relates how the farm servants lounged on 'benches, stools and straw bosses round the fire'.[126] Many people can still remember how these straw bosses (stools) and armchairs were favourite fireside seats, although they might seem dangerously inflammable by today's standards. The term 'boss' and the terms *seas* or *saoistín*, were all names widely used to describe a low straw (or rush) seat. Use of the term 'boss' dates back to the early eighteenth century, enduring until the disappearance of the objects themselves around the mid twentieth century, especially in Munster and south Leinster, and in counties Donegal and Fermanagh.[127]

Straw seating was commonly used all over Ireland within living memory.[128] Twentieth-century dialect terms for straw seats' vary from one district to the next, but seem to originate from the Irish – *saoisteóg*. In Glenties, county Donegal plaited and stuffed stools called 'shaystogs' were still made until very recently, when it became impossible to obtain the necessary hand-cut oat straw with which to make them (figs. 7, 86). In counties Cork and Kerry *saoistín* was the most common reference. These words

in turn may derive originally from the Irish *seas*, (which is still used in county Monaghan) meaning a bench or seat. In county Kilkenny, 'boss' referred to a 'cushion made of special wheaten straw called cotton straw'; such things were known to have been made in the vicinity of Graignamanagh.[129]

In nineteenth-century county Clare, seats were made cheaply with 'square dried scraws of turf covered with plaited straw called *súistíns*'.[130] In some hedge schools the children sat on bosses, or on round stones 'capped with a straw collar or hassock' (fig. 84).[131] A description from the same area, county Tyrone, over a century later, recalled 'A straw hassock is an article that was used by the children of former days in "hedge schools" (and barns used as schools), there being no desks in those days some of the children sat on the floor. Some parents made straw hassocks and sent them to school with their children.'[132] Hedge schools were usually run by learned scholars, often itinerant, who taught local pupils in improvised buildings or sometimes beside hedgerows; hence the name. In the National School in Antrim, conditions were similarly stark, with half the children taught standing (with feet together!), through lack of furniture.[133]

Coiled and bound seats required the longest possible lengths of straw, which were necessarily cut carefully with a scythe rather than by machine. The best time to gather the blackberry briers to make the binding was around November, when the sap was no longer rising. Each one then had to be stripped of its thorns, cleaved into two

or three pieces and cleaned of pith. The long lengths had to be smooth enough to use as a tough thread, for sewing and securing the coiled straw firmly together. Only two basic tools were needed once these raw materials had been prepared. A section of cow horn was usually used to funnel the continuous length of straw into a regular round coil. A tubular 'needle' or awl several inches long and large enough to accommodate the brier binding was used to pierce the straw coils and anchor them neatly with interlocking looped stitches

(fig. 85).[134] In Ireland, this needle was sometimes wooden or of bone,[135] but horn tubing was also probably used. In this way the coils could be built up, beginning with the centre of the seat and working gradually outwards in the manner of a clay coil pot. Chairs, stools and bee skeps usually had coils of between 1 and 2 inches in diameter, but smaller objects like food or seed baskets were sometimes made with much smaller, finer coils. Such strawwork was well suited to the winter months, when both materials had been recently gathered in and there was less work to be done on the farm. Chairmaking was more skilled and complex than bee skep or boss making, as it necessitated the incorporation of truncated lengths of straw in the arms and back (figs. 83, 85–6, 89–92). The demise of the craft of straw skep making began with the bee-keepers' preference for wooden hives, which allowed stocks of bees to be overwintered. Mechanised harvesting of straw was another important reason for the death of the craft.

Plaited boss stools usually have a round seat plan and are often shaped like a slightly swollen drum (far left of fig. 86). Examples of coiled and bound straw stools from counties Clare and Galway are biconical in shape; narrowing inwards towards the mid-

87. *Bothered* from a painting of 1852 by Erskine Nicol R.S.A. (1825–1904). The uneasy subject sits on a 'boss' made of neatly coiled straw, bound with stripped briers, which narrows towards the top. Published in Mrs. S.C. Hall's, *Tales of Irish Life and Character* (1909). Photo courtesy of the N.L.I.

88. Plaited straw armchair, stuffed with straw and with a plaited straw base. Made before 1931 and now in the stores of the N.M.I. Photo courtesy of the Head of the D.I.F., U.C.D.

91. (*facing page, far right*) A coiled and bound straw armchair, with a circular seat plan and four coils forming the armrests. Early nineteenth century, from Birr, county Offaly. After a photograph in the N.M.I's archive.

dle with a central waist (far right of fig. 86). Other coiled bosses, conveniently illustrated in various paintings, had round seats which broadened outwards towards the base (fig. 87).

Nowadays most commercial makers of straw bee skeps (a variant form is now used for collecting swarms) have abandoned the time consuming preparation of brambles in favour of split cane, rattan, or baler twine.[136]

Some of the old straw chairs and stools gained strength from having their seats stuffed with densely packed straw, thus avoiding the need to use valuable timber, but making the whole thing surprisingly heavy (figs. 86, 88, 93). The underneath of these stuffed examples is either neatly coiled and bound in the same way as the top (as is the biconical one, fig. 86), or the stuffing is held securely by a zig-zagging network of string, in the plaited versions. Others had a rudimentary subframe of rough timber around which the straw coils were wound or alternatively two parallel batons where stitched to the underside of the seat (figs. 83, 89–90). When such a timber sub-frame was continued down to ground level it prevented the inevitable wear on the

straw around the base of the chair. The Carlow example, with its rectangular seat plan, has this type of construction (fig. 83). The round seated example of a straw chair from Windgap, county Kilkenny (fig. 90),

89. Straw chair from Enniscorthy, county Wexford, made of coiled straw, bound with stripped bramble bark. Based on a circular plan, the seat is supported by two separate wooden batons, which are stitched to the underside. It has been restored around the base and front edges. Late nineteenth century. Seat 16 in. diameter, 15 in. high, overall height 31 in. Photo courtesy of Enniscorthy County Museum.

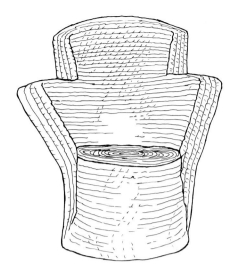

has been faithfully restored this way: a timber framework is clearly visible several inches below the lowest coil. In Abbeyleix, county Laois, a square seated straw chair was similarly constructed; 'Six inches of round leg showed in the front, so the whole straw part was raised off the ground. There was nothing unusual about it, they were in nearly every house.'[137] Other examples which were not made with this raised framework have worn badly around the base.

Seat plans of these coiled and bound chairs, varied from the square or rectangular (fig. 83) to circular (figs. 89–91) or even D shaped (fig. 92). The enclosed arms and backs of these chairs made them warm and

cosy and excluded the draughts of an open fire. They were often favoured for use by old people or invalids. The thermal quality of coiled or plaited straw was also perfect for cradles, which were then warm as well as lightweight and inexpensive. Although plaited straw cradles were still remembered in county Antrim in the 1950s, so far no surviving examples have come to light.[138] The travelling Mrs Hall who was raised in county Wexford, described how a Cork family sat for their meals 'on stools and bosses'.[139] We learn from Patrick Kennedy of the county Wexford 'boss maker' who 'earned his bread by making cradles, and bosses, and chairs, and beehives, out of straw and briers.' Indicating cradles of coiled straw, and that boss-making was his primary concern.[140]

Plaited (as opposed to coiled) straw stools and chairs required no bramble binding. They were made by the same technique as the once common straw mattresses and often by the same people (figs. 7, 8, 86, 88, 93, 248). Straw chairs were common in county Cavan, where in the 1950s it was remembered that:

The seat was made of wood covered with straw ropes. The back contained no wood. Some people made a name for themselves by making these chairs. One man [was] living on the Slieve Russell Mountain . . . and another well known maker lived in the townland of Tomessan. These men also made large straw mats, which were common everywhere in this district but are never seen now.[141]

67

Straw mats are known to have been used as curtains,[142] bedcovers, screens and for the floor, while mattresses were more easily folded and stored when made of two conjoined halves (fig. 257).[143]

Many householders would have acquired the art of making these things for themselves, rather than buying them in the markets. Rushes were used for a similar range of objects in place of straw (figs. 254, 257). In Lisbon market, county Antrim, in the 1830s a straw mattress sold for between five and six shillings, which was the greater part of the average labourer's weekly wage of about seven shillings and six-pence.[144] The manufacture of such 'woven' or plaited straw mattresses nearby in west counties Down, Antrim and Armagh was remembered as recently as the 1960s.[145] Straw baskets as well as bee skeps ('bees caps') were also sold at Lisburn fair, the latter for 10*d*. each, so it is safe to assume that straw seating would have cost even more.[146]

The technique of coiling and binding (favoured for bee skeps) could be employed not only with wheat, rye or oat straw but also from a wide variety of grasses and irises or flags. Materials were doubtless chosen from what was locally abundant: in county Armagh chairs were made from plaited rushes.

The advent of relatively cheap mass-produced chairs, wooden rather than straw beehives and machine threshing and binding of straw have all contributed to the decline in the craft of strawwork. It soon becomes clear why so few of these fragile objects have survived except as memories.

CHILDREN'S CHAIRS

Children's chairs are now rare, although their use in the home was certainly functional rather than decorative (figs. 94–6). The fact that children could be seated on the ubiquitous low creepie stool as easily as adults meant that there was probably less need for specially built chairs for children (fig. 273). The photographer, Robert Welch (1839–1936), shows a child's hedge chair in the foreground of his photograph of the Crawfordsburn Inn (fig. 195), suggesting perhaps that they were also considered curios. An example from The Irish Agricultural Museum (fig. 94) with interlocking arms shows that they were made to the same pattern and method as larger chairs, and doubtless by the same people. One of

94. A child's hedge chair with interlocking arms and rear spindles, mid nineteenth century, from county Donegal. Made of a mixture of pine, ash, oak and chestnut, all its joints are through-wedged, but unlike its full sized counterparts, the grain of the tiny seat runs from front to back. Courtesy of the Irish Country Furniture Society, and the Irish Agricultural Museum.

96. (*right*) Child's chair with interlocking armrests and turned ash back sticks, all through-wedged. The elm seat has been riven and left rough beneath. From a 'big house' at Mount Louise, Balinode, county Monaghan. Seat 16 in. wide, 10½ in. deep, 9–9½ in. high; overall height 20½ in. Courtesy of Monaghan County Museum.

95. Child's *súgán* chair, made of ash, from Inch in county Kerry, its seat recently replaced with seagrass. The back posts, inclined for comfort, and the low stretchers, are typical features of adult *súgán* chairs, but such a decorative back is only occasionally found, in the west. The through-wedges which hold the frame together are clearly visible here. The backrails have been rounded and fitted into through mortices, and then pegged in place. Seat 17½ in. wide at front, 12 in. wide at back, 12½ in. deep, 12½ in. high; legs 1½ in. square; overall height 24½ in.

the 1930s 'Schools Manuscripts' in the collection of the Department of Irish Folklore, recalls how in county Tipperary 'Running stools were made for children learning to walk. They were about a foot and a half high and were fashioned from four pieces of timber. The wheels were generally old cotton reels.'[147] Cotton reels were also used as improvised handles and to make hanging shelves, but no examples have come to light, except in old photographs. In the chapter on settles, it is described how the

settle bed doubles up as a convenient playpen when opened out, and the artist Daniel Maclise (1808–70) illustrates a *súgán* chair laid flat on its back as another safe place to confine a small child (fig. 281). Rattles woven from rush containing hazelnuts or stones were made for babies, but the subject of toys for older children, since they must often have been homemade, would doubtless repay further research.[148]

97. The hearth of an early eighteenth-century house, near Mayglass, county Wexford. The brick smoke canopy is said to have been cracked by the reverberation of floating mines exploding on a nearby beach. An unused bed with low turned posts found new life as a settle (left) and a form (right). The wooden crane is just visible above the fireplace. The floor is of beaten earth.

Chapter 2

SETTLES

Settles and Seats of Various Materials, Turf Seats, Stone Seating, Forms, Open Frame Settles, The 'Carbery Settle', The Settle Bed, Settle Beds and Servants, Other Occupants of the Settle Bed, The Settle Bed for Children, Uses of the Settle Bed, Settle Bed Construction and Variation in Design, Settle Tables

SETTLES AND SEATS OF VARIOUS MATERIALS

Some sat on stones, some sat on blocks,
Some sat on churns, some on wheel-
    stocks;
Some sat on cars some sat on
    ladders,
And, for shift, some sat on
    madders. . . .
The brisk young sparks, with their
    kind wenches
Did place themselves on rushy
    benches. . . .
They both on bench of Rushes sat,
Commixt with flags, both wondrous
    fat;

    W. Moffat, *Hesperi-Neso-Graphia,*
1724[1]

Fireside seats for several people were a common part of the traditional furnishings of all but the poorest Irish houses. Today, most surviving examples are made of painted pine or some other inexpensive timber. However, descriptions from the eighteenth century such as the poem quoted above, suggest that a wide variety of materials other than wood were used to provide people with seating near the warmth of the hearth. As with other designs this improvisation was influenced by what materials were locally most abundant, and such seats often doubled as tables when the need arose. The Reverend James Hall, noted in 1813 that

so poor are many, that there is neither chair, nor stool, nor table in the houses,

98. Early nineteenth-century settle, from county Down made of pine with plaited straw upholstery (figs. 99, 100, 230), covered with flour sacks and later with buttoned leatherette. Photo courtesy of the U.F.T.M.

99. Detail of the back of an early nineteenth-century settle (fig. 98), showing pine frame and plaited straw padding, with string for anchoring the buttons. Photo courtesy of the U.F.T.M.

71

100. The home of American president McKinley, at Dervock, county Antrim, photographed at the end of the nineteenth century by Lawrence's firm. On the right is a settle bed, on the left behind a hooded cradle is a straw upholstered settle (see figs. 98–9). Around the fire, with its double cranes, is a composite seated chair (fig. 39) and a variety of stools. A large salt box hangs beside the doorway into a bedroom, and the ceiling joists have been adapted for storage. Photo courtesy of the N.L.I.

101. *A Poor Place to Call*; the smoky interior of a county Galway cabin, showing a young woman seated on what was probably a bench made of turf. From H. French's *Our Boys In Ireland* (1891).

but round stones about the fire for seats . . . The crook . . . on which they hang the pot over the fire, is of wood, tied by a straw rope to something at the top, and the pot, for boiling potatoes, etc. is not unfrequently turned mouthdownward, and used as a seat . . .[2]

TURF SEATS

Rural houses with their 'seats of sods and roof of straw' are mentioned frequently enough by interested travellers for us to assume that turf (called peat in England) must have been a common seating material.[3] Writing during the 1720s a reporter described how, upon entering a meagerly furnished 'principal farmer's house' on the road from Dublin to Dundalk, he noticed 'a bench on either side of the fire-place made

of turf'. Turf, if extracted in large sections from the bog, could have been cut into shapes suitable for seating and then dried out (fig. 101). A century or so later, Carleton describes how the pupils of a poor 'hedge school' (one of the many improvised schools for the children of the rural poor) either had

72

102. Open fireplace with iron crane, built-in seats (typical of the south and west), and a place to store turf beneath. On the left is a child's cot. Oughterard, county Galway, c.1948. Photo courtesy of Bord Fáilte.

103. Peter MacDonnell's hearth, at Valleymount, county Wicklow, photographed by T.H. Mason, prior to flooding by the Poulaphouca Resevoir, c.1939. On the left is a panelled settle bed, with a narrow shelf along its top. Beside it is a form and a salt box sits on a granite ledge behind the turf fire. To the right of the fire is an ash pit, and a stool. Photo courtesy of Dr F.H. Aalen.

to squat on the floor or were arranged on an ingenious variety of seats. Several of these consisted of 'hobs – a light but compact kind of boggy substance found in the mountains'.[5] In wetland areas, some landlords allowed their tenants to have the use of portions of bog to extract turf for fuel. Making seats from this material was a logical move for those without much furniture. In times of shortage, they could always resort to burning them, which may explain why none have survived today. A few early photographs survive of extraordinary vernacular houses which were built either entirely from excavated turf or from turf which was cut into blocks and used like bricks. A landlord from county Kildare described during the 1830s how hundreds of his tenants lived in such turf houses, adding that 'Their . . . furniture [is] of a piece with the buildings' (figs. 6, 101).[6]

STONE SEATING

Fireside seats made of stone sometimes survive in ruined houses in the southern counties. Single seats inset into either side of a wide hearth and built from the same materials as the walls were common in the south and west (fig. 102). Fireside stone seats were an obvious solution for the poor, who devised inexpensive methods of making them comfortable. In early nineteenth-century county Kilkenny, the Reverend Hall related how people sat on 'stones, set around the fire, with round coils of platted straw by way of a cushion' (fig. 84).[7]

Carleton's hedge school was also equipped with stones for seating: 'Along the walls on the ground is a series of round stones, some of them capped with a straw collar or hassock, on which the boys sit (fig. 84); others have bosses' (see figs. 7, 86–7).[8] Some of these seats were probably made by those who built the houses, as were similar outdoor seats, which were occasionally incorporated into the front wall of stone houses beside the front door. These can still be seen, but there seems to be no distinct distribution pattern as they were probably made at the whim of the builder, in areas where stone was locally available.[9]

An account amongst the manuscripts in the Department of Irish Folklore relates how householders in Muskerry, county Cork, had a seat made of a combination of 'stones, wood and heather sods'.[10]

Schoolteacher Humphrey O'Sullivan recalls in his 1831 diary that Eucharist Thursday was known as 'Corpus Christi of the fine benches' after the old custom of 'spreading fresh rushes, iris, etc. on benches, beside the doors in the country, where old people used to sit telling Irish romantic tales, as the young folks listened'.[11] These intriguingly adorned benches may also have been stone ones, placed out of doors.

The so-called Poulaphouca survey provides detailed descriptions of homes submerged by the creation of the Poulaphouca resevoir in county Wicklow in the late 1930s. Folklorists from the National Museum of Ireland photographed, sketched and recorded oral information about local traditional culture. In one small farmhouse, they noted that 'A wooden seat about 5' long and

2′ wide to the left of the fireplace along the wall, replaces a stone seat which was there formerly'.[12] Photographs taken during the survey (and subsequently) show that such stone benches were once a common feature (fig. 103).

FORMS

Some soap to wash all, shifts, stockings and caul.
A table, three stools and a forum,
All this I will give, and think we may live,
As well as the justice of Quorum,

Anon, 'Thady O'Brady', n.d.[13]

The simple four-legged or board-ended 'form' has existed as a moveable or built-in backless seat for two or more people since at least the early 1600s in Ireland. These forms are mentioned in inventories repeatedly and have also been well represented in early paintings and photographs. They can be seen as forerunners to the more sophisticated settle. They still survive in many rural houses today (see figs. 104, 106–8). The price 'for a boord [table]; and four formes', bought new in around 1630 was thirteen shillings. They were often listed like this together with tables.[14] The term was spelt 'foarmes' and 'formes' when listed in two inventories of the 1640s,[15] and 'formes' a century later in the inventory of a grand Palladian house.[16] This document, with its 'Account of things in ye Kitchen', provides us with an immense list of objects, including '2 formes of Deal' [pine] from which most surviving examples are still made.

In county Wexford these long seats were a common part of the twentieth-century furnishings of the old thatched houses and were pronounced 'furrums' (fig. 97).[17] They are still useful as fireside seats and are often kept alongside a kitchen table, or stored beneath it. Houses built with jamb walls (see figs. 3, 103, 105) often had a built-in or freestanding form along the inner fireside.[18] This long seat was not only conveniently close to the warmth of the hearth but, as mentioned earlier, also provided a preview of approaching visitors through a special spyhole in the jamb wall (known in county Antrim as the 'bole').[19] Sometimes such a jamb wall had a falling table attached to it on the inside which could be lowered for use over a long form. Patrick Kennedy described the arrangement and use of fireside forms in a Wexford priest's kitchen at the beginning of the nineteenth century;

Facing page:
105. *(top) Listenin' to Raison* reproduced from a painting by Erskine Nicol R.S.A. (1825–1904). A couple sit beneath a smoke canopy, supported at one end by a jamb wall, suggesting an eastern location. On the left, against the front wall is the distinctive curved profile of a closed settle bed (see fig. 121). Beside the turf fire is an ash pit, sunk below the level of the flagged floor. From Mrs S.C. Hall's, *Tales of Irish Life and Character,* 1909.

106. *(below) The Schoolmaster's Moment of Leisure,* an engraving from a painting by Howard Helmick (1845–1907). It shows the interior of a comparatively well equipped hedge school. The unfortunate dunce sits on a form with simple angled legs, which must have been wedged into the long seat. The broken round table, was perhaps a gift, but has come down in the world. Its missing foot is supported by one of two tiny stools. The teacher is seated on a hedge chair. From *The Magazine of Art,* II, 1888. Brought to the author's attention by the Irish Traditional Music Archive.

104. A tiny four-legged stool, with through-wedged legs, beside a form with its board legs through-wedged into the top: both nineteenth century and with their original red paintwork. Shown with two turned butter dishes, in the kitchen of the Edmund Rice Centre, Callan, county Kilkenny. Stool seat 14$^{1/2}$ by 7 by 1$^{5/8}$ in. thick, 6$^{1/2}$ in. high.

There is a partition wall as usual between the door and the fire, with a spyhole in the middle. A form runs along this wall, and at the end of it farthest from the fire, is settled a very small round table for the books and the candlestick...There he sits wrapped in a cloak on winter nights; the rest of the form up to the corner next the fire is occupied by the neighbours who drop in...and under them in the very angle is a deep hole to receive the dry ashes.[20]

Forms, being lightweight, were also used around the falling table; where Wexford families ate their meals, 'the forms are arranged, the company take their seats, and if anyone does not make a hearty supper on the best mealy cups [potatoes] and good milk, I don't pity him'.[21]

A rare surviving example of a falling table, examined in a county Kilkenny farmhouse, incorporates in its framework what amounts to a 'falling form' alongside it, on the side furthest from the hearth (figs. 292–3). Both the table and the form can be independently raised up and fastened flat against the kitchen wall. Each is equipped with a single hinged leg at its outer end. Its owners remembered how as children they used to sit at the falling table on this long form for their meals, while their parents were always seated on the more comfortable chairs, nearer the fire (see fig. 292). Like the seats of settles and the tops of tables, the form was painted all over except for its seat, which was worn smooth and kept clean by regular scrubbing with sand.

The Government Reports of the 1830s mention that the poorest people of county Donegal lived in one or two room cabins 'furnished [only] with a few bogwood forms' and beds.[22] These forms were doubtless used as tables as well as for sitting on.[23]

Surviving examples generally conform to one of two basic methods of construction. The simplest type has a seat up to 2 inches thick, through which four independent and carefully splayed legs are wedged from above. This arrangement (which is the same with hedge chairs and stools) means that any legs that become worn down or loose, can be easily replaced or new wedges can be added (fig. 106). The wedges are always

H. Helmick.

75

107. A watercolour of a woman selling salt, from coiled and bound straw baskets made like bee skeps and seats (figs. 89–91) They rest on a long asymmetrical form with diagonal stretchers bracing the odd legs. Another basket has been placed on the back of a tiny chair, presumably because it is too wide to fit on the seat. The sketchbook is thought to have been compiled by Samson Twogood Roche during the 1820s in Waterford market. Photo courtesy of The U.F.T.M.

108. *The Irish Jig*, a watercolour, dated 1845, by Samuel Watson, who used his artist's licence in rearranging the layout of the room to accommodate the party. On the left is a form with its legs wedged into the seat, and another in the foreground has board-ends, braced by stretchers. A cat teases an Irish wolfhound from the safety of a *súgán* chair, and behind it a circular three-legged stool acts as a table. Beside the hearth is a built-in seat, with a salt box over it. Two men with long stemmed pipes, sit at a round table on a built-in high backed settle; above them hams hang from hooks in the beams. The room is lit by reflective candle sconces and a simple chandelier, which can be lowered or raised by a string. Private collection.

driven in at right angles to the grain direction (and length) of the seat, to avoid splitting (see fig. 35). The second type is less economical with timber, consisting of boards the same width as the seat which form two solid ends rather than legs (see fig. 104). These are usually jointed firmly into the seat, a couple of 'through-tenons' being wedged simply from above. Sometimes these board-

ends are provided with additional stabilising supports (right of fig. 107). In both types of construction, the thicker the seat, the more secure the jointing becomes. Both these types of form are illustrated by Samuel Watson in his 1845 illustration *The Irish Jig* of 1845 (fig. 108).

Often just the four legs of old forms are painted, the seat becoming smooth and undulating with wear. The comparatively recent craze for covering table tops and forms with patterned plastic is widespread where traditional homes have not been modernised. It harks back to the use of coloured and patterned oilcloth, a decorative and labour saving feature which has been pinned onto table tops, mantlepieces and dresser shelves since the nineteenth century.

OPEN FRAME SETTLES

One definition of the word settle is 'a long wooden bench with back and arms',[24]

109. An open frame pine settle from Crosshaven, county Cork, c.1800. Traditionally used as a fireside seat or bed. The flat panels are held in place by integral mouldings, which have been picked out in yellow. The way the front legs rise and taper on the insides to meet the armrests is typical of county Cork settles. Courtesy of The Pine Hive (Crosshaven).

yet according to the *Dictionary of English Furniture*, work done on early inventories shows that the terms 'settle' and 'bench' are interchangeable, but 'the distinctive characteristic of the settle is the presence of arms'.[25]

In the south and west of Ireland there survives a type of settle not generally found elsewhere. It was usually constructed with a heavy open framework of pine, morticed and tenoned together and fitted with a panelled or boarded backrest. Unlike the form, it has a seat deep and long enough for a person to sleep on, but without the storage space provided by the purpose-built settle bed (see figs. 109, 110, 114). The extraordinary depth of the seat can make sitting uncomfortable, unless cushions are provided. The deep scrubbed seat and the way the front legs taper to support the armrests are identifiable characteristics of

open frame settles made by Irish immigrants abroad.

The open frame settle does share some of the features of the settle bed. Both often have a high back surmounted by a narrow, sometimes sloping shelf. This feature may be left over from the days of low single-storey cabins. Then, such a ledge would have coincided with the height of the lowest roof timbers, perhaps diverting any dust and drips away from the sitter's back. The odd thing about these ledges or shelves is that they often occur below head height, contributing little to the sitter's comfort (figs. 110–11).

The high panelled back protected fireside sitters from the cold damp walls of the old houses. Throughout Ireland the settle usually took its place against the back wall near the hearth. At the same time their makers sometimes used the panelling as

110. Open frame pine settle, from a derelict house near Skibbereen, county Cork, *c*.1850. Probably made by a wheelwright, with through-wedged tenons and decorative lines and chamfers cut with the scratch stock and drawknife (see detail fig. 111). The pink and white gloss paint was probably applied during the 1950s, over earlier layers of browns and reds, the seat has always been scrubbed. This style of settle, long enough to sleep on, was widespread in the south-west and used less timber than the settle bed.

an area in which to show off their skills, creating eyecatching patterns by mixing contrasting sizes and shapes of panels. This effect was often enhanced in the twentieth century by the application of bright contrasting paintwork (fig. 109).

The open frame settles from Munster rarely exhibit the generous use of timber

111. Detail of the angled top to a west Cork open frame settle (fig. 110), showing hand-planed mouldings and incised lines cut with a scratch stock. The thick pink and white gloss is applied over many previous layers.

found in the construction of some settle beds, with their solid boarded ends. In areas of acute timber shortage examples are found with vertical slats along the back in lieu of panelling (particularly on the west coast, fig. 114). Such slat-backed settles were once the common form on Bere Island, near the Cork/Kerry border. People there still commonly refer to their settle as the 'rack'.[26] Stretching out on such a thing to sleep may have been considered somewhat tortuous; according to the British Government's Poor Reports from early nineteenth-century Kerry, 'A few of them [the poor] have a seat, most justly called a "rack"'.[27]

A feature characterising many of the settles from county Cork is the method in which the front legs rise and then taper to meet and support the horizontal armrests (figs. 109, 110, 113). The arm sits firmly in a bridle joint, often pegged to hold it in place, and is finished with a rounded projecting end, comfortable to the hand. Like the worktops of dressers and the seats of forms, the settle's seat was traditionally left unpainted and instead scrubbed regularly to keep it clean.

The traditional position for these bench-

like settles in the Munster farmhouse was close enough to the hearth to provide the sitter with access to the hand operated Pierce wind machine for fanning the fire. At night the welcomed traveller could stretch out and sleep there in warmth. Placed beside the focal point of the room (the hearth), sitting on the settle, one had a clear view of the front door, front window and the activities of the kitchen in the typically gable-ended Munster farmhouses.

Open frame settles of a similar design to those found in Ireland also occur throughout parts of England and Wales, and in many parts of Europe.[28] Settles were also used in Scotland. There, an open framed settle or seize, from a croft in North Uist, was called a 'deece or deas (from the dais of a hall where they stood).'[29] At Islandmagee, on the east coast of county Antrim, the traditional long fireside seat is also known as the 'dias' or 'dace'.[30] The many links

112. (*above*) Open frame pine settle with tongued and grooved backing boards, in a kitchen near Baltimore in county Cork. It has curved and chamfered decoration at each end and a valance for hidden storage space. *c.*1920.

113. (*above right*) Painted pine open frame settle, from the Beara Peninsula, county Cork. Made in the mid nineteenth century, it has had its base adapted to form a box settle, with space beneath the hinged seat for storage. The dresser has also been altered by the addition of glass doors.

114. This slat-backed fireside settle has been known in some parts of counties Cork and Kerry as the 'rack' since the 1830s. In areas short of timber, settles were often built with such open work backs and armrests, and usually made long enough to act as a spare bed. This early nineteenth-century example is made of pine, overpainted repeatedly, with the most recent layer of pale blue gloss. From the Beara Peninsula (county Cork).

79

between the communities of Scotland and Ulster are no doubt responsible for the use of this ancient terminology.

THE 'CARBERY SETTLE'

An open framed settle, cleverly incorporating a one-legged 'falling' table, was a multipurpose design first heard of through oral accounts in county Cork. Its comparatively lengthy description, and the need to distinguish it from the more common 'settle table' of the south-east, led to the name the 'Carbery settle', after the area in county Cork where it was most commonly used.[31]

After months of fieldwork in county Cork an intact surviving example came to light (see figs. 115, 291D). Many others were remembered but had been cleared from the houses for which they were originally built.

Another example, recently removed to an outhouse, had the attachments for a table in the centre of the back, but the table itself was missing. The one illustrated here (fig. 115) works by fastening the falling table in place when needed, by means of a simple slot and hole attachment (like that of an old roller towelrail). When not required, the table, complete with leg, could be unhooked and folded up for storage. A carpenter making such a Carbery settle would have the advantage of being independent of the blacksmith, who would otherwise be called upon to forge the iron attachments. Making the table hinge directly onto the settle was easier than fastening it into a stone or mud wall. Other examples enabled the table to be fastened up against the wall when not required. One woman in west county Cork explained that the Carbery settle in her kitchen had eventually been scrapped because the table had developed a

115. The 'Carbery settle', named after the barony in west county cork where it once was common. It combines the ubiquitous one-legged 'falling table', with an open frame settle, of a type which was typical of the south-west and west. This mid nineteenth-century example, was originally painted dark red. It is unusual because the table can be removed completely, for storage, by means of slots and dowels. Its single leg is attached with a large single dovetail to a wooden hinge, enabling it to swing freely (fig. 291D). Other versions had a system whereby the table swung upwards and clipped vertically onto a ceiling joist, above. Such a Carbery settle was often the only table in the smallest houses; at night it acted as a spare bed for a traveller, or as a long fireside seat.

116. A unique painted settle, with outwardly curved armrests of pine, reminiscent of the popular upholstered farmhouse *chaises longues*. Made long enough to stretch out and sleep on beside the fire, it originally had long parallel stretchers beneath the seat. Bought near Union Hall, west Cork at auction for a shilling, during the first half of the twentieth century; made in the early nineteenth century. Photographed by Tim Imrie-Tait.

nasty habit of crashing down onto peoples' heads as they sat beneath it.

The example illustrated dates from the mid nineteenth century and was originally painted. People in the Carbery area recalled other examples being used in the smallest houses where space was at a premium. They were also used in much larger farmhouses where an additional table was often needed when the farm labourers came in to eat at the end of a days work.

Eric Cross describes a 'Carbery settle' in his account of the furnishings in the home of *The Tailor and Ansty*: 'Down comes a contraption from the settle. It is a collap-

sable table with a hanging leg. One end rests on the settle and the other is supported by a swinging leg . . . The Tailor is proud of this and enjoys your interest.'[32]

A comparative description from the 1930s of a similar arrangement was recorded from the neighbouring barony of Kinalmeaky:

There was a rail fixed to the wall over the 'settle' the hinges o' the table were got into the rail so that the table would slide along it. They could move the table near the fire if the night was cold or move it away if they wanted. When the table wasn't wanted they'd rise it up on its hinges 'agin' the wall. An the leg would drop down on its hinge by the table. It was fastened up to the wall with a bolt. The manin of having them hanging tables was to give room in the kitchen.[33]

This example was a low backed settle bed, with a table being fixed to a running rail on the wall behind it.

Another example of a settle of similar design to the Carbery one was photographed in a house in county Derry in 1988 by Megan McManus of the Ulster Folk Museum. It was made in the 1940s by Jim Patterson (born in 1902), who based it on a design remembered from his childhood. The falling table was held up to the wall by a brass clip and its hinges and two folding legs were also of brass. The base was made from recycled church furniture and was used for the storage of fuel for the fire.[34]

When searching for the origins of such a remarkable design, it is tempting to conclude that the settle was combined with a falling table, simply because both were widespread and popular and the Carbery settle was the inevitable resulting space-saving hybrid. The fact that it was popular predominantly in one comparatively small region of south-west Ireland, is the result of rural isolation.

Other variations in design of the basic settle include adaptations for particular needs, like the Cork farmer who had special compartments built beneath the settle seat where their young (and vulnerable) turkeys could be kept warm with a heater after hatching. Others have drawers fitted beneath the seat, or occasionally they have a boxed in seat which lifts up to provide storage space (fig. 113). One of the most delightful examples has outward curving arm-rests at each end, reminiscent of the fashionable parlour *chaises longues* (see fig. 116).

Thus, there are many variations in design of these open frame settles, which are particularly noticeable when comparing the work of one maker with another. Some designs did not seem to spread very far inside Ireland. This was doubtless due to communities being more isolated from each other in some cases, because of poor internal communications, than from other neighbouring countries. Coastal regions of

Ireland sometimes seem to be more closely linked with overseas neighbours than with inland Ireland.

Loudon (in his *Encyclopaedia* full of ideas and designs for vernacular furniture), explains somewhat tenuously that on the back of a settle 'a flap might be hung to it, with a jib bracket to serve as a reading or writing table'.[35]

The only surviving English example of similar design to the 'Carbery settle' is illustrated in *The Dictionary of English Furniture* and dates from the late seventeenth century. By comparison it is a complex design, decorated with shallow carving.[36] More similar to the Cork version is the *Cicelu*, or *Zuzulu*; the most typical fireside seat in farmhouses of the Basque region on the French/Spanish border.[37] The Basques were notoriously courageous seafarers so it is possible that the design was transmitted via maritime links between these two coastal regions. In the Lisbon Folk Museum, there is another example of a settle very similar to our 'Carbery' example.

THE SETTLE BED

Willed down, waited for, in place at
    last and for good.
Trunk-hasped, cart-heavy, painted an
    ignorant brown.
And pew-straight, bin-deep, standing
    four-square as an ark.

    Seamus Heaney's 'The Settle Bed',
    1991[38]

The settle bed is a long seat by day, opening out onto the floor upon hinges to create a double bed by night (figs. 117–18). It has been in use in Ireland since the first half of the seventeenth century and probably even earlier. Until about the 1950s settle beds were still in general use and a few examples are still used today as extra beds for visitors.[39] Most surviving examples have been kept in the kitchen as fireside seats, while the folding bed section has often become firmly fixed in place by repeated layers of paint. Others serve as useful repositories for domestic miscellany (see fig. 119).

The earliest known reference to a settle

117. Pine settle bed, recently stripped, with panels decorated by the carved shells. Surmounted by a composite cornice over dentil moulding, the back emulates seventeenth-century architectural panelling. It has fielded panels, integral mouldings and pegged tenons. Mid nineteenth century from east county Waterford.

118. The same settle bed, folded out onto the floor, for use as a high sided double bed. When folded up as a seat, bedding could be stored in the base. The panelled ends, with open work arms, contrast with the boarded ends of examples from further north (figs. 122, 123). Shown at The Irish Agricultural Museum, Wexford; courtesy of the Irish Country Furniture Society.

bed is from a county Waterford inventory of 1640 and is listed as a 'settle bedd or bench bedd contayneinge a flox bedd a boulster a sheete and one coverlett valued £1'.[40] At least half a dozen inventory references to settle beds occur during the seventeenth century, from counties Cork, Waterford, Kilkenny and Dublin. In 1675 another 'Settle Bedstead, two blanketts one rugg' (one can safely assume these were conveniently stored inside the base) was listed in one of the Ormond inventories from neighbouring Clonmell [sic]. Dublin Castle had in 1684 no less than 'Eight Settle bedsteads', listed in the 'Lower fower quarters of the Stable' where stable boys would have slept. No other furniture was mentioned in this area so the 'Eight fflock beds and boulsters, [and] Sixteen Caddowes' must therefore have been stored inside them.[41]

By the second half of the seventeenth century such listings begin to appear more frequently. A 'settled bed' and bedding was amongst the furniture from Burton Hall, county Cork in 1686,[42] a 'settle bedstead [and] flock bed . . . (for servants)' was listed in a Dublin weaver's kitchen in 1694 and another 'settle bedstead' also from Dublin occurred in 1695.[43] These seventeenth-century inventory listings categorically disprove the theory that the settle bed is of 'very late introduction', at least for the eastern parts of Ireland.[44]

Ten entries for settle beds, also mostly from inventories, have been found for the eighteenth century.[45] It is interesting to note how their distribution pattern encompasses most of Leinster, as well as two more from county Cork, one from Tipperary and another from Lecale, county Down. Most of them are listed in the less important chambers of the so-called big houses, castles and homes of the gentry, although one or two were owned by farmers or merchants. As such they took up little space, containing their own mattresses and bedding during

119. Pine settle bed with panelled back and ends, made *c.*1910 by wheelwright/carpenter Patrick Doyle, of Tombreine, Carnew, south county Wicklow. He also made staircases, windows and doors, using timber from the nearby Coolatin estate. He would live and eat with the family for whom he worked. Its present owner used to sleep in it as a child with his two siblings, on a feather mattress. Seat length 72–5 in., 19 in. deep, 21 in. high, width of bed 37½ in.; overall height 49½ in.

120. Pen drawing by Ida Flower of the kitchen of an old house on the Great Blasket Island, off the coast of county Kerry, *c.*1911. The hearth, with its gallows-shaped wooden crane and keeping hole, is covered by one of two half lofts–the back-loft or *cullochta.* Upon it are heaped the 'nets, bags of wool, sails, oars, ladders, [and] panniers for turf-carrying'. To the right is a large panelled settle bed, and a sturdy kitchen table is in its customary place lit by the front window. From Robin Flower's *The Western Island,* 1944. Courtesy Oxford University Press.

the day. In cottiers' and farmers' houses during the nineteenth and twentieth centuries the settle bed was invariably placed in the kitchen, typically against the back wall near the hearth.

It is difficult to draw firm conclusions from their pattern of geographical distribution, as a disproportionate number of inventories survive from the comparatively prosperous southern and eastern counties. The fact that they tend to come from aristocratic homes should not be misinterpreted, because inventories were drawn up more often for large houses than for small.

Together, the seventeenth- and eight-

eenth-century settle bed listings tell us that at least one was made of oak, and that another was yellow, presumably painted to match its 'yellow' room. They are nearly all listed along with the bedclothes which they contained (usually of lesser quality to those described from other beds). A significant number of all these settle beds are described as for servants, or in the servants hall or kitchen. This suggests that the many more inventories (not listed here) which list servants beds, may also have been referring to settle beds.[46]

It was also known as the saddle bed or even the 'Press bed'. Saddle, in counties Down and Armagh, is probably a dialect version of settle. The fact that both 'press beds' and settle beds are folding bedsteads (and that both types of bed were known in the same areas) accounts for this exceptional and confusing cross over.[47] Other variations on the name settle bed include bed settle or simply settle. For simplicity, here it is referred to solely as the settle bed.

Many more references to settle beds do occur after the eighteenth century, but by the nineteenth and twentieth centuries a far greater variety of descriptions (as well as surviving examples), provide us with a wide range of data.

An impressively grand inventory from Ballyhagen, county Armagh, taken in 1817 distinguishes between a 'Settle Bedstead' in the 'New Kitchen' valued at only £1, which must have been for servants, and two 'Settee Bedsteads', one valued at £4. 11*s.* and an-

121. (*facing page, top right*) Settle bed opened down for use as a bed, with substantial boarded ends. Made of pine, from a two-storey house in Ballybritt, county Offaly, *c*.1880. Seat length 75 in., depth 22 in., height 25 in.; width of bed 40½ in.; overall height 50½ in. Courtesy of Roscrea Heritage Centre.

122. Pine settle bed with solid ends and tongued and grooved backing boards, painted shut, *c*.1900. On the seat is a length of *súgán*, wrapped into a ball to prevent it untwisting. On the right is a plaited straw mattress, rolled up ready for storage. Seat length 70–73 in., depth 18 in., height 18½ in., width of bed 20 in.; overall height 42 in. Courtesy of Carndonagh Museum, Inishowen Peninsula, county Donegal.

123. Scrubbed settle bed, shown open, which survived through the famine because it was in the kitchen of a large Presbyterian Manse, and dates from the period when the house was built in 1785. It has been much repaired, the seat has a covering of early linoleum, but was never painted: family tradition relates that it was scrubbed thoroughly every Saturday, so the grain is now smooth and undulating. To its right is a painted meat safe. From the Inishowen Peninsula, north county Donegal. Seat length 74½ in., depth 18½ in., height 20 in.; width as a bed 34 in.; overall height 36 in.

bed was similarly adopted from the 'big house' and adapted to suit the requirements of farmhouses, with their open raftered ceilings.

As mentioned earlier, the employment of servants was by no means confined to the aristocracy in Ireland. Many comparatively small farms employed servants on a seasonal basis to help with the farmwork and the dairying. Their living conditions varied but often they would eat with the family, bed and board being part payment of their meagre wages.

The Ordnance Survey Memoirs occasionally provide descriptions of furniture, in the sections dealing with markets or the 'Habits of the People'.[50] Thus in county Antrim in 1840: 'Most of the farmhouses have . . . a large kitchen with an earthen floor and without any ceiling . . . The furniture of the kitchen is very plain and homely. The servants not infrequently sleep in it in settle beds.'[51] Meanwhile the family were accommodated in a couple of sleeping rooms opening off the parlour. In another county Antrim parish a few months later, the momoirs inform us that

A few of the [smaller] farm cottages possess a half loft over the parlour, in which the domestics sleep. A very wide chim-

124. Pine settle bed with fielded panelling, from Garrycastle in county Offaly, shown open for use as a bed. It was originally grained, but has been repeatedly painted over. Mid nineteenth century. Seat length 72 in., depth 20 in., height 20½ in.; width as a bed 38½ in.; overall height 52 in. with a shelf nearly 6 in. wide across the top. Courtesy of the N.M.I.

125. A high seated pine settle bed, which folds forwards to make a bed 47 in. wide on the floor. Painted brown, over red, its wide seat boards are joined by slotted screws along the edges of boards. The wavy outline above the arms is often found on settles from the provinces of Munster and Connaught..This late nineteenth-century example is from county Clare. Seat length 70 in., depth 21 in., height 29 in.; width of bed 47 in.; overall height 55½ in. Courtesy of the N.M.I.

other, listed as 'furnished' at £14. 15s. 9d.[48] No examples are known to have survived, but these lavishly upholstered 'Settee bedsteads' occur quite frequently in grand inventories and were perhaps of a similar basic design to the settle beds.

However, by the twentieth century this ingenious dual-purposè design had become well known in every county of Ireland.[49]

SETTLE BEDS AND SERVANTS

The settle bed would have become familiar to the less affluent rural population because it was made by country carpenters (rather than by cabinetmakers) and often occupied by servants (who were mainly from rural areas). It was probably widely used in these smaller rural homes by the eighteenth century, although descriptions of it begin to appear from the nineteenth century onwards. This selective adoption of a functional form of bed was perfectly suited to the confines of small kitchens and to the needs of large families. The tester or canopy

126. An early twentieth-century settle bed, with board-ends cut into curves. Made of pine, overpainted repeatedly and finally with cream gloss. It is shown before a traditional house with a flax thatched roof, netted and tied against the wind. Inishowen peninsula, county Donegal.

ney brace impends over a spacious paved hearth, at one side of which there stands a stock or settle bed . . . Their furniture is plain, homely and substantial . . . Stock beds are almost exclusively used.[52]

So it seems that the settle bed was the domain of the servants, at least in the larger farmhouses, while the poorer owners of the 'farm cottages' slept in their settle beds and their servants slept in the loft. Often these farm servants shared beds. Patrick Kennedy, writing of the early 1800s, describes the family retiring to sleep in their bedrooms; 'and the servant girls to their settle bed that rested by the kitchen wall opposite the door', while in contrast the 'male servants retired to their good straw beds in the barn'.[53]

The furnishings of the poorest houses of county Limerick sometimes included 'an abominable thing called a settle-bed'.[54] In houses where space was restricted, as on the Great Blasket Island in the 1870s, the kitchen settle bed often provided sleeping space for several members of a large family.[55] This communal system for sleeping three or more children ocurred in many areas in living memory. It was an obvious solution in crowded conditions and in the winter would have helped people to stay warm. Many people still remember how they were put to sleep this way with their siblings.[56]

OTHER OCCUPANTS OF THE SETTLE BED

'"Wisha" tis many the "stroive" would turn in long 'go for a nights lodging an they'd make a bed in the settle for him.'[57]

Travellers who roamed the countryside were traditionally made welcome and were often accommodated in the kitchen settle bed. During the nineteenth century, 'they were sure to get enough to eat in their regular rounds, and had always their night quarters secured at certain fixed houses'.[58] One Cork farmer related how she preferred them to sleep in the settle bed in the kitchen, where they were less likely to cause an accidental fire (by cigarette smoking) than if they slept in the barn. An account from Carndonagh, county Donegal, relates how 'The journeymen tailors slept in the settle bed in the kitchen'.[59] As mentioned earlier, travelling craftsmen known as journeymen usually became part of the household for whom they worked for the duration of the job. Bed and board was thus an important part of their payment.

Stories of the inebriated being conveniently deposited in this kitchen bed abound. Carleton describes the procedure in his rambling account of a kidnapped schoolmaster: 'Mat was wholly insensible . . . they deposited him in a settle-bed, where he slept, unconscious of the journey he had performed, until breakfast-time on the next morning.'[60] Not only would this have been easier than transporting him through the house into a bedroom, but in Donegal someone wisely concluded that 'The settle-bed was a great place for a drunken man, he couldn't roll out'.[61]

THE SETTLE BED FOR CHILDREN

In contrast, the settle bed has often been linked with the activities of children, as the kitchen with a floor-level fire could be a dangerous place. 'Settle beds were especially safe for youngsters as they were low and they couldn't fall out of them.'[62] Also, when folded down it made an ideal enclosed playpen for the smallest members of a family from south-east county Antrim.[63] A woman from county Tyrone recalls how she had learned to walk within the safe confinement of theirs. An account from county Clare written in the 1940s, described how the farm children usually sat on the settle to eat their meals rather than with the adults at the table.[64]

127. *The Dancing-Master*, engraved from a painting by Howard Helmick (1845–1907). Some of the audience sit on a settle bed, while a woman crouches on a tiny stool by the fire, and above her hangs a wicker birdcage. To the right is a curious three-legged chair, reminiscent of a 'Sligo chair' (fig. 61), suggesting a Connaught location. From *The Magazine of Art*, II, 1888. Brought to the author's attention by the Irish Traditional Music Archive.

USES OF THE SETTLE BED

> The girls by the painted dresser, the
>   dripping men
> Late from the sea and huddled,
> These on the settle, those by the
>   table; the turf
> Sent up faint smoke, and faint in the
>   chimney a light . . .

Robin Flower, *The Dance*, 1944[65]

The settle bed not only served as a double bed at night or a container for bedding and a bench seat in daytime, but also for many other purposes. An account from county Longford in the 1930s mentions how when folded up, the settle bed 'served as a table, or seat during the day'.[66] However, the use of the settle bed as a table was exceptional.[67]

In county Cork, the folded settle bed was 'also used for holding, on top of the seat, the surplus *súgán* or wooden kitchen chairs'.[68] A similar account comes from county Limerick.[69] The removal of these chairs would have created space for the many daytime activities of the working kitchen, where space was limited. In other households, in counties Wicklow, Armagh and Monaghan 'it was usual to keep the crock of spring water on it during the daytime, and sometimes the milking vessels'.[70] Sometimes there was a narrow shelf across the top of the back; this was often used to place household articles or, in one home in county Wexford, it was a repository for boots.[71]

However, the main use for the closed-up settle bed during the day was as a seat, where one could conveniently stretch out and relax or sit next to the fire. There are conflicting accounts as to whether it was a favoured place to sit, because as designs varied, so did degrees of comfort.

SETTLE BEDS: CONSTRUCTION AND VARIATION IN DESIGN

The dimensions of a settle bed probably varied according to the household's needs. If it was to be used as a spare bed, the carpenter could probably afford to create a seat at a comfortable height. However, a writer from county Down recalled: 'It was not a popular seat, too high and too hard with the back too far back to rest against and women and men with short legs looked uncomfortable and ludicrous.'[72] It may be that those in his district tended to have particularly high seats (thus creating extra width as a bed). Dimensions and designs of surviving examples vary enormously and with most dual-purpose design, there tends to be some element of compromise. A perfectly ergonomic seat would obviously create only a small storage space for bedding and a correspondingly narrow bed.

The construction of such a massive and heavy item as a settle bed probably took place in the kitchen, rather than in a workshop elsewhere. This certainly was the normal procedure with dressers, whose size often makes removal through a front door impossible. The fact that settle beds are conspicuous by their absence amongst the detailed Ordnance Survey descriptions of furniture for sale at fairs in the north lends further weight to this theory. The transportation of such cumbersome objects along rough roads by horse and cart would have been slow and difficult.

Most are constructed solidly with butted and nailed box sections and boarded ends, particularly those examples from northern counties. One exception from county Roscommon had its seat carefully joined together by neat through-dovetails, a feature

128. A settle bed with boarded rather than panelled ends, made in the mid-nineteenth century, from north county Cavan. It is remarkable for its three sledge feet (rather than two), which are a feature of settles and dressers from the north. Repeatedly painted, most recently in mustard gloss. From the Derragarra Inn, Butlersbridge, county Cavan.

129. Sketch of a high backed settle showing the configuration of twenty decorative panels of different shapes, and with low armrests. Such workmanship is still legendary along the southern coastal counties, yet few examples survive. This one was from the Comeragh mountains, county Waterford. After a photograph by Patrick Warner.

130. The end of a settle bed from county Tipperary, with a cupid's bow combined with a heart cut beneath the armrest. Painted repeatedly, most recently in two-tone red and white. The seat/bed is kept closed by a wrought iron hook. Early nineteenth century. Courtesy of Victor Mitchell.

that most country carpenters would be unlikely to spend extra time over. It also had renewable 'sledge' feet, a characteristic of most dressers and some settles from the northern half of Ireland. The function of these feet is the same as with the sacrificial sledge feet of many dressers: should the dampness of the ubiquitous earthen or flagged floor pervade them they could be renewed, thereby preventing the rot spreading up to the rest of the settle. Sometimes settle beds are fitted with three rather than two sledge feet, raising the entire seat section several inches off the floor (see fig. 128).

As with other furniture, settle beds from the southern counties usually exhibit an enthusiastic variety of decoration. Instead of the simply shaped boarded ends so common in Ulster, one finds a huge variety of decorative carving, moulding and panelling. Sometimes these amount to a celebration of the carpenter's best skills. High backrests are sometimes made up of panels of every contrasting size and shape. Octagonal, triangular, diamond-shaped and even curved or with arched tops, they are often extravagant and were obviously special conversation pieces (see figs. 117, 129, 132).

Several examples of these especially decorative high backed settle beds originated in the hinterland of Waterford, where they were associated with marriage dowries. A particularly elaborate example with eighteen contrasting panels (with some of them curved) is illustrated in *A Visitor's Guide to the Comeragh Mountains* (fig. 129).[73] Another high backed Waterford settle bed combines carved scallop shell or fan corner details and tall, contrasting fielded panels with distinctly Arabesque or Moorish

arched tops (figs. 132, 23). The maker of this latter example, which was part of a wedding dowry, has also incorporated diamonds, clubs and hearts with a classical dentil moulding beneath the many layered cornice. Few surfaces have been left without ornament and at least two of his distinctive settles are known to have survived. However, others of a similar size, but with less carving, were also being made in southern Munster towards the close of the nineteenth century. Rather like the old fiddle-fronted dressers, these settle beds often display a marked contrast between their lavishly decorative upper sections and their unadorned, functional lower sections (see figs. 117, 132). Thus the seat itself was often left totally plain, with its upper surface scrubbed and unpainted.

The pair of hooks or catches which fasten each settle bed into its closed position were usually the work of local blacksmiths. Their designs predictably vary greatly from one to the next, from the straight and undecorated to the finely wrought, curved and twisted examples. The hook is in most cases attached by a ring to the outside edge of the seat,

131. Detail of the end of a settle bed from county Tipperary, showing one of a variety of designs of wrought iron hooks and eyes made by blacksmiths. They had to be strong enough to bear the weight of several sitters, and such curved designs helped anchor them firmly without splitting the wood.

The settle bed seems to have originated in Ireland and does not occur in the history of furniture from Scotland, Wales or France. Alternatively, the design may have originated from England, but so far only one example, from an inventory of 1641, has come to light. Although there are seats that convert into beds in some other parts of Europe, none follow the same Irish design.[74] The millions of Irish who emigrated to North America, Canada and Australia – particularly around the period of the worst recurring famines of the 1840s – often rebuilt familiar old designs like the settle bed in their new homes. Although constructed with different timbers, these Irish designs are distinct from those of their fellow settlers from elsewhere.

John Mannion has made a study of the Irish settlement in eastern Canada. He shows that these immigrants built settle beds which they called 'stretchers', carrying on the tradition from the 'old world' of placing them along the back wall and using them as beds for their children.[75] Howard Pain, whose definitive book on the vernacular furniture of Upper Canada, also recognises and illustrates the settle bed as a design originating in Ireland. He notes that the French Canadian form of settle bed, known as the *banc lit*, 'was likely adopted from the Irish immigrants'. His eight examples vary in style and tend to be fastened at the centre back of each seat, with only one example fastened by the traditional pair of forged iron hooks and eyes.[76] Russell Hawes Kettell (in his book on furniture from New England) illustrates a panelled back settle bed (with a pair of hooks on the front) suggesting that they also occurred in northern parts of Vermont, Maine and New Hampshire.[77]

Although distinctly Irish designs of dressers and chairs often occur amongst Irish settlements in Australia, it is somewhat surprising that so far no settle beds have been discovered amongst vernacular furniture there.[78] However, the design of some of the many Australian 'open frame' settles (also known as a 'joined open-arm' settle) would not look out of place in an Irish farmhouse. One of these even has a characteristically

while the 'eye' that this hook drops into is screwed onto the front of the bed (figs. 121, 124, 126, 131). Several of the settle beds from the National Museum of Ireland have elaborate curved straps to keep the 'eyes' in place. As considerable strain can be put on these attachments, the blacksmith sometimes made a decorative feature out of the fact that several screws were required to hold the eye in place (see fig. 131). The long strap hinges concealed inside the closed bed were likely to have been purpose made by local blacksmiths as well.

132. One of several late eighteenth-century settle beds, from Portalick Cove, Woodstown, east county Waterford. Classical fluting and dentil moulding flank tall fielded panels topped with contrasting Moorish curves, perhaps a result of nearby Waterford's long history of foreign trade. Shell and cupid's bow motifs (beneath the arms) are less extraordinary in the south-east, where high backed pine settle beds were once common. Carved hearts, diamonds, spades and clubs are nearly obscured by dozens of layers of over painting (see detail fig. 23). Courtesy of the Irish Agricultural Museum.

Irish green paint finish with the seat left unpainted and presumably scrubbed. Like the Irish open frame settles, 'The excessive depth of the seat suggests that it was designed, as were many of these country couches, to double as a bed when needed.'[79]

SETTLE TABLES

The settle table is an example of yet another highly ingenious combination settle. The conversion from a high backed settle into a kitchen table is made by tipping the settle's back through ninety degrees into the horizontal, table position. Pegs or hinges at the rear of the armrest make this possible. (figs. 133, 135, 136, 139–40). There seems to be less of the compromise discernible by the transformation of the settle bed into a seat. However, some examples have a strengthening bar running between the hinges, which would have made sitting rather uncomfortable (fig. 135). Strangely, there is no mention of the settle table amongst the usual commentators on Irish folklife and material culture.[80]

Settle tables were most commonly used in south-east Ireland. Examples have been discovered in counties Wexford, Kilkenny and Waterford (one in the latter county was still in use, with a formica top). A sufficiently large number (several dozen) have survived to be able to draw some conclusions about their design and construc-

tion. Although most examples are strictly functional, a few were made with decorative panelling beneath the table top which would only have been revealed when used as a settle (fig. 136). The same particularly elegant example also has carved scrolls on the sides of the armrests (fig. 137).

One interesting feature is the way in which the legs are sometimes joined beneath the seat with long double stretchers. Such strengthening is commonly associated with the typical Irish kitchen table rather than the settle. The stretchers provide additional rigidity to the settle table, particularly necessary as it would have had to have been moved every time it had a change of use. As a settle, it would have been placed in its usual position against the back wall of the kitchen, but under a window when used as a table. It would probably have been dragged to and fro, since typically the settle

table is heavy and difficult to move. As well as providing extra strength, the stretchers created a raised storage area (figs. 133–5).

Most examples have a deep seat from front to back (as does the open frame settle) which is also long enough to accommodate the occasional sleeper. Many have drawers fitted beneath this seat, sometimes one or two across the front or at each end (figs. 136, 139–40). These would have been useful for cutlery, replacing those usually found under the worktop of the ordinary kitchen table. Some settle tables thus fulfilled the requirements not only of a table or a settle, but also as a spare bed with storage space.

133. Mid nineteenth-century dual-purpose settle table, shown with the table top hinged to the vertical position, for use as a long, high backed seat (see fig. 134). Such settle tables were once common in farmhouses in the southeast of Ireland. From the vicinity of Ballymitty townland, county Wexford.

134. Mid nineteenth-century, dual-purpose settle table made of sycamore with a pine seat, originally painted red. Shown ready for use as a kitchen table (compare to fig. 133). The double stretchers (made from scantlings) are more commonly incorporated into Irish tables, rather than settles. Its joints are either pegged, or through-morticed. Bought at auction near Ballymitty townland, county Wexford. Seat 60 in. long, 21 in. deep, 19 in. high; table top 63 in × 36 in.

135. Pine settle table, probably from southern Leinster, showing the wooden slot and peg mechanism which enables the table top/backrest to be lowered by 12 in. when used as a settle. This early nineteenth-century example, like figs. 133 and 134 has double stretchers beneath the seat. It has the disadvantage of having an uncomfortable strengthening bar across the backrest, unlike that in fig. 137.

136. An unusually ornate,
good quality pine settle
table, with arcaded false
panels across the underside
of the flat table top. The
drawer front is surrounded
by applied mouldings, as
are the panels across the
front of the seat.
Chamfering decorates the
legs and armrests, which
terminate in carved scrolls
(see fig. 137). The joints are
concealed and fastened by
pegs. Repainted in brown
gloss, over brown and black,
with the seat and table top
left scrubbed. c.1800, origin
unknown, but probably
from the south-east.

137. Detail of wear on a
painted settle table (fig. 136)
showing the carved scroll of
the armrest, and chamfered
decoration. Open frame
settles usually have front
legs which taper as they rise
to meet the armrests: here
the maker has made it a
decorative feature.

138. Painted pine settle table, shown with its top folded for use as a settle. It can be lifted and hinged forwards when required as a kitchen table, marked by a pitsaw and an adze, it probably dates from the early nineteenth century. The window behind has drawers built into its sill. Above it is the holy shelf, and to the right is a *súgán* armchair. From Licketstown, south county Kilkenny. Photo courtesy of the Irish Architectural Archive.

Only two examples of single-seater settle tables or chair tables have been discovered (figs. 141–2). Perfectly suited to the smallest cabins, their seats are necessarily heavily built, echoing the open frame settle's design. The long axis of the table top is necessarily altered for these chair tables (compare figs. 140 and 141).

The conversion from settle to table is usually facilitated by a pair of long strap-hinges which fix the underside of the table top (normally serving as the back of the settle) to the rear upper surface of the two armrests. Thus the back can be lowered onto the supporting armrests, overlapping sufficiently at each end to allow the sitters ample leg room beneath (fig. 142). As with the settle bed, during the nineteenth century this transformation sometimes required the services of the local blacksmith to provide such hinges. Sometimes he forged a purpose-made hinge which simultaneously provided structural support for the table top (fig. 139). Alternatively, projecting hard-

139. Pine settle table with one drawer and wrought iron hinges purpose made by a blacksmith. A strip of quarter-round moulding along the back of the seat acts as a draught excluder. Decorated with parallel lines cut with the scratch stock and moulding plane. Late nineteenth-century, from county Wexford.

wood pins were fixed to the rear of the armrests which rotated within corresponding holes drilled into flanges attached to the underside of the table top.

The most ingenious types also utilise a pair of pine flanges attached to the back,

94

140. A settle table with three drawers beneath the seat, the top/backrest is attached by means of strap hinges. This example has a gap along the back of the seat, where some others have a long piece of timber to exclude draughts (fig. 136). Painted red, its top is partially restored. Mid nineteenth century, from Rathgarogue, Parish, New Ross, county Wexford.

141. Chair table, probably from the south-east, shown with its top tilted back for use as a seat. The worn stretchers are the result of decades of use as a kitchen table. The back has cross cleats supporting the table top, which were often covered by a sack of hay hung from hooks, as a cushion. The table top has evidently been turned over; it is worn into ripples from wear and scrubbing on both sides. Partially restored, the base was originally painted brown, c.1800.

142. Chair table, or single-seater settle table, of pine, stripped of its layers of red and green paint. Made with pegged or through-wedged tenons, the arms incised with scratch stock lines. The top, surrounded by a mitred frame, hinges through 90 degrees to become an armchair. From county Wexford, where the larger settle tables were much more common. Mid nineteenth century. Part of The Irish Country Furniture Society's collection, shown at The Irish Agricultural Museum.

each with a long slot in the lower half; into these, fit pegs attached to the back of the armrests. To convert the settle to a table, the back must first be lifted before tipping it forwards (figs. 135, 138). This arrangement lowers the settle's centre of gravity, reducing the possibility of it tipping over backwards. Simultaneously it encloses the potentially draughty gap which some settle tables have along the back of the seat (fig. 140), which is otherwise filled by an extra fixed board (figs. 136, 139).

Decoration of settle tables reflects their functions. Most of the examples examined were originally of painted softwood, usually pine (some have subsequently been stripped and wax polished). Shallow lines have sometimes been made with a simple scratch stock (a home-made tool which works like a marking gauge), outlining and drawing attention to the back, the arms and the drawer fronts (figs. 139, 142). Sometimes the edges of the legs are chamfered, in the manner of the wheelwright, who did the same thing when making wheels and carts in order to reduce their weight (figs. 134, 136, 140).[81] Joints are unselfconsciously through-wedged or pegged for maximum strength. In common with other settles the seat area was left unpainted so it could be scrubbed clean, as was the table top (fig. 136).

The settle table was known, although was not necessarily widespread, in England from the seventeenth century onwards. Only three illustrations of settle tables similar to those found in Ireland have been published. The first, most formal and undecorated example is of oak with an enclosed seat, dating from the seventeenth century, its place of origin unknown. It is the only one of the English examples with the ingenious slotted flange arrangement described above.[82] The second is another seventeenth-century example from Chester, made out of chestnut and sketched from memory.[83] The *Dictionary of English Furniture* illustrates a third seventeenth-century oak settle table acquired by The Victoria and Albert Museum in 1908 (accession unknown), which has a lidded box seat resting on a pair of sledge feet.[84]

It has been suggested that the scarcity of 'chair tables' was due to their being uncomfortable, although they are known to have been used during the sixteenth and seventeenth centuries.[85] A few English examples have been found in Taunton and Wincanton in Somerset: made of pine, they have sledge feet and boarded ends, with storage space beneath the seat. These are thought to date from the early nineteenth century.[86] Gertrude Jekyll illustrates a chair table in her *Old English Household Life*, and it is interesting to note that of the very few examples of chair and settle tables published from England, most are from the west coast, closest to Ireland.[87]

The French favoured a form of open frame and board-ended settle in their farmhouses during the eighteenth and nineteenth centuries. A chair table from the mountainous Savoy region of south-east France bears a close similarity in design to examples from the south-west of Ireland.[88]

In north America it is highly likely that the many Irish immigrants first introduced the design of the settle table. A few examples have been published but with no information about their makers. Settle tables with solid boarded ends, like those from Ulster, were evident in New England. One such example has wide stabilising sledge feet and can be fastened down securely by an extra peg when lowered for use as a table. Single seater chair tables, known there as 'hutch tables', had a hinged box or open chest beneath the table top.[89] Further examples of chair tables were also made elsewhere in America.[90]

Settles in Ireland have been ingeniously combined with a variety of other functions to produce useful and economical furniture, perfectly suited to rural needs. Resourceful woodworkers have adapted the settle more than any other piece of furniture to fulfill a wide range of functions. Hardship has metamorphosed this piece from a high sided fireside seat into a container for bedding, a draught-proof double bed, a kitchen table or an extra table and a place to keep things out of the way of the kitchen routine. Dual-purpose settles fitted well into rural Irish culture, with their emphasis on economy of timber and space.

143. Late nineteenth-century dresser, made by Paddy Crowly (1857–c.1940s), a wheelwright and furniture maker. He saved timber by incorporating the back of the dresser into the parlour wall. The scooped and beaded framework around the shelves characterises his work (fig. 144), but this example is particularly ornate because he made it for his own kitchen. Notice the glass fishing floats along the cornice, a traditional form of decoration in coastal districts. From near Union Hall, west county Cork.

144. White painted dresser, made in the late nineteenth century, by Paddy Crowly. The way the display shelves are surrounded by a scooped and beaded framework is a hallmark of Crowly's dressers (fig. 143) and is similar to much older, high fronted dressers from the same area. Near Union Hall, county Cork.

Chapter 3

THE DRESSER

Introducing the Dresser, Stone Shelves, Ware,
Display Shelves, Spoon Display, Hanging Dressers, Sledge Feet,
Built in Dressers, Coops and Coop Dressers, Small-sized Dressers

INTRODUCING THE DRESSER

> Three noggins, three mugs, a bowl and two jugs,
> A crock and a pan something lesser,
> A red fourpenny glass, to draw at for mass,
> Nailed up to a clean little dresser
>
> Anon, 'Thady O'Brady', n.d.[1]

The Irish dresser is the best known of any of the range of kitchen furniture. Inevitably it is also the most highly sought after by antique dealers. It is easily distinguished from its Welsh and English counterparts because it was traditionally made in one piece, rather than two.[2]

The dresser is unique amongst the furniture of the Irish kitchen because of its primary role as an aesthetic and decorative focal point, a role simultaneously combined with the functional storage of kitchen 'ware' and utensils. More often than not, the dresser was the only item of furniture that the carpenter took extra time to ornament with carved or fretted work, before it was painted. The various dishes, plates, bowls and utensils which the dresser held had an important influence on its overall design. They were prominently shown off to best effect in ways designed to reflect light and avoid dust. The dresser and the ware it held were precious and decorative, highlighting the owner's status and providing a talking point and a link with past generations. One woman from the Glens of Antrim fondly described her dresser as her 'most cherished possession, and each shelf has a history of

its own ... each associated with some part of the past ... Some are still adorned with delph from a shipwreck and are still called "Lake Champagne Delph" from the name of the boat.'[3]

The dresser built by west county Cork wheelwright and furniture maker Paddy Crowly (1857–c.1940) for his own kitchen, was more ornate than any he had built elsewhere in his parish. He knew it would be admired and discussed (fig. 143). A couple from Baltinglass in county Wicklow

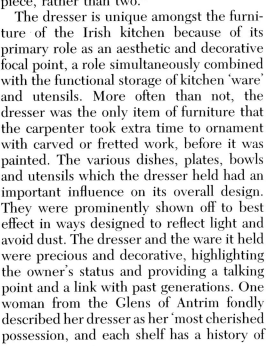

Recessed slate shelving often remains in derelict houses and ruins in Munster, some of which once had wooden doors. Kitchen dressers are mentioned as early as the seventeenth century.[6] Its importance in homes by the eighteenth century is emphasised by the fact that as an inventory item it is often the only object prefixed by the definite article.[7] There are references to such basic arrangements still in use in the 1830s in some of the poorest Irish cabins; 'a shelf in the wall, in lieu of what is commonly called a dresser' for the display of 'a few noggins'[8] is typical of many such descriptions. In 1833, Carleton provided details of a rudimentary dresser from a house 'of the humblest description' with 'a few shelves of deal, supported by pins of wood driven into the wall' (see figs. 127, 286).[9] The British Government Poor Report Commissioners, investigating the housing conditions of farm labourers in county Kerry, described 'some kind of board fixed to the wall to lay one or two mugs on or vessels to drink milk out of, whenever they have chance to have it'.[10]

WARE

A dresser filled with shining delph,
Speckled and white and blue and brown![11]

No description of Irish dressers would be complete without some mention of the so called 'delph', 'delf', 'delft' or 'ware' (short for delftware and spongeware) which they were purpose built to display and store (fig. 145). Paintings, literary descriptions, inventories and government reports all demonstrate the role and function of the dresser as an indicator of wealth and social standing through the centuries. 'In fact your status could be gauged by such remarks as "she has a well plenished dresser" – meaning that you were somebody of value, or vice versa.'[12] Until well into this century, possession of a range of domestic utensils was by no means everyone's privilege, in a society where some were so poor that they could not even afford drinking vessels, but instead improvised with seashells, eggshells or even hollowed out potatoes.[13]

Food was often eaten directly from a

145. The traditional rich mixture of spongeware, transferware and lustre which dressers were built to store and display, and succeeded the woodenware or pewter of the eighteenth century. Jam used to be sold in the hanging 'mugs' (jugs) as a sales incentive. The 'basins' (bowls) are upsidedown, and the plates lean forwards onto bars, to avoid accumulating dust. From a county Cork dresser.

posed in front of the old family dresser for their wedding photographs, rather than by the church where they were married.

This chapter examines the origins and evolution of the Irish dresser, the objects that it was built to display and its variations through time and place.

STONE SHELVES

The first, most primitive forms of dresser were simply recessed stone shelves, set into the thickness of a wall, providing a safe place to hold and display pewter or wooden ware. An early example can be seen at the prehistoric village of Skara Brae, Orkney.[4] Such tiers of stone shelves were also set into the walls of houses on Achill Island.[5]

basket or table top, by hand, rather than with utensils. It is not surprising, therefore, that those who did possess such 'ware' displayed it prominently. China was not discarded when damaged, but still displayed although unusable, emphasising its importance amongst the 'seldom used Willow Pattern china neatly arranged'.[14] Arthur Young noticed 'broken tea cups, wisely kept for shew' in the eighteenth century[15] and in the nineteenth century 'broken plates' were noted in the British Government's Poor Reports.[16] Such fragile treasures still remain on many dressers today, with the chips and cracks hidden from view. During the eighteenth century, most of the 'ware' was made of pewter, wood or earthenware, at which point the use of ceramics was still largely confined to the aristocracy.

Upon his death in 1752, Jonathon Kent, a Protestant small gentleman-farmer from county Tipperary, listed among his possessions 'nine Pewter dishes' valued at fifteen shillings.[17] In contrast, the 'Inventory of ye goods and Chattels of John McNamara' (a broguemaker from county Clare) included a mere two shillings worth of '3 ould platters and abt a Dozen auld trenchers'.[18] McNamara's ware, listed only ten years earlier, was evidently made of wood rather than pewter. There is mention of pewter still being used during the mid-nineteenth century,[19] although it would have been the so-called 'strong farmers', rather than the poor cottiers, who could afford the luxury of 'bright pewter plates . . . ranged . . . in just and gradual order, from the small egg plate to the large capacious dish'.[20] References to pewter in rural homes in the twentieth century occur, but are exceptional[21] and it is now found solely in museums.

Griffiths, who wrote about county Wexford in 1877, explains that each parish used to have its own entourage of tradesmen catering to every rural need. He laments the disappearance of the woodturner who provided the farmers with 'wooden trenchers [plates] . . . with dishes and bowls, from 60 inches diameter to 6 inches – with noggins, and with pails, all wood-hooped, and kept white as snow'. He also explains how the better classes displayed pewter, while in the poorest cabins 'earthen-ware' had come into recent use.[22]

Local availability of ceramics doubtless influenced what was displayed on farmhouse dressers. By the early nineteenth century a range of blue-and-white transfer ware, widely known as 'Willow pattern', became fashionable and available. It was comparatively expensive and would have come into use in the poorest homes later.

Arklow, county Wicklow, was a centre for the production of the colourful hand-printed white ware, known as 'spongeware', so called because it was printed through stencils using sponges.[23] Some spongeware was probably imported from other centres of production in the British Isles, as was the transfer ware. The Belleek pottery in county Fermanagh also made cheap runs of spongeware alongside their usual more delicate ceramics from 1860 to 1920.[24] The Hanbidges, a county Wicklow farming family, were still using wooden trenchers and noggins during the nineteenth century 'which in time were superseded by tin pannicans and very bad white delft plates which improved in their looks by green and blue edges [probably spongeware], afterwards by the blue willow pattern'.[25]

Both types of ware were sold at local markets and shops, while the travelling tinkers sold it from door to door throughout the poorer, more remote districts.[26] On many dressers there are still rows of brightly decorated jugs, sometimes in graduated sets, which were originally sold full of jam.[27] In county Cork these jugs are often confusingly referred to as mugs, while the bowls have been called basins since the early nineteenth century.[28] These ubiquitous 'basins' were used for eating from as well as for drinking tea, milk or porter. Occasionally they are found to have been accidentally discarded in a field, a legacy of their customary use when meals were taken outside by the men working the land.[29]

The dresser is still traditionally the domain of the *bean a ti* (woman of the house), and used to hold pails of water or milk and rows of eggs. More recently a rich miscellany of other objects have found their way onto the shelves: 'crockery mixed here and there with plain tin. A penny ink bottle, a pen and a salt cellar kept them company.'[30]

In county Donegal a dresser was discovered adorned with dozens of wind up

146. A fiddle fronted dresser, a classic example of how panelled doors were added later, according to the fashion around the close of the nineteenth century. Three layers of spongeware bowls are whamelled (turned upside down) on the worktop, while the jugs, teapots etc. are displayed alongside on an auxillary 'hanging dresser'. Photograph by R. Welch at Ballynahinch, county Down, early twentieth century, courtesy of the Ulster Museum.

BOWLS WHAMELLED ON A CO. DOWN FARM DRESSER. R.W.593.

alarm clocks, while another in county Cork had one shelf removed in order to accommodate the most enormous television (it still had spongeware basins on the shelf above). This clearly demonstrates the shifting of the traditional focal point away from the hearth.

The placing of rows of green and blue glass fishing floats above the cornice is a custom which still survives in coastal areas of counties Cork, Kerry and Mayo. When complimented on such a display, one owner complained of the tedium of cleaning the constant accumulation of dust, which perhaps explains why the practice is dying out (fig. 143).

DISPLAY SHELVES

The upper half of most dressers is composed of two, three, or four shelves, and, as mentioned above, reflected the amount of ware owned by the household as well as its status.[31] A good display of ware on the dresser was frequently 'the only bright spot in the . . . dark kitchen',[32] while other ornamentation was unusual in the comparatively sparse rural household, except for religious and political pictures.

In the northern counties of Ireland (county Donegal and what is now Ulster) there prevailed a method of piling the many bowls upsidedown in rows: 'whammeled' in this way their patterned outsides were nicely shown off without collecting dust (fig. 146).

Most nineteenth-century dressers are fitted with removeable horizontal guardrails (figs. 143, 145–6, 151, 165–8 etc.) for leaning the plates on. These enabled more plates to be stored than if they were displayed upright, and like the 'whammeling' of bowls, they prevented unnecessary housework by avoiding the accumulation of dust. The majority of dressers were positioned opposite the hearth, so that the plates, tipped forwards in this way, reflected the firelight and caught the eye.

102

Shelf fronts usually had neatly moulded front edges and occasionally were covered by ornately fretted rails. Less ornate dressers often had coloured oilcloth draped over the shelving, the front flap cut to a wavy edge (see fig. 171).

The display shelves are rarely evenly spaced apart, but instead were arranged to fit the ware, with one shelf built high enough to accommodate the large meat platters.

This system extends throughout Ireland, but generally in the southern counties the meatplates are the lowest row in the display, while further north the top shelf is more commonly used. These large platters were rarely used, except for special occasions like Christmas, Easter or after the harvest. Some dressers have a shelf with a gap of only about 6 inches, for holding bowls or mugs. Many have rows of hooks fixed to the

148. (*facing page*) Late nineteenth-century partition dresser, with later addition of glazed upper doors to save dusting. The confident use of contrasting colours for all the woodwork is a twentieth-century tradition. From the Beara Peninsula, west county Cork.

149. (*above*) Purpose-built glazed top dresser, with a correspondingly shallow worktop. This style becamed popular by the 1930s, when many older dressers had glass doors added to their shelves (fig.

148). Made by Tim McCarthy (1915–42), who often used plywood panels with arched tops, bevelled drawer fronts and glass. Such materials had become easier to buy in rural areas by that time. From near Union Hall, west county Cork.

150. (*top, right*) Glazed dresser painted pale blue and yellow and surmounted by carved sweeping scrolls centred on a scallop shell. *c.*1930. From near Leap, county Cork.

151. (*right*) Elaborate, late eighteenth-century, pine dresser from Lough Gur, county Limerick. The plain fiddle front base contrasts with the rich mixture of ionic pilasters inset with eyecatching cut-glass knobs, carved ropes and flowers. The facia has blind fretwork of celtic interlacing painted in two colours. Photographed prior to the stripping of its two-tone paintwork. Photo courtesy of Shannon Heritage Ltd.

152. Fiddle fronted, built-in dresser, with hanging dresser (displaying spoons) and 'holy shelf', all with traces of brown/red paint. The dresser dates from the building of the farm house (*c*.1723, according to family tradition). A masonry plinth raises it above the earthen floor and a wall divides the base into two. Two doors (far left) were hooked into place when the dresser housed hens. From near Mayglass, county Wexford (see fireplace fig. 197).

153. (*top*) Dressers new and old: the traditional one on the right with sledge feet was made *c*.1900 by Sam Henderson (1876–1953). The left-hand one, with glazed doors and a cupid's bow plinth, was made *c*.1955, by wheelwright David Henderson (1916–90). From a traditional, gaslit, thatched house on the Inishowen Peninsula, county Donegal.

154. Rare kitchen dresser (*c*.1720–30), from a grand farmhouse near Inishteogue, county Kilkenny. It has fourteen spoonholes at one end of its

top shelf, and unusual shaped central shelf brackets due to its extraordinary width (94 in. wide, 25 in. deep, 84 in. high). Later crude supports have been added between its two drawers. Made of pine nearly 2 in. thick, with hearts and diamonds across the facia board, early red paintwork. Hens once lived in the base: now it is used for a miscellany of modern farm paraphernalia.

155. (*top, right*) Dresser with its fiddle front and facia board pierced by mirrored hearts and celtic interlacing, *c*.1840, stripped of its paintwork. From the

reconstructed 'Shannon Farmhouse' at Bunratty Folk Park, county Clare. Photo courtesy of Shannon Heritage Ltd.

156. (*right*) Fiddle fronted dresser of pine with early red/brown paintwork and fluting, reminiscent of classical pilasters, flanking the display shelves. The open base was often used to store large cooking pots and dishes. From a farmhouse near Templemore, county Tipperary, *c*.1810. Shown displaying museum objects. Width 64 in., depth 18½ in., height 80½ in. Courtesy of Roscrea Heritage Centre.

157. An unusually elaborate kitchen dresser, confidently pierced and carved with plant forms, and saw-tooth edging (see details figs. 158–9). Its open base was used to store pans and pots from the hearth. From a single-storey farmhouse near Cloughjordan, north county Tipperary. Pine painted red/brown, *c.* 1880. Width 60 in., depth 20 in., height 87½ in. Courtesy of Roscrea Heritage Centre.

158. The spirally carved shoulder and moulded drawer front of a fiddle fronted dresser (fig. 157) from a farmhouse near Cloughjordan, county Tipperary. Pine painted red/brown, *c.*1880. Courtesy of Roscrea Heritage Centre.

159. Detail of the pierced and carved facia board of a dresser (see fig. 157) from a farmhouse near Cloughjordan, county Tipperary. The cornice has chip-carved 'saw-tooth' decoration, *c.*1880. Courtesy of Roscrea Heritage Centre.

shelf fronts from which jugs, cups and mugs are hung. Shelf spacing varies between makers, regions and the individual needs of the owners. The worksurface of the dresser, also known as the 'bed', was often used for cutting bread (fig. 147), while the 'head' (top) of the dresser was a useful place to keep things out the reach of children.[33]

By the 1930s the movement towards hygiene was a major factor in the introduction of glass doors to dresser tops. Some people simply adapted their old dresser with doors made to fit (fig. 148); others had

160. Unusually wide, low, fiddle front dresser with pierced heart and triangle decoration, made by Willy O'Neal, *c.*1900. Its base stored pails of milk and spring water. From an unused farmhouse near Donard, county Wicklow.

a new style of dresser built incorporating glazing (figs. 149, 153). It cut down the tasks of cleaning and dusting, although it is interesting to note that the old tradition of leaning plates forwards onto a guardrail was still frequently retained behind the glass.[34]

The base of the dresser was open fronted and more recently this space was screened by curtains or cupboard doors. It was rarely decorated and had one pot board for storing bulkier items from the hearth. Large earthenware dishes for milk, buttermaking equipment, kettles, pots etc. were put in this less conspicuous place.[35]

161. (*top, left*) Dresser with a single, central door and three drawers, from county Clare. Decorated with simple cross-hatched pilasters (see fig. 163), its lowest shelf is set back, to create extra space on the work top. Mid nineteenth century.

162. (*bottom, left*) A pine dresser from county Wexford, stripped of its original paintwork, *c*.1880. The narrow central panel and knife drawer are typical of dressers in this county. The twining plant forms along the facia board and the recessed lowest shelf, are features found on other southern dressers (see figs. 189). The chamfered decoration around the door panels suggest that it was made by a wheelwright.

163. (*top, right*) Detail of the projecting corner of a dresser from county Clare, painted red. The naive classical pilaster has vestigial dentil moulding across the top, and carved cross-hatching down the side. Early nineteenth century.

164. (*bottom, right*) A red painted dresser, amongst furniture for sale at the roadside by tinkers. The arcaded top, with its wide cornice, is decorated with incised and chip-carved compass work, rope moulding and sun bursts. The open base is typically left plain. One of several distinctively carved dressers probably originating from Charleville, county Cork, *c*.1800. The peculiarly Irish chair is of a type, with double stretchers, mass-produced in Athlone during the late nineteenth century.

165. Built-in dresser with cupid's bow and shamrock motifs overlaid across the facia board and emphasised by contrasting paintwork. The small cupboards at each end of the worktop are an unusual addition. From near Baltimore, west county Cork, *c.*1870.

166. Late nineteenth-century built-in dresser, incorporated into the parlour/kitchen partition of an island house, off the Cork coast. The home made wooden boats and the two-tone dresser are the kitchen's main decorative features. The single stair-rods bear witness to the former shortage of timber.

167. Dresser with a raised base, a style which was traditional in county Cork up until the late nineteenth century. The facia board displays the repeated cupid's bow motif, and the plates lean forward onto bars to reflect the firelight without collecting dust. Made in the early nineteenth century, from near Union Hall, west county Cork.

112

168. Detail from *A Country Inn Kitchen* (fig. 207) painted by J.G. Mulvany (1766–1838). Amongst the ware of an open based dresser three spoons are held by a leather strap, tacked to a shelf. In 'the room' behind, the end of a draped tester bed, covered by a patchwork quilt, can be seen. Private collection.

169. Detail from *Women Grinding Corn in Ireland*, an engraving of a county Cork interior, showing an open based dresser, lined with hay or straw, and with three spoons prominently displayed in slots in an upper shelf. From *The Illustrated London News*, 1874.

There is a painting by John G. Mulvany (1766–1838) which depicts a scene in a country inn kitchen with an open based dresser against the back wall. It shows that spoons used to be hung vertically at eye level on the dresser, their bowls uppermost (see fig. 168). Three spoons are held in leather loops, which have been nailed to a shelf front.

In 1874, *The Illustrated London News* published an engraving of a county Cork interior in which a distinctive high-fronted Cork dresser has three spoons hung vertically, apparently through holes in an upper shelf (fig. 169). The same custom is shown in *The Illustrated London News* of November 1871. James Brenan's *Committee of Inspection*, 1877, also shows a dresser with about five spoons slotted into an upper shelf (fig. 171).

It is worth making a tactile search of eyelevel dresser shelves for such spoon holes, as their owners are nearly always surprised and amazed by this lost tradition. Many of the dressers recently surveyed have such hidden rectangular slots, cut into the shelf-front behind the customary strip of moulding. It turns out that this simple decorative feature is incorporated most commonly in dressers (and hanging dressers, fig. 152) from the mid and southern counties of Ireland. The earliest examples date from the first half of the eighteenth century (fig. 154), and they continued to be included in dressers made in the first half of the twentieth century. So far no examples of dressers with spoonholes have been found in Ulster. Perhaps this lack can be tied in with the less decorative dressers of the north, where the comparative austerity of design did not encourage conspicuous display of possession.

The Commissioners Poor Reports of 1836 from county Westmeath, describe 'a "dresser" ornamented with a few plates, spoons and porringers', so even the very poorest of homes partook of this type of display.[36] Up to the nineteenth century spoons were a rare commodity amongst the rural poor, but they are nevertheless referred to considerably more often than forks or knives. In mid-nineteenth-century county Wick-

170. Dresser incorporated into the staircase wall of a two-storey farmhouse, facing the kitchen fireplace. It has the raised cupboards which used to be a common characteristic of county Cork dressers until the late nineteenth century (see figs. 166–7, 169). From near Glandore, west county Cork.

low, William Hanbidge's family (who worked a 20 acre farm), 'had no egg cups or egg spoons so we propped them [boiled eggs] up with potatoes and ate them with the ends of the iron spoons with which we used to eat our stirabout . . . as there was not a small spoon in the house safe [sic] six silver ones which father bought when he got married'.[37] Probably their hanging dresser had provision for spoon display as he mentions amongst the trappings of the kitchen 'the little shelves on the wall for spoons and mugs' in addition to 'the dresser with big shelves for crockery'.[38]

The number of spoon holes, like the number of shelves per dresser, varied according to the wealth of the household. Some dressers had none, while some larger dressers have as many as fifteen (always positioned a few inches apart, often at the outer ends of the eyelevel shelf). The carpenters who cut these slots did so early on in the construction of the dresser to suit the households' requirements. The discovery of a row of holes reaching across the entire width of a shelf, on a dresser from west county Cork was unprecedented (fig. 172). Only once spoons were discovered

still in their place, on a hanging dresser in a traditional thatched house in county Wexford (fig. 152). The display of spoons in such slots is a practice which is now largely forgotten and abandoned.

In the eighteenth century, if country people had spoons they were made of iron, horn, pewter or silver and were just as precious as the ware displayed behind them.[39] This method of display helps to explain the absence of drawers in the majority of older dressers, although some kitchens did have special wall-hung boxes for displaying and keeping utensils (see Appendix).

Spoons were displayed on dressers in some other countries, especially the Normandy and Auvergne regions of France. It may be significant that their occurrence in Ireland is common in the south, because there is a long history of trade linking the southern Irish ports with France.[40] The idea of displaying spoons may alternatively have filtered down to the rural population from displays in the homes of the Irish gentry. Some Irish silver flatware, particularly serving spoons, were made during the eighteenth century with turned-over handles, or 'hook-ends', which are thought to

have been used for hanging them up. Such silver spoons would have hung with their bowls downwards, perhaps from the front of a shelf, or dresser.[41] The fact that the vernacular tradition was to hang spoons with their bowls uppermost is because the poor would rarely have had suitable purpose-made spoons and so displayed what spoons they had in the easiest possible way.

HANGING DRESSERS

Before looking at the various different functions and designs of dressers, it is useful to look at its evolution from its poor relation, the hanging dresser. Most homes aspired to such a possession, but there was no point in owning one unless there already existed a collection of kitchen ware to put on display.

In prosperous farmhouses with a lot of

171. *Committee of Inspection*, oil on canvas, painted by James Brenan R.H.A. (1837–1904). A dresser is placed across the room, acting as a divider. Several spoons hang from the end of a top shelf, and fringed oilcloth covers the shelf fronts below. The man inspecting the cloth from the loom, stands with his foot on a tiny stool, his companion sits on a plain carpenter's chair. Photo courtesy of the Crawford Municipal Art Gallery.

172. Detail of an unusual west Cork dresser with slots to display fifteen spoons across an upper shelf. The plates lean forward onto removeable bars to reflect the firelight without collecting dust. Early nineteenth century, from near Ballydehob, west county Cork.

173. Partition dresser from an empty farmhouse in south county Kilkenny, complete with its traditionally displayed 'ware' and a 'hanging dresser' beside it. *c.*1880; the cornice is a replacement.

ware to display, a small 'hanging dresser' provided additional space 'for spoons and mugs' (figs. 152, 173).[42] The hanging dresser was also referred to as the cup rack, the tin rail,[43] the tin rack or simply the rack,[44] presumably due to its display of tinker's tinware. There are lots of different designs (figs. 173–7), the most rudimentary consisting only of a framework of crossed laths into which hooks were attached for hanging up mugs and jugs (fig. 174). The more elaborate types were sometimes composed of small sets of shelves complete with tiny drawers and a pierced facia board, mimicking their full-sized counterparts. Some even had bars attached to lean the plates forward as well as special slots for displaying hanging spoons. In the poorest homes, the hanging dresser or tin rack was often the sole substitute for a full-sized dresser.

The hanging dresser is something which probably grew out of necessity. Fragile wooden noggins, methers (square dug-out vessels, carved from softwood with integral handles, fig. 319), ceramic mugs or jugs all had to be kept safe and preferably on show at the same time. Securing hooks of any sort

115

174. A simple cup rack or tin rail, made of painted laths, with nails for hanging cups. Courtesy of the U.F.T.M.

175. An early nineteenth-century cup rack, painted red, from beneath the stairs of a farm kitchen near Callan, county Kilkenny. Six of its original wooden rods remain, which jut out from the framework, for hanging and displaying ware and utensils (compare to fig. 176). Known there (oddly) as 'the clevy', such simple arrangements were a common addition to, or substitute for, the dresser.

176. A primitive cup rack, which could also act as a drainer, shown as found in an empty county Kilkenny farmhouse. A flat wooden beetle, probably used for clothes washing, rests across the lower rods.

177. One of a variety of designs of hanging dressers, which was sometimes the only place to display ware, or it was an addition to a full-sized dresser. Mid nineteenth century, from south-east Ireland.

into uneven masonry can be tricky, so attaching a lightweight framework of shelves or laths would have reduced the number of difficult fixings. In county Armagh the hanging dresser was described as 'a small dresser with an iron spike attached and which when driven into the wall held the dresser suspended'.[45] Others were composed of slanted pegs which doubled as a draining rack for freshly washed vessels as

well as providing a safe display place (see fig. 176).

In the late 1930s, it was observed that in a number of county Wicklow houses: 'On the wall beside the dresser was a rack. It was almost embedded in the wall, and had stout iron hooks made by the smith on the cross-laths on which tools and vessels were hung. These racks are very common all over the district – I saw one in every other house we visited . . .'[46]

The logical evolution from the hanging dresser is one which has storage space beneath the shelving and is freestanding. The earliest wooden dressers had no doors, instead they had one or two open cup-boards, sometimes with a central balister-shaped splat flanked by half baluster profiles on either side (figs. 152, 154–7, 160, 200). This design of dresser is sometimes referred to as a 'fiddle front' from its similarity to the outline of a violin.

SLEDGE FEET

Freestanding dressers were tall and heavily laden and probably had a tendency to be

179. Pine dresser with twentieth-century two-tone paintwork and sledge feet. (fig. 178) This was a medieval feature which raised the base from the damp floor and could be renewed if necessary. It also helped spread the weight and stabilise the dresser. This late nineteenth-century dresser is from the Mayo byre dwelling at Bunratty Folk Park. Photo courtesy of Shannon Heritage Ltd.

tippy and unstable on earthern floors. This may be one reason for a special type of foot, known variously as the boot, shoe or sledge foot. This the carpenter usually fixed horizontally to the dresser base by means of dovetails (figs. 178–80).

This type of foot is generally associated with furniture from the sixteenth and seventeenth centuries, but if it is a survival of the influence of planted settlers from Scotland and England, it is still remarkable that it went on being made until the early twentieth century in Ireland.[47] It is a feature most commonly found on dressers in the north and parts of the west of Ireland, but it can also sometimes be found, as mentioned earlier, supporting the bases of presses, school desks and settle beds (fig. 128).

There are functional reasons for the survival of the sledge foot in Ireland, compared with its decline in parts of England and Scotland. Housing and hence flooring conditions improved more quickly there, and their increasing prosperity meant fashion altered furniture design more rapidly. The Irish sledge foot spread the weight of the dresser and its load, stabilising it and raising the base cupboards 2 or 3 inches up and away from the damp floor. It acted as a cunning sacrificial element against rising damp: attached by dovetails it could periodically be knocked off and renewed if it became rotten, thereby prolonging the life of the dresser for future generations.[48] This type of built-in renewability, so alien to the built-in obselescence of many designs today, is, as we have seen, also a characteristic of settle beds found in parts of the north, which

often have two or even three sledge feet (fig. 128), and the Irish hedge chairs with their stretcher-less renewable wedged legs.[49]

178. The side view of the base of a dresser, showing a sledge foot, dovetailed on, but renewable should it become rotten from standing on a damp floor. This feature was most common in freestanding dressers from parts of Ulster and Connaught (see figs. 179–80).

180. Cream painted dresser with sledge feet (one rotted from rising damp) with a facia of pierced hearts, interlacing, shamrocks and the favourite 'flying wheel' motif which occurs in the west and south-west as well as parts of France (see also endpapers). It has about six slots for spoon display (figs. 168–9) and the left-hand door is a replacement. From county Tipperary, courtesy of Victor Mitchell.

By the nineteenth century the dresser had become established as an integral part of the fabric of many rural homes. One of the reasons for the survival of dressers in many of the houses surveyed was that they were built in to the walls so thoroughly that to remove them would have entailed considerable structural damage. Innumerable dressers survive whose backing boards form the wall of the parlour or 'room' behind (figs. 143, 148, 166, 170, 173, 186). Where masonry walls have been erected, less timber has been used by fitting the dresser into a special recess. The 1836 Government Poor Reports describe how in county Tipperary 'there is usually a dresser, which answers a double purpose, for the cabins being often built in one room, the dresser is placed across the house by way of a division, thus making a second room'.[50]

Prior to its incorporation into such a dividing wall, the dresser was sometimes placed freestanding across the room (fig. 171).[51] There are many nineteenth-century descriptions of dressers forming partitions between the two main rooms of the cabins, their widespread survival testifying to the strength of this tradition. However, in a considerable number of houses, it acted as a structural support for the loft opposite the hearth, while simultaneously separating the 'room' from the kitchen. In county Limerick where such lofts often formed a small first-floor bedroom, 'the dresser was used to go up to the loft over the room' perhaps by incorporating rungs up one side, instead of the usual portable ladder.[52]

In counties Cork and Kerry there was usually a large food press (cupboard) on one side and the dresser on the other forming 'a partition with a curtain as a door' in the centre.[53] This arrangement often still survives today in Munster but with a wooden door instead of a curtain (like fig. 186). In some of the older houses on the Great Blasket Island during the nineteenth century, 'To divide the house into two a dresser stood out from the wall in the middle of the floor, and a partition met it from the other side'.[54] In a house in Reen townland, west county Cork, the local carpenter had economised with timber by placing the press and dresser side by side, joining them with one continuous cornice (they also act as the parlour wall).

In the northern counties the dresser was sometimes conspicuously placed against the back wall opposite the front door. In houses where people still slept on the ground floor, there were 'two beds in the kitchen, one in the chimney corner and the other in the corner back from the [front] door. The dresser may be placed at the foot of this bed to prevent draughts' but the dresser being placed 'opposite the hearth is regarded as lucky'.[55] Gailey describes this use of the dresser as a bed screen as common in northern coastal areas of Ulster.[56] In Dunfanaghy, county Donegal, the back of a dresser had been incorporated into the structure of a curtained fireside bed (both still in use) in a single-storey house. Such an amalgamation was economical in its use of timber (a considerable amount of 'sheeting' is required for the backing boards of a dresser) as the building of a special *balla beg* (bed wall) was then unnecessary.

Gailey provides a ground plan of the house type where an upper floor is a later addition.[57] When a staircase rises directly facing the front door, the dresser is repositioned, still facing the fire but backing onto the staircase. This arrangement is not uncommon in Munster where the dresser has been moved and reincorporated into the new stairway wall (fig. 170). There are no distinct regional patterns for the positioning of the dresser, depending as it does on the evolution and layout of each house type. However, the favourite place tended to remain opposite the hearth.

COOPS AND COOP DRESSERS

There are enough references to coops for poultry amongst the inventories of large Irish houses, to conclude that the keeping of laying fowl in kitchens was a practice which was widely acceptable by the late seventeenth and eighteenth centuries.[58] Known variously as the coop, coope,[59] coom,[60] comb[61] or coob[62] it was an enclosed area with a slatted wooden front. The different terms seem to have arisen from local pronunciations of the Irish word *cúb* and its English equivalent:

181. *His Iron Will*, painted in 1880 by James Brenan R.H.A. (1837–1904), who was headmaster of the Cork School of Art. Against the wall beside the fire is a two-tier coop: a warm, dry place which encouraged hens to lay eggs during the winter months. Photo courtesy of Sotheby's.

coop. John O'Sullivan (aged 77), a maker of carriages, staircases and furniture, recently described his memories of these straw lined 'cooms' which were in many west county Cork farmhouses, during the 1930s and 40s;

T'would be about six feet long at the lower end of the kitchen . . . And it was made like a press in the bottom, and then there was two rows for two rows of hens and there was always latticed sections and little sliding doors in it where the hens go in . . . They'd slide sideways . . . one section went back of another, and they'd stay there all night the hens used . . . the little laths were beautiful they'd be about an inch and a quarter [wide], and they'd

be beaded lovely around . . . and that was stained like any nice bit of furniture . . . We were terrible interested in them long ago when we were young.[63]

The coop provided a safe, warm, dry nesting place for hatching geese and hens, under the watchful eye of the woman of the house in the kitchen. Arthur Young, writing about agriculture in Ireland in the 1770s, commented that 'much poultry is also reared and fed in all the cabbins by means of potatoes'.[64] In Doyle's *Hints to Smallholders* of 1832 we learn that 'in a gentleman's fowl-yard, there is not an egg to be had in cold weather; but the warmth of the poor man's cabin insures him an egg even in the most ungenial season'. The author explains the several advantages of keeping fowl in 'cottages', 'the warmth of which causes them to lay eggs in winter', which they otherwise would not do. Furthermore 'all the diseases to which poultry of all kinds are subject, proceed from cold moisture'.[65] *His Iron Will*, a painting by James Brenan (fig. 181), shows a two-tier slatted coop (like those shown in figs. 182–4) placed directly beside the hearth, demonstrating that such advice must have been adhered to. There are other accounts of turkeys, ducks, geese and even seagulls being kept in coops as well.

Fowl were traditionally cared for by women in Ireland. They gained an important income from their eggs, flesh and feathers. Doyle reminds his readers that 'You constantly want salt (and I hope soap,) and candles in winter; now a few eggs taken

182. (*below*) Two-tier pine kitchen coop, from Binvoran, Kilmurry, Clonderalaw, county Clare. Like other examples, it never had backing boards, but instead would have been placed against a wall (see figs. 181, 184). Finely made from thin slats, it has its original crazed and flaked red paint. Courtesy of The N.M.I.

183. (*top, right*) Two-tier stripped pine kitchen coop, from county Tipperary. The doors, which slide sideways to give access to the hens and their eggs, have pierced diamond decoration; one is a replacement.

184. A two-tier chicken coop, with shaped central doors which can be slid upwards: made of pine and painted red/brown. The raised front is decorated with incised scratch-stock lines, *c.*1860. Above it hangs a single plaited straw hen's nest. From the Moher farmhouse at Bunratty Folk Park, courtesy of Shannon Heritage Ltd.

185. Early nineteenth-century pine coop, painted black, combining a plate rack in its top layer. The central five slats hinge forwards to release the hens. Its shoulders are shaped like those found on local dressers. Above it hangs an early twentieth-century holy shelf. From the 'Shannon farmhouse' (reconstructed during the building of a runway at Shannon Airport), Bunratty Folk Park. Courtesy of Shannon Heritage Ltd.

to the hucksters procure you these most necessary articles in exchange' and also that 'you may calculate on having a brisk demand for fat poultry for the English markets'.[66]

In the early eighteenth century, even a comparatively wealthy doctor from Tipperary had an 'old coobe' amongst his household possessions, so the practice could not have been considered unhygienic.[67] 'Coops for poultry' were to be found from the cellars of castles to the kitchens of the grandest mansions.[68] Barbavilla, a Palladian house in county Westmeath had no less than two 'chicken coopes' in 'ye kitchen' in 1742, one being described 'with 3 throughts'; this was presumably similar to the three-tiered example from Bunratty Folk Park (see fig. 185).[69]

The historian MacLysaght relates how during the seventeenth century hens were kept inside the smaller cabins at night as protection against the numerous foxes.[70] He recalls 'the woman in the roadway, lamenting her lost fowl', describing how hunting was introduced in Ireland at this time to try to keep down the number of foxes. Even then the rearing of poultry formed a vital part of the economy for the poor majority.[71]

The practice of keeping the fowl indoors did not necessarily mean that the householder had the luxury of purpose-built furniture in which they could be kept; '". . . Av coorse the clocking hen came in an' set under the stairs. Many's the night I heerd her turning the eggs. The goose set under the dresser an' the goslings et their mate up near the hearth fire . . .".'[72] Of the households recently surveyed throughout Ireland, many more recalled keeping fowl in their kitchens than owned coops or coop dressers. A visitor to the Aran Islands in the 1930s discovered that 'beside the hearth there is a small recess in the wall into which brooding hens are put'.[73] Often the early open fronted dressers (see figs. 152, 169) doubled as a place for poultry without any special adaptation. The late Professor Evans mentions 'hen-coops, of straw, wattle or wood' being stored in the bases of open fronted dressers and shows drawings of plaited straw hens' nests from counties Clare and

Leitrim.[74] Hens and ducks were sometimes kept in hatching places under the kitchen table or simply in a box somewhere on the floor.[75] An eighteenth-century open fronted dresser in south county Wexford still has a pair of unhinged doors leaning up against it which were hooked into place whenever it was used for the nesting birds. Its elderly owner recently recalled how 'hens were kept in the bottom of the dresser, broody ones with a clutch of eggs, the cats and the hens put up with each other' (see fig. 152). Other houses had a rope or a perch over the inside of the front door where a cockerel might roost and act as the household's alarm clock.[76]

Enquiries about hens in kitchens are usually greeted with great amusement amongst householders, and most of Ireland's older generations who were brought up in traditional rural homes still remember their antics fondly. From these discussions it transpires that the fowl were in the kitchen most often when they were laying and sometimes at particular times of year. This gave the owner the advantage of knowing where the eggs were rather than run the risk of losing them in the hedgerows or amongst the thatch. Losing hens and their eggs in neighbours roofing material when two thatched houses were adjoined could cause quarrels. The hens tended to nest deeply, completely hidden in all the thatch 'for the hen wouldn't even answer the call to food when she was broody . . . The

children made a mess of the thatch, too, always hunting for eggs'.[77]

Pat Rath, a retired farmer of Kilmuckridge, county Wexford, described how their large farmhouse

> used to have a chicken coop dresser opposite the hearth where the geese used to sit and hatch their eggs. They'd sit there for a month in spring. Every morning they were let out the door. They were in a terrible hurry to get out! You wouldn't believe how clean they were. Terribly clean.

Numerous similar oral accounts, as well as many twentieth-century written descriptions,[78] prove how this seemingly outmoded practice endured within living memory. Ó Criomhthain, writing about his life on the Great Blasket, describes how 'There was a coop against the partition with hens in it, and a broody hen just by it in an old cooking pot'.[79] He recalls the tragic cliff death of his son, as he tried to catch a young seagull, 'for one of those would often live among the chickens in a house for a year and more'.[80]

The historian Kevin Danaher recalls as a boy in county Kerry, 'standing all unaware of danger near in a farm kitchen and being severely pecked on the bare leg by a hatching goose'. It was confined to the base of the dresser with 'its lower section divided into nesting boxes for these birds; these boxes were fronted by upright wooden slats between which the hatching birds could protrude their heads to take food (fig. 186).'[81]

References to 'coops filled with speckled hens'[82] and to hen coops, occur most frequently in Munster and the southern part of Leinster, commonly in counties Cork and Kerry. Mary Carbery writes of life in a county Limerick farmhouse during the late nineteenth century: 'In the lower part of the dresser, instead of cupboards was a long coop in which were sitting hens; it seems to me now that they sat there perpetually except when two geese took their place in early spring.'[83] It was evidently a dual-purpose hen coop and dresser combined, 'gay with willow pattern plates' displayed on the shelves above.[84]

It is unclear when the first combined coop with display shelves above it was built

186. Kitchen partition formed by a decorative press, a door and a coop dresser with a raised front (typical of south Munster, see fig. 166). Photographed by K. Danaher, in 1948, Ballywiheen, Dingle Peninsula, county Kerry. Courtesy of the Head of the D.I.F., U.C.D.

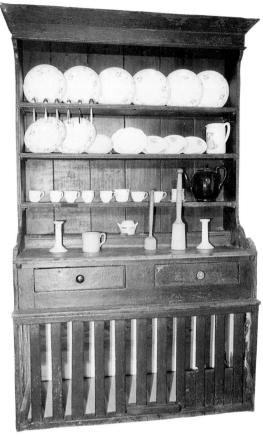

187. Kitchen dresser incorporating hen coops, with iron rodded doors and an unusual cornice, c.1870. A bread-making losset (made by farmer Patrick Hennessy, c.1944) still sits on the scrubbed table top. An abandoned farmhouse near Enniscorthy, county Wicklow.

188. Pine dresser with a two-tier coop incorporated into the base and many layers of paint, the most recent of brown gloss. The base has been restored. From the Dungarvan district of county Waterford, c.1830; courtesy of The Seanachie (near Dungarvan).

189. Dresser with drawers and coop in the base, which would have stood against a wall. Made of pine painted dark red, it has shallow lower shelves, and six slots for displaying spoons. Thought to be from county Tipperary, it dates from the mid nineteenth century. Courtesy of the Irish Agricultural Museum.

190. Dresser with two-tier coops forming the base, a plate rack in the centre and ware shelves above. Early nineteenth century, with unpainted restoration, collected for the N.M.I. from the vicinity of Pallas Green, county Limerick.

191. Side and front views of a dresser with a meal bin base carefully concealed behind false drawer and door fronts. The lid of the meal chest section is sloped, and hinges upwards in the usual way, at the base of the display shelves. Recently stripped and repainted, from county Kilkenny. Part of the Irish Country Furniture Society's collection on show at the Irish Agricultural Museum.

192. (*top, right*) Small pine fiddle fronted dresser with drawers, probably made as a journeyman's sample. Stripped of its original red lead paintwork. Height 22 in.

193. Portable sample dresser, 36 in. high. Finished with brown varnish, from county Clare. Photo courtesy of Shannon Heritage Ltd.

(figs. 186–9). Combination dressers are yet another symptom of the shortage of space and timber in many less affluent homes, as well as the primary concern of rural Irish furniture makers with functionalism. We know that dressers were combined with other functional items of furniture from the references in early inventories (fig. 190). Carpenter built dressers with plate drainer bases were a favourite in the 'big houses'. Many of these survive today.[85] Another combined use in a prosperous house where there were presumably copious quantities of linen to iron was the 'large smoothing dresser'.[86] In the west of Ireland some dressers had meal chests with sloping lids incorporated into the lower section, sometimes disguised by the addition of false drawer fronts. An example of this can be seen at the Irish Agricultural Museum (fig. 191). Others (particularly examples from county Limerick) incorporated spit racks or clevies amongst the display shelves, the spits doubling as convenient rails for plates (fig. '304). One extraordinarily tall dresser has two layers for coops in the base, a plate-draining rack in the middle and a clevy and ware shelf on top (fig. 306). All these combinations illustrate ingenious and economical methods of making the dresser carry out more than its usual utensil bearing function, and like the settle tables, helped save space at the same time.

SMALL-SIZED DRESSERS

Small-sized dressers, have now become rare and sought after objects (see figs. 192–3). It has been suggested that they were occasionally made as toys: at least one is known to have been made for a sick child. Others may have been apprentices' 'masterpieces'. However, the majority of them probably played the role of portable samples of craftsmanship and design for their journeymen makers. These small legacies of their woodworking skills, bear testimony to their determination to seek employment, as they hired themselves out to whoever could employ them.

In the absence of early documentary references to these dressers, it is likely that they were wall mounted and used to hold small decorative items of ware or kitchen

194. *Matchmaking,* engraved after a drawing by Howard Helmick (1845– 1907). An old woman sits by the fire on a low 'creepie' stool. On the wall hangs a salt box, and a tiny dresser. The girl sits on what appears to be a 'Sligo chair', with its distinctive back. Wooden vessels on a woven rush mat, stand before a pad-footed table (*c.*1740), perhaps passed on from a 'big house'. Probably a north Connaught location, from *The Magazine of Art,* II, 1888.

195. Three tiny dressers hung on the wall amongst the miscellany of the Crawfordsburn Inn, county Down. Probably made as journeymen's masterpieces, two of them have fiddle fronts, sledge feet, and bars to lean the plates onto. Below is a small hedge chair with a curved back, made for a child. Photograph by R. Welch, early twentieth century, courtesy of the Ulster Museum.

utensils, in the same way as hanging dressers. They are usually no more than about 3 feet high. Some found their way into the nurseries of the 'big houses'. An illustration by Howard Helmick from the 1880s shows the interior of an Irish cabin: on the wall beside the dresser and dash-churn is a simple miniature dresser upon which is displayed some crockery and a rush light (fig. 194).[87] A slightly later photograph by Robert Welch shows three such tiny dressers hung on the wall amongst the mass of decorative paraphernalia in a country inn (fig. 195). These dressers can be seen to be faithful reproductions of their full-sized open-based counterparts. Two of them even have sledge feet, projecting cornices and retaining bars for tilting the plates forward.

None of the half-dozen or so examples tracked down in Ireland by the author has survived in its original traditional setting. Their portability and the fact that they are worth the same as full-sized examples, has meant that most have now been bought by eager exporters.

Chapter 4

STORAGE OF FOOD & CLOTHES

*The Keeping Hole, Salt Boxes, Ceiling Racks and Hanging Shelves,
Meal Chests, The Stillion, The Ware Press, Food Presses,
Places for Clothes, The Clothes Chest, Dowry Chests*

This chapter examines the traditional places and furniture made for storage: the various types of kitchen and parlour presses, and chests which were universally used in place of chests of drawers or wardrobes. Beginning with embryo forms like the simple keeping holes and clothes lines, it also explains the elaborate presses and bureaux owned by the more fortunate 'strong farmers'.

THE KEEPING HOLE

Literary descriptions of such intrinsic architectural features as 'keeping holes' are unusual. Although they cannot be traced through inventories, their survival in derelict houses throughout the country makes them easy to examine. Visitors who made the popular tour of Ireland, during the 1800s, thinking them a novelty, described how 'in the chimney there were two holes, one very small to place the tobacco-pipe when relinquished; another larger, for the "screeching-hot tumbler" [poteen punch] of old times'. Like other aspects of the Irish house, the *Poll an Bhairc*[2] had local names in different regions. Individual or paired keep holes were called 'boles' in county Antrim[3] and 'coves' in county Cavan.[4] On the Aran Islands, towards the close of the last century, many houses had 'a *cleibhí*, a small square cubby hole set into the wall of the hearth. Pipes, tobacco and perhaps tea,' were often kept in these holes, as well as rosary beads, knitting, bread or anything else that needed a warm dry place, 'ready for use when required'.[5] Tobacco made an important contribution to the poor labourer's social life for talking and smoking around the fire in the evenings was a common pastime in pre-famine Ireland.[6] The contents of these square, round or even triangular recesses (in some Clare houses) vary through time and place. They were usually inset within a few feet of the warmth of the fire in the gable wall (figs. 196).

William Hanbidge, was born in 1813 and raised in a Wicklow farmhouse. He wrote 'the tiny cupboard for salt (for salt was so dear) is in the wall beside the fire'. Salt was probably the most important and expensive foodstuff for which keeping holes were originally built. Spices were kept in a second cupboard along with 'other things that needed protection from damp'.[7]

In coastal parts of county Down, rush lights were made with fish oil held in a small lamp called a 'cruisie'. This could be placed in the right-hand 'wall hole' as there was a special wooden ledge allowing the smell to be wafted up the chimney above.[8] In Gweedore, keeping holes were useful dry places for snuff, pipes and the bog deal spills which were used as matches or lights.[9] One can still see tiny painted wooden doors closing over such keeping holes in parts of Munster and Leinster, hinged with leather. In Armagh some houses had 'safes' which were holes cunningly concealed by closely fitted stone.[11] With the advent of modern food packaging and distribution, keeping holes have lost their original uses and very often (if they survive) now provide a convenient place for an alarm clock (fig. 197).

196. A poor Kerry farm kitchen, Loo, Kenmare, in 1899. A board fixed to the joists acts as a mantlepiece, over a turf fire, with opposite keeping holes. A double-stretchered table and a decorative carpenters' chair stand before an open based dresser with holes instead of drawer knobs. Photograph from the Welch collection, courtesy of the Ulster Museum.

197. Interior of a traditional house on the Great Blasket Island, county Kerry, c.1930. Beneath a half-loft, is a pivoting wooden crane and an alarm clock in a keeping hole. A woman spins, with a recessed press behind her, while her companion sits on a low boarded stool, his back to a meal chest (compare fig. 120). Photo by T.H. Mason, courtesy of the N.M.I.

SALT BOXES

Some salt in a barrel, and for fear we
should quarrel,
Some whiskey to keep us both quiet . . .
Salt butter a store, and salt herrings
galore,
With good praties as much as she
wishes.
Two pots and a griddle, a sive and a
riddle,
A slate for a tongs, to bring fire on,
A pair of pot hooks, and two little
crooks,
To hang up the salt box and grid iron.[11]

Salt was a precious commodity amongst the poorer classes as it formed a vital part of the most meagre diet. Salt boxes were probably the next step up the evolutionary ladder from recessed 'keeping holes' in terms of storage. A large percentage of the population – whose diet during the nineteenth century consisted mainly of potatoes – used salt (amongst other things) to 'kitchen'

126

or flavour their meals. The following extract from a poem of 1807 describes a county Down cottier's home and diet:

But words I will not multiply,
Potatoes all our meals supply;
A little milk to them we add –
And salt, when that can not be had.[12]

Salt was also the vital ingredient for preserving meat and fish. During the seventeenth century it was listed amongst the considerable stock in trade of a Dublin grocer, as '130 Barrels of salt; £46-10-00'.[13] By the eighteenth century such items of furniture as 'One Sault chest and Small Sault Box' are frequently mentioned in the 'Kitchings' of castles and houses of the gentry.[14]

The habit of storing the salt in a box beside the fire was established in the poorer rural homes by the second half of the eighteenth century. Hincks illustrates the ubiquitous salt box with its sloping lid, hung up by the hearth in his stipple engraving of fireside

yarn-spinning in the late eighteenth century (fig. 69). Many nineteenth-century paintings depicting hearths, show the distinctive wall-hung salt box (figs. 198, 207). They occur all over Ireland and are usually between 1 and 2 feet wide and a foot high; the sloped lid echoes that of its larger relative, the meal chest, which slopes at about 45 degrees and is hinged at the top. An account from the 1950s indicates how common they were.

When closed it looked like a house with a high wall on one side slanting down to a lower one and roofed over . . . [in county Down, there was] a house this shape and it's called the Salt-box still. These boxes held about a stone weight of salt. The old woman of the house was very careful about salt.[15]

Although such containers have vanished from today's domestic scene, a photograph from Wicklow in the late 1930s shows a salt box still placed on a stone ledge beside the hearth (fig. 103).

199. A slatted press attached to ceiling joists above the kitchen fireplace, stores home-cured bacon, its long door closed by a turnbuckle. From the townland of Fowlerstown, north county Dublin, c.1959. Photo courtesy of the N.M.I.

teriors amongst the Lawrence and Welch collections of photographs also provide evidence for ceiling space having been utilised for storage at the turn of the nineteenth and twentieth centuries (figs. 100, 196, 264).

Ceiling storage was often in the form of a few seemingly insignificant batons nailed to the underside of the joists of the kitchen ceiling. These provided a space equal to the depth of the joists for storage, were fixed up by the householder and used very little timber.[18] Ceilings in traditional houses are often so low that reaching these racks would have presented no problem. One poor home in county Kerry used a long board nailed up to the joists in place of a mantlepiece (fig. 196). The ceiling of Conagher's Farm in county Antrim (former home of United States President McKinley), was the resting place for a veritable mass of objects ranging from shoemaking lasts to a large rifle (fig. 100). These things were also safely out of reach of children.

Huge iron hooks in the ceilings of old kitchens are now all that remain of the once widespread tradition of hanging rows of home-cured hams from the rafters or joists. They would first have been salted, then smoked high up in the wide chimney space (eg. see Samuel Watson's *The Irish Jig*, fig. 108), then hung for dry storage near the fireplace. In some homes the beam from which the flitches were hung was called the 'meat stick'.[19] Being large, valuable items of food, this conspicuous system kept them safe, as well as out of the way (see figs. 207, 218). Similarly, fish were also salted and nailed up to the ceiling for storage (fig. 204).

Such displays of food were impressive. An account of a farmhouse in early nineteenth-century county Wexford tells of 'entering the large comfortable kitchen, with the bacon flitches in the chimney, and sundry seasoned delicacies hanging from racks fastened to the ceiling'.[20] With the advent of fridges and freezers, few such racks still survive. However, fig. 199 shows an elaborate system for long-term storage of bacon. Presumably from a comparatively prosperous farmhouse, this 'bacon safe' is described as 'a press attached to the ceiling joists above the kitchen fireplace for storing home cured

CEILING RACKS AND HANGING SHELVES

The separation of food from marauding mice, rats, dogs and cats gave rise to various systems of suspended shelving, ceiling racks and hooks. In many traditional houses such ceiling racks still remain, as evidence of past habits. The fixing of battens and hooks into the parallel rows of unclad ceiling joists presented less of a problem than making attachments into masonry. In 1735, county Meath's Killeen Castle had '1 Rack over head' in the larder as well as a 'Large hanging rack' in the kitchen, both of which must have been for safe storage of food.[16] Around the same time, the kitchen of a grand Palladian house in county Westmeath included 'one wooding Rack, one Large Rack' and 'Two small Racks' in its huge inventory. A little later in 1760, Killiane castle in county Wexford listed 'a meatrack' in the 'Kitching' as well as '1 cheese rack' and a 'hanging shelf' in the vault amongst other utensils.[17]

Hanging racks are commonly listed in other grand eighteenth- and nineteenth-century inventories. Documentary evidence for their use in poorer houses is more difficult to trace. However, such contrivances are visible in many of the paintings of ordinary country homes and public houses (e.g. figs. 198, 207). The rare shots of in-bacon'. Its base is slatted, providing ventilation, with a long door which hinges open downwards or is held closed by a turnbuckle (a simple wooden latch commonly found on cupboard doors). A 'hanging rack in the kitching' was amongst nearly a thousand pounds worth of goods sold at Captain Balfour's auction in 1741. It fetched the princely sum of 16s. 3d., as much as a 'Blunder Buss' in the same sale.[21]

Some houses still have a stout pole fixed between two joists, sometimes supported by a pair of horse shoes. Others rested a beam across the rafters or through the branches of a tree.[22] These all served as places to hang up a slaughtered pig and collect the blood to make black or white pudding.[23]

MEAL CHESTS

A fine thing is a dairy-herd and a
    holding,
wheat and barley for reaping,
meal in the chest and a fire in the
    evening
and shelter for the travelling man,
a shirt and a coat at mass on a Sunday,
a fashionable hat and a coat.[24]

The term 'meal chest' is one of several

that refer to a high sided wooden chest built to store various kinds of food. Others include 'meal bin', 'flour chest', 'flour bin', 'meal ark', 'hutch' or 'corn bin' according to use and region. The poet's mention of 'the chest' here is a casual reference to an item of furniture that used to be more common and more essential than the dresser in nineteenth-century rural homes (fig. 200).

Towards the close of summer all those involved in food gathering were traditionally invited by the farmer to celebratory 'harvest home' feasts. Such occasions marked the end of summer and the onset of the difficult months of winter. The most prosperous, large farms of the south and east, employing considerable numbers of workers, sometimes feasted in the barn rather than the kitchen.[25] Such rural cultural customs often have interesting bearings on furniture. At harvest time the grain was brought inside for storage until the following year in 'the flour bin, with two [or sometimes three] compartments, one for flour and the other for meal,' which might be 'yalla meal'.[26] 'In some houses the grain for human consumption, or the meal, especially the oatmeal, was kept in large chests, when packing the meal in, the children used to stamp it down firm with their bare feet.'[27] This excluded air and helped to keep it fresh.

The indoor storage of meal in such chests has been a traditional part of the farming routine for centuries. As early as 1686 '2 meale tubbs' were listed in the inventory of a grand house in county Cork.[28] The more fortunate farmers during the seventeenth century, had substantial chests, judging by the county Kildare account of 'the jest ... to lock her up in a greate wooden [sic] chest (which they call a hutch, and has an arched cover: it will hold sometimes eight or ten barrels of corn or more) which was in the room'.[29] By the eighteenth and early nineteenth centuries, inventories often mention 'a binn'[30] and during the 1830s British Government Commissioners reported of the poorest cottiers in county Louth: 'for the meal they generally go into debt, paying a high rate for credit'.[31]

Such a meal chest was generally kept against a kitchen wall, often close to the fire to help keep the stores dry (fig. 202). Carleton confirms this with his description of a poor

200. A substantial farm kitchen, photographed in 1912 by R. Welch, near Ballynahinch, county Down. The built-in dresser has an open fiddle front, to its left is a meal chest and one of two cup racks. Beside the table, with its bread-making losset, is a *súgán* chair with a spindle back. On the right is a creepie stool. Photo courtesy of the Ulster Museum.

to have . . . one formal dish, whatever else they have, which some call, stirabout or hasty pudding, that is flour and milk boiled thick; and this is holden as an argument of the good wives good hus-wifery, that made her corn hold out so well, as to have such a dish to hold summer fare with; for if they can hold out so long with bread, they count they can do well enough for what remains of the year until harvest . . . they are so formal, that even in the plentifullest and greatest houses where bread is in abundance all the year long, they will not fail of this dish, nor yet they that for a month before wanted bread.[35]

Such sensible customs continued well into the twentieth century.[36]

An account of 1915–20 from county Wex-ford shows how common the chests once were: 'In most farmers kitchens there was a meal bin. They had sloped lids and when opened there was a narrow shelf in the back of some of them which contained bread-soda, cornflour, sugar etc. in packets or in jam jars. The bins held flour, wheaten meal [and] oatmeal produced by the local mills.'[37] The narrow inside shelf was also a useful place to keep sieves and perhaps a mug or

201. Pine meal chest, in use in a three-roomed house in north county Cavan. It is painted brown and inside is divided in two, with a narrow shelf along the back, all lined with wallpaper. Bastable bread cooks in a pot oven with embers on its lid, suspended from the crane above the turf fire.

cabin's furnishings in the 1830s: 'opposite the bed, on the other side of the fire, stood a meal chest, its lid on a level with the little pane of glass which served as a window'.[32] This positioning was also convenient for cooking over the hearth (fig. 201).

Significantly, it is one of the only items of furniture sometimes fitted with a lock, or hasp and staple (figs. 202–3). Until fairly recently, meal chests were also to be seen behind some shop counters. A general store in Rosscarbery, county Cork, had until recently such a brown painted chest for storing loaves of bread. Eric Cross's lively account of the tiny home of a Cork tailor at the end of the last century is revealing: 'Upstairs are the bedroom, with the great box-bed, and the small room beyond where Ansty keeps the meal and corn so that even at night when she is asleep she can still guard it from the pilfering of the rats and the mice.'[33] One of Jack Yeats' verses proves that Ansty's fears were justified;

Or the kettle on the hob
Sing peace into his breast;
Or see the brown mice bob
Round and round the oatmeal chest.[34]

When times were hard people struggled to make their supply of meal last between harvests. In the seventeenth century the passing of lean winter months was celebrated with a customary Mayday ritual

202. 'The girl from county Leitrim', a county Galway interior showing the meal chest, padlocked, in a dry place beside the fire. A round potato skib is at her feet, and a staved noggin on a creepie stool. From *Hall's Ireland*, by Mr and Mrs S.C. Hall, 1840. Courtesy of the N.L.I.

203. Built-in pine meal chest, in the kitchen of a large county Wicklow farmhouse. It predates the kitchen partition, and is a different colour in the next door dairy. The unusual fall front, enables one to reach into the base. Its original shaped bracket feet have been covered over by a plinth. c.1810, from near Kiltegan.

Amusingly, it has been painted pale blue on one side of the new wall and brown and white on the other, blending with the colour schemes in each room. Like so many built-in dressers, this incorporation into the fabric of the house may have contributed to the chest's survival. It is still used for flour, but like other meal chests that remain in place, this flour is now stored inside tupperware boxes, amongst loaves of bread, stainless steel sieves and cooling racks.

Some meal chests (like other food storage places and canopy beds), were habitually lined with wallpaper. This would have been easier than painting inside a chest, which was rarely empty for the job. It also excluded dust and kept the meal from escaping through knot holes or gaps in the boards. The meal chest from county Wicklow, with its conspicuous front flap, is repapered annually when the kitchen is redecorated, using a contrasting piece of wallpaper from last year's scheme. In common with most other examples, its sloping lid is hinged a few inches away from the wall, creating a narrow shelf, so that when opened, it can be propped up. It would have been used every day, so possibly the top sloped to prevent an annoying accumulation of objects on the lid. The horizontally placed boards of such chests are generally nailed together, but unusually for Irish vernacular furniture, a few surviving examples have carefully dovetailed construction. The role of oral history has been especially vital in the research of this object, as it has now become an extremely rare sight, even in the older houses. Diets have changed and flour and oatmeal can now be bought conveniently packaged, so it is not surprising that these huge chests have largely been banished, providing space for more modern kitchen equipment.

Only one example has been found where the maker has spent some time disguising and decorating it. It was in county Kilkenny, with a set of false drawer fronts adorned with white porcelain handles, in the manner of a dowry chest. Carleton's 1830s account of 'the stations' at Maynooth, with the inevitable scrubbing, painting and spring cleaning of the kitchen, mentions that 'it so happened that this man was needed to assist in removing the meal chest to another part

cup which acted as a scoop. Some chests had compartments for two or even three types of meal.

In county Cork meal chests often tapered inwards a few inches towards the base, at the front. This would have provided foot space and made reaching into the bottom rather less awkward. Elsewhere the bins have parallel sides and fronts.

Like the dresser, the chest's size reflects the scope of the surrounding farm. The example illustrated (fig. 203) comes from a so-called 'strong' county Wicklow farmhouse. It is so tall that a special fold-down front has been incorporated to avoid accidents when reaching towards the base of the bin. Originally it was raised off the ground by nicely shaped bracket feet; subsequently these feet have been covered over by a plain plinth. Its antiquity is suggested by the partition wall (complete with incorporated dresser), built a century or so ago right over the top of the chest.

of the house; this was under Katty's super-intendence, who seeing the fellow sit ... called him ... to assist in removing the chest'.[38] It may be that such a functional object was considered unworthy of the neighbours gaze, or that it took up too much valuable space when the kitchen was to be filled with people.

Storage of other foodstuffs varies from place to place. We know from Ó Criomhthain's description that potatoes were stored underneath the high post beds, which were a couple of feet from the ground, providing the necessary dark place without taking up extra space. He also mentions that all the houses on the Great Blasket (in county Kerry) kept fish stored in barrels, which must have been salted.[39]

Another system of storing potatoes, from the north of Ireland, is provided by Carleton in his passage concerning the furnishings of a humble dwelling in the 1830s, 'In the lower end of the house stood a potato-bin, made up of stakes driven into the floor, and wrought with strong wickerwork.'[40] It is impossible to say how typical such an in-

genious arrangement was, as this is the only description and (not surprisingly) none have emerged during fieldstudies. However, the concept of 'earth fast' timber as a structural basis for buildings has long been familiar to historians of vernacular architecture. It was used for furniture in county Wicklow up until the 1930s, where a tailor had his own work table made in this substantial way, with tree trunk legs protruding from the ground. It was a clever solution to the problem of building a table strong enough for him to sit crosslegged on while sewing (see fig. 298). Another house nearby was equipped with a fireside stool made using stakes driven into the ground.

THE STILLION

'Stillion' is an ancient term that still survives amongst the language concerning the traditional house. In county Wexford it means a fixed slate shelf, inside the front door, upon which pails of milk or water are placed as they are brought from the spring. The term

204. A poteen maker's kitchen, showing a bucket resting on a jutting stone stillion, with another recessed shelf above. Photographed by R. Welch between 1890 and 1904, who noticed 'The top stone of a quern which grinds corn for meal and barley for poteen'. Inishmurry, county Sligo. Photo courtesy of the Ulster Museum.

132

The stillion[43] was originally a wooden framework which kept barrels off the ground. A surviving slate example, set into and supported by the masonry (fig. 205), was better suited to its purpose as it was both cooler and more durable than the wooden equivalent. Like the comparatively primitive wall recesses, stone shelves would in some areas have been more easily obtainable than those of wood. Several Irish historians have noticed that 'A strong wooden stool, or a stone slab in some cases, stood near the back door and supported a couple of buckets of clean water for drinking, cooking and making tea'; or in the north that 'the porch is sometimes used as a cool storage place for drinking water . . . [with] a niche . . . set in the stonework of the side most sheltered from the sun', but neither account recorded a local name (fig. 204).[44]

Before the days of mains water supply, water was often carried considerable distances by hand or horse and cart to people's houses (fig. 206). A habitual resting place for such pails, out of reach of animals, was important. William Hanbidge recalls at the turn of this century how 'for over a hundred years every drop of water for the house was carried from the Hayden's spring, down by the riverbank a quarter of a mile away . . . This heavy labour ceased only a few years ago when a well was sunk in the yard by the house.'[45] A poem of 1807 describing a poor man's possessions in county Down, mentions such things;

A jug in which we daily bring,
Our humble bev'rage from the spring.
In order, on a shelf of stone,
(For chest, or cupboard here is none)
A dish, and three old plates are plac'd'.[46]

205. 'The stillion', a cool slate shelf, built in beneath the steep stairs of an early eighteenth-century house, inside the front door. Stillions of stone or wood were traditionally placed where pails of water could be kept cool, straight from the spring. South county Wexford.

206. Drawing water, c.1935, county Louth. Photo courtesy of the D.I.F.

was used in the seventeenth century, when Burton Hall in county Cork had a 'Stilling Room' as well as '25 Hogsheads stillinge . . . 5 stillings' in the cellars and the Ormondes at Clonmel (county Tipperary) had '1 stellen' in their 'seller'.[41] From this and several subsequent inventory entries from the eighteenth[42] and nineteenth centuries one can deduce that the term meant a stand for casks (of wine, beer etc.) and that it filtered down into more general social use as a place for standing containers of water or milk.

207. *A Country Inn Kitchen,* by J.G. Mulvany (1766–1838), oil on canvas. It shows a late eighteenth-century kitchen in the south of Ireland. An open based dresser has spoons displayed at eyelevel. In 'the room' beyond, is the corner of a draped tester bed. A hanging shelf and some hams dangle from the ceiling. Diners await their meal before a panelled ware press, one of its four doors ajar. Six different low stools support a variety of things, including the artist's signature. Private collection.

Although the word stillion is now falling out of use, having become obsolete with the introduction of indoor running water, some old houses (particularly in the south-east of Ireland) still have such a recess or shelf beside the door, a reminder of times past.

THE WARE PRESS

A roadside inn this summer saturday: –
The doors are open to the wide warm air,
The parlour, whose old window views the bay,
Garnished with cracked delph full of flowers fair.[47]

In some of the more substantial farmhouses, there was a cupboard in which special china was stored and sometimes displayed (figs. 207, 216, 218). In smaller homes such a display cabinet might be in the form of a glazed corner cupboard which was generally kept in the ground floor parlour or the 'room'. Such 'ware presses' or 'three corner presses' held any fortunate overflow of extra ware which otherwise was displayed on the dresser. Such a press was recalled in a county Cork household during the surge of activity in anticipation of the Stations:

Cleaning and painting finished, the next target was the big ware press in the parlour. Out came delicate china which had been in the family for years. My mother's respect for the Stations weighed against her fear of breakage, but the Stations won every time. Once when a precious jug was broken she mourned it for days, telling us how long it had been in the family. Finally, Dan, our part-time travelling farm worker, said: 'Misus, if it was here that long it was time to break it'. And that was the end of that.[48]

134

208. (*above*) Parlour corner press with an open arcaded top, shell spandrels and curved and moulded shelf fronts. The hollow half-round pilasters on each side, are made up of wide reeding. Guilloche interlacing, built up with applied fretwork, decorates the facia (detail fig. 20). The door panels are a simplified version of linenfold. Painted thickly and repeatedly in red, pink, cream, pale green etc. Late eighteenth century, probably from county Tipperary.

209. (*top, right*) Large 'three corner press' for displaying ware, of pine, painted brown and with scumbled shamrocks. It has panels with carved shell corners, and a central drawer flanked by fluted pilasters. Presented to the Irish Agricultural Museum, by Baroness de Breffny, probably from Kilmacow, south Kilkenny, *c.*1860.

210. (*right*) Late nineteenth-century corner ware press, with applied decoration in the form of elongated stems with curled tendrils. The carved corner fans on the door panels are traditional in many parts of the south, and also occur on its arcaded interior. The brown paintwork, with white doors, is the traditional combination for these pieces, but has been recently applied. Possibly from county Limerick.

211. The seldom used parlour of an eighteenth-century farmhouse, as found. An early nineteenth-century built-in ware press has its doors ajar to reveal an arcaded interior and display of ware. A mass-produced 'Connecticut clock' (imported since the Great Exhibition of 1851), is surrounded by religious prints, portraits of the family and of Parnell. The door of a small press, recessed into the hearth wall, is on the left.

The habit of having such luxury display cabinets probably originated with the fashionable astragal glazed display cases of the gentry, with their thirteen panes of glass per door. Many of the surviving 'three corner presses' are glazed in this way (with varying degrees of success) but the painted pine glazing bars are necessarily wider and sturdier than their aristocratic ancestors. On opening the glazed upper doors, the inner shelves are sometimes emphasised by a surrounding decorative framework a few inches wide (figs. 209–11, 214, 220–1). Often such cabinets were built permanently into the corners of the parlour, thus requiring the minimum of materials, being composed mainly of shelves and doors. Like the dressers, the main carcase of the piece was often built in its intended room. The storage space inside such a press was comparatively small, but as it was intended for show this was not a disadvantage (figs. 211–12). Surviving vernacular examples have often been grained carefully in imitation of the other dark oak or mahogany parlour furniture.

Inside such cabinets was a variety of precious objects, usually things too delicate or precious for daily use, alongside objects brought by relatives from abroad. They were links with the past, rich in sentiment and nostalgia. A measure of the value placed upon such luxuries can be gauged from W.M. Thackeray's description of how they were shown to him in 1843; 'a grand service of china for dinner and desert. The kind young widow shows them with no little pride, and says with reason that there are few lodging-houses in Cork that can match such china as that. They are relics of happy old times.'[49]

The three corner press echoed the parlour itself, both being late eighteenth-century innovations emphasising display rather than usefulness. Some examples are richly decorative, suggesting that more time was devoted to this piece than to any others in the house. Classical style pilasters, dubiously derived and naively executed, sometimes flank the doors of the upper section (figs. 208–9), while the base, with its panelled doors, might be raised on shaped bracket feet (figs. 212, 214). The Ulster Folk Museum has an ornate bow-fronted example, complete with pilasters, bracket feet and panelling, combining all that was extravagant and symbolic of status in Irish furniture. These delicate features could survive in the cloistered environment of the 'room'. It was the only ground floor space in most

136

212. Shallow glazed press, for the display of special 'ware', built into the parlour wall of a farmhouse at Screen, south county Wexford. Each door is made up with eighteen, rather than the usual thirteen panes of glass. Early nineteenth century.

213. Bureau bookcase of pine, with an unusual low glazed top (compare to figs. 215–16) and scratch-stock lines imitating drawer beading. Most bureaux were made during a period of rising prosperity for the 'strong farmers', after the great famine. Presented to the Irish Agricultural Museum, by Baroness de Breffny, probably from Kilmacow, south Kilkenny, c.1870.

214. Corner ware press, made around 1880, of pine, and painted in two-tone white and brown, in the mid-twentieth century. The arrangement of the low panels with their carved shell corners, is repeated on the arcading inside the top, and on other southern vernacular furniture (see fig. 223). From a farmhouse in Ballacolla, county Laois. Width 42½ in., height 72½ in. Shown at Roscrea Heritage Centre; courtesy of Victor Mitchell.

215. A tall bureau bookcase, pine painted red and more recently green, c.1860. The design, copied from fine examples of walnut and subsequently mahogany, would have been seen in 'the big houses' since the early eighteenth century. The extra glass panels (compare fig. 217), carved shell decoration and nailed construction make it unmistakably vernacular. Thought to be from Castleblaney, county Monaghan. Part of the Irish Country Furniture Society's Collection, at the Irish Agricultural Museum.

216. Oil painting on canvas by John G. Mulvany (1766–1838), probably of the upstairs room of a town or farmhouse. Beside the fireplace is a bureau and some rush seated chairs, painted green. Bureaux and desks were a fashionable luxury and very few vernacular examples have survived (see figs. 213, 215) On the left a press has one door open, displaying the ware inside. Private collection.

217. Built-in, painted pine 'three corner press', each upper door having thirteen panes, and the lower doors disguised, strangely, as six dummy drawer fronts. Such false drawer fronts were common on Irish parlour furniture (see fig. 239). First half of the nineteenth century, from the parlour of a farmhouse near Union Hall, west county Cork.

farmhouses which was sometimes fitted with a suspended rather than an earthen floor, making bracket feet a possibility. The ceiling was sometimes intricately panelled and painted, in contrast to the open joists of the kitchen.

Occasionally one finds a three corner press displayed in a large farm kitchen, rather than in the parlour. J. G. Mulvany's *A Country Inn Kitchen* shows ware on display in a press with panelled upper doors, which have been left open for an impressive display (fig. 207). Another of his paintings shows a similar display, in a smarter upstairs room, probably of a modest town house (fig. 216).

One west county Cork kitchen used to have such a ware press which was recessed into the rear kitchen wall, it was closed off by means of a hinged falling table which folded down in front of it. Other ware presses are small and recessed into a parlour wall with only one glass door hinged to the front. One example, built into a county Cork parlour, has six dummy drawer fronts on the lower doors (fig. 217). These were a hastily contemplated attempt by the maker (or perhaps a suggestion by the owner) to make it look grand, drawers were after all an expensive feature; but six of them could never run into a corner!

Three corner presses with panelled doors and no glass may date from times when glass was difficult to obtain. Such examples have been found in parlours and doubtless they were used in the same way as the glazed ones, but with the upper doors swung open for display (figs. 211, 225).

FOOD PRESSES

In some traditional Munster homes there are still vast food presses which often form one side of a room partition, with a dresser on the other side and the parlour door between (fig. 186). Thickly painted and lined with pastel coloured wallpaper, a lingering smell of cabbage sometimes betrays their former use. Other tell-tale signs like the network of interconnected mouse and rat holes, reveal how their contents encouraged theft. Monumental in size, it has been suggested that their design harks back to the enormous furniture of the traditional Irish tower house (fig. 218). Often

218. *The Interior of an Inn*, by Nathaniel Grogan Snr. (1740–1807), who was born and worked near Cork; pencil, pen, grey ink and watercolour. A large panelled ware press has a door ajar to display its contents. People carouse around tables, seated on a form, a barrel and chairs. A tall tester bed and clothing draped on a rope, are visible in the adjacent room. Photo courtesy of Christie's, London.

219. Pine 'four door press' painted brick red and with three central drawers, from Cloghadreen, Old Pallas, county Limerick. The configuration of panels on the doors, and the spiralling chip-carved motifs, are the same as on fig. 221, indicating the same maker. The shelves have strips of wood attached for propping up and displaying plates. Both examples originally had plinths. With unpainted repairs. Courtesy of the N.M.I.

220. The interior of the 'four door press' in fig. 219. The shaped shelf fronts and decorative arcading suggest that it may have been intended for the display of ware. Original backing boards missing. Courtesy of the N.M.I.

they are about the same height and width as the dresser in the same kitchen (where they always stood). They defy all postmodern ideas about shallow, orderly shelving, encouraging 2 feet deep of what tends inevitably to be chaotic storage. Everything from cabbage to potatoes, left-over food, packets and bottles, string and jars of jam or bread soda, could be hidden from view behind the brightly painted panelled doors. Such immense size was conducive to private hoarding and characteristic of thrift.

Such food presses were not necessarily found in every home. Unlike the three corner press, which was a luxury and a status symbol, the food press was useful. The British Government's Poor Reports of the 1830s frequently described the furnishings of the poor as 'very scanty'[50] and hardly referred to presses at all. However, they do mention that in county Tipperary they had 'sometimes a press or cupboard and a dresser',[51] while others in county Carlow had to improvise with 'a shelf fixed up to the wall, serving as a cupboard or press'.[52]

Some food presses are composed of shelving hidden by a pair of large doors, others are divided into four doors and accordingly are usually called 'four door presses' (figs. 218–21, 224, 226–8). Many more take the form of recessed cupboards along-side the hearth (fig. 229).

Decoration of these doors was often in the form of multiple panelling (fig. 219). Sometimes the panels had carved triangular scallop-shell corners or carved rope moulding (both characteristic of the south-east of Ireland) or naive fluted pilasters, capitals

and friezes. Some examples have a pierced and fretted arcading around the inner shelves, in the same manner as the three corner presses (figs. 220–1). Raised and fielded panelling, using pine an inch or so thick, was another favourite device (figs. 224, 226–7).

As we have seen with other furniture, decoration was largely the hallmark of indi-

221. (*above*) Large pine 'four door press', repeatedly painted, most recently in pale blue and cream gloss. Lavishly decorated with shaped panels, carved scrolls, symmetrical rope mouldings and a many layered cornice (see detail fig. 17), it also has an arcaded interior. Mid-nineteenth century, from Ballynaclogh, county Limerick (the same area and maker as figs. 219–20). On loan from the N.M.I., at the Irish Agricultural Museum.

222. (*top, right*) The bog oak turnbuckle of a four door pine corner press. The diagonal carving across the centre is the sole decoration, other than black and brown paint, on this late nineteenth-century press, which is built into the parlour of a farmhouse at Toomavara, county Tipperary.

223. (*right*) Pine press, made *c.*1750–75, with early brown paint applied over layers of red and then green (detail fig. 18). The carved shell motifs are repeated on

the corners of the interior arcading. Mouldings have been applied diagonally across the facia, beneath a cornice with vertical reeding, echoed around the drawers and reminiscent of cross-banded veneer. Holes have been drilled in the right-hand side for ventilation. Simple incised interlacing decorates the long drawer. Partially restored, bought by the Irish Country Furniture Society from a county Limerick dealer, shown at the Irish Agricultural Museum.

224. Pine 'four door press,' plain inside, lined with wallpaper and used for food storage, c.1830. Original red paintwork with subsequent varnish. The doors, with fielded panels, are surrounded by flat reeding, and surmounted by carved oval paterae, linked by dentil moulding. Finely carved rope mouldings run across the cornice and beneath each vestigial capital. From Creevagh, Clonmacnoise, county Offaly, shown at the Irish Agricultural Museum, lent from the collection of the N.M.I.

225. (below) Corner press with small central drawers and patterned and scumbled paintwork, reminiscent of seventeenth-century kingwood graining. The sides are flanked by classically inspired, simple fluted pilasters. Mid nineteenth century, from county Kilkenny. Photo courtesy of Chalon (U.K.).

226. (top, right) Four door food press, built into the parlour/kitchen wall of a farmhouse near Leap, west county Cork. Made of pine in the early nineteenth century, with fielded panels and fine saw-tooth moulding along the underside of the cornice.

227. (below, right) Four door press, made c.1850–75, from county Tipperary, with graining in contrasting colours which highlights the fielded panels. The bracket feet are replacements, the cornice is damaged. Courtesy of Victor Mitchell.

228. Built-in pitch pine and white pine 'four door press', with a long central drawer. Made around 1900 by Paddy Crowly, a wheelwright and carpenter (see his dressers figs. 143–4). The pitch pine is likely to have been salvaged from a shipwreck. He also made the pair of carpenters' chairs and probably the traditional pine double-stretchered table too. From a farmhouse in west county Cork.

230. (*facing page, below*) An 'Irish mountain farm kitchen', in Glenshesh, county Antrim, *c*.1890–1910. The hearth has four keeping holes. To its left is a recessed cupboard and a straw upholstered settle (see figs. 98–100, 104). A braced *súgán* twister hangs from the ceiling. Carpenters' chairs stand on the rough floor and beyond in the 'room' is a three corner press, displaying glassware. Late nineteenth-century photograph from the Welch collection, courtesy of the Ulster Museum.

vidual makers and regions. Cornices were sometimes delicately underlined with tiny saw-tooth mouldings (fig. 226) or built up layer upon layer like architectural mouldings (figs. 221, 225). The door panels were usually small and the upper ones were sometimes intricately shaped (figs. 219, 221, 227), reflecting the widespread shortage of large dimension timber. These panels were emphasised by grained paintwork imitating more expensive woods (figs. 225, 227), or during the past century, picked out dramatically with contrasting colours (figs. 221, 226, 228). In common with other furniture made in coastal areas, fieldwork has uncovered presses made from pitch pine and even oak, perhaps made from the gleanings of a ship-wreck or from a deckload of timber which was sometimes jettisoned in stormy weather.

Some of these presses have drawers either centrally positioned between the upper and lower cupboards, or beneath them. Drawers were comparatively time consuming and therefore expensive to make. The wheelwrights and house carpenters who made these pieces rarely took the extra time to

cut dovetails, so usually the drawers were simply butted and nailed together. Handles were sometimes white porcelain knobs, but when these were unobtainable, cotton reels or even diamond shaped holes took their place (see fig. 196).

PLACES FOR CLOTHES

The word wardrobe is rarely mentioned even amongst the inventories of the grandest houses and most surviving examples are of no great antiquity or are the products of machine manufacture. The word 'press' crops up far more frequently in the bedroom lists, suggesting that this was indeed the common name for a place to store clothes (or food, as already described, in the kitchen). Although inventories rarely detail the purpose of objects specifically, one from county Armagh of 1716 does list 'a press for hanging cloaths in at £1.0.0.'.[53]

Poor people during the eighteenth and nineteenth centuries did not own many clothes, indeed there was a thriving trade in second-hand garments, so purpose-built furniture to accommodate them was a low

229. (*above*) Recessed cupboards flanking the hearth of an empty two-roomed weaver's house near New Ross, county Wexford. On the right is a fire fan made by Pierce of Wexford.

priority. Writers travelling along the west coast of Galway at the close of the last century peered in through the doorway of a poor cabin, haughtily describing what they saw: 'Across the room was stretched a clothes-line, upon which fragments of something that might possibly have been clothes, at some time or other, were hanging' (fig. 231).[54] The same arrangement was recalled in more detail, half a century later by a folklorist, who wrote of county Armagh; 'The sole wardrobe of the cabin was a rope line attached to two swivel hooks built into opposite walls about the middle of the cottage. Each person had a certain part of the line as their own. The hooks were specially made by blacksmiths and can still be seen in many houses.'[55] Such a system has not been observed recently but another example of it can be seen in H. O'Neill's painting of a Lauga Law Kitchen Interior, from county Wicklow.[56] Estyn Evans described the *súgán* which was hung across the cabin near the fire, saying merely that it was used as a drying place for clothes.[57] Clothes are still hung near the fire (or over the stove which has taken its place) to dry, on a pole or on lengths of string tied to the clevy. This would also have been a useful place to store clothes in the absence of a purpose-built chest or wardrobe (fig. 242). The fact that this method of hanging clothes is recorded in three such diverse areas,

143

231. *A Cottage Interior, Clare Island*, with the clothes line strung across the kitchen, probably made of straw rope. A simple way to keep clothing away from damp floors and walls, this alternative to a chest or wardrobe was often described by visitors to the homes of the poor (see fig. 218). From *The Illustrated London News*, 1886.

Strangely, very little has been written by the usual commentators on Irish material culture on the subject of clothes chests and storage. For the prosperous minority, a typical way to store clothes was in 'a good oak clothes-chest', as was the case with a thriving Kilkenny Druggist in 1767.[61] Such 'Indian and Mohogany Cloaths Chests' or 'Chamber Chests'[62] are frequently mentioned amongst the possessions of the wealthier Irish householders in the seventeenth and eighteenth centuries,[63] providing a precedent for their widespread use by the less fortunate classes.

The fact that the poorer classes adopted this method of storing their clothes and bedding (if they were fortunate enough to own it) is proven by the frequent references to them amongst the British Government Poor Reports of the labourers' cabins during the 1830s. The descriptions of furnishings frequently list only 'an old deal table, a few stools, and an old chest for the clothes and provisions (fig. 232)'.[64] Many of the most destitute had no need for such a chest, as in county Clare at that time the reports state that 'The clothing of the labourer is generally very bad; so bad that great numbers are prevented, from shame, from going to chapel on Sundays.'[65]

Carleton, in his *Tales of Ireland*, amusingly describes an elopement somewhere in the north of Ireland: 'At length it occurred to her mother to search the chest in which Peggy kept her dress; and no sooner was this done, than it appeared that her absence was voluntary and premeditated, for her best clothes had been secretly removed from the chest, and could no where be found.'[66]

Mrs Hall, in common with many of the other foreign travellers around Ireland, somewhat pompously published 'suggested improvements' to the life-styles of the peasantry. On the subject of the ubiquitous Irish clothes chest she wrote: 'If a deal chest-of-drawers can be substituted for the universal and unwieldy "box", into which the women huddle their "bits of clothes" in a most untidy manner, so much the better; it is ... a decided step to domestic improvement.'[67] What Mrs Hall failed to con-

indicates it was once a widespread habit.

In county Clare, the expression 'first up, best dressed' is said to have arisen from the use of a simple row of wooden pegs set into the wall, where the family's clothes were hung in lieu of a wardrobe.[58] All sorts of things which needed to be kept away from dust, smoke and the damp of the floor, were hung up in bags, particularly sewing and knitting paraphernalia.[59] Two such draw-string bags, can be seen clearly in Samuel Watson's 1845 depiction of *The Irish Jig* (fig. 108).

A century ago, Edith Somerville and Martin Ross had occasion to describe the parlour furnishings of a Connemara cabin, where they stopped to stay the night:

'Back in the room' was a small whitewashed place with an earthen floor as clean, though not quite as dry, as the one in the kitchen. A big four-poster bed filled one end of it ... The walls were lavishly hung with fervidly coloured religious prints ... and drapery's adventitious aid was lent by the suspended wardrobe of the family, both male and female, which relieved the severities of the bedposts, and gave a little air of interesting mystery to the corners of the room.[60]

232. *Molly Carew*, from a painting by Erskine Nicol (1825–1904). Inside the door, is a large chest, of a type widely used in the nineteenth century for storing clothes. Its plinth is deliberately raised up away from the damp floor, a feature also found in existing examples (fig. 239). On the right is a red-painted dresser and in the room behind is a bed with blue curtains and a valance, hung from the ceiling. Reproduced in Mrs S.C. Hall's *Tales of Irish life and Character*, 1909. Photo courtesy of the N.L.I.

233. Clothes chest made of pine, with spliced rope handles and original black paint, *c*.1870. Notice the double twisted straw ropes which tie down the unlined thatch. From an upstairs bedroom of an eighteenth-century house in south county Wicklow.

sider was that such people could never afford a chest of drawers, with its comparatively lavish use of timber. Things other than clothes could also be conveniently secreted away in the chest, as Elizabeth Smith discovered in 1847, when one of her tenant farmers gave her 'seven pounds [which] he produced from the secret drawer in his chest', for the farm rent.[68]

Although few of these boxes, or *cófra*, now survive outside museums, a description of traditional furniture 'no longer made' in county Longford during the 1930s reveals how they looked:

Clothes chests . . . were just square or oblong boxes about five feet long and four feet high. But the size varied . . . They had a lid, which fitted closely, and to which a lock was fitted. They rested on four short thick stands. Sometimes they had a drawer underneath. They held blankets, bed linen, wearables etc. They were substantial and durable and practically every house in the neighbourhood has still one in use.[69]

The same writer provides a rough sketch, showing such a chest with a lock and a long single drawer occupying the full width of the base.

These large coffers, rather like the English form of blanket box, doubled up easily for other purposes, with their horizontal rather than sloping lids. In county Tipperary the commissioners found such 'chests serving as tables in some poorer houses',[70] while the Reverend Hall was surprised to come across 'a wake, where the corpse of a woman dressed in her grave-clothes, was laid on a chest . . . dressed in a plain cap and black ribbon as when alive'.[71]

The chests varied in size according to space and requirements and were common in the single room of the poorest dwellings (fig. 233). The poem 'Thady O'Brady', which effectively provides us with a rare single-room cabin inventory all in rhyme, was probably written at the start of the nineteenth century. It demonstrates that the pine clothes chest was kept close to the fireside bed;

First, a neat feathe-bed and a four posted 'stead, . . .

145

234. An unusual clothes
chest, as found, combining
drawers and doors, made of
pine and painted dark
brown. The gallery with its
carved foliage, surrounds
the top of four shallow
drawers, which are set back
from the base. Made in 1906
by Andy Bergin (see dresser
fig. 292), from near Callan,
county Kilkenny.

And a neat deal board chest at our feet
too,[72]

Two-roomed homes (those divided into a
kitchen and a smaller 'room' or parlour)
sometimes had such a chest in the parlour.
Ó Criomhthain recalls their two-roomed
home on the Great Blasket: 'There were
two beds in the lower portion . . . A great
chest was kept between the two beds up
against the gable end.' This must have been
for keeping the family's clothes in.[73]

Danaher describes curtained alcoves
serving as spaces to hang up clothes in the
bedrooms, early in the twentieth century,
adding that the wealthier homes did have
clothes cupboards and wardrobes. Aromatic
herbs, lavender and bog-myrtle were kept
amongst the clothing to discourage the
attacking clothes moth.[74]

Somerville and Ross mention seeing
'a huge American chest with a washing
apparatus [A jug and basin] on it' in 'the
room' (as the parlour bedroom was commonly called) of a Connemara cabin.[75] Their
reference to an 'American chest' is a typical
one, originating from the massive exodus
of Irish to America around the period of
the worst famines. They carried with them
pitifully little in the way of baggage except

for the 'emigrants little tin trunks'.[76] Tin
trunks are still referred to as emigrants'
trunks in many households.

DOWRY CHESTS

The dowry chest, whose name is linked
with a vanished social marriage custom, is a
more elaborate and expensive version of
the simple rectangular clothes chest. Its
design, sometimes called a 'chest on chest',
is recognisable as a transitionary stage in
the evolution of the simple rectangular
clothes chest towards the chest of drawers.
However, chests of drawers never became
a typical part of traditional vernacular furnishings in Ireland (fig. 234).

Such dowry chests were used most
commonly in the southerly counties of
the country. Surviving examples were
found during recent fieldwork in counties
Kilkenny, Waterford and Wexford, where
they still formed part of the traditional furnishings of old houses.[77] These surviving
examples give weight to a description of the
dowry chest written during the 1950s, which
states that it was 'a large, well made box
with a flat top, in almost every house. These
were very well made by certain carpenters
and no nail was used in their construction; the
sides being "dovetailed" into one another.'[78]

Perhaps it was a dowry chest that was mentioned as having been in the upstairs 'store-
room where mother kept her dovetailed
chest, books, linen, spinning wheels and
many other things' in a large county Limerick
farmhouse.[79] The historian Timothy O'Neill
mentions that brides brought with them
as dowry, linen, frieze, thread, wool and
blankets in a chest, adding that textiles
were often stored unused as heirlooms for
generations.[80]

The dowry chest is one of the only pieces
of furniture which consistently had so much
trouble taken over its construction. Dovetails were very rarely used on other furniture.
The fact that the chests were used to store
money and valuables suggests that the
dovetailed construction was for reasons of
security rather than aesthetics (particularly
as they were subsequently hidden by
paintwork). One example, in a derelict
eighteenth-century farmhouse in county

235. Finely decorated dome-topped pine dowry chest, which comes apart in two sections. The front is flanked by naive fluted pilasters, the symmetrically carved rope moulding is typical of the south-east. Its original honey coloured paintwork may have been imitative of satinwood. From Ballingarry, county Kilkenny, first half of the nineteenth century. On show at the Irish Agricultural Museum, from the collection of the Irish Country Furniture Society.

236. Pine dowry chest with original scumble woodgraining, c.1800. From a house in Carrigbeg, Doon, county Limerick, where the rest of the woodwork was grained to match. Partly restored, with its handles missing, such early finishes are usually overpainted (see detail, fig. 18). The carved chevrons and rope mouldings were often used to decorate these chests. Shown at the Irish Agricultural Museum; courtesy of the N.L.I.

carving, false drawer fronts (deliberately making them look even more expensive and elaborate), classical pilasters and even, on one example, an arched lid (fig. 235) all point to an object held in high esteem. Their painted and grained finish is usually in imitation of fashionable mahogany, oak or even satinwood (figs. 235–7).

The fact that the chests were usually made in two separate halves, presumably for ease of carrying, is significant when considered in the light of their use as a marriage chest. No other large heavy items of Irish furniture could be separated for transporting in this way. Some examples have a sloping lid, which may have been useful as a writing slope, as well as discouraging people from placing objects on the lid (fig. 238). Others have small shelves or drawers inside; all these features are reminiscent of the meal chest.

The same 1950s description opens by saying that the dowry chest was 'allied to the dresser'.[81] Presumably this alliance lies in their common emphasis on status and decoration, characteristics which are of secondary importance in other items of Irish furniture. The Roscommon account continues: 'It was called a "dowry chest" because the daughter got one as part of her dowry, and the chest contained quilts, blankets, sheets etc for her new home . . . My mother got one when she was married about the year 1876.'[82] Such an object was treasured and filled with special things in anticipation of a wedding.

During fieldwork, no dowry chest has ever been found in a kitchen, they were more likely to have been fashionable parlour pieces, as they were highly desirable and within financial reach only of the more prosperous farmers. So it is rather surprising to learn that 'Sometimes the box was used as a "bin" for holding flour meal or groceries etc . . . Each box was fitted with a good lock and was often used as a safe for anything of value.'[83] Perhaps after the marriage, the bedclothes stored in the dowry chest could be moved elsewhere, perhaps into the settle bed, leaving the upper section free for use as a meal chest.

The tradition of providing a dowry with the bride was a customary feature of Irish marriage up to the nineteenth century. The

237. (*above*) An unusual pine dowry chest, made in one piece and painted to imitate mahogany. The drawers, with their diagonally carved fronts, are flanked by square holes which were intentionally left unfilled. Mid-nineteenth century, from Kyleagree, Limerick Junction, county Tipperary. Courtesy of the N.M.I.

Kilkenny, was made out of fine wide elm boards, rather than pine, although it had nevertheless been painted. Its lower drawers were still filled with books and family papers. Such cabinetmaking, as opposed to carpentry, was the domain of the most highly skilled woodworkers, hence the reference quoted earlier to 'certain carpenters'. The careful attention to decorative detail on these pieces, involving time consuming

239. Two pine dowry chests from different parts of north county Limerick, for storing bedclothes and clothing. The mulberry coloured one on the right, made in the mid-nineteenth century, is from Ballytrasna, Pallas Green. Width 40 in., depth 23 in., height 42 in. Both examples have incised lines delineating the drawers, but the left-hand example, grained like oak, has additional false drawer fronts. Its bracket feet are decorated with lines of dots, and raised to keep it away from a damp floor. Notice the uneven carving of the rope mouldings. From Ballynagally, Grean, Barony of Coonagh. Courtesy of the N.M.I.

238. (*facing page, below*) One piece dowry chest in 'the room' or parlour of a farmhouse in Licketstown, county Kilkenny. Made of varnished pine in the late nineteenth century, like some other examples (figs. 232, 239), it has raised bracket feet. The kitchen chairs on the right, are typically Irish, with their double stretchers beneath the seat. Photographed in 1986; courtesy of the Irish Architectural Archive.

dowry was a particularly significant aspect of marriages amongst the Munster cattle-owning families.[84] This is of interest in relation to the dowry chests, the distribution of which coincides, as they occur mainly in the southernmost counties.

Patrick Kennedy, writing about the matchmaking and dowry system of the early nineteenth century, discusses how country people hoped to gain social standing or material possession through their marriages. 'The custom of making expeditions into the county of Carlow to get wives and large fortunes was prevalent in the early part of the twentieth century in county Wexford . . . The bride brought so much money or stock to her new home; and if she became a widow within a short period of her bridal, she returned, if she chose, to her own people, and her dowry went back with her.'[85] Details of the 'stock' likely to have been put aside for a wedding are scarce, but Kennedy conveniently mentions how a man once put off a wedding because the bride's 'niggardly father digusted him by refusing to include a good quilted linsey-woolsey petticoat, on which he had staked his peace of mind'.[86] This is further evidence that clothing was something which was stored up as dowry, presumably in the purpose-built chests.

The sums of money which changed hands were sometimes immense, 'seventy or eighty pounds . . . on the day of the *hauling home*'[87] at a time when in comparison 'a pottle of thick milk [four pints] cost a penny' and 'a large sized fat pig' cost about three pounds.[88] Writing during the same period, Mrs Hall mentions how the size of a dowry was 'a common way in Ireland of estimating the possession of wealth', siting an example of people living in poor looking housing who were in fact rich enough to 'give a marriage portion of a hundred pounds with a daughter'.[89]

Chapter 5

BEDS

Thorough Beds and Shake-downs, The Outshot Bed, Bedrooms,
Bed Cords and Bedding, Plaited Straw Mattresses, Low Bedsteads,
Enclosed Beds, Tester Beds, Canopy or Camp Beds, 'Covered Car Beds',
Box Beds, Alternative Forms of Enclosed Beds, Wicker Beds,
Built-in Beds, Bed Hangings, Bed Folklore

THOROUGH BEDS AND SHAKE-DOWNS

And in a corner by the wall,
We have a bed which *cannot* fall,
But let this not create surprise-
Securely on the ground it lies;
To furnish it no flocks of geese,
Were plundered of their downy fleece,
Plain straw it is . . . and o'er this bed,
The ruins of a quilt are spread.

P. McClabber, 'Cabin Comfortless', 1807[1]

In the poorest homes, when people could not afford a wooden bedstead or many bedclothes, the usual alternative was to sleep close to the warmth of the hearth. This practice of communal sleeping on the floor, with parents and children huddled together, was known variously as the 'thorough bed', 'sleeping in stradogue' or on a 'shake-down'. It was remarked upon as early as the sixteenth century, when one of the Spanish Armada captains wrote that the Irish 'sleep upon the ground, on rushes, newly cut and full of water and ice.'[2]

It may seem bizarre to open a chapter discussing beds with descriptions of people who did not have them. However, such conditions persisted amongst the poorest households up to the 1830s, when the British Government's Poor Inquiry shows, the practice was widespread throughout Ireland.[3] Government reporters provide little information pertaining to terminology, since their purpose was merely to describe what they saw: they do not use terms like the 'thorough bed', 'stradogue' or the 'shake-down'. Literary accounts using these terms

occur most frequently amongst the many curious travelling foreigners, who tended to spend more time describing such things. Travellers' accounts substantiated by dictionaries, show that 'stradogue' comes from the Irish *sráideog*, defined as 'a shake-down . . . a mat, a coverlet, [or] a bed on the floor'.[4] Similarly, the 'thorough bed' is also a bed on the floor, but usually it appears to describe one slept in by several people.

This mode of sleeping was, for the poor, not a matter of choice. We learn from the ransacking of the grand Maynooth Castle in 1534 that 'great and rich was the spoile, such store of beds, so manie goodlie hangings', so evidently the rich did not have to contend with such discomfort.[5] A bed was also a reflection of ones status within the household. John Stevens, writing in 1689, noted: 'In the better sort of cabins there is generally one flock bed, seldom more, feathers being too costly; this serves the man and his wife, the rest all lie on straw, some with one sheet and blanket, others only their clothes and blanket to cover them.'[6] It was only the poorest sections of society who habitually slept on beds of straw, rush or bracken on the floor, as descriptions of beds and bedsteads, amongst other sections of the rural population, are numerous. Some descriptions infer however that sleeping in stradogue close to the warmth of a fire was not always such a hardship. John Dunton, a seventeenth-century explorer, when travelling through Connemara found there were 'no inns, nor indeed any roads', and so accepted the hospitality of some people who lived in

150

240. A cottier tenant and family sleeping communally 'in stradogue' amongst their animals and before the fire. Such privation was widespread throughout Ireland amongst the poor up until the nineteenth century. Drawn in 1830 by their landlord James Connery, and published in his book, *The Reformer* (1832). Photo courtesy of the N.M.I.

some 'little hutts' there. He spent the night on a long bed of freshly gathered green rushes, wrapped up in clean, soft, white 'breadeen' blankets. Initially he was perturbed when some cows and sheep were ushered in to lie beside him (for fear of wolves). But he soon remarked upon the sweetness of their breath 'and the pleasing noyse they made in ruminating or chawing the cudd [which] would lull a body to sleep as soon as the noys of a murmuring brook and the fragrancy of a bed [of] roses.'[7]

According to Arthur Young 'A "shake-down" when I was in Ireland [1776–8] meant some clean straw spread upon the floor, with blankets and sheets.'[8] The preparation of a 'thorough bed' in a single-room hut, with a central fireplace, comes from a description of the Rosses, county Donegal in 1788;

> All the family lay together in one bed . . . the youngest men were sent out for heath or bent-bushes; which they spread across the floor, to a length sufficient for the number present, and in breadth about six feet: over this litter . . . a long plaid or blanket, on which the others, having stripped off their clothes, lay down as fast as they could; men and women together, all naked: then the mistress having drawn the rest of the blanket over them, lay down last herself.[9]

Caesar Otway, travelling through county Mayo around 1800, learnt of the carefully regulated formula of people 'sleeping in

stradogue'. First the floor was thickly strewn with fresh rushes, and the whole family covered themselves with blankets or clothes. Then they 'lie down *decently*, and in order: the eldest daughter next the wall farthest from the door, then all the sisters, according to their ages; next mother, father, and sons in succession, and then the strangers, whether the travelling pedlar, or tailor, or beggar [with] great propriety of conduct.'[10]

James Connery, a landlord in the 1830s, provided no proper explanation as to why he had occasion to visit his tenants at four thirty one March morning. He does however, describe how he found 'the man, wife, and six children, snoring in a bed of very coarse heath, on the cold ground . . . before the fireplace in the kitchen, with the heads of half of them reversed, having but a small share of covering'. The father of the family was a 'cottier tenant or small farmer who occupied about nine English acres of land' in county Waterford. Connery's drawing of the scene shows that they had a table and seats and even a dresser (fig. 240). Apparently the man had been forced to sleep on the floor as 'the fleas ejected him some time before from the bed in which he usually lay, in a dungeon of a room he had.'[11]

A French baron exploring county Limerick in 1887, described a similar arrangement of 'sleeping "straddogue"', adding that 'this rather primitive couch is still used in many houses'.[12] In county Wicklow, three servant women had to sleep like this before the kitchen fire, even though they worked in a comparatively grand house; and even the children of a farmer with 80 acres, slept 'on straw laid on chairs'.[13] People were obviously well aware of the dangers of sleeping so close to the hearth, taking the wise precaution in county Cavan of placing stools along the edge of the hearth 'to keep the bed from taking fire'.[14]

In county Derry in the 1830s, those compiling the Ordnance Survey Memoirs noted that the poor man usually had '1 or 2 plain bed frames . . . and the extra beds wanted [presumably for travellers] supplied by shakedowns of straw or bracken upon the cold floors and raised daily unless when a sick person lies on one of them'. During a cholera outbreak in 1832 in county Kilkenny, such 'John's Wisps' were burnt and people were provided with free straw to replace them.[15]

In Tullaghobegly, Gweedore, county Donegal, the teacher at the National School claimed that amongst a population of over 9,000, they had only two feather beds and eight chaff beds. 'Their beds are straw – green and dried rushes or mountain bent: their bed-clothes are either coarse sheets, or no sheets, and ragged filthy blankets.'[16] As a result of this letter to the Lord Lieutenant of Ireland, an anonymous English donor arranged for the distribution of clothing and bed-ticks.[17] In the following extract, a Gweedore poet praises the 'noble' landlord, Lord George Hill, who eventually helped improve their conditions:

I lay upon a green rush bed,
Bestrewn upon the floor;
I never thought to've laid my head,
On *pillow*, at Gweedore.

I've lain upon the self-same bed,
With master, man, and maid,
And in the same apartment where
The cows and sheep were laid.

One cov'ring did us all, you see –
('Tis true, 'twas summer weather,)
And as we had no other choice,
We all lay snug together.

R.M. 1845[18]

In the poorest homes in county Kildare, a bedstead, however inferior, was 'considered by the owners as the article of most value'.[19] Like many other traditions in Ireland, this practice continued and in some areas people still resorted to shake-downs and shared beds (particularly for children in large families) well into the twentieth century. A temporary shake-down was still made for the occasional visitor to a west Kerry farm in the 1930s. Sticks were arranged 'criss-crossed' on the kitchen floor before the fire, which were then covered by old Indian meal or bran sacks filled with loose straw to raise the sleeper from the draughty and possibly damp floor.[20]

One of many cultural links between Ireland and Scotland can be also seen here. The Scottish highlanders during the eighteenth century positively preferred to sleep upon heather, with the brush uppermost,

refusing to sleep in ordinary beds during their trips to the south.[21] 'Shake-downs' were also referred to and described during the 1750s in the north of Scotland.[22]

There are many disparaging references to various types of bed in the cabins. An account from county Louth of 1712 mentions how a householder slept on 'a straw bed, with napy [hairy, downy] blankets and sacks stuffed with straw for a Bolster'.[23] Better than sleeping on the floor would have been the combination of 'pallet, straw and quilt' mentioned as a bride's dowry in nineteenth-century county Wexford.[24] 'Trussing beds' and 'truckle' or 'trundle beds' on wheels, are listed in Irish inventories from the 1500s onwards, and in south county Down there was 'a Trundle bed in [the] boys room, pushed under [the] double bed in daytime', in the early twentieth century.[25] Traditionally these truckles were for servants: they had wheels and were designed to be pushed beneath a larger bed during the day. Although none survive, they would probably have had a simple low wooden frame, with *súgán* or bog fir ropes slung through a series of holes to support the bedding, called 'the bed'.

Most homes were rarely large enough to contain two bedsteads, so there would be a bedstead for the parents and the children would sleep together on the floor. A Galway labourer managed ingeniously to make a raised bed with no tools; 'Two holes in the wall . . . answer instead of the two head bed-posts . . . two forked sticks driven into the floor answer for the end bed-posts; resting on these are two stretchers or long sticks, and across these stretchers are laid wattles upon which the straw is spread.'[26]

While the 'thorough bed', directly before the fire, was the warmest place to sleep, those who could afford more permanent wooden bedsteads tended to place them on one side of the hearth, where it was still warm but out of the way of the many kitchen activities. Usually it would be set up against the rear or back wall in the corner. A bed raised up from the damp earth floor was highly desirable for a number of reasons. Not only was it drier, but it also helped avoid the inevitable low-level draughts inherent in any house with a constantly burning floor-level fire.

242. Padraig O'Docherty and his fireside bed, at Portacloy, county Mayo in 1957. The arrangement of the form alongside the low four-poster, with its low valance and draught-excluding drapes, is typical. Photo courtesy of the N.M.I.

In order to keep the useful working space before the fire unobstructed while simultaneously creating a draught free sleeping place, an architectural annex of some antiquity known as the 'bed outshot' evolved. This semi-enclosed area accommodated the bed within the rear wall of the house, whilst setting it back away from the hearth. The use of masonry in the construction of such outshots, with built-in ledges on the inside, meant that a raised bed frame could the constructed using the minimum of timber (fig. 241). Outshots with beds intact are now rare outside museums.

The main areas in which bed outshots occurred are in the north and west of Ireland: counties Donegal, Derry, Tyrone,[27] Mayo and Sligo have all been shown to have had examples of outshots, as have parts of counties Leitrim, Fermanagh, Galway, Roscommon, Antrim and Armagh.[28]

Names for the outshot vary from one region to the next. In highland areas of counties Derry and Fermanagh it was called the *cúilteach*, whereas other regions knew it as the *cailleach*. Anglicised versions of

241. A wood engraving taken from an original by R.C. Woodville Jnr. (1856–1927), who was known for his accurate and highly finished art work. It shows *A Fisherman's Cabin in Connemara*, with a stone-framed fireside wall-bed with its own window, which may be in an outshot. The simple furniture includes a hanging dresser, a carpenters' chair and an unhooded cradle. From *The Illustrated London News* (1880).

these Irish terms include 'cooltyee' and 'haggard', while in county Tyrone some referred to the outshot as the 'cooskyee' and in Mayo as *An cailleach* or the 'hag bed'. *'Póca'* or in English *'pocket'* or 'bed pocket' was an apt term used in north-west county Mayo, or 'pouch' in county Sligo.[29] The eldest members of the household were traditionally allocated this bed. Amongst the centre of activity and close to the warmth of the hearth, which was the focal point of the home (fig. 242). The names given to this type of projecting 'wall-bed' reflect its associations; the position in the rear corner of the kitchen and its use by elder family members. Hence the uncomplimentary 'hag' bed, and the various terms such as *cailleach* – 'old woman', and *cúilteach* – 'back-house'. References to such architectural projections have been traced back to the ninth century, although the earliest examples may have been kitchen storerooms rather than beds.[30]

The size of the alcove varied, from beds which were recessed only very slightly into the corner wall with no external extension visible, to larger projections clearly visible at the rear of the house, with a special projecting area of roof above (fig. 5). The length of the alcove was typically sufficient for the length of the bed and no longer. Some of the examples in the south were only 3 feet 7 to 4 feet 1 inch wide, big enough for a double bed. When the outshot bed encroached upon the kitchen space, the foot end was sometimes enclosed by wooden boards, which were (like the in-

243. A kitchen fireside wall-bed, probably in an architectural outshot. The foot end is boarded and wall papered and the curtains could be drawn across to hide the bed during the day. Note the customary position of the form and the hearth 'keeping hole'. From Teebane East, Glenhull, Omagh, county Tyrone. Photo courtesy of the N.M.I.

245. The wall-bed or fireside outshot bed, draped with patterned curtains for privacy and to exclude draughts. The foot of the bed appears to be enclosed by a masonry, rather than a timber wall, which has been papered from four feet upwards. Probably county Tyrone, c.1940s.

244. Canopy bed shaped to fit beneath the thatch, in the loft bedroom in which it was originally built during the late nineteenth century. Made of pine and lined with wallpaper, it is unusual for its lack of paint. From a thatched house in south-eastern county Wexford.

sides of the beds) then covered in wallpaper (figs. 243, 245). This arrangement retained the basic principle of only one long side being open beside the fire. In one area of acute timber shortage, outshots were built with a stone rather than timber internal wall at the foot of the bed (rising to nearly the same height as the rest of the walls in the house, fig. 241).[31] The remarkable height of this and several other examples of kitchen beds was perhaps to help keep out any animals which might be found in a byre dwelling. This suggestion is reinforced by the fact that the pig in the county Mayo illustration is asleep on a layer of straw beneath the bed, which must also have provided additional warmth (fig. 241). In the examples from counties Donegal and Tyrone there were special ledges and slots

in the masonry upon which a timber bed frame could be laid.

In common with some other types of Irish bed, the outshot bed was often draped with curtains, giving a measure of privacy and usually kept drawn closed during the day, hiding the bed from the kitchen (figs. 243, 245). Early examples were probably screened by straw mats, later replaced by locally woven cloth curtains. In the north-west some outshot beds were hidden from view by wooden doors, which would have been another good way to exclude the animals in byre dwellings and fitted into the Irish tradition of box beds (fig. 264). Outshot beds with doors were described in 1913 by George Birmingham (in his book *Irishmen All*), as being common in the 'old fashioned' farmers' homes:

There are doors, like the doors of cupboards, by which the bed can be cut off from the room, and these are often closed when there is someone in the bed. Nothing could be more abhorrent to modern ideas of sanitary sleeping-places than these beds. Fresh air is an impossibility . . . For the window of the room [as he called the outshot] is very small, about a foot square, and it cannot be opened.

As with other types of enclosed beds, the fact that they lacked proper ventilation must have contributed to their demise in the first half of the twentieth century.

There are many references to beds in the corner of kitchens; some of these undoubtedly would have been outshots especially in the regions already mentioned where they have been found to exist. A wall-bed was one inset into the thickness of a wall, without neccessarily projecting visibly at the rear of the house.

246. Paired and curtained beds, lined up foot to foot along the rear wall of 'the room'. Their nineteenth-century painted pine framework originally had horizontal wooden roofs or testers. The beds in this example are entirely separate from the enclosing frame. From the Inishowen Peninsula, county Donegal.

247. The Inishowen paired beds with the upper valance folded back to show the pine cornice and frame, which has been grained to imitate oak. The angled cornice and facia board echoes those found around the tops of dressers and presses.

Bed outshots which were equipped with a small window giving a view from the rear of the house, must have made life more interesting for bedridden occupants, who could make use of the daylight for reading or sewing (figs. 3, 241). Others were furnished inside with framed prints, holy pictures, small sets of wall mounted shelves, wall recesses or sometimes a tiny container for holy water.

Other areas where bed outshots have been documented include the Orkney and Faroe Islands with their 'half-neuk' wall-beds, and the sleeping niches of the Hebridean black houses. In the Gower area of Wales, bed outshuts [sic] were positioned near the hall hearth and had cupboard

doors. Examples of outshots have also been noted in other parts of western Europe.[32]

The equivalent of the old fireside bed can now be seen as the settle bed, or in the south-east the open frame settle, made long enough to sleep on. These settles often still occupy a similar fireside position when elsewhere other kitchen beds have been removed.

BEDROOMS

As housing conditions improved, particularly after the famine, an increasing number of people began to divide up or build additional bedrooms on to their homes. Accordingly during the twentieth century the instances of beds beside the hearth became less common.

Large farmhouses would have had provision for bedrooms, leading directly off the kitchen, behind the gable ends or on an upper floor. The parlour or 'the room', which in rural Ireland was an early nineteenth-century innovation, was often partitioned off at the lower end of the kitchen furthest from the fire. This was a formal room provided for the entertainment of important guests and therefore seldom used; it frequently doubled as a bedroom (figs. 246–7).

Lofts over the fire or over the lower end of the kitchen provided a warm place to sleep.[33] Sometimes this loft was enclosed and access was made possible via a ladder (fig. 155). These lofts were sometimes so close to the apex of the roof that little light penetrated, especially when there were two or three bedrooms in a row; the centre one would have no gable window. In a county Wexford farmhouse in the nineteenth century, we learn that 'on sharp wintry nights it is a very cosy room to sleep in, the warmth penetrating from . . . the wide chimney and being prevented from passing into the outer cold air by the thickly scrawed and thatched roof'.[34]

Farm labourers were often provided with beds in a stable loft when there was not enough space in the house, with animals as their only source of heat.[35] Where enclosed wooden beds were found in upstairs rooms they were nearly always made *in situ*, because of the problems associated with

155

manoeuvring such a large object up steep stairs. A rare surviving canopy bed was found during fieldstudies in county Wexford. It could only have been made in the bedroom where it stood as the stairway and the bedroom door were both far to small to have allowed it through (see fig. 244).

BED CORDS AND BEDDING

An inventory drawn up in 1756, upon the death of Richard Ryan of Nenagh, Tipperary, includes some interesting details about bedding. His bed consisted of '1 Bedstead, 1 Feather Bedd and bolster, 1 blew Quilt, 1 Blankett and 1 Bedd corde'.[36]

The base of these wooden framed beds was made by threading various types of rope through a series of holes drilled in the frame for that purpose. Such bed 'cordes' are often mentioned in Irish inventories since the seventeenth century.[37] 'Corded Bed Steads' were used during the eighteenth century for servants in castles and big houses, as well as by the poor to raise their bedding off the floor.[38] A county Antrim resident provided the following account as recently as 1964 of 'a wooden bed with a chaff or feather bed-tick stretched on a [bog] fir rope frame'. The ropes were threaded through holes in the sides and ends of the bed.[39] The widespread use of bog timber has been well documented and was not only used to make the bed frames but also cleverly made into durable and elastic ropes for bed cords (fig. 66).[40] MacEvoy wrote at the close of the eighteenth century that poor people living around bogs made a trade from the twisting of bog fir for bed cords; about 20 yards of such rope was needed per bed. They used the roots and filaments for rope making, and the resulting cords were said to last much longer than hemp ropes.[41] In 1837 these bog fir bed ropes were made in Castle Wellin, and sold at Lisburn market in county Antrim for 4 *d*. per set, but prices varied in different areas.[42] For the uninitiated, it is hard to imagine how rope could be made from semi-fossilised wood, but one of the Ordnance Survey Memoir collectors was sufficiently curious to write an account of the extraordinary technique in 1834;

The fir timber when raised out of the bog is cut across at fixed lengths varying from 3–6 ft. and when partly dry it is beetled [beaten] with a sort of wood sledge all round the piece and when brought to a pliable state the outside part is drawn of the length in string about the thickness of a straw, and when outside ring is off the piece of timber is again beetled all round till made pliable and so continues ... place the piece of timber brought into the aforesaid pliable state beside him standing on one end and place a common four footed stool [upsidedown] across his thighs and he then fastens the end of a few plats of fir to one foot of the stool by a string and then draws of the wood ... with his teeth and feeds and forms and twists the rope with his hands [fig. 66] and as he advances the length of the rope he turns the stool round foot after foot and so continues leaving the rope outside the stool feet, till the rope is finished.[43]

'Deal bedsteads' could then be bought at market for 7*s*. to 9*s*. per set, and having threaded up a bed cord, the buyer had a choice of either new or secondhand bedding. Lisburn market offered 'Straw mattresses [at] 5*s*. to 6*s*. each'. These came from Lurgan, about 13 miles away and judging by their high price, must have been plaited (figs. 8, 248).[44]

On top of the cords and straw mattress (or palliasse) was either a tick or bed (another type of mattress) filled with loose straw (often misleadingly called chaff), flock, goose feathers or (in county Wicklow) white bog cotton (in Irish *ceannbhán*) according to ones means.[45] Ticks filled with chaff were refilled every thrashing [threshing] or in springtime when the straw had dried.[46] In county Kerry people re-used the hessian

248. Plaited straw mattress made to fold in half, from the upstairs bedroom of a two-storey farmhouse at Breen, Armoy, county Antrim. It was used in one of two end to end, or paired beds, beneath a feather mattress. Photo courtesy of the U.F.T.M., who acquired it in 1985.

sacks, which Indian meal or bran came in, filling them with newly thrashed straw and placing them beneath their goose feather ticks. Many beds had high boarded sides to accommodate this considerable depth of bedding. Straw was sometimes used to stuff the bolster, and duck feathers were used for the pillows. Flour bags laid out into the sun to bleach, together with scraps of material from worn out clothes and blankets were carefully stitched into patchwork quilts.

Feather merchants usually set up their businesses in towns, supplying feather and down from both domestic and wild birds, for pillows, mattresses and upholstery.[47] The task of separating the feathers and down from the quills was tedious and the '4 feather tubs' listed amongst objects in a castle kitchen in 1760 are a legacy of that activity.[48] Farmers who kept geese generally sold the feathers after supplying themselves with their own feather ticks.[49] Goose feather mattresses were very warm and a comparative luxury, and like beds and bedsteads, were often handed down in wills.[50] When brass and iron beds became popular in the second half of the nineteenth century, straw mattresses were still used under the feather ones in order to protect them from the rust of the iron beds.[51] In county Kerry and county Clare the marriage dowry was known as the 'fortune', and a bride customarily took her own bed and bedclothes with her to her new home.[52]

PLAITED STRAW MATTRESSES

There are still a few surviving examples of straw plaited mattresses or palliasses in museums (fig. 248).[53] Plaiting of straw was a technique used for a variety of other objects such as straw mats, hens' nests, armchairs and low seats called bosses. Lack of timber encouraged the use of alternative materials and straw was even woven to make bed coverlets and curtains.[54] The makers of plaited mattresses were probably responsible for making these other related things, and oat straw with its golden colour, and rush were favoured materials (fig. 248). Plaited straw mattresses, sometimes designed to be folded in half, would have been made and sold locally. Three or four

inches thick and of considerable weight, they could also be rolled up for storage, not unlike a present day futon, and stored inside a closed settle bed (fig. 122). The National Museum of Ireland recorded the survival of this ancient craft during the 1960s, so there are photographs of such mattresses being made (fig. 8). There are many references to their widespread use. In county Wexford they were regarded as superior even to feather beds, and they would undoubtedly have been less expensive.[55]

LOW BEDSTEADS

The survival of lathe-turned low four-poster beds of regular patterns with simply shaped wooden headboards, in areas such as county Cork (where otherwise very little lathe turned vernacular furniture remains), suggests that they may have been the products of centres of small-scale mass-production. These beds are often discarded amongst the furniture left in houses which have been derelict for a long time. Since the surviving examples never display any makers' marks it is hard to ascertain their origins, but they followed a wide variety of simple patterns. These wooden beds must have been inexpensive and widely available, judging by their relatively high rate of survival (fig. 249).

249. Lathe-turned low four-poster bed, c.1875–1900, with worn traces of its original reddish-brown paint, from west county Cork.

Bedsteads with four squared corner posts about 4 or 5 feet in height, with simply slatted ends, were probably equally common and would have been made by local carpenters or by the householders themselves (fig. 242).[56] In the wake of the medical profession's advice against enclosed beds, tall four-posters and so called 'canopy' beds were sometimes cut down to make low four-posted bedsteads.[57] Surviving examples should therefore be examined carefully for signs of conversion.

However, the number of surviving brass beds, which were mass-produced and sold in market towns towards the end of the nineteenth century, now far outweighs the number of wooden beds (fig. 280). The doctors' advice had a strong bearing on the design of beds. They advised against poorly ventilated enclosed beds on the grounds of health and brass beds were encouraged because they were less likely to harbour vermin than their wooden counterparts. Another innovation in bedding along with the 'dismantlable' brass bed and its wire springs, was the horsehair mattress, which replaced the more fragile straw ones (fig. 248).[58] Brass beds have now become a common sight in the Irish countryside, taking their turn to act as gates and to prevent farm stock from straying.

ENCLOSED BEDS

Two sets of questionnaires sent out to approximately 220 people during the 1950s and 1960s provide valuable information about the traditional beds used in rural Irish homes, up until the mid-twentieth century. These questionnaires Sent out by the Department of Irish Folklore University College. Dublin and the Ulster Folk and Transport Museum, County Down have been combined with a variety of earlier evidence, from documents and illustrations, to examine the range of different enclosed beds which were used, as surviving examples outside museums have now become extremely rare.[59] Although there are common themes linking the different bed types in particular areas, lack of consistent terminology has resulted in contradiction between historians. The fact that the two

questionnaires dealing with the subject of beds also used contrasting terminology, may have contributed to such confusion.

Although in the past attempts have been made to categorise types of bed, none has combined material from the two main questionnaires with fieldwork and documentary research throughout Ireland. This has shown that enclosed beds were usually built-in, rather than freestanding, and were curtained, or screened by wooden doors. A range of these enclosed bed types have been identified, and for convenience are grouped loosely under various headings according to their structure.

TESTER BEDS

Now widely known as the 'four-poster', this consisted of a raised bedstock, with four posts supporting a wooden (or occasionally cloth) canopy known as a tester.[60] Accordingly it was known as the tester bed, but also (because of its height) as the 'high standing bed',[61] the 'standing bed' or simply the 'post bed'. Testers and standing beds begin to occur regularly in Irish inventories from the 1500s, with their 'hangings' or 'curtains' to enclose the raised bedstock and exclude draughts.[62] The finest fashionable examples must have looked grand and imposing as they were evidently hung with fine textiles, which matched the window curtains and other upholstered furniture. One from county Armagh was described simply as 'Slabb and sticks, one Standing bed and bedstead', in 1712.[63] Another mid-eighteenth century example from county Offaly had a 'deal teaster' while a third had a 'Suite of hangings for a beed [and] one Bed Teaster'.[64] It was not only the gentry and the so-called strong farmers who slept in such 'standing beds'.

As these grand prototypes evolved into lighter, more elaborate examples of fine upholstery, the vernacular versions focussed increasingly on the functional priorities of shelter. Houses heated by only a single fire were often cold and draughty, and sometimes had leaking roofs. The tester beds were used predominantly in Ulster, as well as in counties Louth, Cavan, Mayo and

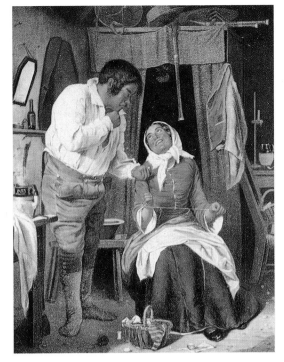

house, dates from the early 1900s and provides a rare glimpse of a primitive 'four poster'.

> First, a neat feathe-bed, and a four
>   posted 'stead,
> A bolster, quilt, blanket, and sheet
>   too,
> A straw curtain one side, to the
>   rafters well ty'd,
> And a neat deal-board chest at our
>   feet too,[66]

Other descriptions of beds enclosed by curtains or mats of straw show that they were quite common among those who could not afford cloth curtains. Carleton wrote in the 1830s of a dwelling of the 'humblest description': 'To the right of the fire was a bed, the four posts of which ran up to the low roof; it was curtained with straw mats, with the exception of an opening about a foot and a half wide on the side next the fire, through which those who slept in it passed.'[67] The Government Poor Inquiry of the 1830s, stated that in county Meath, 'some of them . . . have rude bedsteads made of bogwood, which are commonly set to one side of the fireplace; mats made of straw are fastened to the posts by way of curtains to shelter them'.[68]

A description of furniture in the small houses on the Great Blasket Island off Kerry at the end of the nineteenth century, mentions how potatoes were stored beneath some of the beds, and

> The rest of the trumpery in the house was stuffed under the post-bed for the night. This bed was more than a couple of feet from the ground, and it was often made of wood or iron. Some of the houses had no division to make a room, but there was a post-bed in one corner and a bed on the floor in the other.[69]

Ó Criomhthain explains how in a house with a big family one would find a post bed beside the fire (which may have looked like fig. 251) where the 'old people' used to spend the night, smoking a pipe which was lit from the fire with a wisp of straw.

Galway.[65] On the other hand, some versions of these 'post beds' dispensed with the addition of a flat tester, perhaps where there was a shortage of timber, or if the roof was considered sound, yet they retained the posts from which curtains were hung (fig. 251).

A verse from a song which wryly describes the meagre contents of a poor man's

252. An upholstered canopy bed belonging to a feather-dealer at Thomas Street, in the Liberties of Dublin, c.1798. Such beds were copied, but with wooden roofs for use in rural houses (fig. 253). Drawn by H. MacManus in Mr and Mrs S.C. Hall's in *Ireland, Its Scenery, Character etc.* (1842).

253. Detail of a watercolour considered to be an interior at Listowel, county Kerry (see fig. 282). It shows part of a draped canopy bed with an arched wooden roof, upon which rest baskets. It is in 'The room' of a public house. Private collection.

CANOPY OR CAMP BEDS

The second of the three main types is the 'canopy' or 'camp' bed, which in its vernacular form is apparently unique to Ireland. It also had roots in the seventeenth century tradition of enclosed beds draped with curtains (figs. 251, 259), but used more timber in its construction. Usually, it had wooden sides and back as well as a top 'canopy' made of wood. The 'front' (actually a long side) was hung with straw mats or cloth curtains according to the householder's purse. This distinctive bed owes its name to the covering canopy: a tester which arched down to shelter the sides, as well as the top. Shapes of these canopy beds varied from the simplest rectangular fronted types (fig. 244), to arched topped ones (figs. 252–3, 256) or hipped-roof ones (figs. 255, 261).

Although their early prototypes were elaborately hung upholstered beds, which by the eighteenth and nineteenth centuries tended to incorporate an increasingly minimal timber superstructure, the vernacular canopy bed was unusually lavish with timber. Initially this roof-like canopy must have been a functional development, to keep the sleepers warm and dry, but as they became popular, some makers revelled in creating decorative and comparatively ornate versions. A nicely carved canopy bed with an arched hood from county Waterford (fig. 256), incorporates decorative motifs which are reminiscent of the bed's lavish origins (fig. 252).

254. Detail of one of the rare woven rush mattresses which were made for the paired canopy beds, from county Roscommon (fig. 257). A rare and possibly unique survival of an ancient craft. Courtesy of Victor Mitchell.

160

255. (*top, left*) An early
nineteenth-century 'canopy
bed' with a hipped roof,
made of painted pine.
Broomfield, Castleblaney,
county Monaghan.
Courtesy of Victor Mitchell.

256. (*top, right*) Pine
canopy or camp bed from
county Waterford, with
fluted decoration inspired
by classical pilasters, on the
front posts. The cleverly
carved front arch, imitative
of crimped ribbon, is
reminiscent of the high
fashion upholstered beds
which originally inspired
these uniquely Irish wooden
counterparts. The bed was
dismantled and reassembled
for display in The Irish
Agricultural Museum,
where it can now be seen.

257. (*right*) Late nineteenth-
century paired 'canopy
beds' from county
Roscommon. Originally
these two double beds were
built in and the front facia
board, with its oak graining,
would have reached the
ceiling. It is decorated with
diamonds, a central heart,
and a cornice with
classically inspired dentil
moulding. The curtains
which screened the fronts
are lost, but the original
woven rush mattresses are
still intact.
Courtesy of Victor Mitchell.

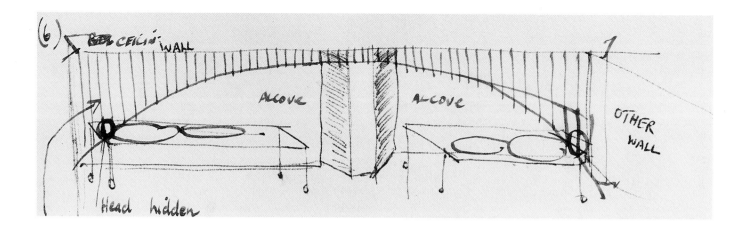

258. Paired beds in alcoves, as drawn in a response to a questionnaire sent out by the D.I.F., in 1957. The arched framework, was made of 'slats of wood usually wallpapered . . . [the] wooden canopy hid the head of the sleeper'. The canopy reached up as far as the ceiling of the room. From Follom Big, Roslea, county Fermanagh.

261. (*facing page, below*) Paired canopy or camp beds in a bedroom at Limerick Junction, county Tipperary. The right-hand one with its hipped roof, is decorated inside with stencilling. Both fronts have interlaced decoration, and scratch-stock lines. The left-hand bed is lined with wallpaper. Both shapes were particularly popular throughout southern Ireland during the nineteenth century. Both beds, painted white, are 48 in. wide, 74 in. long and 72 in. high, and the occupants slept foot to foot. Photo *c.*1950, courtesy of The N.M.I.

Although there is no wooden prototype to these arched top or hipped-roof beds amongst finer Irish furniture, their silhouettes echo some of the shapes used for fashionable beds hung with drapes since the seventeenth century, as do the names applied to them. However, their purpose was primarily as a form of shelter, as a resident of county Kilkenny put it 'the canopy was put over the bed to keep out the dust, rain drops and particles from falling from the roofs'.[70] A questionnaire respondent from county Longford, also mentioned the dust from thatch as being a particular reason for the 'standing beds' with roofs; several others remembered seeing such beds specifically in thatched houses.[71]

A rare example of such a canopy bed still *in situ*, is in the loft bedroom of a thatched house in county Wexford (fig. 244). It demonstrates the suitability of such a bed to its environment, as the underside of the thatch is unlined (fig. 233). Such a close relationship between architecture and the furniture it houses is a recurrent feature; the dressers (and some settles) with their renewable 'sledge feet' are comparable. The Wexford bed is simple and undecorated (apart from its 'drapes') and was left unused after the wake of the owner's mother, at which point she was laid out in it.

The curtains and drapery – which the householders probably added themselves – formed further embellishment and brought them closer to their fashionable origins (fig. 253). Evidence for prototypes with similar shapes and names occurs amongst the inventories of 'big houses'. '4 Cannopy bedsteads' with 'suites of curtains and hangings' were listed as early as the 1680s in the nursery of Burton Hall, county Cork.[72] In 1735 we find reference to a 'Camp Bed Stead' amongst the furniture from a castle in county Meath.[73] By the 1820s 'Eliptic roof bedsteads' in mahogany and 'Waggon Rooffed' bedsteads with curtains were a popular part of the gentry's furnishings.[74]

The canopy bed was well known in southern and western Leinster, parts of Connaught and throughout Munster (where a common alternative name was the camp bed). In southern Leinster, terms such as 'canopy bed', 'roofed bed' and even 'the crib' were applied to these enclosed beds (figs. 244, 252–7).[75] Other terms were popular in Munster, where they remembered them as 'Canopied or Canopy beds' or as Camp beds, which in west Cork was how the British Government Poor Report described them in the 1830s.[76] A questionnaire respondent from Clare recalled two distinct types; one with a flat roof called a 'Castor bed' and another with a 'pointed roof' known as a 'Cant bed' (with oblique sides or corners), but unless a hipped-roof bed was meant, examples of the latter do not appear to have survived.[77] The fact that canopy beds with hipped roofs were well known in county Clare is probably why this particular shape has been tagged a 'Clare bed' by antique dealers. There is however, no known documentary precedent for this term and hipped-roof canopy beds were often found elsewhere (fig. 255). Canopy beds with hipped roofs were known in Irishtown, county Mayo and in Galway as 'Tent beds', a term which was also used to describe popular draped Victorian beds.[78]

162

The occurrence of different shapes of canopy beds within a county, and indeed within a room, is established both from the documentary sources and from old photographs (fig. 261).

'COVERED CAR BEDS'

A variant of the canopy bed called the 'covered car bed' should not be confused with the fashionable 'covered bed' of the late seventeenth century. It was so named because its draped canopy resembled those seen on popular horse-drawn vehicles. The term 'covered car bed' is now widely used to apply (somewhat indiscriminately) to a variety of enclosed beds and deserves explanation here to avoid further confusion.

The origin of the term 'covered car bed' lies in a distinctive form of public horse-drawn transport which plied its way through Waterford, Cork, Killarney, Limerick and various other Munster towns during the nineteenth century (fig. 260).[79] The 'covered car bed' or simply the 'car bed' was originally a curtained canopy bed. Long after the vehicles went out of use, the beds were still referred to in this way, particularly in counties Cork and Tipperary.[80] According to one account, the covered car actually had 'four uprights from the corners, with a roof on top and curtains all around', and from such a description alone it could equally well be a traditional canopy or tester bed.[81] The similarity lies predominantly in the waterproof oilcloth curtains, which made the vehicle popular for long journeys among tourists in the frequently rainy south. Mrs Hall considered it compromising, and in 1840 she wrote that it was 'a comparatively recent introduction, its sole recommendation being that it is weatherproof, but it effectually prevents a view of the country, except . . . by tying back the oil-skin curtains behind.' The Halls 'endeavoured to remedy the evil of confinement by stopping at every promising spot and either getting out or making the driver turn his vehicle around so that from the back we might command the prospect we desired'.[82] The covered car or 'jingle' was one of the two most popular horse-drawn cabs in Cork city and was still in use after the First World War: its slightly domed roof (not apparent in

259. *The Doctor's Visit, 'Out of Danger'*, by Erskine Nicol R.S.A. (1825–1904). In the background the patient is confined to a bed which is screened by an upper valance and curtains, hung from the ceiling rather than from a tester or canopy. The type of turf spade on the left indicates that the house is in county Galway, where Nicol is known to have painted. Courtesy © 1969 Sotheby's, Inc.

260. A 'Covered Car': a weatherproof public jaunting car that had 'four uprights from the corners, with a roof on top and curtains all around.' Its name became locally synonymous with the common curtained beds, hence 'Covered Car Bed'. From H.W. French's *Our Boys in Ireland* (1891).

262. *A Card Party* by Erskine Nicol, R.S.A. (1825–1904). A stool is being used as a card table, one player on the right sits on a coiled and bound straw boss, another on a low *súgán* chair. In the foreground is a potato skib and a tiny 'creepie stool'. In the background may be a pair of box beds, one with door ajar. Nicol probably used artist's licence with the room layout, but the furniture is meticulously recorded. From Mrs S.C. Hall's *Tales of Irish Life and Character* (1909). Photo courtesy of the N.L.I.

263. Jack B. Yeats's 'The Cuttle Fish', is a kitchen scene showing a fireside box bed in the background, with its wooden roof, sides and front. Its narrow entrance is screened by a curtain and pot lids are hung near the fire light. From J.B. Yeats's *Life in the West of Ireland*. Reproduced by kind permission of Anne Yeats.

the drawing: fig. 260) is distinctive amongst the Cork traffic photographed by the firm of Lawrence at the turn of this century.[83]

BOX BEDS

The third main type of enclosed bed is the box bed. Although it was well known in parts of Holland, Portugal, France, Scotland and Wales, in Ireland it was used predominantly in the north-east. Box beds appear to have been well known up until the first half of the twentieth century in Ulster, especially in county Antrim, indicating a transmission of design from the common box beds of neighbouring Scotland; there is also the possibility of influence from the Netherlands, where box type beds with draped fronts (and high valances) were common.[84]

The Irish box bed was totally enclosed on all sides except the front, which usually had a door or pair of doors. Square box-like enclosed beds with curtains hiding the front and a valance along the top, were also sometimes described as box beds. Like the tester and canopy beds, a warm atmosphere could quickly be created by the occupants' body heat. It has been suggested that box beds were a nineteenth-century innovation, and they are rarely specifically described or listed in inventories. However their wide distribution suggests a longer established tradition.[85]

Inevitably, adaptations and hybrid types of the three basic tester, canopy and box bed forms also occur. Box beds are known to have been made by enclosing the four posts of an old tester bed with timber sheeting.[86] J.B. Yeats illustrates a fireside box bed which has a curtain hanging across its narrow central opening, rather than doors (fig. 263); and a late nineteenth-century photograph from county Donegal shows what appears to be the front of a box bed which has been built into a recessed bed outshot (fig. 264).

All three types of enclosed beds provided a measure of privacy in those houses which otherwise had no separate bedrooms, and could be closed or curtained during the day to hide the bed. Box beds with wooden doors were especially suitable in 'byre dwellings' occupied both by people and their animals.[87] In the 1930s a county Tyrone gamekeeper had her Winchester rifle 'safely shut up in the box bed "to be out of people's view."' and she considered it 'the best corner in the house'.[88] The study of such

164

The Reverend Hall, in his tour of Ireland in the early nineteenth century, made a fascinating but perhaps not wholly exceptional find; 'In one house [in county Limerick] I observed a bed of extremely neat wickerwork, sufficient to contain two grown people, shaped like a cradle; the head jutting out as if it had been one.' The weaving of wicker beds may have been a local tradition, although no surviving examples have so far come to light. Woodworm are inordinately keen on devouring wickerwork, and like strawwork, it is inherently fragile and wears out quickly. He mentions that in Kerry as well as in Limerick he finds 'the common people extremely fond of wicker-work. Their doors with padlocks, windows, cradles, beds, chairs, etc. etc. are, in general, all of wicker-work.'[91]

264. Photograph by R. Welch of a farm interior at Teelin, Carrick, county Donegal, c.1900. Between the open based dresser and the cobbled hearth is a box bed, probably in an outshot, with its central narrow door, slightly ajar. On the right is a potato skib and there are batons attached to the joists for storage. The spongeware bowls on the dresser are lined up on their sides, or 'whammeled'. Photo courtesy of the Ulster Museum.

beds is made difficult by the way they were repeatedly altered, built on to or dismantled. Canopy beds were sometimes adapted from low bedsteads by the addition of roofs and sides. By the close of the nineteenth century however, doctors were widely disapproving of enclosed beds and many were adapted to make low four-posters, sometimes known as stump bedsteads.[89] The curtains have usually been lost by the time such rare beds reach the antique dealers yard, yet in their heyday the tester beds were often largely obscured by drapes.

A form of tester bed which again relates to fashionable eighteenth-century examples, is described as 'half roofed', having only half a canopy or tester which projected over the sleeper's head. No surviving genuine examples are known to have survived. The vernacular version of the 'half-tester' or 'angel' bed, as it was known in England in the early 1700s (and elsewhere in Europe a century earlier), was described by questionnaire respondents from counties Galway, Armagh and Monaghan.[90]

The words tester bed or standing bed, canopy bed and camp bed, have continued to be used well into the twentieth century to describe vernacular versions of their grand predecessors.

BUILT-IN BEDS

For reasons of material economy, beds were often built into the fabric of the dwelling, resulting in hybrid forms derivative of tester, canopy and box beds. Fireside beds created a comfortable, warm place to sit, with one's back to the bed (figs. 242, 251). Often there was a form placed there, or the bed itself became a fireside seat. The bed-rail which was away from the wall and closest to the fire was known as the 'stuck' in county Fermanagh, as the 'stock' in county Antrim, and south in county Wexford as the 'Natch'; the latter may have been a derivation of the Irish for the side-rail of a bed: cnaiste.[92] When there was a second room off the kitchen the beds were again placed along a wall, reducing the number of curtains needed (fig. 259). Often there were two beds placed along a rear wall, which could be entirely screened off and hidden from view by a line of curtain, usually with a length of valance along the top (figs. 246–7, 257–8). This pairing was a traditional arrangement and was done with many different designs of bed. In Donegal, as many as three beds were sometimes placed end to end along the rear wall, like the carriages of a train, in larger farmhouses.[93] When the second room doubled as a parlour, the beds could easily be made unobtrusive behind the curtains (fig. 246).

Such paired beds were particularly common throughout Ulster during the nineteenth century. They were also known in counties Roscommon, Clare and Tipperary. An example recently discovered in a two-roomed thatched house in the Inishowen peninsula of Donegal had a built-in wooden framework behind the curtains, with a projecting cornice like that of a dresser running along the top of the front edge (fig. 247). The framework was meticulously grained to look like oak and housed a pair of relatively modern beds with low head- and foot-boards. Originally it also had a flat wooden tester built in above both beds but typically the local doctor had advised its removal to improve ventilation. Fortunately they only removed the roof and not the rest of the structure.

An example of paired canopy beds from county Roscommon was probably made towards the close of the nineteenth century and used a great deal more timber than the Donegal pair (fig. 257). Extracted from the house where they were originally built-in, their arched roofs are conjoined with a facia board that would have reached up to the ceiling across the rear wall of a bedroom or parlour. Accordingly only this front has been grained in imitation of oak, with diamonds and a large central heart decorating the two entrances. Inside they have been repeatedly lined with wallpaper (a widespread tradition), which was torn off when the beds were dismantled and reassembled.[94] Their slatted pine bases support a pair of fragile woven rush mattresses: rare and possibly unique survivals of an ancient craft (fig. 254). Although the curtains have been lost, lines of pinholes indicate that they were once attached around the front of the two arches.

Another rare survival of a curtained fireside bed, was discovered in Fulcarragh in north county Donegal. This one was so thoroughly well disguised that upon entering the kitchen the uninitiated would not have realised that there was a bed in the fireside corner at all. It defies simple categorisation. The foot end was made from tongued and grooved boards attached to a framework of four upright posts, 3 by 3

inches thick and decorated by corner chamfering. It was made in the 1920s by John McFadden (1905–85) and painted blue, matching the rest of the furniture in the room. This type of bed was similar in appearance and position to the ones that used to be built into an architectural outshot, and arises from the same tradition.

Some built-in beds had a stone wall enclosing the foot end instead of a timber screen.[95] In county Donegal some houses without outshots had this *balla beag* (little wall or bed wall) at the foot of the bed, which was the same height as the tester (between 6 feet 6 inches and 7 feet) and presumably acted as a support for the tester as well as a draught excluder.[96] Such a stone structure also occurred during the 1840s in county Wicklow (where houses were not traditionally built with bed outshots), 'to protect the bed from the wind of the door'.[97] Another method of saving timber favoured in parts of counties Donegal and Antrim, was to incorporate the foot of the kitchen bed with the back of the dresser, which then faced the front door and acted as a screen.[98]

The need for enclosure of the bed area against draughts must have been acute in the poorest houses, some of which had doors made from woven sticks, twigs and straw ropes. However, in the same houses that had such flimsy doors and internal walls (in county Kerry), they had substantial enclosed 'Camp beds' to keep them warm at night.[99]

BED HANGINGS

The traditional use of curtains to drape the canopy and tester beds saved the expense of timber. They could either be woven by the householders from straw (as already described), or from cloth. In the absence of surviving examples of such coloured curtains, paintings and contemporary descriptions help recall them. Accounts vary locally but 'Heavy cloth' was used in a house in county Monaghan, and as elsewhere, the curtains were sometimes drawn closed at night.[100] A diarist and landlady from county Wicklow during the hungry 1840s wrote how 'Peggy Dodson has chintz [fashionable printed cotton/linen] curtains to her bed and many other little indications of well doing'.[101] Another type of printed cotton – cretonne – was used for drapes in county Antrim, along with 'flowered muslin', a product of local home industry.[102] An article from the 1880s describes the interior of a labourer's house:

> in a corner a great four-post bed with patchwork quilt, wherein scarlet predominates, and scarlet and white curtains; the whole, lacking the ordered neatness of an English peasant's cottage, but picturesque to a degree, with dancing flame and Rembrandtesque masses of shadow, and high lights on occasional spots of colour.[103]

J.B. Yeats and J.M. Synge travelled together to investigate the so-called 'Congested Districts' of county Mayo in 1905 for *The Manchester Guardian*. Yeats drew and Synge described the 'large wooden bed with a sort of red covering, and red curtains above it', which they observed beside the fire of a poor byre dwelling (fig. 251). Apart from this impressive bed, there appears to have been very little furniture in the room.[104] Another curtained bed, painted by Erskine Nicol (1825–1904), is draped in blue cloth, and evidently has a solid wooden tester, as a number of objects are resting on top of it. What appears to be a bunch of red flowers or fruit (arbutus?) is dangling from the inside of the tester, put there perhaps for their fragrance or as decoration (fig. 250). Another blue (or perhaps originally green[105]) draped bed with a wooden roof is in the background of a watercolour of a shebeen. The roof is arched, with a number of baskets resting on top (fig. 253). One observer of such interiors remarked how 'the native dyes . . . are rich and harmonious, seldom subdued, however, because the Irish are Oriental in their love of bright colours'.[106]

A few vernacular tester beds had top canopies made entirely of cloth rather than wood, as did many of the eighteenth-century ones after which they were modelled, although descriptions of such details are disappointingly rare.[107] People often used the wooden tester as a storage shelf.[108] In one east-county Monaghan home, hens were allowed to roost on top of the tester,[109] whereas in a county Antrim household the top of the tester was considered a safe place to keep a gun.[110] The roof of the canopy bed painted in fig. 253 is the resting place for a number of baskets and 'band boxes' – for hats were also stored conveniently on top of such beds.[111]

BED FOLKLORE

Beliefs and customs associated with beds abound. Some of them are to do with their position in relation to the house or the compass, others to the types of materials used. In some areas it was the custom to take a dying person from his bed and put him on a straw heap on the floor called a 'shake-down'.[112] As well as straw beds being burnt during cholera epidemics[113] the sensible practice of burning straw bedding occurred during the seventeenth century as described in the letters of John Dunton; 'For the death of anyone they carry out their bed, which is commonly of straw . . . and set it on fire before the door of the house, with such sharp and loud cries as pierced my head quite through, to give notice to the neighbourhood of the decease.'[114] This and the practice of whitewashing bedsteads with lime water later came to be associated with the prevention of disease.[115]

After a death in a Catholic household, the corpse was usually laid out, sometimes on a bed, for the wake. Whereas in Victorian England it was customary to use black hangings for mourning, at Irish wakes they only used black drapes when old people died. White drapes, perhaps with black bows, were considered appropriate for younger deaths.[116] We are told how a child at one such wake in county Wexford was 'greatly taken with the white curtains about the poor corpse, and the ribbons tying them about the bed-posts'. The bed was evidently a four-poster.[117]

Chapter 6

PRESS BEDS & OTHER DISGUISED BEDS

A folding bed which when closed up resembles a cupboard, the 'press bed', is so called because the word 'press' is still widely used rather than 'cupboard' in Ireland.[1] It is another example of a variety of cunningly concealed and disguised beds, which used to be a familiar part of the furnishings of traditional homes throughout Ireland. Confusingly, in a very few instances in county Tyrone and south county Antrim, the term 'press bed' was used to describe the settle bed, but for clarity 'press bed' will here only apply to the type of folding bed contained in a cupboard.[2] Indeed, in county Down, where they were often used, the press bed was also known as the cupboard bed.[3]

Usually kept inconspicuously in the parlour, the unwary would never suspect the presence of a double bed hidden away behind the doors of a cupboard or sideboard (figs. 265–70). They were convenient, unobtrusive and economical with space, requiring only a position where they could be opened up and folded down onto the floor. Ideally suited to the typically cramped conditions of the smallest (but nevertheless hospitable) Irish dwellings, it is disappointing that so few have survived, although about a dozen examples have been discovered dotted around Ireland. When examined alongside documentary evidence, it becomes clear that the press bed was once widespread throughout Ireland, but predominated in Ulster and Munster.[4] It may be that in some of the poorest nineteenth-century housing (mainly in the westerly counties of Mayo, Sligo and Galway) people were less likely to spend money on the elaborate concealment of beds in the seldom used luxury of a parlour. Since the settle bed is a rather more useful item of furniture when closed (doubling as a fireside seat for several people) the press bed may have lacked popularity by comparison.[5]

Press beds can be conveniently divided into two main types: high and low. The former contains a bed which folds once by means of hinges near the head end, to be concealed by a pair of cupboard doors. The mattress is stored upright alongside the bed frame inside the cupboard. Several surviving examples have an additional drawer or cupboard below, or occasionally above, the double doors (which is odd, as it is very hard to use a drawer above eye level). This provided storage space for any extra bedding, or even for clothes. All the examples surveyed had slatted wooden base boards.[6] The short legs which are fixed or fold out to support the foot end of the bed are often made of a durable hardwood such as oak, in contrast to the pine used for the rest of the bed, which was all painted apart from the bed frame.

An archetypal example of a high press bed was found in a small traditional house in county Cavan (fig. 268). The parlour off the kitchen was small and meant that the room had to be carefully rearranged for the bed to be unfolded. However, it was still recently being used to accommodate visiting relatives, and a foam rubber mattress was stored inside ready for such an occasion. The house had all sorts of traditional furniture still in use, and bastable bread was still cooked there over the fire (fig. 201). It is significant therefore that

168

265. Mid nineteenth-century pine press bed with a low drawer for storing bedclothes, painted red and then overpainted with brown. The curved cornice is damaged on the left-hand side, location unknown. Courtesy of the N.M.I.

266. High pine press bed, showing how the bed is tilted back for storage, and attached via a single steel rod across its base to acts as a pivot, instead of hinges. Its mechanism requires the press to be unusually deep (42 in.). Courtesy of the N.M.I.

267. High pine press bed, opened out for use as a substantial double bed. The bed is particularly high (21 in.) because of the drawer beneath it. The integral footboard has lathe turned corner posts and the bed frame is through morticed and nailed together. Location unknown. Courtesy of the N.M.I.

there was no settle bed, nor was one remembered: one space saving bed was evidently considered to be enough.

The second, low type of press bed, doubled by day as a sideboard or chiffonier (figs. 269, 270), and so was well disguised, as well as being useful in the parlour. Instead of the bed folding out onto the floor all in one piece, it was cleverly hinged to open out in three pieces. However, it took up slightly more floor space than a high press bed, with none of the extra storage space. Unless the top of it was made to hinge upwards, there was not enough head room to enable one to sit up in bed. The lower, chiffonier type appears to have been more popular in rural Ireland than the high variety. An English illustrated catalogue shows that factory produced press beds (known as 'dess' beds) were hidden behind a wide variety of elaborate disguises by the early twentieth century.[7] Press beds are known to have been used since the seventeenth century in wealthy English houses as well as in the homes of the Irish aristocracy.[8] The scarcity of English press beds is probably due to their popular conversion back into hanging wardrobes, by the removal of the hinged bed.[9] This may also explain

268. Painted pine high press bed in the parlour of a three-roomed house in county Cavan, near the border with counties Monaghan and Fermanagh. The cornice is decorated with dentil moulding and the mattress has been removed to show the wide backing boards. The bed has been repaired with packing cases and is relatively high when folded out because of the low drawer. Early nineteenth century.

269. Low pine press or chiffonier, containing a folding bed (fig. 270), which is held in place by pine turnbuckles. For use in a parlour, it has false drawers, and is painted black over red. Late nineteenth century, from Ballyluddy, county Limerick. The chiffonier is 46 in. wide, 22$\frac{1}{2}$ in. deep and 42$\frac{1}{2}$ to 70 in. high. Courtesy of the N.M.I.

270. Low pine press bed, which folds out in three sections to form a bed. The footrail is dovetailed onto the siderails for strength. Late nineteenth century, from Ballyluddy, Ballynaclough, Coonagh, county Limerick. The bed is 72 in. long and 42 in. wide. Courtesy of the N.M.I.

why so few survive in Ireland. Their economy with space meant that they were particularly suitable for English town houses, which was the same reason that made them a popular feature of rural Irish homes.[10]

Although many Irish inventories list beds and bedding in somewhat insubstantial terms, enough of them are described as press beds or bedsteads to warrant analysis. Seven such descriptions from between the 1680s and 1817 show that these beds were used in large Irish houses, and like settle beds they were frequently allocated to servants.[11] These inventory entries show that the press bed was a parlour piece even in some wealthy homes (as it certainly was in the majority of ordinary rural homes), although it is hard to imagine how the bed could have been hidden when it was 'glass-framed, resembling a book-case, and done in the neatest manner', as described in 1755.[12] Some of these inventories listed both settle beds and press beds, the former were most often in the kitchen, whereas the press beds were usually in bedrooms or parlours.

Their origins may lie in the more ancient type of bed that was recessed into a wall. Christopher Gilbert suggests that in England they were inspired by the un-enclosed 'turn-up bed-steads' (like a high press bed without its cupboard), but so far no surviving examples of these have been

found in Ireland.[13] The only description which probably refers to an unenclosed 'turn-up bed' comes from the Great Blasket Island. An islander recalls that during the late nineteenth century 'a family may keep a bed upright against the kitchen wall and tip it down when it is needed at night' with no mention of an enclosing press.[14] However, in the 1920s in county Cork, an old man 'who lived in a *Cruinnteach* (round house)' with a central hearth, had only one room which contained not only a dresser and a press bed, but also a settle bed.[15] These are the only descriptions of such folding beds being placed in the kitchen other than one from Ballymena, county Antrim, which folded 'into a cavity in [the] wall to appear as a wall press during the day'.[16]

A later account written in the 1930s from county Longford relates how the press bed was 'generally set up in a room [parlour] rather than in the kitchen'. It was 'about six feet high, three feet wide and a foot and a half deep . . . It was generally set into an alcove . . . so that the front of the press was level with the wall.'[17] Another description from 1888 states that: 'in some of the old houses I have seen a press-bed – press, *anglice* cupboard - which turned up on end into the wall, its two doors folding over it by day; in one such, a late sleeper of tender years was turned up by accident and found himself standing on his head.'[18] This was one of several accounts mentioning that the sleeper's head was usually placed towards the press.

J.C. Loudon, in his *Encyclopaedia of Cottage, Farm and Villa Architecture and Furniture* of 1833, describes press beds disparagingly: 'they are objectionable, as harbouring vermin, and being apt soon to get out of order when in daily use'. This is another possible explanation for their present rarity. 'They have however, one advantage, which is, that persons sleeping in them are generally obliged to get up betimes in the morning.' He illustrates one similar in concept to fig. 269. They 'are sometimes made to imitate chest of drawers, or a secretary, in front; in order, if possible, to prevent the real use of the article from being discovered: a proof that beds of this kind are not held in much repute; because they indicate a scarcity of bedrooms.'[19]

The fact that they were well disguised perhaps accounts for the comparatively few early descriptions of them. The efficiency of their camouflage is proven by the following account from county Wexford.

I remember a 'Press Bed' doing its work in 1921. A party of British military raided a house in search of wanted men. An officer and two privates went into the sitting room, in which there was one of these 'Press beds'. It certainly looked exactly like a press. The officer opened this press. When suddenly the bed crashed down upon him. He didn't like it.[20]

OTHER DISGUISED BEDS

Without the evidence of surviving examples, it is difficult to draw conclusions as to the nature of the various 'table beds' and 'desk beds' which occur in eighteenth-century inventories. Six 'table beds' are listed in two grand inventories from counties Meath and Westmeath in the early eighteenth century.[21] The inventory of Killeen Castle in county Meath contains three such references. The first was '1 Oake table bed with 3 drawers, 1 feather bed and boulster with a pair of blanketts & Rugg'; nothing else was listed in this 'Yellow Room'.[22] Elsewhere it is listed simply as the 'table bed' (with bedding). Perhaps the table bed allowed space for storage of bedding during the day, with the table top hinged up and out of the way when it was required for sleeping. Such a design probably functioned like the settle table, with a bed where the seat would normally be (fig. 136). In both inventories it is listed in rooms of lesser importance: 'the Lobby' or 'ye Dressing Roome' or the 'House keeper's Roome' or as a subsidiary bed in a grander room, suggesting its use by servants.

'Desk beds' also feature in Irish inventories, and were presumably similar to the low press beds, but with a bed folded up and disguised behind the dummy drawers of a desk. Like the table beds, no vernacular examples of these seem to have survived, but they may have resembled one of the designs from the Gillow Estimate Sketch Books of 1788.[23]

171

CRADLES

There are many similarities between the common canopy bed and its tiny relative, the cradle. Both objects are shaped by their essential function – to provide a warm dry sleeping space raised up from the floor – and are covered, particularly over the sleeper's head, with some sort of canopy (fig. 271).

Like the beds, cradles nearly always had such a canopy, except for the very poorest, most basic examples, often from the west of Ireland. These can be seen in early photographs and illustrations: with or without rockers, they are usually in the form of low rectangular boxes (figs. 241, 272-3). However, the British Government Poor Inquiry of 1836, shows that the households of the poorest classes of labourers and cottiers had no cradles at all, improvising with alternative babies' beds.[1] Recent research into cradles made in Ulster shows it was customary for new born babies to sleep at their mothers' sides, a cradle being used during the day.[2]

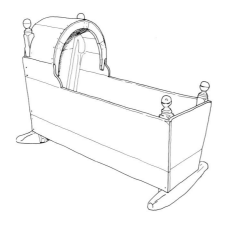

271. Pine cradle with turned corner posts and an arched hood, the main body of the cradle is nailed together, painted in yellow ochre and dates from the last quarter of the nineteenth century. Courtesy of Carndonagh Museum, Inishowen, county Donegal.

The following extract describes all the furniture of 'Thady O'Brady', whose basic possessions indicate that he must have been a poor cottier, in the early 1800s;

> But we must think of young Thady, and
>   have flannel ready
> With pineady to keep him a feeding,
> A cradle see saw, and a red lobster's
>   claw,
> To give to the brat when he's teething.[3]

Cradles were most frequently made out of pine and had a pair of rockers. In working households, such as amongst a family of weavers, the cradle was an important, functional object, allowing the mother to do other things while minding the baby. Mrs Hall describes such a scene in a small weaver's 'cottage' in county Down where 'the man was working at his loom; his wife was spinning, rocking the cradle with one foot, and turning her wheel with the other; while the elder girl was carding flax.'[4]

Comparatively few surviving wooden cradles have panelled sides (fig. 274). They are usually simply constructed from nailed boards, tapering inwards towards the base. The boarded sides rise at the head end providing a small canopy, which in thatched houses protected the childs' face from drips or dust which might fall from above, as well as providing shade (figs. 274-7, 283-4). The loosely fitted base-boards sometimes have holes for ventilation and are removable. The most elaborate examples have curved hoods (figs. 271, 274-5) (like some canopy beds) or pierced decoration around the hood area (fig. 275) with a turned

Far right:
274. (*top*) Pitch pine cradle made in 1889 by Richard Harvey, of Tandergee, east county Armagh, for his nephew Robert Harvey. He has taken trouble to decorate the hood, footboard and the ends of the rockers with curves, and it is finished with dark varnish. The framework has chamfered edges around the panels, and the inner base board is of recycled, grained pine. Length 37 in., width 19 in., height 28 in. Courtesy of Armagh County Museum (66.60).

275. (*middle*) Pine cradle painted matt mulberry red, with turned corner posts and a simply pierced facia board around the inside of the hipped hood. Mid nineteenth century, from county Clare.

276. (*below*) Early nineteenth-century boarded pine cradle with traces of blue and more recent red paint. Its corner posts have been smoothed and polished by touching. The flat hood (which is slightly damaged) with its sloped sides, is a type which was once widespread in the north-east of Ireland. From near Cornafean, county Cavan. Length 44 in., width 14 in., height 28 in. Courtesy of The Pighouse Museum.

finial handle at each corner. A piece of string could be attached to one of these handles and tugged to make the cradle rock. Simpler versions have chamfered handles or none at all. In common with other items of rural Irish furniture, cradles were often grained to imitate oak or mahogany, or simply painted in reds, blues or two-tone combinations of colours (fig. 283).

The cradle would be placed in the kitchen during the daytime, close to the woman of the house and the warmth of the hearth (figs. 281–2, 284). Bedding varied according to locally available materials, but as with adult beds, a plaited straw mat was often used which could be placed on the boards beneath a mattress. A collection of cot or cradle covers in the Ulster Folk and Transport Museum shows that they were often cut down from full-sized bedclothes.

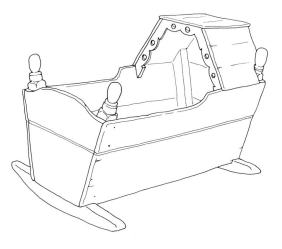

However, an inventory from Munster in the 1740s shows that those who could afford to provided their babies with 'a cradle with a bed and quilt and two pillows [as well as] three cradle blankets'.[5]

In areas where timber was in short supply, it was recycled and driftwood was often

277. (*top, left*) Pine cradle with a double curved and raised hood, and shaped sides. Its projecting corner posts have turned finials. The main body of the cradle is painted brown, with carefully shaped and black painted rockers. From the vicinity of Ballymoney, county Antrim. Courtesy of the U.F.T.M.

278. (*below*) Wickerwork cradle with decorated half canopy, on pine rockers, which are fastened through the wicker base to two parallel pine batons on the inside. From Castlefin, county Donegal, it was made in the early twentieth century. Shown outside a reconstructed byre dwelling with opposite doors, courtesy of the U.F.T.M.

279. (*top, right*) Basketwork hooded cradle with open work decoration along the sides, from Inisheer (the most easterly Aran Island), off county Galway. The vertical rods are fixed into round holes in the pine subframe, which is fixed with through-tenons to the rockers. The base is of pine slats. 36 in. long, 24 in. wide and 32 in. high. It had been recently made when acquired by the N.M.I. in 1957.

used (fig. 283). Sally (willow) was another easily obtained and popular material for weaving cradles. Referred to in inventories as 'Twigg' cradles they were used at every level of society, at least since the seventeenth century (figs. 278–81).[6]

A traveller exploring the south-east of Ireland before the great famine, was obviously impressed with the healthiness of the children of the poor. He wrote:

In England, you often find, in the splendid mansions of the great, puny, sickly children, in mahogany cradles. In Ireland, you often see on straw, in a piece of coarse wicker-work, which moves roughly, a child, which gets scarcely any thing after it is half-a-year-old but potatoes and milk, looking better than the son of a prince.[7]

This description suggests homemade wicker cradles, and that straw mattresses were used. Basketwork cradles were not only cheaper than wooden ones, but also lighter and easier to carry.

Synge, on his visit to the Aran Islands at the turn of the twentieth century, noticed that the 'home-made cradles, churns and baskets, are full of individuality, and being made from materials that are common here, yet to some extent peculiar to the island, they seem to exist as a natural link between the people and the world that is about them' (fig. 279).[8] Thirty years later, another keen observer of culture on the Aran Islands, wrote that their wicker cradles, in common with the wooden ones found on the mainland, 'are objects of great sentiment [passing] from mother to daughter for many generations'.[9]

A photograph taken in the early 1900s, of Cork city market illustrates that a variety of designs of wicker cradles were on sale, along with other items of furniture and basketry (fig. 280). These particular cradles had square or rounded hoods and some were fitted with carrying handles. The Cork photograph makes it clear that not all of them were provided with wooden rockers – woodwork not being the basket-maker's primary trade. Perhaps householders added their own rockers if so desired. These light, woven cradles which are still used in some parts of Ireland, are widely referred to as 'Moses baskets'.[10] An example made recently in county Antrim (an area with a well established tradition of basketmaking) is raised up on a special bent wood stand.[11]

280. Late nineteenth-century photograph of 'Paddy Market, Cork' from the Lawrence Collection, showing new and secondhand furniture for sale. Basketwork cradles with decorated square or round hoods and conical-topped birdcages, are stacked amongst brass beds and bedding. Upholstered parlour chairs are raised up on a parlour pedestal table and an old washstand. A woman stands with her hand on a plain carpenters' chair, flanked by framed prints and patterned carpets. Large items like dressers, which were often built-in, are conspicuous by their absence. Barrels and boards form tables for the heaps of vegetables, fish and old clothes. Courtesy of the N.L.I.

281. An etching by Daniel Maclise, A.R.A (1808–70), showing the cramped conditions of a single-storey house, probably in the west of Ireland. On the left is a basketwork cradle with rockers, handles and a high arched hood. In the foreground the animals have wandered through the half door, and a small child is confined amongst the legs of a *súgán* chair, laid on its back for the purpose. Grandmother crouches before the cobbled hearth on a very low creepie stool. From J. Barrow's, *A Tour Round Ireland, Through the Sea-coast counties, in the autumn of 1835* (1836).

Various illustrations of wicker cradles show that their designs varied considerably between one maker and region and the next (figs. 278–9, 281).

Cradles were made not only by the householders but also by those specialising in working with straw. Although no Irish examples of straw cradles are known to have survived, we learn from one of Patrick Kennedy's nineteenth-century tales of the Wexford man who 'earned his living by making cradles, and bosses [stools], and chairs, and beehives, out of straw and briers'.[12]

Straw cradles were probably just as common as wickerwork ones. Like the once ubiquitous straw chairs, coiled straw was an excellent form of insulation. Coiled straw-work was known in England (but not in Ireland) as lip-work or 'beehive work', because the craft was frequently practised by those who made straw bee skeps.[13] Sadly, the craft of straw-and brierwork in Ireland has virtually died out, along with the making of bee skeps.[14]

The plaiting method was also deployed to make straw cradles, in the same way as with mattresses and cushions, although the resulting cradle would have looked quite different from the smoother, neatly coiled and bound beehive technique.[15]

Literature and paintings provide evidence for the past existence of straw cradles their rarity exacerbated by their inherent fragility (fig. 282). Evans mentions them, explaining that they were sometimes suspended from the roof. This somewhat precarious-sounding arrangement might

282. An anonymous watercolour thought to be the interior of an inn at Listowel, county Kerry, c.1842 (also detail, fig. 253). The woman wearing a white cap, near the fire, appears to be rocking a high hooded cradle, made from straw. On one of the dressers is a tall staved jug with one handle, amongst bottles, a pewter plate, a book, ink and a quill pen. Children and animals share the warmth of the fire. Private collection.

284. Handcoloured print No. 61, *A Cradle Song*, by Jack B. Yeats, showing a cradle with an unusual pointed hood, and panelled sides, probably county Galway or Mayo. c.1904. Courtesy of Anne Yeats and The Cuala Press Ltd.

explain the occasional lack of rockers and another use for the 'carrying handles' mentioned above.[16] Kidney-shaped, coiled straw baskets for sowing seeds, were known in Wales and county Wexford as seedlips; round straw baskets were also used in Ireland (fig. 107).[17]

283. Panelled pine cradle, with elm rockers made from recycled wheel felloes. Made in the mid-nineteenth century by wheelwright and joiner Con Coakley, from near Leap, county Cork. It encompasses all the wheelwright's favourite devices: wedged and pegged tenons, decorative scratch-stock lines and panels held by chamfered posts. One post must have been driftwood, because it has the distinctive large bore holes of the marine Toredo worm. Inside are the remains of leather straps and buckles. 36 in. long, 20 in. wide to the tips of the rockers, 31½ in. high.

Cradles were traditionally handed down through the generations of families, sometimes being used for literally dozens of children, but they have now become rare. A cradle made by a wheelwright in county Cork (fig. 283) has rockers made from the worn and recycled 'felloes' of the outer rim of a wooden cartwheel, with clearly visible spokeholes. Wheelwrights were known for their ingenuity and resourcefulness, recycling whatever they could in an economical way, including the spokes of old wheels as rungs for ladders.[18]

Chapter 8

TABLES

The Variety of Tables, Improvised Tables and Potato Skibs,
The Baking Board, The Falling Table,
The Kitchen Table

THE VARIETY OF TABLES

Of Rushes there was Benches made,
On which the meat was partly laid:
But all the mutton that was sing'd,
Was laid on Doors that were unhing'd;
. . . The rest was plac'd in stately sort
On Planks which Firkins did Support,

W. Moffat,
Hesperi-Neso-Graphia, 1724[1]

Significantly, this early eighteenth-century poem, about a feast in a nobleman's house, describes an improvised table, despite the fact that they could afford to eat meat. One of the earliest illustrations of an Irish table is another 'improvised' one from a sixteenth-century illustration of men feasting out of doors beside a fire. They have a long board which rests on their legs as they sit on the ground (fig. 285).[2]

In Ireland, as we have seen, the hearth has always been emphasised as the main focal point of the home rather than the kitchen table; tables are considered by many Irish historians to be of comparatively recent origin.[3]

When they existed in a kitchen, tables were rarely positioned centrally, but instead placed under a window against a wall (fig. 120). Some of the earliest ones were probably little more than simple boards. According to Evans, in county Donegal there were still houses without tables as recently as 1957. He illustrates a tray-like table with short stumpy legs, hewn from a single piece of timber and discovered in a country Armagh bog. It has a hole in one side which could have been for hanging it on the wall.[4]

Many households in Ireland did not possess tables in their homes at all.[5] Patrick Kennedy wrote that a school in county Wexford in the early nineteenth century 'had *some* wooden seats, though it had not reached the dignity of a table' even though it was 'one step higher than the unsophisticated hedge-school'.[6] Many of the people in county Cork were so poor during the same period that there was 'neither chair, nor stool, nor table in the houses, but round stones around the fire for seats'.[7] Grant records that in the poorest houses of the Scottish highlands, tables were also conspicuous by their absence.[8]

However, there is evidence that even in comparatively wealthy Irish houses in the early eighteenth century, many farmers possessed merely the most meagre of furnishings. In county Louth, in 1728, a farmer with five children and a maid-servant possessed neither a dresser nor a table.[9] The fact that furniture was sometimes taken by landlords in lieu of rent probably deterred people from amassing it. A century or so later, further evidence of a notable lack of possessions amongst those who could clearly afford them is sighted by Mrs Hall, who mentions the phenomenon of tenants concealing wealth; 'We ourselves have known instances where the purchase of a single piece of furniture, or the bare indication of thrift . . . was a certain notice to the landlord that it was his time to apply for rent'.[10]

285. An Irish chieftain's feast, in 1581, showing people apparently eating off a long board resting on their knees, which acts as a table. From J. Derricke's The *Image of Ireland*. Photo courtesy of the N.L.I.

IMPROVISED TABLES AND POTATO SKIBS

Three stools, one larger than the rest
Our table when we have a guest:
A basket variously employ'd,
Tho' nearly by old age destroy'd,
It holds potatoes raw, or boil'd,
And serves to rock our youngest child.

P. McClabber, 'Cabin Comfortless', 1807[11]

Families would often use a stool to serve on, rather than a table, sitting around it on the floor (or on low seats) near the hearth (figs. 262, 286).[12] This habit seems to have survived since the seventeenth century, especially in counties Galway and Mayo.[13] Dr Pococke, who was a guest in a rural Mayo 'Cabbin' in 1752, wrote that 'their table is a long sort of stool about twenty inches high and broad and two yards long'.[14] The lowness of such tables must have been due to people wanting to sit with their heads beneath the usual pall of peat smoke as was the case with many chairs, and stools. Various other accounts describe flat-topped chests, inverted creels or barrels being used to eat off in the absence of a conventional table. Sometimes a door was taken off its hinges providing a place to put food, or a board was laid on top of the cast-iron cooking pot.

For those without tables, the most com-monly described and ingenious dual-purpose substitute is as follows; 'In some houses the potatoes, when boiled, are turned out on a flat home-made basket – a 'scrahag' – which is placed on a pail in the middle of the floor. The family sit round it on stools, each with a noggin of buttermilk in his hand to 'kitchen' [flavour] the repast.'[15] Although this description was as recent as 1930, the practice was born of long established tradition. There are numerous accounts of families eating potatoes from around a flat basket, which was either placed on their knees or on top of the steaming hot pot in which they had just been boiled (fig. 287). The latter would have kept both the family as well as their food warm while they ate. After eating, the basket would be hung outside on a south facing wall to dry. It was not only the poor who ate this way. Knight, a traveller through Mayo in 1813, described the same arrangement when eating with a farmer and his family 'who had one hundred head of black cattle and two hundred sheep' and 'was said to be very rich besides'.[16]

The round, shallow basket was often homemade and widely known as a potato skib (from the Irish *sciob*). Local names include a 'scuttle' (Clare), a 'sciath' (Kilkenny), *bascáid geal* or *an losaid* (Donegal), or a *ciseóg* in Galway.[17] A woman from county Louth, born in 1871, said such *sciobs* were known locally as 'Sally Saucers' because they were 'made out of sally-rods [peeled osier]: It would be all very white, real white: when it would get dirty or stained we used to take the Sally Saucer to the river and scrub it till it was white again. We bought them in Dundalk . . . They cost a shilling.'[18]

THE BAKING BOARD

Linked by terminology and use to the *sciob* is the *losaid*. Translated from the Irish *losaid* (or 'losset') means either a kneading trough, a table spread with food, a food tray, a collapsible small table or a shallow food basket. All served as tables in the poorer households.

Bread-baking was a daily activity in most homes and the kneading trough or baking board was usually made like a wooden tray with three of its four sides raised to contain the precious flour (fig. 288). The dough was kneaded in it or food was eaten from it in the manner of a *sciob*. While not in use it was hung on the wall. The baking board is still referred to as the 'losset' in county Wexford, as it has been since the mid-seventeenth century. A county Waterford merchant had a 'greate lossett valued at 4s.' in his kitchen in 1640, and a 'small Losett for macking bread' was listed amongst kitchen items from a grand county Westmeath house in 1742.[19] A few examples of them still survive today in the older houses.

On the Great Blasket, Ó Criomhthain described the islanders' tables at the beginning of this century as,

rather like a kneading trough – a board with a raised frame round it to keep in the potatoes or anything else they put on them and a stand of tripod shape that could be folded up so that the stand and the kneading trough could be hung up on the wall till they were needed.

Meals were eaten off these seemingly precarious arrangements and he goes on to describe how one day;

The tripod frame was standing ready, [for a meal] with the kneading trough on it, full of potatoes and whatever 'kitchen' went with them. A good-sized potato fell from the trough. Off went the dog after it. He carried the stand away with him, and the trough and all its contents rolled every way through the house.[20]

Although in many houses a version of a

baking board or kneading trough might have been the main table, in the more comfortable homes and into the twentieth century, they would have been used on top of a larger kitchen table when preparing bread (fig. 288).[21]

THE FALLING TABLE

The falling table could be considered to be the next step up the evolutionary ladder from the simple baking board. Unfortunately, very few examples of this ingenious space-and timber-saving device have survived intact outside museums. The principle of its design is that the minimum of timber is required; the table top is usually hinged via projecting pegs which fit into metal rings in the wall, while the other end is supported by one or two legs. It saves space because when not required the table can be swung upwards to a vertical position and held there by a wooden turnbuckle, a leather strap, a hook or a nail and chain to the wall or ceiling. The single leg, which is also hinged, hangs parallel with the table top once it is raised up, thereby leaving space in the kitchen for the other activities (figs. 289–94).

The falling table is almost invariably the victim of modernisation, but its removal sometimes still leaves a pair of telltale iron rings set in the wall. Surviving examples are now extremely rare.

Over 200 responses to questionnaires

289. A falling table from a farm kitchen, Cooneen, county Fermanagh, c.1966. This variety could be moved towards or away from the fire, by means of a bar fixed to the wall (as fig. 290). Or it could be folded up out of the way. Notice the Connecticut clock and the stretcherless chairs with their interlocking arm-rests. Photo courtesy of the U.F.T.M.

about traditional furniture, sent out in the 1950s and 60s,[22] combined with recent field work show that falling tables were once found in rural homes throughout every county of Ireland.[23] They were also widely known as 'hanging' tables or *bord crochta* and 'folded' tables (Kerry); 'folding tables'/ 'the falling table' (Antrim); poetically the 'falling leaf table' (Longford); the 'fallen table' (Fermanagh); the 'wall table' (county Roscommon) or the 'let down table' in county Kilkenny (figs. 292–3).[24] One respondent from county Down observed that 'poor people used the single leaf, richer the dropleaf'.[25] Details of use and design were equally varied (figs. 291).

This huge range of local names, which sometimes varied even from one household to the next, makes the study of early 'falling tables' from inventories problematic. Many entries suggest that such a thing is being described. A 1712 inventory from county Armagh lists 'a table frame and one board hanging in the kitchen',[26] while another from the same parish has 'one fall table at 0.2.0.' in the 'kitchine': its comparatively low value providing a further clue.[27] Their widespread use in Ireland until the first half of the twentieth century, indicates that they probably survived from a tradition of several centuries standing. Gate-leg tables were usually listed in Irish inventories as 'spider tables', but care must be taken to avoid confusing inventory entries which may actually be describing drop-leaf tables.

Early literary descriptions of such tables are rare. But the British Government Poor Inquiry reporters wrote that, in the meagerly furnished cabins of county Kerry, there was usually 'some kind of a board fixed to the wall serving as a table'.[28] The ingenuity of design of these tables also caught the eye of Patrick Kennedy, describing in fascinating detail the interiors of farmhouses in counties Carlow and Wexford in the 1820s;

a table frame that has been kept upright along the wall by a hasp at its upper end, and two pivots that fit in grooves at its lower corners, is brought to a horizontal position, and from its front an excuse for feet dangles to the floor, and keeps it up. A cloth is spread on the table, and the overlapping edges are raised up at each

290. Elevation of a falling table hinged to a long wrought iron bar (attached to the front kitchen wall). It could be moved along the bar, adjusting its distance from the hearth (on the left), or raised to act as a window shutter (compare with fig. 289). After a sketch sent in response to an U.F.T.M. questionnaire, c.1961, from Ederney, north county Fermanagh.

291. Variations in design of falling tables (See also figs. 289–90, 292–4).
A   Falling table with wooden hinges, shown down and up, from county Donegal. After a sketch by Coltman, courtesy of the Head of the D.I.F., U.C.D.
B   Falling table attached with wrought iron eyes fastened into the wall near the hearth, held upright by a leather strap, with chamfered and through-wedged legs. Sketched by the author in 1987, in a farmhouse near Kiltegan, county Wicklow.
C   Falling table or wall table, hinged partly onto the back of a chest, held upright by a leather thong. From a house subsequently submerged by the Poulaphouca Resevoir, county Wicklow, c.1930s.
D   The removeable falling table detached from the Carbery Settle (fig. 115), west county Cork, showing the single leg attached by a dovetailed pine hinge, c.1850.

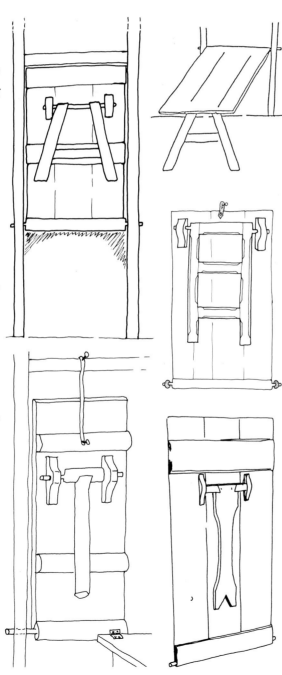

side by the youngsters, to prevent the potatoes from falling off when spilled out upon it . . .

The family are described as eating directly off the table cloth, though previously Kennedy described how the dresser was bedecked with plates.[29] Another reference to such a design is betrayed in conversation, at the end of a meal '". . . rise the table." (The table was a falling one that when not in use stood up flat by the wall.)'[30]

Variations in falling tables occurred when one end of a table was hinged to a wooden framework that was fixed to the wall (rather than to iron rings buried in the masonry), which would have been easier for the average householder to build himself. In the Barony of Carbery in county Cork another version of the falling table, which was hinged to the centre of a high backed settle, used to be common. Labelled for convenience the 'Carbery Settle' it is described in the chapter on settles (pp. 80–2, figs. 115, 291D).

There are many variations in design and size with these 'one legged' tables.[31] Like the dressers, their size related to space and use. They were often about 3 feet wide and 4 feet long. A farmer from Killybegs, county Wicklow, remembers particularly the 'swanky' diamond-shaped wooden clip which held his 7-foot long table up against the wall. It was fixed beside the fire in a high-ceilinged farmhouse, occupied by a large family.

They often existed as the sole table in a kitchen in smaller homes. In larger, more prosperous farmhouses (especially in land-lords' houses), they served as an additional eating place on the occasions when farm labourers were fed as part of their day's work on the estate.

The falling table was usually attached to the back wall of the kitchen (away from the front door) and within a few feet of the hearth. But they were also found in the parlour or 'room' and in Ballinrobe, county Mayo, there was one in the school. In Lackan, county Wicklow, the falling table was fixed over one end of a hearth-side seat; 'It could be lowered on to the floor and also swivelled about on the stake which held it to the wall. In this way the end of it could be brought close to the fire.'[32]

292. 'The let-down table' (also fig. 293) lowered for use: an extremely rare mid nineteenth-century example of a design once common throughout Ireland. In this farmhouse the children used to sit on the form, while their parents nearer the fire (on the left) had chairs. The top, usually covered by oilcloth, is deeply scored by knife marks, a legacy of the annual pig kill. The dresser, with sixteen holes for displaying spoons, was made in 1906 by John Bergin.

Fieldstudies in the Wicklow mountains shows that these tables were very common in the farmhouses and cabins, within living memory. They were often used for playing cards on, as well as at meal times. An example recently found in county Kilkenny has a surface deeply grooved and scored from decades of cutting up pig carcasses. It is unusual because it has a falling form which hinges beside it (figs. 292–3). It is still in use and when let down reveals a portrait of Jesus.

Another such table found during fieldwork at Killybegs, county Wicklow, was made of pine; its top covered by two layers of printed and patterned oilcloth, fastened with pins. The top consisted of four boards, 3 feet wide and 4 feet long. It had a double leg built like a chamfered ladder with three rungs, which was painted dark green. This swivelled freely by means of a pair of projecting dowels fixed to the underside of the top by a pair of blocks (fig. 291B). The other end of the table was similarly attached by two more projecting dowels into iron rings fixed firmly into the wall. The whole table was comparatively low due to the absence of an apron or frieze rail beneath the top. It was held in the upright position by a leather strap. In 1987 the house was derelict; it has since been modernised and the falling table has been removed.

Fieldwork near Enniscorthy in county Wexford, has shown that falling tables were once common in nearly all the houses. Local historian Patrick Hennessy recalled that

some of these tables had special holes drilled in their tops, near the edge, for eating boiled eggs out of. In many poor households, eggs formed an important part of the diet, and such a detail made more sense than spending precious money on eggcups. Apparently there would be as many of these 'egg holes' as there were places around the table for sitting. They were especially useful when there was a 'thrashing' [threshing] and all the neighbours who had helped with the harvest came to eat together in the house.

Falling tables were sometimes attached to a length of iron rail along which they could be moved to an alternative position, near the fire in winter and away from it in summer. One example, from a house in county Fermanagh, could be slid along a rail about 7 feet in length. Others could be moved and fastened in the upright position in order to provide a window shutter at night (fig. 290).[33] Another near Union Hall in west county Cork used to be dropped down to reveal a recessed ware cupboard, when raised it served as the cupboard door.

In county Leitrim, these tables were apparently 'very much in vogue' at the beginning of the twentieth century. One example 'was attached to a horizontal bar in the wall, on which it could swing, hingelike . . . Frequently the bar to which it was attached ran the full length of the wall . . . It was a very useful device, and had no disadvantages.'[34]

293. 'The let-down table', elsewhere known as a 'falling table', folded up against the back kitchen wall alongside its let-down form. Both are held up by an iron pin which slides into a hole in the supporting framework. Both have hinged legs, that of the form is recently replaced. From a farm kitchen, near Callan, county Kilkenny. Table 72 in. × 36 in. by 21 in. high. Form 82 in. long by 9 in. wide, 16 in. high.

294. The 'falling table' or 'wall table', which hinged up against the wall when not needed, with its folding legs. In Eliza Short's house near Valleymount, county Wicklow, before inundation by the Poulaphouca Resevoir, c.1930s. Photo courtesy of Dr F.H. Aalen.

The falling table epitomises the two most common constraints of Irish furniture making: economy with timber and space. It was perfectly suited to homes on the treeless islands off the west coast, where timber shortage was acute. Could it have been a falling table that Arthur Symons saw when he mentioned that '. . . the table lounges on an inadequate number of legs . . .' in the Atlantic Hotel on Inishmore in 1918?[35]

THE KITCHEN TABLE

The kitchen table was a common sight in the typical English cottage well before the nineteenth century. It has, however, already been mentioned that most Irish households could not afford the luxury of a full sized, four-legged and therefore movable table. The grander houses and castles, however, are known to have contained many varieties of table since the sixteenth century and probably long before that.[36] Killiane castle in county Wexford, for example, had twenty-one tables in the mid-eighteenth century.[37] Enough Irish kitchen tables survive from the nineteenth century to demonstrate that they had characteristics of design which set them apart from the usual English tables.

The typical Irish design varies in size but often has a top 4 feet wide by 6 or 7 feet in length. Often there is a place for a drawer at each end or in the centre of one of the long sides. The legs are nearly always square in section rather than turned (they were built for stability rather than aesthetics) and are linked near the floor by a pair of long parallel stretchers which run lengthwise beneath the table top (figs. 295–7). Closely aligned and out of the way of chairs and sitters' feet, they form a framework which considerably

295. Rare late eighteenth-century kitchen table, its top worn thin from scrubbing, with typically Irish double stretchers beneath. The base is repeatedly painted, most recently with pale green. From a farmhouse at Cranford, Gorey, county Wexford. Courtesy of the Irish Agricultural Museum.

strengthens the table as a whole. These stretchers are sometimes cross linked, like a ladder, forming a useful low shelf upon which bowls of milk or cooking equipment can be placed off the floor (fig. 288). In county Armagh the practice of placing the corpse during a wake on these low laths gave rise to the reference 'waking table'.[38] Placing pails beneath the table top had the advantage of preventing things from falling into them from the thatch above, which was a real possibility;

The man of the house was sitting at the head of the table, with a wooden mug full of milk beside him. He'd just put his hand to his plate, to take out a piece of fish, when he saw some object fall into the mug. He looked down, and there was a lump of something drowning in the milk . . . 'It's a young chicken . . . they're falling from above'.[39]

The arrangement of the parallel stretchers provided valuable storage space without utilising any more timber than the English tables, which often had four stretchers linking the legs.[40] This useful design occurs in all areas of Ireland and seems to have no English precedent. Some tables simply have one central stretcher instead. They are usually constructed with 'through-wedged' mortice and tenon joints throughout, characteristic of the Irish furniture makers' attention to the priority of durability and functionalism over aesthetics.

The old established practice of scrubbing table tops daily was widespread and laborious. Water and white river sand or 'shelly' sand was used as an abrasive before the introduction of commercial cleaning fluids.[41] In many households, the twice-daily scrubbing is still recalled as an arduous chore, eventually giving the surface a bleached and smoothly ridged texture not unlike driftwood. The recent introduction of manmade formica tops with aluminum edging, known in Ireland as 'Beauty Board', was welcomed and quickly became fashionable. These were easily wiped clean, came in a variety of colours and could be glued into place on top of the old scrubbed top. Inevitably these beauty-board tops have now become more common than the original pine tops (fig. 297).

Most of these kitchen tables were made out of pine, the least expensive and most widely available timber. There are occasional references to oak tables, in the more prosperous farmhouses or in well furnished parlours.[42]

The large kitchen table was most often placed against the front wall of the traditional house under the window, leaving the central part of the kitchen free and providing daylight and a view for anyone working at it. Other authors have provided useful ground plans of traditional houses and furniture, which nearly all show tables placed in this way.[43] Even now, most traditional homes keep their tables against the wall, despite the introduction of cookers and fridges, which has moved the pattern of domestic activity away from the hearth.

The kitchen table was used for many tasks other than for preparing food and eating. There are numerous references to the 'tailor making clothes for the family . . . sitting cross-legged on the kitchen table'.[44] Perhaps he was taking advantage of a clean area with a good light source for his intricate work. Fig. 298, a photograph taken in the late 1930s shows an ingenious table in the house of Michael Fox, a tailor. Instead of having a freestanding table beneath the window, his table top is set onto four large logs which are 'earth fast' – in other words they have been sunk firmly into the beaten earth floor.

296. 'Eviction scene' photographed by the firm of Lawrence during the last quarter of the nineteenth century, and considered to be on the Vandaleur estate, county Clare. Four simple *súgán* chairs, are heaped around a typically Irish double-stretchered kitchen table, with a scrubbed top. Although some such scenes may have been 'staged' for the photographers, the furniture is nonetheless local. Courtesy of the N.L.I.

297. A kitchen table with a recent 'beauty board' top and double stretchers linking the legs (fig. 288). Both probably made by wheelwright Paddy Crowly (1857–1940s), who also made the removeable clevy over the fire. From Reen, west county Cork (figs. 143–4).

298. This rare photograph, taken before inundation by the Poulaphouca Resevoir, shows 'the Tailor's table, standing on 4 logs, set in [the earthen] floor'. Such 'earth-fast' furniture was easily made, but short-lived. 'The Tailor's House', Woodend Bridge, Butterhill, county Wicklow, c.1930s. Photo courtesy of Dr F.H. Aalen.

Some well-off households had more than one table, as Kennedy – describing a spring day in 1820 – explains,

Edward . . . introduced me to the family, and we sat at dinner at a table necessarily large, for it had to accommodate twelve individuals. The heads of the house and the eldest daughter used a smaller one near the fire.'[45]

The custom of entertaining guests in the adjoining parlour or 'room' rather than in

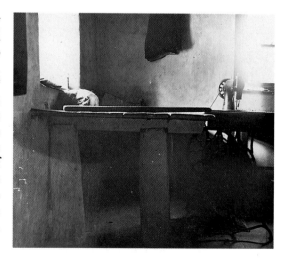

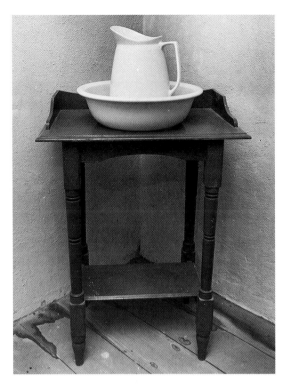

299. A painted bedroom washstand, late nineteenth century, with a jug and basin (which in many examples was sunk into a hole in the top). Such lathe-turned examples were often made in batches in small workshops. Photo courtesy of Shannon Heritage Ltd.

300. These spindly 'gypsy tables' were sold by the roadside by travellers, and are early twentieth century. Made of unworked branches, stripped of their bark and nailed together, they have thin pine tops, recycled from boxes and covered with wallpaper. From near Callan, county Kilkenny. 26 and 30 in. high, both tops 17 in. wide.

the kitchen, is often mentioned in nineteenth-century Irish literature. Some could not afford the luxury of furniture which was rarely used, so;

> the table was removed into the adjoining room, and a touch from the finger of the matron was the signal for me to follow her in to supper. On a naked deal [pine] table stood a plate of potatoes and a jug of milk. The potatoes must be eaten from the hand, without fork, knife or plate; and the milk taken in sups from the mug . . . It must be remembered that a sup of sweet milk among the poor in Ireland, is as much a rarity as a slice of plum-pudding in a farm-house in America. After supper we returned to the kitchen.[46]

Styles of tables other than the ones outlined here would also have been found in the traditional dwelling house. By the twentieth century small, light washstands, sometimes with turned front legs and a round hole in the top to take a bowl and jug, had become popular. Usually, they had a three-sided raised gallery around the top and a lower shelf beneath and were used

for washing in the bedrooms (fig. 299). Occasionally there exists an upstairs room divided off for use as a bathing room for the whole family, containing one of these stands. Many of them follow such similar patterns of shape and design that it is likely that they were being mass-produced and possibly even imported. Like the rest of the furniture they were repeatedly painted. Tables kept in the parlour were sometimes made of polished oak or mahogany, and were regarded as something of a status symbol. Parlours were widespread in farmhouses but rare in smaller cottiers' houses by the 1830s.[47] They varied in richness of decoration; some doubled as bedrooms while others (in county Antrim) were much grander, 'furnished with modern chairs and tables of mahogany, a cupboard well stocked with china, delf, glass, and some silver spoons, and each of them has a clock.'[48] Parlours were generally rather damp and stuffy from lack of use. According to Danaher, special visitors were 'incarcerated there, and entertained by members of the family taking turns one by one'. Some of the furniture was made by local craftsmen in the latest and most fashionable styles.[49] Mass-produced clocks imported from Connecticut (fig. 289) after the Great Exhibition (London) were much less expensive than the previously popular wall clocks (figs. 54, 218).

The high seated settle bed sometimes fulfilled the function of a table by providing a resting place for pails of spring water or milk during the day. Both settle beds and settle tables are discussed in the chapter on settles.

Chapter 9

THE HEARTH &
THE SHRINE

The Use of Roasting Spits, The Clevy or Spit Rack,
Regional Variations in Clevy Design, The Origin of the Word Clevy,
The Crane, Holy Shelves and Shrines

THE USE OF ROASTING SPITS

Meat on spits, and wild fowl from the ocean;
Music and song, and drinking bouts;
Delicious roast beef and spotless honey,
Hounds and dogs and baying.

Egan O'Rahilly, poet, eighteenth century,[1]

Before discussing the clevy or spit rack, it is important to examine the evidence for the consumption of meat amongst the rural working population. Although long forgotten now, there is plenty of evidence that iron spits were once used for roasting meat over the fire.[2] In some areas this seemingly medieval practice continued up until the first half of the nineteenth century.[3] Iron tripod stands, which stood a few feet apart on either side of the hearth, enabled the roasting spits to be suspended at various heights over the fire. One end of the spit had a handle for turning, while the centre was flattened to grip the meat.[4] A dripping pan would be placed beneath the meat to collect the juices. In the absence of built-in ovens[5] and before the advent of the stove, a spit would have been the most convenient way to cook meat, other than cooking it in a pot oven or bastible over the fire.

In the country, meat was eaten regularly only by those lucky enough to be able to afford it. According to schoolteacher Humphrey O'Sullivan, writing in his diary of 1827, 'the dwellers in country hovels eat meat only three days in the year: Christmas day, Shrove Tuesday and Easter Sunday'.[6] The following year he observes 'people bringing home the shrovetide little juicy joint: five pence a pound for pork, four pence halfpenny for mutton, four pence for beef'.[7] One of the many questions put by the British Government's commissioners investigating the state of the poor (at around the same time), pertained to trades and diet. In Queen's County (now county Laois) they reported that 'tradesmen eat milk and potatoes and butter and unlike labourers get meat twice a week'.[8]

The great majority of the rural poor ate little or no meat, as demonstrated by county Down poet Andrew M'Kenzie in 'The Poor Man's Petition' of 1807:

The cruel butcher's murd'rous knife,
For me deprives no beast of life; . . .
But words I will not multiply,
Potatoes all our meals supply;
A little milk to them we add –
And salt, when that can not be had.[9]

Contemporary observers of Irish life during the nineteenth century often commented that the pigs reared by the poor were sold to pay their rent, rather than being kept to eat. Fowl were sometimes kept for special occasions, so although meat was a scarce commodity spits would have been required for roasting. It has already been described in the chapter about dressers, how large meat plates were given a special tall shelf for storage and display, despite the fact that in many households they were seldom used (see dresser illustrations).

(fig. 301). The memory of such a clevy being built to hold a spit is now lost to oral history.

The following description of this typical old county Cork feature, emphasises its twentieth century use.

> Over the fireplace is 'the clevy', a shelf filled with tins. One contains sugar and another tea. There is a box of pepper and one containing caraway seeds, which Ansty mixes with tea. The remainder of the tins are mysteries. Never during any operation in the economy of the house are they opened . . . Perhaps they are but tins without contents and simply are, as the collection of dishes and plates on the dresser, awaiting an occasion still buried in the future.[10]

The makers of such clevies had long forgotten their original use; some are actually far wider than the fireplace openings above which they are built.[11] Others have been built over recently installed stoves. They are usually painted in the same colours as the rest of the kitchen furniture. The two vertical spit-holding elements form a vital system of support for the long mantlepiece, often being attached to the low ceiling joists for support (fig. 302). Some fixed clevies had provision for more than one spit, others were decorated with moulded fronts to the shelf or had chip carving on the supports. These decorative features often correspond to those on the dresser. Sometimes the whole thing is covered by a length of oilcloth, which may be cut with a decorative fringe hanging down in front. Beneath the clevy a long string or strip of timber is usually attached for drying clothes.

Later versions built around the 1950s retain the familiar and traditional outline, but no longer have slots cut to hold spits. Some built around the turn of the twentieth century are attached by means of iron rings and pins to the ceiling, facilitating their removal for instance, in order to hang new wallpaper on the chimney-breast (fig. 302B). Another from a farmhouse near Ballydehob, county Cork, still has a small cupboard placed at each end of the shelf.

301. Built-in clevy originally made for holding a long spit, incorporating a shelf, as was typical in county Cork farmhouses. Fixed to the wide beam over the hearth and to a ceiling joist, it is thickly overpainted, recently with brown gloss. From a farmhouse near Rosscarbery, west county Cork.

THE CLEVY OR SPIT RACK

Spits may have held the same significant status as the large meat platters, as the survival of considerable numbers of racks or clevies to hold them testifies. The clevy or timber spit rack was an integral part of the mantlepiece well into the first half of the twentieth century in county Cork. Old habits die hard and it may have been the strength of this tradition which persuaded carpenters to continue making the elaborately curved wooden hooks for storing spits, long after the spits themselves had gone out of use. These two (or more) vertical elements also served as a support for the long storage shelf above the fireplace

302. Side views of various painted pine clevies from above farmhouse hearths in west county Cork, originally for holding spits. Their horizontal shelves are indicated by dotted lines, ceiling joists by cross-hatching. a) Made by Hayes, from near Glandore, *c.*1930; b) made by Paddy Crowly of Maulicorrane, Union Hall, *c.*1890 (see figs. 143–4), removeable by means of wrought iron brackets; c) from near Skibbereen, *c.*1850.

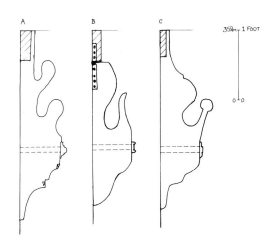

Clevies vary in appearance from one district to the next. The fixed mantlepiece type of clevy was once a common feature of traditional houses on the south county Kilkenny border (fig. 303) as well as in county Cork. Another design of clevy (more like a hanging dresser with slots), was widespread throughout Munster and southern Leinster and was not neccessarily directly positioned over the fireplace (figs. 304–5). In the Comeragh mountains in county Waterford, reference is made to the 'cleevy', attached to the wall above the settle and forming 'a complicated rack where there was a place for each of the spits'.[12] This Waterford type resembles a hanging dresser, with its square shape and shallow shelves, surmounted by a cornice. With two or three spits in place, plates could be leant forwards onto the spits in the manner of the bars of a dresser, combining the two functions of storage and display in the time honoured way. Some surviving examples incorporate long batons, which enabled the plates to remain tipped forwards, even when the spit was removed for use (fig. 304).

In county Limerick a number of dressers survive which combined a spit rack, a plate rack and an area for plate storage, all surmounted on a coop for the storage of live fowl (fig. 306).[13] Nearby in north county Cork, some houses had 'a "clevvy" for holding ware mounted on a hen-coop' as well as an ordinary dresser.[14] These examples emphasise the close association between fowl and the means of cooking them. The hanging dresser type of clevy, with room for

303. (*below, left*) The wide hearth of a farmhouse in Licketstown, county Kilkenny. A double-hooked clevy is fitted above the long shelf. Notice the recessed presses and 'keeping hole', adjustable pot hanger, and on the left the fire bellows, which are turned by hand. Also the *súgán* armchair and the 'windsor' type armchair, with its distinctively Irish paired stretchers beneath the seat. Photo courtesy of the Irish Architectural Archive.

304. (*top, right*) Clevy made to hold three spits horizontally resting in deep hooks (detail fig. 305). Thickly painted with red/brown, the craquelure is particularly noticable along the cornice, c.1790. Plates were lent forward onto the spits and onto the wooden baton (across the lowest layer). It also has nails for hanging jugs and mugs. 47 in. high by 45 in. wide, depth 5–9 in. Collected in the Pallas Green area, county Limerick, courtesy of the N.M.I.

305. (*below, right*) Detail of a clevy (fig. 304), showing two of the deep hooks made to hold iron roasting spits. Collected in the Pallas Green area, county Limerick, courtesy of the N.M.I.

306. An unusual dresser combining a two-tier hen coop, with a plate rack, surmounted by a clevy and a shelf for ware. The clevy, with its deeply cut slots to hold a spit (as fig. 305), also displayed plates. Decoration is confined to scratch-stock mouldings and incised criss-crossing along the facia (compare fig. 190). Painted repeatedly, its brown/red paint has craquelure, with unpainted repairs. Early nineteenth century, collected for the N.M.I. from the vicinity of Pallas Green, county Limerick.

three layers of spits, is also well known in county Limerick (figs. 304–5, compare to fig. 177).[15]

Prototypes for these spit racks may be found in some of the castles and grand houses of Ireland. The sheer size of these grander versions reflects the wealth (and appetite) of their owners. One surviving example from county Tipperary consists of two layers 15 feet in length. 'Spitts' and 'wooden Racks over ye chimney' occur frequently amongst inventories from all over Ireland, between the sixteenth and eighteenth centuries.[16]

THE ORIGIN OF THE WORD CLEVY

The clevy (both as a word and an object) was almost certainly transferred by early planted settlers from England and Wales, where they rarely survive now, but can be seen depicted by early nineteenth century artists such as Thomas Rowlandson.[17]

The word 'clevy' seems to have originated from the English word 'clavel', meaning a beam or shelf over a fireplace. During the nineteenth century it was pronounced 'clavy' in various parts of the west of England.[18]

In Ireland, clevy originally meant a spit rack and a combined shelf or shelves for storage. As spits fell out of use, clevy or *cléibhi* carried on being used as words to denote places of storage. By the end of the nineteenth century in the Aran Islands, the *cléibhi* was the common word for the hearth 'keeping hole' for pipes, tobacco and tea.[19] In counties Kilkenny and Clare 'clevy' still denotes the hanging dresser, the use of which is no longer necessarily associated with the hearth.[20]

THE CRANE

The crane, that most essential piece of farm-house furnishings, is illustrated incidentally throughout this book, and so deserves some explanation.

Before the advent of mass-produced stoves, hearths were usually equipped with devices for suspending pots and kettles above the fire, for cooking. The most simple device was a chain, attached to a cross-bar in the chimney, with 'S' shaped hooks for hanging the pots at particular heights.

Like most things in Irish material culture, names for such devices vary greatly from one place to the next. A visitor to a poor county Cork house in 1813 observed 'The crook, as it is called, or hook, on which they hang the pot over the fire, is of wood, tied by a straw rope to something at the top'.[21] Such a crook, rack, hook, or crane of wood, must have been the common type up to the nineteenth century, although only a few survive now, and even fewer are still in use (figs. 97, 197, 307–8).

The word 'crane' is particularly apt, as the device was pivoted, enabling large, heavy, hot pots to be swung easily away from the fire, and as such must have been a great improvement on the simple chain. The danger of such a wooden device catch-

FIRE ORNAMENTS

307. A rare wooden crane, for hanging pots over the fire, in the kitchen of an empty farmhouse in the Wicklow mountains. It pivots on a stone jutting from the hearth wall.

308. A family seated on a settle and *súgán* chairs, by a turf fire, with a partly painted wooden crane. Notice the 'keeping hole', recessed press and the decorated 'holy shelf'. Photo 1930 by T.H. Mason, on the Great Blasket Island, county Kerry. Courtesy of the Head of the D.I.F., U.C.D.

ing alight, was sometimes lessened by the base of the pivot being raised a foot or two from the ground and set into projecting stonework (fig. 307). Some surviving examples are whitewashed, reducing inflammability; others are blackened by soot. However, their rarity now is probably due to the danger of them catching fire; a diary of 1829 describes how a county Kilkenny 'cottage' burned to the ground in less than a quarter of an hour. It is significant that the 'The pot-rack (wooden-) pin and the pot rack itself were burned'.[22]

Many more sophisticated, wrought-iron,

blacksmith-made cranes survive from the nineteenth and early twentieth centuries. Some incorporate decorative twists, others are large enough to accommodate several pots at different heights. Sometimes people lit more than one fire beneath them for different cooking operations, and oven cooking of bread (without yeast), in particular, was done by means of a bastable pot with a lid. Soda bread, or bastable bread 'which is baked in a pot oven over a turf fire, is delicious. Glowing pieces of turf are placed on the lid of the pot so that gentle heat is distributed evenly, thus producing beautifully baked bread.'[23] Considerable skill is required to cook it, as the lid cannot be lifted until the process is complete (see fig. 201).

HOLY SHELVES AND SHRINES

The kitchen shrine used to be a common sight in Roman Catholic homes and was the resting place for a variety of coloured plaster statues of holy figures. Most sur-

309. (*facing page*) Colour print from a drawing by Jack B. Yeats, showing a woman selling blue, white and pink 'fire ornaments', which presumably hung on either side of the fireplace, as decoration. Probably from county Mayo or Galway, published in 1912 in J.B. Yeats's *Life in the West of Ireland*.

This page:
310. (*top, left*) A mid nineteenth-century shrine, with a celtic cross in a gothic style, made of oak and painted grey. Such shrines were usually placed on a special shelf in the kitchen and housed plaster figures of the holy family. This pitched-roof shape is typical of examples from Catholic houses in the south-east. From a farmhouse in south county Wexford.

311. (*top, right*) A simple shrine from the loft of a small farmhouse near Shillelagh, county Wicklow. Early twentieth century, probably home-made, of pine painted with cream gloss.

312. (*right*) A simply adorned 'holy shelf' and red votive lamp, in the kitchen of a small west Cork farmhouse.

viving examples have a pitched 'roof' surmounted by a cross (figs. 310–11). One late nineteenth-century example from county Wexford is elaborately carved out of oak and adorned with gothic motifs, more reminiscent of church furniture than that of the rural dwelling (fig. 310). In county Clare in the 1940s, 'the religious shrine of the "Blessed Lamp" and the Sacred Heart picture before which the family prays the "Family Rosary" at night' were traditional features.[24] A surviving example from the west of Ireland is large and unusually elaborate, with three arched sections reminiscent of a triptych, carved and fretted on every surface and inset with glass of three different colours. Although these symbolic and decorative shrines are no longer commonly found (many have now been relegated to the attic) many traditional houses in Munster still retain the small 'holy shelf' upon which a red votive light constantly shines (figs. 308, 312–13). This was an important focal point. Sean O'Casey makes recurring references to such a lamp, throughout his play *Juno and the Paycock*

193

313. The 'holy shelf', decorated with flowers and a lamp, and surrounded by religious prints, both formal and realist. These were often bought from travellers and traditionally were hung tilted forwards. The underside of the thatch, supported by bog timber and rough branches, is lined with scraws (sods of matted grass and roots), which turf smoke has blackened. Moycullen, county Galway, *c*.1948. Photo courtesy of Bord Fáilte.

(1924). Some of them are similar to the French domestic shrines (*niche à Vièrge*) found in rural Brittany, which hold a statue of the Virgin Mary, and have a glass door in the front.[25] In Ireland these little shelves and shrines usually bear the same decorative details and are painted in the same colours as the rest of the kitchen furniture.

194

SMALL FURNISHINGS

*Domestic Utensils, Tinsmiths' Work, Woodturners' Work,
Coopers' Ware, The Mether or Madder,
Basketry*

314. Stepped kitchen spoon or cutlery rack of painted pine, similar to examples from Wales. Early nineteenth century, from Clearystown, county Wexford. Courtesy of the Irish Agricultural Museum.

315. A 'knife brick box' of grained pine, from Carndonagh, county Donegal. Abrasives were kept in the box, which was laid flat when used for honing steel knives, using its elongated back. Mid nineteenth century.

DOMESTIC UTENSILS

Two pots and a griddle, a sive and a
    riddle,
A slate for a tongs, to bring fire on,
A pair of pot hooks, and two little crooks,
To hang up the salt box and grid iron . . .
Three noggins, three mugs, a bowl and
    two jugs,
A crock and a pan something lesser,
A red fourpenny glass, to draw at for mass,
Nailed up to a clean little dresser
Some starch and some blue, in two papers
    for you,
An iron and a holder to hold it,
A beetle to whack and a stick horse's back,
To dry your cap on 'fore you fold it,

Anon, 'Thady O'Brady', *c.*1800[1]

This extract from 'Thady O'Brady', an anonymous 'comic song', lists lightheartedly some of the meagre contents of a poor man's cabin and what he proposes to provide for his future wife. In its entirety, it provides an accurate rhyming inventory of the wide variety of domestic utensils common in even the poorest dwellings.[2] Griddles (for baking or grilling), sieves and riddles (for sifting), all crop up regularly in inventories and early illustrations of interiors and were essential in the preparation of food (fig. 318). The 'red fourpenny glass' was a special one, doubtless for use during 'the Stations' (when Roman Catholic Mass was said in a private house, see pp. 21–3). The starch and blue were for stiffening and whitening the washing and the 'stick horse's back'

must have been a wooden clothes horse for drying clothes indoors, in front of the fire (fig. 198). Although such things are in the strictest sense paraphernalia rather than furniture, they provide a valuable insight into the daily routine and illustrate the varied skills of the craftsmen.

The various painted wooden boxes for holding spoons and other cutlery, which usually hung beside the dresser, were often decorated with pierced motifs, such as the flying wheel, the heart or the cupid's bow, and painted to match the rest of the kitchen furniture (figs. 314–15). They were made in a variety of shapes and sizes while some had internal dividers, and they were often simply nailed together. An example of a wall-mounted, stepped spoon rack, from Chearystown, county Wexford, is remarkable for its similarity to examples from Wales (fig. 314). Their proximity and a long history of communication between the two areas probably accounts for the similarities in design.[3]

195

The knife box or knife brickbox was not intended to hold knives, but hung on a nail and contained an abrasive substance such as rottenstone, bathbrick or sand, for sharpening and cleaning steel knives. It had a board 2 to 3 feet long attached to the box which could be laid flat on the kitchen table and used with the abrasive for honing knives (fig. 315).[4] These painted boxes with their bare and rounded honing boards were sometimes listed amongst kitchen paraphernalia during the eighteenth century, but their functional design is likely to be even older.[5] They were a common part of kitchen furnishings throughout Ireland, and can still be seen in the smallest local museums from county Donegal to county Cork.

TINSMITHS' WORK

All the functional objects pertaining to cooking, washing, dairying and preserving food had their place in the kitchen and many people displayed them thoughtfully to provide an extra element of decoration. The travelling tinsmith's wares included mugs and pails for holding milk or water (figs. 204–6). In south county Armagh, 'These along with can-lids, were diligently scoured with a damp cloth and turf ash, well polished, and then imprinted with spirals by placing the thumb down hard and twisting an imprint on the polished tin. At night, these gave a coruscating effect which caught the light from every angle.'[6] One of Jack Yeats's drawings, *The Cuttlefish*, shows a collection of pot lids hung near the hearth on the side of a box bed, which must also have reflected the firelight nicely (fig. 263). Elizabeth Smith, who kept a meticulous diary of her activities in county Wexford during the 1840s, noted upon entering one of her tenants' small farmhouses the 'clean, very clean kitchen, bright fire, dresser well filled, wall hung with polished pots and covers', which evidently created an eye-catching display.[7] The tinsmiths also made the graters used to make boxty bread, which required grated raw potato (one hangs from the top of the dresser in fig. 264).

A writer brought up in early twentieth-century county Antrim, described the re-gular summer visits of a variety of 'beggars and journeymen'. Amongst them was the tinker, who would repair with lead solder 'large cans with lids for milk or water, watering cans, saucepans, teapots and tin mugs with handles'. In return he was paid and fed breakfast, dinner and tea. He carried a flour bag, carefully knotted in the middle to hold flour at one end and oatmeal at the other. This 'mealbag' he carried over his shoulder, along with a tin box of 'pickle tea and sugar'; both these would be replenished by the householder before he departed.[8] Many such 'tramps' travelled around nineteenth-century Ireland this way, the food which they gathered was often cooked by the hospitable providers of a night's lodgings. The tinsmith's work is also discussed in the chapter about dressers.

WOODTURNERS' WORK

Their platters are of wood,
By cunning turners made.
But not of pewter (credit me)
As is our English trade.

Derricke, 1581[9]

Woodturners provided a huge variety of dishes, plates, bowls, ladles and butter stamps and such 'turners dairy utensils' were sold in markets and shops up until the late nineteenth century (fig. 317).[10] The number of surviving vernacular chairs incorporating turned work is comparatively small, but a huge number of turned domestic utensils instead provides evidence of the turner's skill. The 'beetle to whack', mentioned above in 'Thady O'Brady's comic song', refers to a range of pounders: club-like implements which were widely used to beat and compress straw before twisting it into rope (*súgán*), for beating flax, for clothes washing or perhaps most commonly to mash potatoes. These can often be seen in illustrations amongst kitchen implements (fig. 188). Most surviving examples were turned on a lathe, but flat beetles were also known (fig. 176).[11]

Most of the turner's income would have been generated by making and selling a range of bowls and plates, often using sycamore, chestnut or lime. By the late

316. Wooden 'jugs', sketched from a dresser and said to be 'common drinking vessels' used for milk or whiskey. Top right was widespread and sometimes known as a *lámhóg*; below right is a staved and wood-hooped vessel. Drawn by H. Hill, engraved by Sly, from Mr and Mrs Hall's *Ireland: Its Scenery, Character, etc.* (1841).

317. A stripped fiddle fronted dresser, from Lough Gur, county Limerick. Its facia board is decorated with interlacing, made of blind fretwork: an arrangement favoured in the west. The shelves, which display turned wooden dishes and trenchers, *lámhógs* and staved noggins, are framed by carved rope-mouldings. *c.*1800. Photo courtesy of the N.M.I.

nineteenth century, in county Wexford, as earthenware began to take their place, it was recalled how commonplace were the 'wooden trenchers all the size of the earthen-ware dinner plate of the present day – with dishes and bowls, from 60 inches diameter to six inches'.[12] The pole lathe, powered partly by the elasticity of a sapling tree, would have been the turner's main means of production. The suggestion that people were turning bowls as large as 5 feet in diameter must be an exaggeration: their work was evidently of an impressive size, but a county Armagh woodturner stated that the largest he had turned was 24 inches.[13]

This so-called 'wooden ware', which also included large bowls for buttermaking (figs. 104, 317), is regularly mentioned in documents, becoming less common towards the end of the nineteenth century.[14] Turned containers for liquids, some with a projecting handle, were widely used and came in a variety of sizes (figs. 316–17). Mrs Hall illustrated some in 1841, which were displayed on a dresser in county Kerry (fig. 316). She explained how they were 'the common drinking vessels of the Kerry peasantry', several of whom had followed her party up the mountain in the hope of selling whiskey or milk to her from such wooden 'jugs'.[15] In county Kerry such 'timber ware' was remembered well into the twentieth century.

There was timber mugs and bowls and plates, and big dishes ... made by a turner. The timber mugs used be four pence each. These mugs would hold about four cups of water ... These used be as white as snow when they was washed and cleaned. They used be scoured first with heath [probably heather], and then washed with boiling water, and put outside the door to dry and cool.[16]

Hence,

A churn and a dish to make the cream
    splash,
Some boiling hot water to fill it,

Anon, 'Thady O'Brady',[17]

COOPERS' WARE

Coopers were responsible for supplying a whole range of staved containers or casks, from the smallest drinking vessels, the larger tubs used for carrying water or for washing clothes, right up to the ubiquitous dairy dash-churn (figs. 168, 194, 316–18). All these products varied in design from one maker or region to the next.[18] The largest of all – barrels – were used for

318. A three-legged stool, and a small piggin for buttermilk. The 'borrane' is made of scraped sheep-skin drawn round a hoop: it can be used as a sieve when winnowing corn, holds carded wool or feathers during plucking, or acts as a tray or drum. Drawn in county Cork by J. Franklin, engraved by Walmsley, from Mr and Mrs Hall's *Ireland: Its Scenery, Character, etc.* (1841).

salting, preserving and transporting fish or meat, and were often then recycled for use as seats (figs. 218, 282) or containers for other foodstuffs.[19]

In 1877 it was recalled how 'In all farm-houses the dresser in the ample kitchen was covered . . . with noggins, and with pails, all wood hooped, and kept as white as snow – whilst tubs and casks, all wood hooped, were in abundance.'[20] These containers with their hoops of willow or sometimes ash, soon began to be replaced by those bound by blacksmith-made iron hoops. On the Aran Islands, people had tankard-shaped 'milk jugs' with projecting lug handles, made up of staves bound by three iron hoops.[21]

In the 1840s, Caesar Otway, who often wrote about the west of Ireland, descri-bed 'vessels called noggins . . . composed of small staves, and bound together with hoops' which he examined in a cabin in county Mayo.[22] Small bound wooden drinking vessels known as noggins were used through-out Ireland at all levels of society. The word noggin also applies to a spirit measure of less than a quarter of a pint.[23] They were useful as dippers or measures and their contents were frequently shared at markets, a custom sanctioned by the nineteenth-century saying 'there's no luck in a dthry bargain.' Hence:

> I bought it myself at the market,
> From big Conny Collins, that made it,
> For two shillins, an' the share of a naggin.[24]

Kennedy, writing of nineteenth-century rural Wexford, described how a guest was offered the choice between 'a tumbler of spirits and water and a noggin of mixed milk'. Although in some areas 'Porridge and milk used to be eaten out of noggins',[25] a noggin was defined as 'a small mug or cup'.[26] Such things were skilfully made by the 'noggin weaver' (who may have been a specialist cooper) and in counties Cavan and Tyrone were made of oak staves, cle-verly bound together with one or two wide strips of interwoven ash. One stave was left longer than the others and served as a handle, which was usually comfortably shaped or pierced (fig. 317). Another exam-ple from county Donegal had staves of bog-

fir bound together by two separate strips of sally (willow).[27]

A piggin (known also in England and similar in shape to the Scottish 'luggie'), was another staved vessel, similar but con-siderably larger than a noggin, which was often used as a milking pail, as well as for drinking out of (fig. 318).[28] Defined as a 'small pail or tub', it had a projecting 'lug' as a handle.[29] Roughly hewn stone lids were sometimes used as covers, serving a dual purpose in keeping the water or milk cool while protecting it from marauding animals.[30]

Both noggins and piggins were often mentioned amongst the objects listed in the poorest houses right up to the kitchen or dairy of a 'big house' and were commonly used throughout the eighteenth and nine-teenth centuries.[31] They were available in a variety of shapes and sizes, from a noggin of a mere 3 inches high to a piggin capable of holding $1\frac{1}{2}$ pints or more.[32]

Similar staved vessels were known to have been used on the Continent and related examples, also of circular shape, bound with bronze and dating from as early as 50 BC have been recorded.[33] The terms piggin and noggin were both in use by the first half of the seventeenth century, so the Irish examples may easily stem from an ancient and widespread tradition.[34]

THE METHER OR MADDER

> Usquebagh to our feast in pails was brought up,
> A hundred at least, and a *madder* our cup.
>
> Swift and McGauran, *c.*1720[35]

319. Methers or Madders: traditional communal drinking vessels, dating from the medieval period through to the nineteenth century. Usually hewn from a solid block, with an inset base: made from a variety of local timbers. Lower right is from Corry, county Armagh. Upper right, a late nineteenth-century example of Yew from Killarney, county Kerry. Others of unknown origin. From the Department of Antiquities' collection, N.M.I.

The terms 'mether' or 'madder', both apparently Anglo-Irish derivatives of the Irish *meadar*, describe a large wooden drinking cup, square in plan, the main body of which is usually hewn from a single block of wood.[36] Examination of dozens of methers in the National Museum of Ireland shows that the base of each vessel was usually made from a separate piece of wood, inserted into a groove (or croze) and made watertight with a mastic-like substance. This collection of methers (pronounced like weather) shows that many are of ancient origin, and were still being made well into the nineteenth century (fig. 319). Two examples in the National Museum's collection, both from Kerry, are markedly different in appearance. Although many of them were originally found preserved in bogs, these two, made of yew, had never been buried and upon

close examination showed no signs of any great antiquity (fig. 319, top right).[37] Most of this collection have two integral handles, each on opposite sides.[38] Slightly fewer examples have four handles, one on each side, while others have one or no handles.[39] Sometimes the four handles are elongated below the line of the base, raising the whole vessel by an inch or so (fig. 319, top left).[40] They vary considerably in size, capacity, timber type and workmanship, but generally share the quadrangular top which tapers inwards to a round base. Some small ones without handles are of horn, while others are decorated with incised or poker-work patterns and symbols.

Their use and manufacture appear to have declined drastically towards the second half of the nineteenth century. The considerable size of some of the earliest examples suggests that they were popular at a time when large dimension timber was still commonly available. Lack of suitable timber at this later period may have contributed to their demise.

Wooden drinking vessels had been offered to travellers in northern Connaught since the seventeenth century, when Dunton drank milk, strained through a filter of clean grass, out of a 'meddar'.[41] While in Mayo in the mid-eighteenth century, the touring Dr Pococke wrote of the country people, 'all their vessels are of wood, most of them cut out of solid timber'.[42] A century later, Carleton described familiarly the 'old Irish drinking vessel, of a square form, with a handle or ear on each side [and as suggested in the poem, above], out of which all the family drank successively, or in rotation.' He also quoted a proverbial expression for a stormy night; 'the wind ris, and the rain fell as if it came out of methers'.[43] Such a saying surely arose as a result of the mether's considerable capacity, which was 'about a gallon' according to Caesar Otway. Otway, upon searching for a drinking vessel in a poor Mayo dwelling, was surprised when 'nothing was forthcoming but a wooden meather, carved out of a block of soft wood'.[44] An example of such a 'mether', discovered in a county Armagh bog in 1833, was described in *The Dublin Penny Journal* as made of 'crab tree. Its height is $7^{1/2}''$ and its circumference is $10^{1/2}''$; it holds about three pints . . . the usual size and form; but it is sometimes found of considerably greater size.'[45] Surviving examples range in height from only 4 to about 10 inches (fig. 319).

By the close of the nineteenth century these methers had become rare outside museums. A county Tyrone curator whose museum had dozens of these vessels in the mid nineteenth century, noted their connection with examples found in Scotland. He wrote of his collection that 'They are of various dimensions, some so small as to hold not more than the contents of a wine glass, whilst others are large enough to contain several gallons'.[46] Other commentators on methers cite examples which were made of silver, while an ancient wooden example from the Hebrides was described as being set with embossed silver and coral.[47] Stories abound of the great mirth caused by watching the uninitiated (usually English) attempt to drink from these peculiarly Irish square-topped vessels. One such account from the 1830s relates how a Lord Townsend

had two massive silver methers made in London, where they were regularly introduced at his dinner parties; the guests more usually applied the side of the vessel to the mouth, and seldom escaped with a dry neckcloth, vest, or doublet. After enjoying the mistake, usually called on his friend, the late Colonel O'Reilly . . . to teach the drill and handle the mether in true Irish style.[48]

Another distinct type of dug-out vessel, still in use in the nineteenth century was the narrow necked churn, examples of which have often been excavated from bogs.[49] Confusingly it was also known as a mether, but it was one of a wide variety of wooden containers which held butter. These bog butter-methers have often been preserved with their contents for centuries, although whether they were hidden or buried to conserve their contents is unclear.[50] Others are depicted in early illustrations or survive in museums all over the country.

It is interesting to compare methers with other solid or dug-out objects. Carving from the solid to make containers or chairs is generally considered to be one of the primary stages in the evolution of furniture construction, so it is remarkable to find such techniques being used as late as the nineteenth century. The dug-out chair, which went on being made up until the start of the twentieth century (fig. 80) has resulted from the same woodworking techniques of laborious gouging and carving as the methers. Dug-out examples of Irish kneading lossets, of shallow, oval form, were also known.[51]

Another distinct type of solid wooden vessel was the *lámhóg*,[52] a tall lathe-turned cup with a small projecting lug handle, narrowing towards the base and usually with a projecting foot rim (figs. 316–17).[53] This was partially turned on a pole lathe, and then finished off by carving. The shapes of these turned wooden mugs and goblets vary considerably and many show signs of having been made as recently as the nineteenth century, although like the methers, they arise from a more ancient tradition. The *lámhóg* and the mether are of particular interest, because unlike the many other wooden vessels which were commonly used, their designs seem to be peculiar to Ireland.

BASKETRY

'The wicker round,' he said, 'the skib,
In which potatoes from the pot are
    poured;
The creel that brings the turf up from
    the bog;
The kish that holds them by the
    fireside:
There's no one marks them with a
    craftsman's name
Scanted they are as commons of the
    house.'

Padraig Colum[54]

The basketmaker was the provider of a vast range of containers, from the fireside turf basket or kish, to the potato skib and the cradle. The subject of basketry in Ireland is complicated by the huge variety of basketwork objects that were made and used around the farmhouse and because their names and shapes varied greatly from one region to the next. Creels, as baskets for carrying were commonly known, were useful for a variety of jobs outside the home; huge carrying creels formed an integral part of the primitive Irish block-wheel carts: smaller creels with hinged bottoms were slung on one's back for transporting seaweed or turf. Basketmakers wove the frameworks of boats, lobster pots, shallow containers for holding 'long lines' for fishing or on a smaller scale calves' muzzles and babies' rattles. Here, a few of the most common or interesting basketwork items used inside the home will be described (the round potato skib or *sciob*, or original Irish kitchen table, has already been described in the chapter on tables. (fig. 203).

Sally (willow) was used all over Ireland, growing best in damp areas near lakes and rivers. Basketwork dating back to neolithic times has been found in bogs in counties

Westmeath, Longford and Tipperary. By the nineteenth century, two main regions were noted for basketmaking; around Lough Neagh in Ulster[55] and in the Suir Valley in northern Munster.[56] Sally was used not only by itinerant basketmakers, but also by specialist basketmaking firms and by many people who wove their own baskets whenever the necessity arose.

Arthur Young complained about the lack of proper osier grounds in Ireland, during the late eighteenth century, having observed that a shortage had resulted in 'considerable importation of them from Portugal' into Cork.[57] However, some people grew their own, as Young 'observed with much pleasure, that [near Limerick] all the cottars had their little gardens surrounded with banks well planted with osiers'.[58] The Reverend Hall, travelling through Limerick some thirty years later, wrote that in 'Kerry, and elsewhere, I found in the county of Limerick, the common people [were] extremely fond of wickerwork. Their doors with padlocks, windows, cradles, beds, chairs, etc. etc. are, in general, all of wickerwork.'[59]

An octogenarian basketmaker from county Offaly recalled recently how in his youth 'nearly every man could work rods' and that most people had their own 'sally garden'. The golden osier or green sally (and many other species), were tended and cut, to season for their own use or as a source of supply for any basketmaker who they might employ.[60] Woven wicker or wattle covered by clay was commonly used to fashion the tapered chimney canopies of traditional houses and such combinations of timber and wicker were used to make furniture as well.[61]

Carleton, writing during the 1830s, described how in a byre dwelling 'of the humblest description' there was 'a potato-bin, made up of stakes driven into the floor, and wrought with strong wickerwork'.[62] Dorothy Hartley, a keen observer of craftsmanship, noticed on a trip to county Wicklow in the 1930s, a chair made from 'bent sallies and a naturally bent piece of apple bough, wedged into a wooden seat, and four strong, straight, axe squared legs [that] were painted black.'[63] Wicker armchairs were also made and can be seen in early photographs, for sale in street markets and outside shops.[64]

In the same house as the wicker potato-bin, Carleton described how 'Above the door in the inside, almost touching the roof, was the hen-roost, made also of wicker-work'.[65] Wild birds also were caught in woven traps and then kept in wicker bird-cages, which can be seen hanging up in many nineteenth-century illustrations (eg. figs. 54, 127). Dorothy Hartley noticed a caged bullfinch hung in the porch of a Wexford farmhouse in the 1930s, kept perhaps for its musical song or colour.[66] In nineteenth century county Tipperary, linnets, goldfinches and jays were kept indoors in wicker cages.[67] These round birdcages, often with conical tops, can be seen amongst a huge range of other wicker-work items, photographed by Lawrence in the street market in Cork, at the end of the nineteenth century (fig. 280).

In a country where the design of verna-cular furniture was strongly influenced by timber shortage, it is not surprising that sally and dozens of other pliant materials were used as alternatives. Unfortunately the low value and fragility of the resulting objects means that disproportionately few examples have survived. Dry willow is one of the woodworm's favourite foodstuffs.

Although several authors have touched on basketmaking in Ireland in books on Irish history and culture,[68] there is still a need for further study, to do this fascinating subject justice.

Gazetteer

The following is a list of the main museums with Irish vernacular furniture in their collections. Those prefixed with an asterix have the most substantial collections, the others have a few pieces which are representative of locally typical designs. Many more smaller village museums managed by local committees are worth visiting, and may be open at weekends in summer, or upon request. For details of opening hours, see S. Popplewell, *Exploring Museums Ireland* (H.M.S.O. London, 1990).

Armagh County Museum, The Mall East, Armagh, county Armagh

Bunratty Castle and Folk Park, Bunratty, county Clare

Carlow County Museum, Carlow, county Carlow

Craggaunowen Project, Nr. Quin, county Clare

Damer House, Roscrea Heritage Centre, Roscrea, county Tipperary

De Valera's House, Bruree, county Limerick

Donegal County Museum, High Road, Letterkenny, county Donegal

Edmund Rice Museum, Callan, county Kilkenny

Enniscorthy County Museum, The Castle, Enniscorthy, county Wexford

Enniskillen County Museum, The Castle, Enniskillen, county Fermanagh

Glencolumbkille Folk Museum, Glencolumbkille, county Donegal

The Irish Agricultural Museum, Johnstown Castle, Wexford, county Wexford

Knock Folk Museum, Knock, county Mayo

Monaghan County Museum, Hill Street, Monaghan, county Monaghan

Muckross House, Killarney, county Kerry

The National Museum of Ireland, Kildare Street, Dublin (substantial collection, all in storage at time of publication)

Patrick Pearse's House, Rosmuck, county Galway

The Pighouse (Folk) Collection, Corr House, Cornafean, county Cavan. Telephone in advance: 049 37248

Ulster American Folk Park, Camphill, Omagh, county Tyrone

The Ulster Folk and Transport Museum, Cultra, Holywood, county Down

Wilson House, Dergalt, Strabane, county Tyrone

320. The entrance to Ceim Hill Museum, near Union Hall, west county Cork, showing a stool made from one of a pair of winch covers, with three splayed and through-wedged legs. These were salvaged from the wreck of the steamship *Asian*, which sank on the nearby Stag Rocks in 1924. The stools, originally painted brown, were made by the present curator's father, Denis O'Mahoney. By kind permission of Therese O'Mahoney.

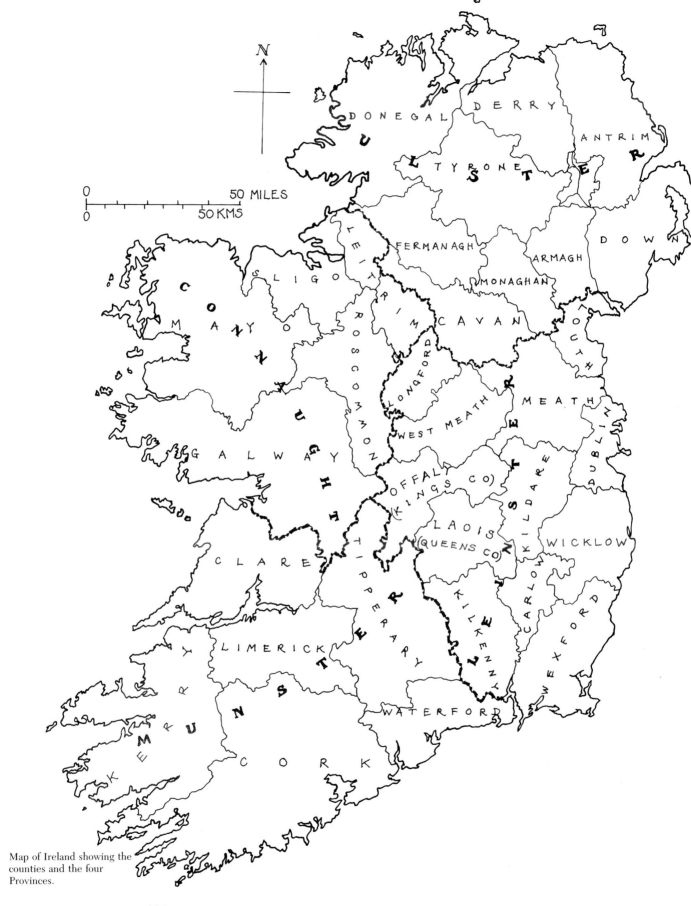

N

0   50 MILES
0   50 KMS

DONEGAL   DERRY

ULSTER   ANTRIM

TYRONE

FERMANAGH   DOWN

ARMAGH

MONAGHAN

SLIGO   CAVAN

LEITRIM

CONNAUGHT   ROSCOMMON   LONGFORD   LOUTH

MAYO   WEST MEATH   MEATH

GALWAY   OFFALY
(KINGS CO)   KILDARE   DUBLIN

LAOIS
(QUEENS CO)   WICKLOW

CLARE   LEINSTER   CARLOW

TIPPERARY   KILKENNY   WEXFORD

LIMERICK   MUNSTER

KERRY   CORK   WATERFORD

Map of Ireland showing the
counties and the four
Provinces.

204

Glossary of Terminology

This glossary is intended as a quick guide to the meanings of some of the terms used in the main text. Irish equivalents, translations or origins (given in italics) are only occasionally included where the author considers them relevant. This is not intended as a comprehensive set of etymologies and translations, as many other regional terms in English and Irish exist which are unlisted.

BASIN   A bowl used for eating or drinking out of.

BATH BRICK   A brick-shaped piece of earth made of carbonate of lime or of calcium, kept in a KNIFE BOX for sharpening or cleaning knives.

BED-OUTSHOT   See OUTSHOT.

BEETLE   A pestle-like wooden implement used for washing clothes, mashing potatoes or beating straw before twisting it into rope etc.

BENT   A type of reedy grass cut from sandy coastal areas, used for twisting into rope for chair seats, plaited mats, coiled SKEPS etc.

BOG-WOOD   Oak, FIR, yew etc. found preserved in peat bogs. Bog oak is hard and black like ebony, polishes well and was highly valued. Bog yew was said to resemble rosewood. Bog fir (sometimes known simply as FIR), was useful for building, fuel, lighting, furniture etc.

BOOT FOOT   See SLEDGE FOOT.

BOSS   A round seat or hassock made of straw, either coiled and bound or plaited, or of rushes. (In Irish, variously *súistín, súisteog, saoistín, saoisteog*)

BOX BED   A rectangular box-like bed, often built-in, but enclosed on three sides and above by wood, the front covered by wooden doors or sometimes by curtains.

BYRE-DWELLING   A dwelling which combined accommodation for people at one end of a room and cattle at the other. Used to be found in the provinces of Munster, Connaught and Ulster.

CABIN   A poor or landless mud- or turf-built dwelling.

CADDOW   A woollen covering or coverlet.

CAMP BED   Another local word for a CANOPY BED, especially in Munster.

CANOPY BED/CAMP BED   In Ireland, a bed with an arched wooden TESTER over it, or 'canopy', generally with a curtained front.

CARBERY SETTLE   An OPEN FRAME SETTLE incorporating a FALLING TABLE, once common in west county Cork.

CHAMFER   A bevel resulting from the removal of a right-angled edge.

CHICKEN COOP   See COOP.

CLARE BED   Antique dealers' term for a hip-roofed CANOPY BED.

CLEVY   (From English dialectal *clevy, clavel* a mantelpiece) A pair of hooked brackets in various forms, for holding a spit. Also a local word for a KEEPING HOLE or HANGING DRESSER.

COOB   See COOP.

COOM   See COOP.

COOPER'S MARE   A low woodworking bench-vice upon which a chairmaker sits astride to shape chair legs etc.

COOP/COOB/COOM/CHICKEN COOP/HEN COOP   (Hence Irish *cúb*, anglicised as coob/coom) A slatted straw-lined cage, one to three layers high, for confining laying fowl indoors.

COOP DRESSER   A dresser incorporating a HEN COOP in the base.

COTTAGE   A small dwelling house. Until the late nineteenth century, often used as a derogatory term.

COVERED CAR/JINGLE   A horse-drawn public conveyance, used in southern counties from the early nineteenth to the early twentieth century, surrounded by an upper valance and rainproof oilcloth curtains.

COVERED CAR BED   In southern counties, a bed enclosed by curtains, so called because of its resemblance to a horse-drawn COVERED CAR.

CRANE   A pivoting device of wood or iron for hanging pots, kettles, griddles etc. over the fire at fixed heights, and for swinging them away from the fire when the contents are cooked.

CREEPIE/CREEPIE-STOOL/CREEPY   (From the verb to *creep*) Particularly in the northern counties a common low fireside stool, with three or four legs (and in Scotland a church stool of repentance).

CUP-RACK   See RACK.

DEAL   Pine or FIR, usually sawn into boards or planks.

DELFTWARE/DELFT/WARE   Glazed ceramic plates, bowls, mugs and jugs made in Ireland or imported from abroad, sold at fairs and by itinerants, and displayed decoratively on Irish dressers.

DONKEY'S BREAKFAST   A straw bed taken by a departing emigrant on a boat.

DOWRY CHEST   A two-part clothes chest with drawers in the lower half, usually surmounted by a chest with a sloping, lockable lid: found predominantly in southern and south eastern counties.

DRAWKNIFE/DRAWING KNIFE   A double-handled cutting tool used by basketmakers and chairmakers for shaping chair legs, CHAMFERING etc., which cuts when drawn towards the user.

DUG-OUT   A chair, LOSSET, METHER, etc., which has been hewn or gouged from a single block or trunk of wood. Hence DUG-OUT CHAIR.

FALLING TABLE/FALLING-LEAF TABLE/FOLDING TABLE/ HANGING TABLE/WALL TABLE (Irish *bord crochta*) A space-saving and timber-saving table hinged to a wall, supported at its outer end by a hinged leg(s). It lifts upwards and can be fixed flat against the wall. Some examples are hinged to a long wall bar, and can be slid along to double as a window shutter or to be closer to the fire. Once known throughout Ireland, it is now rare.

FAMINE CHAIR   Antique dealers' term for a HEDGE CHAIR.

FEATHER TICK   See TICK.

FELLOE   One of the outer, curved rim sections of a wooden cart-wheel.

FIR   See BOG-WOOD and DEAL.

FOLDING TABLE   See FALLING TABLE.

GRAINING   See WOODGRAINING.

GYPSY TABLE   A small three-legged table sold cheaply by tinkers at the roadside. The legs, of unworked slender branches, were nailed together.

HANGING DRESSER   See RACK.

HANGING TABLE   See FALLING TABLE.

HEDGE CARPENTER   An unqualified carpenter who made pig troughs, fences, wooden ploughs, etc., often utilising naturally bent KNEES and found timber.

HEDGE CHAIR   A slab-seated chair, often made by a HEDGE CARPENTER or householder, from local timbers, with legs and back fixed into a slab seat by unconcealed through-wedged joints.

HEN COOP   See COOP.

HUTCH   See MEAL ARK.

JAMB WALL   An internal dividing wall between the entrance and hearth, often fitted with a spy hole (or logie hole) to provide a glimpse of approaching visitors. A common feature of traditional houses in parts of eastern and south-eastern Ireland.

KEEPING HOLE   (In Irish variously *poll an bhairc*; hole in hob, or *poll an phaidrín*; the hole for the Rosary beads, etc.) A recessed hole set into the fireplace wall of a kitchen, for safe, dry storage of small articles, knives, etc. Sometimes fitted with a wooden door.

KITCHEN   (Irish *Anlann*, sauce) A term used to denote various additions to a staple meal of potatoes, eg. milk, butter, butter-milk, salt, fish, meat, etc., added to improve the taste or consistency.

KNEE   A naturally bent piece of timber, used in shipbuilding, also by makers of HEDGE CHAIRS for curved back rests.

KNIFE BOX   A wall-hung box with a long extended back. The box was used to store ROTTENSTONE or BATH BRICK, and its long back was laid flat and used for sharpening and honing knives.

LIP-WORK   The technique of making chairs, stools, bee SKEPS, containers etc., from straw which is coiled and bound together, usually with stripped briars. A term not traditionally used in Ireland, but described here instead as 'coiled and bound work'.

LOSSET   (Irish *losaid*). A kneading tray to contain dough and flour when making bread. Usually hung up on the wall when not in use.

MADDER   See METHER.

MEAL   Oatmeal, flour, Indian meal etc.

MEAL ARK/MEAL BIN/MEAL CHEST/HUTCH   (Irish *Airc*) A tall kitchen chest with a sloping, hinged lid and narrow internal shelf, for safe, dry storage of oatmeal, flour etc. between harvests.

METHER/MADDER   (From Irish *meadar*) A drinking vessel of ancient origin, square topped, the body hewn from a single block of wood, with an inset base and usually with two or four handles.

NOGGIN   (Hence Irish *naigín*) A straight-sided mug or dipper, about 3 inches high, made of bound staves, with one longer stave serving as a handle.

OPEN FRAME SETTLE   A SETTLE made of framed-up small pieces rather than of wide boards, found mainly in the west and south west.

OSIER   A shoot of willow not grown to maturity, cut annually for basket making.

OUTSHOT/BED-OUTSHOT   (Regional Irish forms include *cúilteach*; literally 'back house', and *cailleach*; 'an old woman'). An alcove usually set into the rear wall of a kitchen corner near the hearth, to accommodate a bed which was often concealed by curtains or wooden doors. Used to be built into traditional houses in parts of the north west and west.

PAILLASSE/PALLIASSE   (From French *paille/straw*) A mattress of straw, sometimes plaited.

PIGGIN   (Irish *pigín*) Larger version of a NOGGIN, a small, staved pail or tub for milk or water, sometimes covered and kept cool by a stone lid.

PITSAW   A large, two-man saw, usually operated in a pit, or on a raised framework, for sawing up tree trunks into boards.

POST BED   In Ireland, usually a built-in four poster bed, with or without a TESTER, and draped by curtains.

PRESS   The usual word for a cupboard.

PRESSBED   A two-door cupboard containing a wooden-framed bed and bedding which can be folded out onto the floor for use.

RACK   (Irish *Raca*) Term used in county Kerry to describe a slat-backed fireside SETTLE.

RACK   A wooden framework fixed to a wall for hanging cups and utensils on hooks, and locally known as a CUP-RACK/HANGING DRESSER/TIN-RAIL. Also a CRANE for hanging pots over fire.

ROOM, THE   The usual name for the parlour, or in some areas of western Ireland the WEST ROOM, usually leading off the kitchen, and sometimes doubling as a bedroom.

ROTTENSTONE   A friable siliceous limestone used for sharpening knives.

SALLY   The willow or osier, grown for basketmaking, hence sally garden.

SALT BOX   A wooden box kept near the hearth to store salt, with a sloping lid and sometimes with leather hinges.

SCRAW   (From Irish *scraith*). Green sod, matted grass and roots, used to line the underside of thatch.

SETTLE   A bench with a high back and arms, usually made long enough to sleep on. Also used as an abbreviation for SETTLE BED.

SETTLE BED   A bench with hinges which can be folded out onto the floor, to make a high-sided floor-level double bed, often used to accommodate a traveller or several children. By day it is a long seat, with the mattress and bedding stored inside out of sight.

SETTLE TABLE   A SETTLE with a back rest, which converts into a table by folding downwards by means of hinges at the rear of the arm rests. Used in parts of the south east.

SHAKE-DOWN   (Irish *sráideog*) A temporary bed made daily on the floor from straw, bracken, rushes.

SHOE FOOT   See SLEDGE FOOT.

SKEP   An old-fashioned beehive, dome shaped, of coiled and bound straw.

SKIB   (Irish *scib, sciobóg, ciseóg* in Galway, *bascáid geal* in Donegal) A shallow, round or boat-shaped basket, commonly used for straining potatoes. It was often also used to eat potatoes out of, supported on a three-legged pot instead of a table.

SLEDGE FOOT/BOOT FOOT/SHOE FOOT   A renewable foot which runs from the front to the back of the base of a dresser or SETTLE, especially in northern and western counties. Considered to be of medieval origin.

SPIDER/SPIDER TABLE   Used in inventories to denote a gate-leg table: one with drop leaves which are supported by hinged gates.

STANDING BED/HIGH STANDING BED   Usually a four-posted bed draped with curtains and covered by a TESTER.

STATIONS, THE   The occasion of Roman Catholic Mass and Confession being held in a private house, usually with a celebratory meal.

STILLION/STILLING   A stone or wooden structure on which pails of water from the spring were placed. In early inventories, a stand or gantry for casks.

STRADOGUE   (From Irish *Sráideog*) A family slept 'in stradogue', top to tail, before the fire, on an improvised bed or SHAKE-DOWN of straw, rushes, heather etc., usually covered by clothes or a blanket.

STRAW CHAIR   An armchair made either of thickly plaited straw, or of coiled straw, bound together with stripped briar. The seat of either type was stuffed, or had a rudimentary wooden supporting framework.

STRETCHER   A piece of timber fixed as a brace between chair or table legs.

SÚGÁN   (Irish *Súgán*) Twisted straw or hay rope, used for weaving into chair seats, hence SÚGÁN CHAIRS. Also for many other uses like tying down thatch, tethering animals, making harness etc.

SÚGÁN CHAIR   Any chair originally intended to have a woven SÚGÁN seat. Most have now had their seats rewoven with fishing twine or string.

TESTER   The wooden canopy above a bed.

TESTER BED   (Hence Irish, *Leaba théastair*) A bed fitted with a (flat) wooden canopy above, the top surrounded by a VALANCE, and hung with curtains made originally of straw, or later of cloth.

THRAWHOOK   (From Scots, literally throw-hook, numerous local Irish terms) A northern Irish word for a particular implement for twisting straw or hay rope.

THREE CORNER PRESS   A corner Cupboard, usually built into the parlour, with glazed upper door(s), for special WARE, glass etc.

TICK   A mattress of straw, flock, feathers etc. (hence FEATHER TICK), covered with sackcloth, linen or cotton cloth (hence ticking).

TINKER/TRAVELLER   Originally an itinerant tinsmith, mender of pots, and seller of WARE.

TIN-RAIL   See RACK.

TURF   Peat cut from peat bogs and dried for use as fuel. Up to the nineteenth century, was sometimes made into the walls of houses and into seats; Irish *saoiste ceathrar cúinneach*, a quadrangular seat of turf.

TWISTER/THRAW-HOOK   An implement for twisting rope from various materials (straw, hay etc.).

VALANCE   A strip of cloth running along the top and/or across the base of various types of enclosed or curtained beds, often gathered.

VERNACULAR   Local, indigenous. A term originally used by architectural historians, but used here to denote furniture built for vernacular dwellings, where otherwise the terms 'regional', 'common' or 'country' might be used.

WALL TABLE   See FALLING TABLE.

WARE   See DELFTWARE.

WEST ROOM   See ROOM.

WOODGRAINING   Paint of two colours applied in imitation of expensive decorative woods such as oak, mahogany, satinwood etc.

Bibliographic Note

A separate bibliography is not included here, because the number of publications devoted to Irish Vernacular Furniture can be counted on the fingers of one hand, and all the documentary sources used can be found in the footnotes. The sources drawn on here are deliberately as varied as possible, and are combined with the findings of field-studies of surviving furniture from all over Ireland. Evidence is drawn from a combination of early photographs, paintings, drawings, newspapers, journals, diaries, poems, songs, oral history, inventories, museum and university questionnaire responses, insurers' reports, government reports and surveys, and literary descriptions from Irish inhabitants and their visitors, through the centuries. With the exception of Nicholas Loughnan's *Irish Country Furniture*, a pamphlet written for the Irish Heritage Series (1984), articles touching on furniture have tended to be written by architectural historians or folklorists, for specialist journals about particular areas of Ireland.

Any student of Ireland's material culture owes much to the work of such folklorists as the late Professor Estyn Evans, whose book *Irish Folk Ways* was one of the first to address the details of everyday life, including a chapter about furniture, and a bibliography. Since his fieldstudies during the 1940s and 50s, many objects, particularly those of straw, have almost vanished from the domestic scene, and his writings on such furniture have therefore been referred to here as a rare modern source. The more recent publication of Caoimhín Ó Danachair and Dr P. Lysaght', *A Bibliography of Irish Ethnology and Folk Tradition* (1978), is an invaluable source of further reading. Ó Danachair has also published

widely on Irish culture and some of his photographs are reproduced here.

Further information came from the British Government's Poor Reports, some of which related to housing conditions during the 1830s. Similarly, housing and interiors were included amongst the descriptions of local topics accompanying the Ordinance Survey maps of Northern Ireland (from the 1820s). These manuscripts are now being published by the Royal Irish Academy (Dublin) in conjunction with the Institute of Irish Studies (Queen's University of Belfast). Inventories of Irish houses are comparatively rare, few of them surviving through the centuries of upheaval. However, Rosemary ffolliott has almost single-handedly published a considerable number of inventories not only from 'big houses' but also from farmhouses, in *The Irish Ancestor* (an annual journal).

The diverse mixture of literature referred to amongst the footnotes, includes travellers' descriptions of interiors; particularly interesting are those from the first half of the nineteenth century by William Carleton and Patrick Kennedy.

More recent information relating to furniture can be found amongst the manuscripts and 'Schools' Collection' volumes dating from 1935 and housed by the Department of Irish Folklore (successor to the Irish Folklore Commission), University College, Dublin. In the same archive are the responses to questionnaires about furniture, which were sent out in the 1950s. The Ulster Folk and Transport Museum near Belfast, subsequently sent out similar questionnaires, to respondents throughout the nine counties of Ulster; covering a broad range of subjects and responses, some of which are also illustrated.

Notes

Abbreviations used in References:

Two sets of questionnaires about furniture are particularly useful in ascertaining regional differences and styles. The first was sent by the Department of Irish Folklore (part of University College, Dublin) in the 1950s, and is referred to thus: eg. D.I.F. Ms. Vol. 1663 or 1664 (*c*.1957) 71. The last figures refer to the respondent's number . It was sent to about 120 people throughout Ireland. It would repay further study by an Irish speaking scholar, as some of the responses are in Irish.

The second questionnaire was sent to over 100 people by the Ulster Folk and Transport Museum in 1964, concentrated, in unequal numbers, on the old nine counties of Ulster. It is referred to as 'U.F.M. Quest (1964) Q1b/71'. The final figure again is the respondent's number, and the other refers to the questionnaire number. Combining both sets of responses provides answers from every county, but disproportionately: once combined, county Leix (Laois) for example has only three responses, whereas county Antrim is represented by thirty-three.

Brit. Mus. Add. Ms.	British Museum Additional Manuscript
D.I.F.	Department of Irish Folklore, University College, Dublin. (Irish Folklore Commission collection). numbered responses to questionnaires on all aspects of folklife, including furniture, sent out in the 1950s to over 120 respondents all over Ireland.
H.C.	House of Commons Poor Inquiry (Ireland). Reports of the Commissioners of Inquiry into the Conditions of the Poorer Classes in Ireland (1836).
N.L.I.	National Library of Ireland, Dublin.
O.S. Mem.	Ordnance Survey Memoirs of Ireland. 1820s and 1830s, Institute of Irish Studies, Queens University Royal Irish Academy, Dublin.
P.R.O.N.I.	Public Record Office of Northern Ireland, Belfast.
U.F.M. Quest.	Ulster Folk and Transport Museum Questionnaires; numbered responses to questionnaires on all aspects of folklife, including furniture, sent out in the 1960s to over 100 respondents in the 9 counties of Ulster.

Introduction

1 For more on dress, the following is highly recommended; M. Dunlevy, *Dress in Ireland* (London, 1989), 111–13.

2 A. Day and P. Williams eds, O.S. Memoirs of Ireland, V, Parish of Leckpatrick (1821), county Tyrone (I.I.S./ R.I.A., Belfast, 1990), 124.

3 Day and Williams eds, O.S. Memoirs of Ireland, X, Parish of Island Magee (1839–1840), county Antrim (I.I.S./R.I.A., Belfast, 1991), 37, 102.

4 J.C. Walton, 'The Household Effects of a Waterford Merchant family in 1640' in *The Journal of the Cork Historical and Archaeological Society*, LXXXIII, No. 238 (July–December, 1978), 102.

5 C. Gilbert, *English Vernacular Furniture*, 1750–1900 (London, New Haven, 1991), 2.

6 G. Stokes ed., *Pococke's Tour in Ireland in 1752* (Dublin, 1891), 87, 117–20. The condition of the streets of Cork may be attributed to the fact that vast numbers of cattle were driven through them to Cork slaughter houses, to victual the British and French fleets during the 18th century. For more about the state of roads and transport see J.L. McCracken, 'The Age of the Stage Coach' part 4 in K.B. Nolan ed, *Travel and Transport in Ireland* (Dublin, 1973), 55. He explains that 'In other parts there were no signposts because, it was said, the poor would have cut them down for fuel as soon as they had been put up.'

7 F. Page ed, *Letters of John Keats* (Oxford, 1954), 3–9 July 1818, 140. The author is grateful to Christopher Gilbert for pointing out this text. See McCracken, 'The Age of the Stage Coach', 52–3. Examples of sedan chairs can be seen in Enniscorthy Castle Museum, county Wexford and the Ulster Folk and Transport Museum, Belfast.

8 O.S. Memoir, Box 5 II 13 (1837), 14, 101. This has subsequently been published as, Day and Williams eds, O.S. Memoirs of Ireland, VIII, Parish of Blaris (1837), county Antrim (I.I.S./R.I.A., Belfast, 1991), 70–7. For definition of 'Bent grass', see Glossary, p. 205. These 'bent bottomed' chairs are likely to have been similar in range of design to *súgán* chairs from elsewhere.

9 These settle tables (chair tables) have been photographed (but not published) by Gabriel Olive, to whom the author is grateful; also to Christopher Gilbert for drawing her attention to them.

10 R. Ross Noble, 'The Chairs of Sutherland and Caith-

ness: A Northern tradition in Highland Chairmaking?' in *Regional Furniture*, I (Leeds, 1987), 33–40. There are many other connections, such as the word 'creepie' being used in both regions, to describe a small low stool.

11 See A. Fenton, *The Island Blackhouse* (H.M.S.O. Edinburgh, 1989), 19–23. D. Jones, 'Box Beds in Eastern Scotland' in *Regional Furniture*, V (Leeds, 1991), 79–85. See also chapter 5: Beds, in this volume. Also Gilbert, *English Vernacular Furniture*, 129–32, cites examples of outshut [sic] beds, similar to the outshot [sic] beds of north-western Ireland.

12 To make connections between Irish designs and those found in Canada see H. Pain, *The Heritage of Upper Canadian Furniture: A Study in the Survival of Formal and Vernacular Styles from Britain, America and Europe, 1780–1900* (Toronto, 1978), 128, fig. 314, 159–63, 210–11, 235, 300, fig. 809. Also J. Mannion, *The History of Irish Settlement in Upper Canada* (Toronto, 1974), 152–8.

13 For examples see T. and J. Hooper, *Australian Country Furniture* (Victoria, 1988), 27, 78. Also T. and J. Hooper, *Australian Country and Colonial Furniture and Folk Art Exhibition Catalogue* (1988), lot 50, from Young, New South Wales; 'Early blue painted dresser with Irish stylistic features, large dovetails to the sleigh feet' illustrated amongst lots 41–58. Further examples of forms, chairs etc. of Irish origin are published in G. Cornall, *Memories, A Survey of Early Australian Furniture in the Collection of the Lord McAlpine of West Green* (Perth, 1990), 55–7, 72, figs. 2–3, 72, fig. 3, 115, fig. 2, 130, fig. 4.

14 J.M. Synge, *The Aran Islands* (1906, Belfast, 1988), 18.

Irish Vernacular Architecture

1 Quoted in M. Harkin and S. McCarroll, *Carndonagh* (Dublin, 1984), 170.

2 Notably A. Gailey, *Rural Houses of The North of Ireland* (Edinburgh, 1984). E.E. Evans, *Irish Folk Ways* (London, 1957, 1979), 39–58. K. Danaher, *Ireland's Vernacular Architecture* (Cork, 1975). A. Gailey, 'Vernacular Dwellings in Ireland' in *Revue Roumaine d'Histoire de l'Art., Serie Beaux-Arts*, XIII (Bucharest, 1976), 137–56. A. Gailey, 'The Housing of the Rural Poor in Nineteenth-Century Ulster' in *Ulster Folklife*, XXII (Belfast, 1976). C. Ó Danachair, 'The Bothán Scóir' in E. Rynne ed., *North Munster Studies* (Limerick, 1967), pl. XXI and 489–98. W. Pfeiffer and M. Shaffrey, *Irish Cottages* (London, 1990), good as an illustrative source. In addition see articles published on this subject in Irish journals by A. Gailey, E.E. Evans, F.H.A. Aalen, K. Danaher (C. Ó *Danachair*), D. McCourt, A. Cambell.

3 Dr A. Gailey, the leading authority on vernacular architecture in Ulster, first warned the author away from the use of the term cottage. He has gone into the word's history in depth, studying its use since the 1600s in Ulster. See Gailey, *Rural Houses*, 197–205. 'Only people from towns refer to one storey country houses as "cottages", and earn the secret annoyance and resentment of the owner . . . The term in south Armagh vernacular was "a house of one bay". It is of primitively simple structure . . .' from M.J. Murphy, *Mountain Year* (Dublin, 1964), 9.

4 Each aspect is described fully in its appropriate typological chapter.

5 In some instances the walls of traditional houses have actually been demolished beyond repair in order to remove such furniture. Free-standing dressers, for example, were often built within the confines of the kitchen so furniture dealers often resort to cutting them in half (horizontally) to extract them. So called 'three corner presses' were usually simply a wide front framework surrounding glazed and panelled doors, fitted across an existing corner, with shelves behind.

6 The Census of Ireland for the Year 1841, quoted in C. Woodham-Smith, *The Great Hunger* (London, 1987), 20. Also Ó Danachair, 'The Bothan Scoir', 489. Also Gailey, 'The Housing of the Rural Poor', 34–58.

7 For more precise details of distribution of particular materials, floor plans and the overlapping of types etc. see C. Ó Danachair, 'Some Distribution Patterns in Irish Folk Life' in *Bealoideas*, XXV (Dublin, 1957), 108–16. And more recently, Gailey, 'Vernacular Dwellings in Ireland', fig. 16, 149.

8 Except in areas where it was locally mined and abundant.

9 Gailey, 'Vernacular Dwellings in Ireland', 138–9. B. O'Reilly, 'The Vernacular Architecture of North Co. Dublin' in *Archaeology Ireland*, V, No. 2, Issue. 16 (Summer, 1991), 24–6. O'Reilly has recorded the survival of both these two distinct house types and some hybrid forms, all within county Dublin.

10 Danaher, *Ireland's Vernacular Architecture*, 12.

11 There are inevitably exceptions to these guidelines and Gailey explains how where the two contrasting regions meet there are often confusing hybrid types combining characteristics from both categories.

12 W. Hanbidge, *The Memories of William Hanbidge, Aged 93, 1906, An Autobiography* (St Albans, 1939), 20.

13 U.F.M. Quest. (1964) Qlb. 73; shows a house plan with a '½ wagon wheel' fender, which was apparently quite common and presumably was made of the iron rim of a cartwheel.

14 U.F.M. Quest. (1964) Qlb. 71.

15 Evans, *Irish Folk Ways*, 62.

16 Very few earth floors still survive in use.

17 W. Carleton, *Traits and Stories of the Irish Peasantry*, II, 4th edn, (Dublin, 1835), 287.

18 Arthur Young, who toured Ireland in 1777, illustrates a single-roomed cabin with no windows or chimney and a plume of smoke issuing from the door. His description of how poor people actually prevented smoke from escaping by blocking the chimney or doorway to conserve heat and fuel is quite typical: C. Maxwell ed, A. Young, *A Tour In Ireland with general observations on the present state of that Kingdom, made in the years 1776, 1777 and 1778* (Cambridge, 1925), 84–5, 187.

19 H.C. Parliamentary Papers: Report of the Commissioners (II) 1836. Supplement to Appendix (E). XXXII. County Kildare, Union of Clane, 59.

20 H.C. Parliamentary Papers: Report of the Commissioners (II) 1836. Supplement to Appendix (E). XXXII. County Meath, Baronies Navan upper and lower, 111.

21 European countries where byre dwellings were also well know included parts of Denmark, Germany Holland, Belgium, France and Britain according to Ó Danachair, 'Some Distribution Patterns in Irish Folk Life', 114–16. See also C. Ó Danachair, 'The Combined Byre and Dwelling in Ireland' in *Folklife*, II (Cardiff, 1964), 58–75.

22 Reconstructions of byre dwellings can be seen at Bunratty Folk Park, Limerick and the Ulster Folk and Transport Museum, Cultra, county Down.

23 T.H. Mason, *The Islands of Ireland, their Scenery,*

People, Life and Antiquities (London, 1938), plate 54, fig. 59, 35. Mason goes on to describe the radical transformation of these conditions wrought by the Congested Districts Board (set up in 1891), who had by 1936 rehoused such 'cottagers' and banished livestock from the houses.

24 D.I.F. Ms. Vol. 782 (Parish of lack, county Kerry, 1941), 393.

25 M. Doyle, *Hints to Small Holders, on Planting, Cattle, Poultry, Agricultural Implements, Flax etc.* (Dublin, 1832), 54–7. Doyle also mentions that since labourers were unlikely to have enough grain to fatten poultry for the market, keeping them in indoor coops helped fatten them quickly as they took less exercise. The author is grateful to Dr Austin O'Sullivan for drawing her attention to this text.

26 C. Otway, *Sketches in Erris and Tyrawly* (Dublin, 1841), 28. A similar hanging straw partition is described in further detail near Kilkenny, by Revd. J. Hall, *Tour Through Ireland, particularly the interior and lesser known parts etc.* 2 vols, I (London, 1813), 86.

27 D.I.F. Ms. Vol. 782 (Parish of Lack, county Kerry, 1941), 393.

28 This arrangement of a dresser forming a partition, in a weaver's house, is depicted in an oil painting by James Brenan (1837–1904) 'Committee of Inspection' in the Crawford Municipal Art Gallery, Cork, Cat. No. 292.

29 T. Ó Criomhthain (1856–1937) describes typical byre dwellings partitioned by furniture from the Great Blasket Island in his youth in *The Islandman* (Oxford, 1937), 26–8.

30 This type of partition, 'seven feet high, ornamented in front by a dresser' separating a county Wexford farm kitchen from its parlour, is described in P. Kennedy, *Evenings in the Duffrey* (Dublin, 1869), 61.

31 A disproportionate number of surviving dressers in traditional houses remain because they were incorporated into such walls.

32 For a description of such a sleeping loft divided into three 'apartments' see P. Kennedy, *The Banks of the Boro* (London, 1876), 170.

33 'The loft at the bottom of the house is *an lochta* – the loft proper – while *cullochta*, the back-loft, overhangs the hearth.' from R. Flower, *The Western Island or the Great Blasket* (Oxford, 1944, 1985). 42. Also see 'Thallage' in G.B. Adams, 'Glossary of Household Terms', appended to A. Gailey, 'Kitchen Furniture' in *Ulster Folklife*, XII (Belfast, 1966), 31–4.

34 Flower, *The Western Island*, 42.

35 Many 'paired beds' were in the form of enclosed beds, i.e. with three sides and the top enclosed and a curtain which could be drawn across the front. For evidence see U.F.M. Quest. (1964), Q1b and D.I.F. (c.1950) Mss. Vols. 1663–4. The author's fieldwork has also shown that a few examples still survive in use, particularly in county Donegal.

36 Many surviving 'rooms' have decorative ceilings, formed by complex geometric arrangements of painted 'tongued and grooved' pine, contrasting with adjacent kitchens with their open joist ceilings.

37 J.M. Synge, *The Aran Islands* (Oxford, 1907, 1985), 14.

38 Flower, *The Western Island*, 42.

39 H. Glassie, *Passing the Time, Folklore and History of an Ulster Community* (Dublin, 1982); see fig. 'Mrs Cutler's Cooker', 389, 390.

40 Gailey, *Rural Houses*, 64–5.

41 G.Ó Tuathaigh, 'The Distressed Society, The Struggle for Emancipation and Independence, 1809–1918', in B. de Breffny ed., *The Irish World, the History and Cultural Achievements of the Irish People* (London, 1986), 192–5.

42 Conditions in the old houses were for many damp, cramped and dirty. Micheal O'Guiheen, poet and storyteller of the Great Blasket Island, described his family's move to one of the new houses built by 'the Board' at the beginning of this century: 'We were all delighted to be leaving the horrible old hole, where we were smothered alive. However hard my mother [Peig Sayers] tried to keep it clean and tidy she failed.' The new place was considered a dramatic improvement: 'There won't be a cow or an ass tethered inside this house of a night. Your father will have to put up a shed against the house for them.' From M. O'Guiheen, *A Pity Youth Does Not Last, Reminiscences of the Last of the Great Blaskets Island's Poets and Storytellers* (Oxford, 1953, 1982), 8.

How Ireland's Timber has influenced Furniture Design

1 Anon., 'Lament for the Woodlands' quoted from F. O'Connor, *Kings, Lords and Commons* (New York, 1959), 98–101.

2 D. Corkery, *The Hidden Ireland, A Study of Caelic Munster in the Eighteenth Century* (Dublin, 1924, 1986), 35.

3 'A considerable quantity of timber for the rebuilding of London after the Great Fire of 1666 came from Ireland. The regular export of Irish timber to England continued throughout the century.' From E. MacLysaght, *Irish Life in the Seventeenth Century: After Cromwell* (1939), 143–4: Footnotes referring to Daniel Defoes 'Tour', I (1724–6), 141. Also mentioned by E. McCracken, *The Irish Woods Since Tudor Times, Distribution and Exploitation* (Institute of Irish Studies, Belfast, 1971), 77. For information about earlier export of Irish timber see T. O'Neill, *Merchants and Mariners in Medieval Ireland* (Dublin, 1987), 100–2, who explains: 'In medieval France, Irish oak was considered to be especially suitable for furniture and sculpture.' The choirstalls of Rouen Cathedral utilised it in 1465–9. Irish oak was also favoured by the builders of English churches: it was used for Salisbury Cathedral in 1224.

4 J.H. Andrews, 'Land and People, c.1685, in T.W. Moody, F.X. Martin and F.J. Byrne eds, *A New History of Ireland, 1534–1691* (Oxford, 1976), 468.

5 McCracken, *The Irish Woods*, 15. Also E. Neeson, *A History of Irish Forestry* (Dublin, 1991), 63: 'the substantially forested Ireland of 1600 [became], by 1750, a treeless wilderness and a net importer of timber'.

6 McCracken, *The Irish Woods*, 45, 13–56, 90–6. Dr Pococke mentions working ironmines and ironworks and others already closed down near Lismore in western county Waterford in G. Stokes ed., *Pococke's Tour in Ireland in 1752* (Dublin, 1891), 123. M. Scott ed., *Hall's Ireland, Mr and Mrs Hall's Tour of 1840*, vols, I (London, 1984), 103.

7 A. Young, *A Tour In Ireland made in the years 1776, 1777, and 1778*, II (London, 1780), 162.

8 Ibid., 161–2.

9 W.M. Thackeray, *The Irish Sketchbook* (London, 1843), 146–7.

10 T.M. Truxes, *Irish-American Trade, 1660–1783* (Cambridge, 1988), 218–21, 292–6. Corkery, *Hidden Ireland*, 34–6. McCracken, *The Irish Woods*, 28.

11 Stokes, *Pococke's Tour*, 155–6.

12 J.B. Sykes, *The Concise Oxford Dictionary* (Oxford, 1985), 244; Deal; 'piece of sawn fir or pine wood of

standard size; a quantity of these; fir or pine timber'. McCracken, *The Irish Woods*, 169: 'Glossary ... *Deals*. [In Ireland] The term was first applied to softwood imported from the Baltic. While the size of deals varied it lay between certain limits: in the eighteenth century a standard deal was 12 ft long, 11 in. wide, and 1½ thick, but Christiana deals were between 10 and 12 ft long and 3 in. thick. A load of Danzig deals was 50 cubic ft.

Although the current nomenclature is red deal for Scots pine and white deal for Norway spruce, in the eighteenth century deals were referred to as either Norwegian or Spruce – a corruption of Prussia.' Young, *Tour in Ireland*, II, 161, 'The Baltic fir supplies all the uses of the kingdom, even those for which nothing is proper but oak.'

13 McCracken, *The Irish Woods*, ch. 5, 112–21.
14 C. Woodham-Smith, *The Great Hunger, Ireland 1845–1849* (London, 1962, 1987), 208.
15 Ibid., 208, 206–38.
16 J. McEvoy, *Statistical Survey of the County of Tyrone* (Dublin, 1802), 187–9.
17 Ibid., 188. Describing the state of timber in county Tyrone, McEvoy stresses how important bog fir is amongst the sources of timber, because 'The prices of timber are very high, and it is difficult to procure'. The Tyrone bogs were the source of abundant bog timber, but bad roads and difficulties with extraction made it difficult to exploit. Bog fir was sold at 'half a crown the cubic foot', for making looms and millshafts, roofing, lofting, laths and for twisting into bed cords (20 yards for 10*d*.).

By comparison, see H. Dutton, *Statistical Survey of the County of Clare* (Dublin, 1808), 283–6: Dutton states that bog fir is preferred to bog oak for 'inside work'. He claims that huge dimensions of bog fir are frequently found. He tells of a tree recently extracted near Kilrush, which 'measured at the thickest end thirty-eight inches in diameter, and at upwards of sixty-eight feet long, thirty-one inches; it was very sound timber, and produced him upwards of £36'. For more similar details of prices and availability of bog timber and other timber, refer further to the other Statistical Surveys of particular counties written during the first decades of the nineteenth century.

Although very little vernacular furniture survives made of bog fir or bog oak, it has been shown to have been widely used in areas of bogland. This is one of comparatively few aspects of Irish vernacular furniture to have been researched; methods of extraction, the general use of bog-wood and its particular regional use for furniture – the latter based largely on the Department of Irish Folklore's Mss. – are discussed in A.T. Lucas, 'Bog Wood, A Study in Rural Economy' in *Bealoideas*, The Journal of the Folklore Society of Ireland, XXIII (1954), 71–134, esp. 74–81, 87–92. Since Lucas seems not to have examined the Government Poor Inquiry reports in depth for this study, the following references to householders with bog-wood furniture form a small addition to his work: H.C. Parliamentary Papers: Report of the Commissioners (II) 1836, Supplement to appendix E, XXXII; county Kildare; [unlisted amongst Lucas's regions] 59, county Cork; (fir seats) 179, county Donegal; (bog-wood forms and bedsteads) 304, 319.

Bog oak in particular was highly prized for its blackness and was used in 'fine furniture', for the 19th-century souvenir trade and in marquetry both by Irish cabinetmakers and abroad. See G. Bernard Hughes, 'Irish Bog-Wood Furniture' in *Country Life*, CXLI No. 3859 (London, 1971), 1318–21. See also E. Pinto, *Treen and other Wooden Bygones* (London, 1976),

fig. 15; L, M, 56–7, 192, 438, for examples of bog-wood jewellery, drinking vessels etc. For information about Killarney production of bog oak souvenirs etc. read, B. Austen, *Tunbridge Ware and related European Decorative Woodwares, Killarney, Spa, Sorrento* (London, 1989), 41, 177–8, 180–2, 185–6.

18 McEvoy, *Statistical Survey*, 187. E.E. Evans, *Irish Folk Ways* (London, 1957, 1979), III: Evans mentions how the planting of ash in 'ditches and closes' was encouraged by the government of Ireland within the English Pale, during the 16th century.
19 MacLysaght, *Irish Life*, 271.
20 See T. Ó Criomhthain, *Island Cross Talk, pages from a diary* (Oxford, 1928, 1986), 50, 113; M. O'Guiheen, *A Pity Youth does not Last* (Oxford, 1953, 1982), 36–8.
21 T. Ó Criomhthain, *The Islandman* (1929, Oxford, 1987) 184–6.
22 Ó Criomhthain, *Island Cross Talk*, 113.
23 D.I.F. Ms. Vol. 1833, 333–4; 'They used make household furniture out of substantial pieces of wrack [sic] after bringing them to the sawmill in Galway.'
24 This example of wreck furniture can be seen in Ceim Hill Museum, Union Hall, west county Cork. It was made by the present curator Therese O'Mahony's father, Denis O'Mahony. The nicely turned winch cover lent itself perfectly to the requirements of a seat, through which three legs were fixed by 'through wedging' in the traditional way (see fig. 320). Details of the circumstances surrounding the wreck of the *Asian* and the rescue of crew and wreckage can be read in *Lloyd's List Weekly Shipping Summary*, July–December 1924, XXXIX, No. 3548. (London, Wed. 24 September, 1924), Marine casualties, notes on Wireless Operator's Communication; Steamer *Asian*, 2.
25 Ó Criomhthain, *The Islandman*, 239. The wreck of a ship from New York and the excitement of the whole village is described as they gather wreckage in M. O'Sullivan, *Twenty Years A Growing* (1933), 160–1, chs. 12–13; 'When we came above the Sorrowful Cliff it was an astonishing sight. Nothing but wreckage! Without a lie, you could have walked out from the Spit of Seals' Cove and gone ashore in Inish Túiscirt without wetting your foot, with all the cotton bales, chests, boxes, and appurtenances on the sea ... a curragh coming to the quay with a load and another leaving, the coves ringing with the sound of blows on the boxes out to sea. Every curragh had an axe, and when they found a box too big to bring ashore they split it open on the spot.'
26 T.H. Mason, *The Islands of Ireland* (London, 1936), 13.
27 E.E. Evans, 'Traditional Houses of Rathlin Island' in *Ulster Folklife*, XIX (Belfast, 1973), 16.
28 A. Taylor, *To School Through the Fields* (Dingle, 1988), 107.
29 H.C. Parliamentary Papers: Report of the Commissioners (II) 1836. Supplement to Appendix E, XXXII, 64. Also, see P's, 'Ancient Irish Chair' in *The Dublin Penny Journal*, I, No. 8, (Dublin, 18 August 1832), 64: 'An ancient oak chair ... has been used for firing during a severe winter, being deemed by its owner as a useless and inappropriate article of luxury.'

The Variety of Furniture Makers

1 'In Memory of Major Robert Gregory', quoted from A. Norman Jeffares ed, *W.B. Yeats Selected Poetry* (London, 1974), 65–8.
2 Evidence demonstrating that householders made their own furniture is widespread amongst the many

surviving examples examined during the author's Irish fieldstudies, as well as in documents. For instance, H.C. Parliamentary Papers: Report of the Commissioners (II) 1836. Supplement to Appendix E. XXXII, 143; Wexford, barony of Gorey, Ballaghkeen; 'The occupier of the cabin furnishes it himself'.

3   A. O'Dowd, 'Baskets' in D. Shaw-Smith ed, *Ireland's Traditional Crafts* (London, 1986), 127.

4   The work of wheelwright Con Corkley is discussed in detail in C. Kinmonth, *Irish Vernacular Furniture, 1840–1940, A Neglected Aspect of the History of Design*, unpublished MA thesis for the Victoria and Albert Museum/Royal College of Art joint History of Design MA course (1987- May 1988), 163–6.

5   *The Indentures of William Cunnane dated 1895*, Ms. in the possession of Knock Folk Museum, county Mayo. Also in J. Gallagher (ex curator). *A Look into the Past, Our Irish Heritage* (Knock, 1990), 35–6.

6   V. Gookin, *The Great Case of Transplantation Discussed* (London, 1655), 17; quoted by E. MacLysaght, *Irish Life in the Seventeenth Century: After Cromwell* (Dublin, 1939), 40, 439.

7   W.S. Mason, *Survey, Valuation and Census of the barony of Portnehinch* [Queen's County] (1819), 14; 'This barony is mostly in a state of agriculture: The farmers and labourers far exceed in number those of any other occupation; as to trades or occupations the weavers are the most numerous.' Mason provides a table of occupations for the local population of 12,374 'souls'. Of this total, there are amongst the variety of tradesmen 34 masons, 53 carpenters and wheelwrights, 3 sawyers, 14 coopers, 62 Smiths and nailers, 64 shoe and brogue makers, 36 tailors, 191 servants, 1 painter and [significantly, only] 1 turner.

8   For illustrated examples see P. O'Donovan and J. Murphy, *Irish Shopfronts* (Ulster, 1981).

9   The work of several individual Irish woodworkers and furniture makers are written up as case studies in Kinmonth, *Irish Vernacular Furniture*, 148–74.

10   H.C. Parliamentary Papers; Report of the Commissioners (9) 1836, Appendix C. XXX, Parts I and II, 37: Cork City, Parish St Peter.

11   A. Gailey, 'A Wicker Coffin from Ballyshiel Graveyard, Annaclone, county Down' in *Ulster Folklife*, XVII (Belfast, 1971), 89–90.

12   R.E. Colby, *The Ordnance Survey of the County of Londonderry*, I (Dublin, 1837), 199: See table to show rates of wages of 'the humbler classes'.

13   C.C. Ellison, 'Setting up House – 1825 Style' in *The Irish Ancestor*, VIII, No. 2 (Dublin, 1976), 75–80. The list of carpenter's work done by John Fox at Kilgeffin; 'Bookcase, hat stand; 2 dressing tables and basin stands; night chair; 2 servant's bedsteads; dresser and [plate] drainer; 2 forms; 4 kitchen chairs, 2 kitchen tables; tray for servant woman; paste board and chop board.' The servant's bedsteads were almost certainly wooden settle beds, as they were often referred to in that way. John Commins, 'Kitchen furniture and lamp manufacturer' of 59 Henry Street, is also mentioned, having supplied a parlour lamp at £2 and an oil bottle at 3s.

14   Colby, *Ordnance Survey*, 199: See table. For a description of a hedge carpenter's work see W. Rose, *The Village Carpenter* (Cambridge, 1937, 1987), 61–7.

15   G. Hill, *Facts from Gweedore* (facsimile reprint of 5th edn, of 1887, Belfast, 1971), 37.

16   Mrs A. Nicholson, *Annals of the Famine in Ireland in 1847, '48 and '49* (New York, 1851), 44–5.

17   'Early records for the town of Galway' quoted by Dr Pococke in G. Stokes ed., *Pococke's Tour in Ireland in 1752* (Dublin, 1891), 106.

18   H. Dutton, *Statistical Survey of County Clare* (Dublin,

1808), 185.

19   Colby, *Ordnance Survey*, 199.

20   The Corkley family is discussed in further detail in Kinmonth, *Irish Vernacular Furniture*, 163–6.

21   H.C. Parliamentary Papers; Report of the Commissioners (9) 1836, Appendix C. XXX, Parts I and II.

22   Ibid., 33.

23   Ibid., 23, 26.

24   Ibid., 33, 38.

25   Ibid., 39.

26   Ibid., 163.

27   L.M. Cullen, *Life in Ireland* (London, 1968), 112–15. Cullen explains how in linen spinning areas, a 7-year-old child earned 1d. per day and further south in wool spinning regions as much as 2d. per day. He also discusses the working patterns of the numerous migrant and seasonal labourers.

28   H.C. Parliamentary Papers; Report of the Commissioners (9) 1836, Appendix C. XXX, Parts I and II, 63.

29   D.I.F. Ms. Vol. 1664 (1957), county Cavan, 87; 'Some people made a name for themselves by making these [straw] chairs...[they] also made large straw mats, which were common everywhere in this district but are never seen now.' Also 'The boss maker' as described by P. Kennedy, *Legendary Fictions of the Irish Celts* (Dublin, 1866), 100.

30   H.C. Parliamentary Papers; Report of the Commissioners (9) 1836, Appendix C. XXX, Parts I and II, 33; City of Cork.

31   *The Indentures of William Connane dated 1895.*

32   See C. Kinmonth, 'The Role of Oral history in Researching Irish Vernacular Furniture' in *Oral History; The Crafts*, The Journal of the Oral History, XVIII, No. 2 (Autumn 1990), 64–5. Also Kinmonth, *Irish Vernacular Furniture*, 172–4.

33   Ms; 'The Eagle 2/- Diary for 1939'. Farm activities diary for Seaview Farm, Carragillihy, west county Cork. Private Collection. August-September 1939.

34   G.C. Bonthrone, 'Childhood Memories of County Antrim' in *Ulster Folklife*, VI (Belfast, 1960), 42.

35   J. Manners, *Irish Crafts and Craftsmen* (Belfast, 1982), 15. Shaw-Smith ed, *Ireland's Traditional Crafts*, 74–5.

36   T.P. O'Neill, 'Coopering' in Shaw-Smith ed, *Ireland's Traditional Crafts*, 64.

37   *Downpatrick Recorder* (8 June 1850), quoted by A. McClelland, 'Folklife Miscellanea from c18th and c19th Newspapers' in *Ulster Folklife*, XIX (Belfast, 1973), 71.

38   D. Thomson and M. McGusty, *The Irish Journals of Elizabeth Smith, 1840–50* (Oxford, 1980), 113, [c.1847] 116. The author is grateful to Dr F.H. Aalen for drawing her attention to this diary.

39   A few surviving census returns for 1821 were transcribed before the Four Courts fire of 1922 and have been subsequently published. They provide details of age, occupation and status of the population of two complete parishes in the barony of Iverk, county Kilkenny and show how common it was for farmers and the owners of comparatively small amounts of acreage to keep servants. Out of 230 households, only four carpenters and one cooper are listed, one of these carpenters having an apprentice and servant. See R. ffolliot and E. Walsh Kelly ed, 'The 1821 Census Returns for the Parishes of Aglish and Portnascully, county Kilkenny' in *The Irish Ancestor*, VIII, No. 2 (Dublin, 1976), 113–24.

40   E. MacLysaght, *Irish Life in the Seventeenth Century* (Dublin, 1939), 40, 176. For more information about pit-sawing see; W. Linnard, 'Sweat and Sawdust: Pit-sawing in Wales' in *Folk Life*, Journal of The Society of Folk Life Studies, XX (Cardiff, 1982), 41–55. See also R.A. Salaman, *Dictionary of Tools* (New York, 1975),

442–3. M. MacManus, *Crafted in Ireland, an Ulster Folk and Transport Museum Exhibition Catalogue* (Belfast, 1986), 55–6; McManus explains that the pole-lathe is thought to have been used in Ireland since the Iron Age and that it survived alongside more sophisticated lathes up until the 1930s.

41 M. Heverin, 'James O'Keeffe – A Master Craftsman', in Kilmore Parish Journal (Wexford, 1979–80), 26–7. S. O'Keeffe, 'The Common Hall', in Kilmore Parish Journal (Wexford, 1987–88), 31–2. Guided tours of south county Wexford encompassing areas of particular O'Keeffe interest, have been conducted by Nicholas Furlong and by Dr Austin O'Sullivan. Dr O'Sullivan has collected a splendid range of J. O'Keeffe furniture and memorabilia which are on exhibition in a special room in the Irish Agricultural Museum, near Wexford. The Irish Country Furniture Society have also been interested in preventing the export of his work. The National Museum of Ireland has two O'Keeffe pieces in their county Offaly stores which are published here for the first time (figs. 13, 14). The author is particularly grateful to Seamus O'Keeffe for providing information.

42 O'Keeffe, 'The Common Hall', 31–2. The author is grateful to Dr Austin O'Sullivan for drawing her attention to articles and items of furniture made by J. O'Keeffe, and for accompanying her on fieldstudies of O'Keeffe furniture in county Wexford.

43 Illustrated in Ibid., 31.

44 The sideboard is illustrated in Heverin, 'James O'Keeffe', 27. Another detail of his carving is illustrated by N. Loughnan, *Irish Country Furniture* (Irish Heritage Series No. 6, Dublin 1984).

45 *Freemans' Journal*, 2 January 1890, and 27 January 1894.

46 Dr J.B. Burgess, *Know Your Town*, typescript Burgess Mss., III in Athlone Branch Library.

47 *Journal of the Department of Agriculture and Technical Instruction in Ireland*, VI (1905–6), 738–41. The author is grateful to Dr William Crawford for drawing her attention to this text.

48 Special Correspondent, 'Ardee gave me a chance of Sitting Pretty' in *Irish Furniture and Furnishings Magazine* (March 1951), 31–3.

49 Special Correspondent, '81 year old John O'Sullivan tells me about Windsor Chairs' in *Irish Furniture and Furnishings Magazine* (March 1951), 33–5.

Painted Furniture

1 W. Carleton, *Traits and Stories of the Irish Peasantry*, 2 vols. (Dublin, 1835), I, 16, II, 160.

2 A. Jouvin de Rochefort, *Ireland Under The Restoration* (1667), quoted in F. Murphy, *The Bog Irish: Who they were and Where they Lived* (Australia, 1987), 139–40.

3 P. Corish, *The Irish Catholic Experience, A Historical Survey* (Dublin, 1985), 134.

4 Ibid., 189.

5 S.J. Connolly, *Priests and People in Pre-famine Ireland 1780–1845* (Dublin, 1982), 50.

6 Ibid., 93.

7 Jouvin de Rochefort, *Ireland Under The Restoration*, quoted in F. Murphy, *The Bog Irish*, 139–40.

8 G. Stokes ed, *Pococke's Tour in Ireland in 1752* (Dublin, 1891), 60.

9 Carleton, *Traits and Stories*, II, 286–7.

10 A. Taylor, *To School Through The Fields: An Irish Country Childhood* (Dingle, 1988), 8–11.

11 Ibid., 16–17.

12 K. Danaher, *The Year In Ireland: Irish Calendar Customs* (Cork and Dublin, 1972), 70.

13 Ibid., 71.

14 E. Cross, *The Tailor and Ansty* (Cork and Dublin, 1942), 20.

15 C. Kinmonth, 'The role of Oral History in researching Irish Vernacular Furniture' in *The Journal of The Oral History Society*, The Crafts, xviii, No. 2 (Autumn 1990), 65.

16 P. O'Donovan and J. Murphy, *Irish Shopfronts* (New York, 1981), 4, 34, 70, 75, 78, 82–4, 88, 94. This small book of colour photographs concentrates on shopfronts from southern Ireland, the references listed are those which have been 'grained'. The people who built and painted shopfronts frequently also supplied locally made furniture when the opportunity arose. Similarities in styles of construction and decoration are therefore frequently apparent.

17 F. Oughton, *The Complete Manual of Wood Finishing* (London, 1982), 144–52. For more detailed descriptions of 'graining' techniques and of materials such as scumble.

18 D.I.F. Ms. Vol. 1664. County Limerick, 57.

Chapter 1 STOOLS AND CHAIRS

An Introduction to Seating

1 G. Hill, *Facts from Gweedore* (1845, reprint of 5th edn, of 1887; Belfast, 1971), 16. Lord George Hill was a landlord who bought land in Gweedore, county Donegal. He made considerable changes and improvements and successfully opened the subject of Irish poverty up to political debate.

2 A. M'Kenzie, *Poems and Songs on Different Subjects* (Belfast, 1810), 117–21, quoted in A. Gailey, 'The Housing of the Rural Poor in Nineteenth-Century Ulster' in *Ulster Folklife*, XXII (Belfast, 1976), 50.

3 K.M. Harris, 'Extracts from the Committee's Collection' in *Ulster Folklife*, VI (Belfast, 1960), C.G., county Derry, 19.

4 O.S. Mem., Box 15, VI, 1 (1835), Racavan, county Antrim.

5 W. Carleton, *Traits and Stories of the Irish Peasantry*, 2 vols. I (Dublin, 4th edn, 1835), 17.

6 House of Commons Parliamentary Papers: Report of the Commissioners (II) 1836. Supplement to Appendix E. XXXII. County Meath, Baronies of Upper Deece, Denifore, 101.

7 J.M. Synge, *The Aran Islands* (Oxford, 1907, 1985 edn), 16.

8 T. O'Neill, *Life and Tradition in Rural Ireland* (London, 1977), 23–4.

9 W. Hanbidge [1813–1906], *The Diaries of William Hanbidge. Aged 93. 1906. An Autobiography* (St Albans, 1939), 20. The author is grateful to Dr F.H. Aalen for drawing her attention to this text.

10 E. Cross, *The Tailor and Ansty* (Cork, 1942, 1987 edn), 18–19.

Low Stools

11 W. Moffat, *Hesperi-Neso-graphia: The Western Isle Described.* (Dublin, 1724), Canto II, 7.

12 See A.T. Lucas, 'Contributions to the Study of the Irish House: Smokehole and Chimney' in A. Gailey and D. Ó hÓgáin ed. *Gold Under the Furze, Studies in Folk Tradition* (Dublin, c.1982), 57–9. Lucas provides dozens of mainly 19th-century examples from all over Ireland of descriptions of labourers' cabins and hovels without chimneys or simply with 'holes for chimneys'.

13 J. Stevens, *Journal* (1689–91) quoted in F. Murphy, *The Bog Irish Who they were and How they Lived* (Australia, 1987), 51.

14 G.T. Stokes, ed., *Pococke's Tour in Ireland in 1752* (Dublin, 1891), 87. This also provides an insight into what the stillions of that period looked like.

15 C. Otway, *Sketches in Erris and Tyrawly* (Dublin, 1841), 4, 159.

16 H. Dutton, *Statistical Survey of the county of Clare, with observations on the means of improvement* (Dublin, 1808), 143. Literary descriptions are supplemented by evidence from paintings and drawings depicting rural interiors, where such stools can be seen to have fulfilled a wide variety of less obvious functions (figs. 207, 286).

The Effect of Flooring upon Seat Design

17 O'Neill, *Life and Tradition*, 16.

18 Stevens, *Journal* in Murphy, *The Bog Irish*, 51: 'The cabins have seldom any floor but the earth.' Carleton, *Irish Peasantry*, I, 287, describes during the preparations for the Station; 'Several concave inequalities, which constant attrition had worn in the earthen floor of the kitchen, were filled up with blue clay, brought on a car from the bank of a neighbouring river, for the purpose.'

19 A. Gailey, *Rural Houses of the North of Ireland* (Edinburgh, 1984), 128, 202, 205, 215.

20 Harris, 'Extracts', 20.

21 In many traditional houses this slope is still quite distinct; it presumably helped any water to drain away from the hearth area and accordingly has its effects on chair and settle design. I examined several settles in houses in west county Cork, which had considerably longer legs at the end furthest from the fire, to compensate. The same thing is often said to have been done with chairs.

22 Dressers and settles (particularly from northern counties) were often fitted with special sacrificial 'sledge' feet to cope with the rising damp; see appropriate chapters that describe these features.

23 D.I.F. Ms. Vol. 654 (1939), 99. (The Poulaphouca Resevoir Survey).

24 This is what is written on the back of the original black-and-white print of this table, from 'The Tailor's House' (Mr Michael Fox) Woodend Br., Butterhill (Map A), see fig. 299. Part of a collection of prints and documents from the Poulaphouca Resevoir Survey kindly lent to the author by Dr F. H. Aalen.

25 W. Carleton, 'The Courtship of Phelim O'Toole', in *Six Irish Tales* (Dublin, 1833), 26.

26 The American painter Howard Helmick (1845–1907) painted a Galway scene of nine people gathered outside an inn, in 1880. Entitled 'News of the Land League' the group are seated around two minimal tables and three seats which appear to be 'earth fast': they have been made by driving boards into the ground (fig. 25). A fourth seat is a firkin or small barrel. The painting is part of the collection of the National Gallery of Ireland, Dublin; Helmick, N.G.I. 4507.

27 A good example of such a chair with sawn off and renewed legs can be seen at the Pig House Museum, county Cavan.

28 D.I.F. Information recorded by P. MacDomhnaill, collector, from Cappawhite Parish, county Tipperary: D.I.F. Ms. Vol. 407 (24 October 1937), 285. The use of the word 'knee' here probably means a naturally curved backrest, fixed onto a series of vertical spindles by through wedged tenons.

Improvised and Recycled Stools

29 R. Flower, *The Western Island* (Oxford, 1st pub. 1944, 1985 reprint), 45. Here Robin Flower contrasts the interiors of the old houses on the Great Blasket Island, county Kerry, with the newer two-storey ones which were being built by the Congested Districts Board at the beginning of the 20th century.

30 H.C. Parliamentary Papers: Report of the Commissioners (II) 1836, Supplement to Appendix E. XXXII. County Roscommon, Barony of Roscommon, 38.

31 Ibid., Carbery West, East division, Castle Ventry. 179.

32 Ibid., Baronies of Navan, upper and lower, 111.

33 The rafters for the barn opposite Fullers Stores, in Union Hall, west county Cork, are of mahogany salvaged from a wreck.

34 *Lloyd's List Weekly Shipping Summary*, XXXIX, no. 3548 (July–December 1924), *Steamer Asian*, 24 September 1924, 2.

35 A. Taylor, *To School Through the Fields, An Irish Country Childhood* (Dingle, 1988, 1990), 107–9.

36 E. Cross, *The Tailor and Ansty* (Cork and Dublin, 1st pub. 1942, 1987), 18.

Stool Terminology

37 The term 'creepie' is used by E.E. Evans in *Mourne Country* (Dundalk, 1951, 1989), 200. Also by L. Maclintock, *Jamie Freel and the Young Lady* in W.B. Yeats *Fairy and Folktales of the Irish Peasantry* (London, 1888); In Fanad/Fannet' county Donegal; 'and then sat down on a "creepie" in the chimney corner', 55. The long history of northern Irish and Scottish connections may explain its traditional use in both areas. In some other texts it is spelled 'creepy' instead.

38 'P.', 'Ancient Irish Chair' in *The Dublin Penny Journal*, I, No. 8, (Dublin, 18 August 1832), 64.

39 H. Glassie, *Passing The Time, Folklore and History of an Ulster Community* (Dublin, 1982), 358.

40 D.I.F. Ms. Vol. 1404 (April 1955), Ballinamore, county Leitrim, 501–2.

41 Taylor, *To School Through the Fields*, 99.

42 *Mist's Weekly Journal* (London, 1728).

43 R. Ross Noble, 'Chairs, Stools, and Settles: The Vernacular Tradition in the Highlands' in G. Cruickshank, ed., *A Sense of Place, Studies in Scottish local History* (Edinburgh, 1988), 163–73.

44 For example Hanbidge, *William Hanbidge*, 20. This mentions 'four legged deal stools scrubbed like the table white with river sand'. Also Carleton, *Traits and Stories of the Irish Peasantry*, II, (Dublin, 1835, 4th edn.), 289; 'Hitherto, all hands had contributed to make every thing in and about the house look "dacent"; – scouring, washing, sweeping, pairing, and repairing', on the eve of 'The Station'. Also Carleton, I, 17.

45 H.C. Parliamentary Papers: Report of the Commissioners (II) 1836. Supplement to Appendix E. XXXII. County Mayo, Baronies of Clanmorris, Carra, Costello, 21. Also in county Wexford 'the occupier of the cabin furnishes it himself.' 143.

46 O.S. Memoirs, Box 5, II, 13 (1837), 1–117 and Box 5, II, 8 (1837), 1–17. Some of these O.S. Memoirs have now been published by the Intitute of Irish Studies, Queens University, Belfast, in conjunction with the Royal Irish Academy, Dublin.

Hedge Chairs

47 This is discussed in C. Kinmonth, 'Beside an Irish

Hearth' in *Country Life Magazine*, CLXXXV No. 21 (23 May 1991), 110–11.

48 Notes from Northern Ireland Home Service Transcript, 'The Carpenter' (9 November 1959), BBC.

49 H. Dutton, *Statistical Survey of the county of Clare* (Dublin, 1808), 185.

50 O.S. Memoirs, Box 5, II, 13 (1836) 1–117 also D.I.F. Quest; Chair Types (1980), Ms. Vol. 2072, 83: this short questionnaire illustrated a hedge chair and a *súgán* chair, without naming them. It asked if 'either of the types of chair . . . is the traditional kind made by wood workers in your locality'. One respondent from county Tipperary wrote 'This seems to be like the old kitchen chairs'.

51 K. Danaher, 'Furniture' in D. Shaw-Smith, *Ireland's Traditional Crafts* (London, 1986), 71. Danaher refers to the 'backed stool type' of chair as the 'Windsor', without putting forward any specific evidence for Windsor influence.

52 J. Gloag, *A Short Dictionary of Furniture* (Canada, 1965), 505–8.

53 T. and J. Hooper, *Australian Country Furniture* (Victoria, 1988), figs 28 and 31; 27.

54 W. Rose, *The Village Carpenter* (Cambridge, 1937, 1987), 61.

55 John Brown, *Welsh Stick Chairs* (Newport, 1990), 80–5. John Brown explains with words, photographs and drawings, the techniques and philosophy behind the making of his own (traditionally made and influenced) design of 'Welsh stick chair', some examples of which are quite similar to Irish hedge chairs. He also looks at the history of Welsh chairs, explaining their development through technical processes.

Interlocking Arm Chairs

56 Dr M. Gahan, 'The Development of Crafts' in J. Meenan and D. Clarke eds., *The Royal Dublin Society, 1731–1981* (London, 1981), 258–60. John Surlis's work has been immortalised by one of a series of television programmes by David Shaw-Smith, entitled 'Hands' and his accompanying book. Shaw-Smith ed., *Ireland's Traditional Crafts*, 74–5.

57 Another similar style of chair was produced since the 1960s by revivalist Al O'Dea, who originally founded Corrib Crafts (of Tuam, county Galway). The firm still make an assortment of traditional styles of chairs inspired by vernacular patterns.

58 For examples see Hooper, *Australian Country Furniture*, 27, fig. 31. Also H. Pain, *The Heritage of Upper Canadian Furniture. A Study in the Survival of Formal and Vernacular Styles from Britain, America and Europe, 1780–1900.* (Toronto, 1978), York County, fig. 314, 128. Figs 313 and 315 also look as if they could have sprung from the Irish tradition of hedge chairmaking.

Gibson Chairs

59 Danaher, 'Furniture' in Shaw-Smith, *Ireland's Traditional Crafts*, 71. The term 'Gibson' suggests that there was once a maker by that name, although unfortunately no primary material has come to light to support this theory. Danaher, a folklore specialist and Irish historian who uses the term Gibson or alternately 'fool's chair', describes them as coming from Oldcastle, county Meath. Like the name famine chair, 'fool's stool' and 'fool's chair' are probably terms adopted for convenience by furniture dealers, as no documentary evidence has been discovered to support

their traditional use. The author would be interested to hear from anyone who knows more about the origins of this chair and its various names.

60 Irish Agricultural Museum accession No. ICFS 018., at Johnstown Castle, Wexford, county Wexford. N. Loughnan, *Irish Country Furniture* in Irish Heritage Series No. 46 (Dublin, 1984), 5., here Loughnan describes the Gibson chair as an 'Irish Windsor', but provides no documentary evidence for such an English influence.

Hedge Chairs with Composite Seats

61 According to Fionnuala Carragher of the Ulster Folk and Transport Museum, who is familiar with their collection.

62 H. Glassie, *Passing the Time, Folklore and History of an Ulster Community* (Dublin, 1982), 359. Glassie shows a drawing of one from county Fermanagh, he also notices that the 'left arm and front leg, which would rest nearest the fire, are replacements'.

'Sutherland Chairs' and their Derry Relatives

63 'Sutherland chairs' were first mentioned briefly by I.F. Grant in her book *Highland Folk Ways* (London, 1961), fig. 21(A), 172. They were more recently illustrated and described in far greater detail by Ross Noble, curator of the Highland Folk Museum in the Scottish Highlands. Noble explains how most of the examples that he has studied came from the Sutherland district of northern Scotland, with related types from neighbouring Caithness: See R.R. Noble, 'Chairs, Stools and Settles: The Vernacular Tradition in the Highlands' in G. Cruickshank, ed., *A Sense of Place* (Edinburgh, 1988), 163–9. Also R.R. Noble, 'The Chairs of Sutherland and Caithness: A Northern Tradition in Highland Chairmaking?' in *Regional Furniture*, I (1987), 33–40, especially figs. 1–6.

64 This is pointed out and illustrated by R.R. Noble, 'Chairs, Stools and Settles', *Regional Furniture*, I (1987) 164, 167, fig. 37; This figure shows a plough made from a naturally bent fork, which has been cleaved to provide two matching 'Y' shapes.

65 Two of these are amongst the Ulster Folk and Transport Museum's collection at Cultra, Belfast (illustrated here), a third is in a private collection in the city of Derry and the fourth is owned by the Cathedral of Derry. The Cathedral authorities apparently consider that their example dates from the seige of Derry (1689), and that it was made from the famous gates of Derry.

66 A good example of this remarkable chair type migrated to southern Australia via a Scottish emigrant named McBean, and is illustrated in the lavishly illustrated book which catalogues the collection of Lord McAlpine's bush furniture: G. Cornall, *Memories, A Survey of Early Australian Furniture in the Collection of the Lord McAlpine of West Green* (Perth, 1990), fig. 2, 68. For the Romanian example see R. Capesius, 'Mobilierul Taranesc Romanesc' in *Muzeul Etnografic al Transilvaniei* (Cluj, 1974), plate V, 7–8. The author is grateful to Dr Alan Gailey for drawing her attention to this text.

Comb Back Chairs

67 See Brown, *Welsh Stick Chairs*, plates 6–8, 1–13, 17, many examples are from Carmarthenshire and north Wales. See main text for details of construction tech-

niques. C. Gilbert, *English Vernacular Furniture, 1750–1900* (New Haven, London, 1991), 100, plate 186, shows stretcherless comb backed 'Windsor chairs' painted in 1746, but with higher backs than the Irish examples. Such comb backed chairs, without stretchers, were also known in the west of England. Also B. Cotton, 'Unconventional Windsors from the Cotswolds' and 'Shadford, Shirley and the Caistor Workshop' both in *Regional Furniture*, II (1988), figs. 1 and 3 respectively.

68 Armagh County Museum; Accession notes of Chair: 57, 1966. This accession is further endorsed by a footnote concerning this event in M.M. Curnock ed., *The Journal of Rev. John Wesley*, VII (16 June 1789), 511.

Carpenters' Chairs

69 Ms. in author's collection; Taped and transcribed conversation between author and John O'Sullivan, aged 73; carriagemaker and general woodworker of Skibbereen, county Cork, 9 January 1988. Transcript No. 8804, 16.

70 For more about the Robinson brothers fine cabinet-making read Shaw-Smith, *Ireland's Traditional Crafts*, 84–6.

71 O.S. Memoir, Box 16, IV 22 (January 1840, with additions from draft Memoir [*c*.1834] received April 1835) Parish of Templecorran, county Antrim. 51.

The 'Sligo Chair'

72 To view such chairs on display visit the Irish Agricultural Museum, Johnstown Castle, county Wexford, where at the time of writing there were two examples. A dozen more are in the county Offaly stores of the National Museum of Ireland, where access is unfortunately limited.

73 'P', 'Ancient Irish Chair' in *The Dublin Penny Journal*, I, No. 8, (Dublin, 18 August 1832), 64. Another version of this drawing appeared about thirteen years later in P. Parley, *Tales about Ireland and the Irish* (London, *c*.1845), 202. However, it is so similar (although a mirror image), that it was probably copied from *The Dublin Penny Journal's* illustration and has therefore not been reproduced here.

74 Mrs S.C. Hall, *Ireland, The Scenery Character etc*, III (1841–3), 294.

75 Accession notes for one of a dozen of these chairs which are in the N.M.I. stores at Daingean, county Offaly. Accession No. F1931: 114; indicates that this one was presented to the museum in 1931. Information, amongst the notes about the chairmaker, was provided, presumably at that time, by Owen MacNeill, and is in Irish. The author is grateful to Dr Anne O'Dowd (N.M.I.) for her translation of these notes.

76 Ibid., N.M.I. F1931: 114 Accession notes.

77 See Danaher, 'Furniture' in Shaw-Smith ed., *Ireland's Traditional Crafts*, 73, where he claims that it is 'known as the 'Tuam chair' because in recent times it has been confined to the Tuam area of Galway'. Presumably he was referring to their manufacture by Corrib Crafts (p. 76), rather than the N.M.I. collection. My fieldwork in the Tuam area discovered three more dilapidated 19th-century examples.

78 R. Edwards, *The Dictionary of English Furniture*, I (Woodbridge, 1983), 227–8, figs 8–9, 11–13. Edwards describes them as of a 'French type' where they are widespread and varied. The English example, in the

Victoria and Albert Museum, came from Devon. The author has examined several early examples in collections in Scotland, where they seem more common than in England.

Súgán Chairs

79 O.S. Memoir., Box 5, II 8 (21 June-21 July 1837), Parish of Blaris, county Antrim, 15. Many of the O.S. Memoirs footnoted are in process of publication at the time of writing.

80 P.R.O.N.I. T1062/27 (1725) An Inventory of... James Stevenson of Derrycreew, parish of Loughall and county of Armagh; '4 rush bottomed chaiers at £0. 2. 0 [6*d*. each]'.

81 P.R.O.N.I. T1062/29 (1729) Inventory of Joseph Williamson... of Creangh in the parish of Kilmore and county of Armagh; '6 bullrush chaiers at £0. 3. 0 [6*d*. each]'. Also P.R.O.N.I T1062/25 (1728/9) An Inventory of... John Scott of Dunughlaghan in the parish of Kilmore and county of Armagh; '3 bullrush chaiers'. Also P.R.O.N.I T1062/24; (1728/9) An Inventory of John Reed of Ballyberoan... parish of Loughgall and county of Armagh; 'seaven bullrush chaiers at £0. 5. 10.'

82 It is significant that of over a hundred questionnaire respondents' descriptions, none mention ladder backed chairs. D.I.F. Quest., (*c*.1957), Ms. Vol. 1664: county Donegal; 'It was common to see wooden chairs with straw-ropes wound neatly round the rungs left for the purpose – 'Rope-bottomed' chairs'; 101. County Down; 'rope or sugan' 112. County Armagh; 'called rope chairs', 75, 'no other name but a rope chair', 77.

83 Brit. Mus. Add. Ms: 31,882., 47; Court Book from the Diocese of Killaloe (12 December 1732) An Inventory of what goods and etc. Mr Richard Dennis... had or was proposed at the time of his death.

84 H.C. Parliamentary Papers: Report of the Commissiones (ii) 1836. Supplement to Appendix E. XXXII. County Tipperary, Baronies Clanwilliam etc. 234; county Limerick, 225; county Clare, Kilkeady, 158.

85 D.I.F. Quest., (*c*.1957), Mss. Vols. 1663–4. This furniture questionnaire covers every county and although the relevant question is not perfectly worded, it is possible to ascertain that *súgán* chairs were known in each county, although not consistently by that name. Wherever there is doubt, the author has found evidence through fieldwork, early photographs and alternative documentary sources to substantiate this claim.

86 O.S. Memoir., Box 5, II 13 (6 March-19 May 1837), Parish of Blaris, county Antrim 12.

87 According to N. Webster, *Webster's New Twentieth Century Dictionary* (New York, 1983), 173; Bent means '1; the stiff flower stalk of certain grasses. 2; any of various reedy grasse. 3; any of a number of related grasses, chiefly low growing and spreading; also called *bent grass*.'
The author is grateful to Dr A. O'Sullivan (of the Agriculture and Food Development Authority, Johnstown Castle, county Wexford) for the following information about Bent: 'There is a common grass, *Agrostis tenuis* which is commonly known as Bent-grass. It was once a common constituent of old-meadow hay on unmanured pastures. However there is a grass of coastal sand dunes, *Ammophila arenaria*, whose common name is either Marram grass or Sea-bent. This grass is large and coarse and was commonly used for thatching in coastal areas.' Castlewellan, county Down, where these chairs were being made, is close to the coast, so either type of grass could have been the type used for seats. The custom of using grass for chair seats was remem-

88 O.S. Memoir., Box 5, II 8 (21 June-21 July 1837), 15.

89 See P.R.O.N.I T1062/27 (1725) county of Armagh; '4 rush bottomed chaiers at £0. 2. 0 [10s. each]'. Also P.R.O.N.I. T1062/29 (1729) county of Armagh; '6 bull-rush chaiers at £0. 3. 0 [10s. each]'. Also P.R.O.N.I. T1062/24; (1728/9) county of Armagh; 'seaven bullrush chaiers [sic] at £0. 5. 10.' The latter listing is evidently from a larger house than the others, and it is interesting to note the higher price, suggesting perhaps more elaborate chairs.

90 D.I.F., Ms. Vol. 707 [Parish of Ballynakill, county Galway], 456. D.I.F., Ms. Vol. 513 [83-year-old informant of Castlegregory, county Kerry, 1938], 278. D.I.F., Ms. Vol. 469 [82-year-old informant of Dunquin, county Kerry, 1938], 248. All three Mss. quoted in A.T. Lucas, 'Bog Wood A Study in Rural Economy' in *Bealoideas*. The, Journal of the Folklore Society of Ireland, XXIII (Dublin, 1954), 109.

91 Lucas, 'Bog Wood', 109, 71–134. This impressive article traces the history of use of bog timber for a wide variety of purposes, as well as explaining techniques for bog wood extraction, manufacture of rope etc.

92 Gahan, 'The Development of Crafts', 258.

93 Christopher and Noirin Sullivan of Lauragh, county Kerry, still make *súgán* chairs, using oat straw grown because of its golden colour for the purpose. Their operation is not highly mechanised and their methods stem from traditional techniques.

Corrib Crafts, a small firm in Tuam, county Galway make these chairs on a larger scale, with alternative forms of woven seats. Both productions are illustrated and described by Shaw-Smith ed, *Ireland's Traditional Crafts*, 76, 141–3.

Súgán Chair Construction

94 D.I.F. Ms. Vol. 1664 (1958), county Limerick; 'Chairs made of bog deal, seats made of straw/rushes-sugan'.

95 E.E. Evans, *Mourne Country, Landscape and Life in south Down* (Dundalk, 1989), 187.

96 Ash is frequently mentioned as a favourite timber for these chairs; U.F.M. Quest. (1962), Q.1/163, county Down; 'chairs usually made over an ash frame'. D.I.F. Ms. Vol. 1664 (1958), county Kerry, 49; 'Ash frame and twisted hay, or straw seat'. Ms. Vol. 1663 county Kilkenny, 55; 'ash *súgáns*'.

97 All the aforementioned uses are described in detail by E.E. Evans, *Irish Folk Ways* (London, 1979), 52–4, 65, 103, 200, 204, figs. 68, 207.

98 U.F.M. Quest. (1962), Q.1/County Down; 5, 7, 23 'clews', 66, 75, 160, 163, county Tyrone; 131. County Armagh; 118.

99 *Mist's Weekly Journal* (England, 27 July 1728). U.F.M. Quest. (1962), Q.1/159 (county Antrim). (Leggings); 'I have seen some farmers using straw ropes to tie to the legs of their trousers when they were working in wet soil (ploughing etc.) to keep them clean.'

100 U.F.M. Quest. (1962), Q.1/159.

101 Revd. J. Hall, *Tour Through Ireland, particularly the interior and lesser known parts etc.* 2 vols, I (London, 1813), 199–200.

102 U. O'Connor, *Celtic Dawn* (London, 1985), 287–90.

103 U.F.M. Quest. (1962), Q.1/23 (county Down).

104 U.F.M. Quest. (1962), Q.1/118.

105 D.I.F. Ms. Vol. 1664 (c.1958), 59.

106 The technique of twisting *súgán* and of seating an Irish *súgán* chair is illustrated and fully explained by Olivia Elton Barratt in K. Johnson, O. Elton Barratt,

M. Butcher, *Chair Seating, Techniques in Cane, Rush, Willow and Cords* (London, 1990), 118–20. The technique for replacing a trapezium-shaped rather than a square seat plan is explained by S. O'Toole, 'Sugan Chairs' in *The Basketmakers' Association Newsletter, An Irish Issue*, No. 56 (Winter 1991), 17–18.

107 As in the seat of a *súgán* armchair in Yeat's Tower House, Thoor Ballylee. Another seat of this unusual square pattern was illustrated with a sketch, drawn by a questionnaire respondent from county Armagh; U.F.M. Quest. (1962), Q.1/118.

108 Evans, *Mourne County*, 187.

109 M. McGrath ed., *The Diary of Humphrey O'Sullivan, 1827–32*, XXX (Irish Text Society, 1928–31), 9 August 1827, 5, 111.

Other Unusual Chairs And Dug-out Chairs

110 British Museum Add. Ms: 31, 882; Court Book from the Diocese of Killaloe. Inventory of William Mewstead of Derrynaslin in the county Of Tipperary, deceased 22 April 1749. 158. '12 chairs @ £1. 4. 0. 1 Arm Chair £0. 2. 6.'

111 Infra-red photographs helped to show up the otherwise difficult to decipher date as 1690.

112 D.I.F. Ms. Vol. 435 (1937), Parish of Tullaghobeghy, county Donegal, 211. Translated from Irish by Dr Patricia Lysaght, D.I.F.

Chairs made of Straw

113 U.F.M. Quest. (1962) Q.1/C.J. McQ: Kilskeery, county Tyrone: 'Bee skeps are still made of ropes or plaits of straw'. Shaw-Smith, (*Ireland's traditional Crafts*, 139–40), shows step by step photographs of the late Jack Carey, Clonakilty, west Cork, making a coiled straw and brierwork bee skep. His technique is also recorded in one of Shaw-Smith's excellent series for television entitled 'Hands'.

114 Such a straw seed basket (or seed lip) was vividly described to the author by Phil Tobin of Kilmacoe, Curracloe, Wexford, county Wexford (17 August 1991). He could remember using one which was kidney shaped in plan, 9 or 10 inches deep, with a leather strap which went over his shoulder. 'Made of coiled straw like a bee skep, sowing seed properly meant that a lot of it landed on your hat.' The author is grateful to Nicholas Furlong for this introduction.

115 E.E. Evans, *Irish Heritage* (Dundalk, 1945), 128, fig. 77; Evans describes and illustrates such a basket of coiled straw (a 'kishaun') from the Aran Islands. Round in plan, narrowing towards the open top and with a strap, for carrying food and keeping it hot. C. Kickham, *Knocknagow, or The Homes of Tipperary* (Dublin, 25th edn, 1887), 63; 'a straw basket heaped up with meal, with a bright tin measure on the top of the heap'.

116 U.F.M. Quest. (1962) Q.1/C.J. McQ: Kilskeery, county Tyrone: 'Carpenter's tool kits were made of straw, or straw ropes, or plait. Straw ropes were used for making mats for dogs to lie on.'

117 C. Otway, *Sketches In Erris and Tyrawly* (Dublin, 1841), 28; 'this habitation consisted of two rooms – one the general receptacle for all the animals . . . and was divided from the other by a long straw mat that hung from the ceiling, and served for a door.' Also W. Carleton, 'The Courtship of Phelim O'Toole' in

Six Irish Tales (Dublin, 1833), 26; 'a bed, the four posts of which ran up to the low roof; it was curtained with straw mats'. Also H.C. Parliamentary Papers: Report of the Commissioners (II) 1836, Supplement to Appendix E. xxxII. 331 (county Down), 113; county Meath; 'mats made of straw are fastened to the posts by way of curtains'.

118 Because straw seats are so extremely rare in Ireland (outside museums) the author published descriptive appeals to try and locate more of them: C. Kinmonth, 'The Last Straw?' in *Carloviana*, Journal of The Old Carlow Society, No. 39 (1991/1992), 2–3, 9. Also P. O'Leary and C. Kinmonth, 'Our Country Furniture' syndicated in three south-eastern newspapers; *New Ross Standard, Wexford People, Enniscorthy Guardian* (24 October 1991), C4. The author is grateful to Nicholas Furlong for this article's publication. Confusingly, in the parish of Ballee, county Down, the word 'boss' was used to describe a pigeon's nest, rather than a stool; U.F.M. Quest. (1962) Q.1/160.

119 Evans, *Irish Heritage*, 129, fig. 79; A tall tapering conical hen's nest from county Clare, is illustrated here. U.F.M. Quest. (1962) Q.1/C.J. McQ: Kilskeery, county Tyrone: 'Straw ropes were used for . . . Kishogues for hens' nests, for the hens to lay in. These nests were hung against the wall by a straw handle or loop.'

120 Made by Johnny McDonagh of Geevagh, county Sligo in 1912, who also made baskets, donkey's creels, willow calves' muzzles and willow scallops for thatch.

121 W. Carleton, *Traits and Stories of The Irish Peasantry*, II, (Dublin, 1835, 4th edn.), 156–7.

122 Evans, *Irish Heritage*, 128. Evans mentions 'lipework' (rather than lip-work) being common in Wales, but there is no known use of this word in Ireland, except as an adopted term. See J. Geraint Jenkins, 'A Cardiganshire Lip-worker' in *Folklife*, Journal of the Society of Folk Life Studies, III (Cardiff, 1965), 88–9, who explains that the term lip-work, is of Scandanavian origin.

123 For illustrations and descriptions of these Orkney chairs see Gilbert, *English Vernacular Furniture*, 145–7, figs. 237–8.

124 H.C. Parliamentary Papers: Report of the Commissioners (II) 1936, Supplement to Appendix E. xxxII. Parts I and II, Ulster, county Fermanagh, 63.

125 Kickham, *Knocknagow*, 51 (55, 59, 71); 'Sitting in a straw arm-chair, near the kitchen fire'. P. Kennedy, *The Banks of The Boro, A Chronicle of County Wexford* (Dublin, 1875, 1989 reprint), 294.

126 P. Kennedy, *Legends of Mount Leinster* (Dublin, 1855, 1989 reprint), 50.

127 The Revd. Dean Swift, *Gulliver*, bk. iv. ii. (1727) quoted under the definitions of boss, in J. Wright, *The English Dialect Dictionary*, vol. 1, A–C: 'Round which they sat on their haunches upon bosses of straw'. D.I.F. Ms. Vol. 1663 (1957): County Galway; 'siosrogs' [from *suidhisteog* = seat, diminuitive] 4. County Carlow 'a boss' 42. County Kilkenny 'Bosses and sugan chairs made in Graignamanagh' 54, 48. County Longford 'hammocks' 70. D.I.F. Ms. Vol. 1664 (c.1958): County Tipperary, a seat called a boss 'made by winding sugans around in the form of a firkin' and 'bas made of twisted hay or straw', 61, 64. County Kerry; 'called *saoistin*', 48. County Cork, Castlehaven; 'sheesteen'-20, Minane bridge; '"Boss", a straw chair, or a sisteen'-26. County Donegal, Gweedore, 'parrdog' [*Pardog* = pad, mat, pannier] also named '*saoisteog*' 102, 89, 98, 100. County Monaghan, '*seas*' or 'suiosrog' [*suidhisteog* = seat, diminuitive or straw mat]. There were references to straw seats in every county, but only

the ones with names have been listed here. Also in Clare, Limerick, Cork and Tipperary 'bosses (seats made of straw)' mentioned in H.C. Parliamentary Papers: Report of the Commissioners (II) 1836, Supplement to Appendix E. xxxII. 89–90 (Clare, Limerick), 164 ('seesteens'-county Cork), 245 (Tipperary).

128 Extensive study of the hundreds of replies to two museum questionnaires covering all the counties of Ireland, prove that straw seats and chairs of various types were undoubtedly known in every area. They are: D.I.F. Ms. Vols. 1663–4 (c.1957–8) Questionnaire: Certain Articles of Furniture; 'Q.5; Where seats or chairs ever made from twisted or plaited straw? If so what was their name?' plus U.F.M. Quest. (1962) Q1, Questionnaire – Straw Ropes, questions 8–9; For what purposes were straw ropes used? etc.

129 The translations of Irish words which were still occasionally used by the museum and folklore questionnaire respondents, combined with their descriptions, show wide overlapping of terminology to describe straw seats – *seas, suidhiste, suidhistin/ saoistin* [diminutive] and straw mats – *suidhisteog/ saoisteog*). The range of words chosen may indicate an accompanying variation in size and shape of the straw objects.

130 D.I.F. Ms. Vols. 1664 (c.1958), 4 [from *suidhiste* = seat].

131 Carleton, *Traits and Stories of the Irish Peasantry*, II (Dublin, 1835, 4th edn) 206.

132 Harris, 'Extracts', 31; M. McK., Kilrudden, Clogher, county Tyrone. Hassocks, one made of 'wheat straw, bound and sewn as they used to make the old straw beehives' and another made of 'plaited rush grass', were discovered in an old church in Lusk, county Dublin and are described by Dorothy Hartley, *Irish Holiday* (1938), 29–30.

133 G.C. Bonthrone, 'Childhood Memories of county Antrim' in *Ulster Folklife*, 6 (1960), 38.

134 This technique, which is essentially the same as that used for making bee skeps, is described and illustrated step by step in F. Alston, *Skeps, Their History, Making and Use* (Mytholmroyd, 1987), 20–5.

135 Evans, *Irish Heritage*, fig. 77; Evans illustrates such a bone pin which he says was used while making the coiled straw 'kishaun' for food carrying, from the Aran Islands.

136 Those considering practising this craft should be wary of using blue baler twine as a binder, which may have been pre-treated with degenerating chemicals.

137 This account was provided by James Mulhall, of the Carlow County Museum. His childhood recollection of the chair was heightened by the trouble he got into for tweaking out loose bits of straw from it. His grandmother would use a cushion and sit by the fire in such a chair, in the corner; she 'never stirred, always kept in the one place'. It was thrown out after she died. The device of raising the chair up on legs would have protected the base against wear.

138 D.I.F. Ms. Vol. 1664 (1957), 70; Mrs Rose Emerson, Glens of Antrim, 'baskets for babies were also made from plaited straw'.

139 Mr and Mrs S.C. Hall, *Hall's Ireland*, 2 vols. I (Dublin, 1841–3, London, 1984), 37. Information about Mrs Hall from J. Delaney, *Baskets and their Uses in the Midlands* in Gailey and Ó hÓgáin eds, *Gold Under The Furze*, 226.

140 Kennedy, *Legendary Fictions of the Irish Celts*, 100–1.

141 D.I.F. Ms. Vol. 1664 (1957), 86–7.

142 Carleton, 'The Courtship of Phelim O'Toole' in *Six Irish Tales*, 26.

143 K.M. Harris, 'Plaited Straw-work' in *Ulster Folklife*,

IX (1963), 53–60. This article discusses a far greater range of straw objects than there is scope for here.

144 O.S. Memoirs, Box 5, II 13 (6 March-19 May 1837), 13. Also 'Rates of Wages of Humbler Classes' from *Ordnance Survey Memoir of the county of Londonderry*, I (Dublin, 1837), 199.

145 U.F.M. Quest. (1962) Q.1/5, 19, 159.

146 O.S. Memoirs, Box 5, II 8 (21 June-21 July 1837), 16. There were 6 stalls selling the straw baskets, at 'various prices' and a further 8 stalls selling the bee skeps. O.S. Memoirs, Box 5, II 13 (6 March-19 May 1837), 101, 'straw baskets and beehives are brought from the neighbourhood of Ballinderry'. The author is grateful to Megan McManus for bringing these and other related documents to her attention.

Children's Chairs

147 D.I.F. Ms. Vol. 750 (1937), 462. The accompanying sketch depicts a T shaped handle raised to a convenient height and attached at floor level to a simple three-wheeled framework, the whole cross shaped in plan.

148 O'Neill, *Life and Tradition*, 97.

Chapter 2 SETTLES

Settles and Seats of Various Materials

1 W. Moffat, *Hesperi-Neso-graphia: The Western Isle Described, in eight cantos* (Dublin, 1724), 10–11. This bawdy description of an Irish nobleman's feast provides a useful insight into the variety of seating resorted to in the absence of proper chairs. The reference to them (Gillo and his wife) sitting on a 'Bench of Rushes' which were 'Commixt with Flags' probably describes one of rushes and Iris, plaited together to form a large boss-like bench; see section on straw seats. pp. 63–8.

2 Revd. J. Hall, *Tour Through Ireland, particularly the lesser known parts etc.* 2 vols., I (London, 1813), 199–200. Here Hall is describing conditions in the poorer cabins of county Cork, between Blarney and Millstreet.

Turf Seats

3 C. Otway, *Sketches in Erris and Tyrawly* (Dublin, 1841) 47; Quotes from a presumably anonymous poem 'published in the year 1689'.

4 *Mist's Weekly Journal* (England, 27 July 1728).

5 W. Carleton, *Traits and Stories of the Irish Peasantry*, II (Dublin, 1835, 4th edn. corrected), 207. These hobs were evidently used elsewhere also; 'Seated upon a hob at the door . . . a toil worn man, without coat or waistcoat', 159.

6 A. Gailey, *Rural Houses of the North of Ireland* (Edinburgh, 1984), figs. 34, 35 and 36 show turf houses; 45–7. H.C. Parliamentary Papers: Report of the Commissioners (II) 1836. Supplement to Appendix E. XXXII, Union of Clane, county Kildare. 59: 'Some attempt walls, with large blocks or squares of turf . . . Some of these huts are mere excavations of the dry bog'.

Stone Seating

7 Revd. Hall, *Tour Through Ireland*, 86.

8 Carleton, *Traits and Stories, of the Irish Peasantry*, II, 206.

9 I have noticed such stone seats in areas as diverse as county Donegal, county Waterford and county Cork. They can be likened to the hearth 'keeping holes' (pp. 125–6) and to the now rare, stone stillions (pp. 132–4), for placing pails of water or milk inside the front door. All these integral features would have to have been made when the house was built.

10 D.I.F. Ms. Vol. 45 (translated from Irish), 68.

11 M. McGrath ed., 'The Diary of Humphrey O'Sullivan, 1827–32' (2 June 1831) in the *Irish Text Society*, XXXII (1930), 49.

12 D.I.F. Ms. Vol. 654 (1939), *Poulaphouca [Resevoir] Survey*; Butler's House, 60. I am grateful to Dr F.H.A. Aalen for drawing my attention to this material as well as providing me with photographs and manuscript from this survey.

Forms

13 Anon, 'Thady O'Brady, Favourite Irish Comic Song' (*c.* early 19th century), National Library of Ireland, unreferenced book.

14 *Ormonde Household Accounts* ['Ormonde Inventories'] (1629–32), National Library of Ireland, Ms. 2549, 17.

15 J.C. Walton, 'The Household Effects of a Waterford Merchant Family in 1640', *Journal of the Cork Historical and Archaeological Society*, LXXXIII, No. 238 (July–December, 1978), 102; 'one draweinge table with two foarmes 2£ [sic] 18s.' Also D. St John Seymour, 'The Household Furniture of Castletown Waller in 1642', *North Munster Archaelogical Society Journal*, I (1909–11) 255–8; 'fformes'.

16 R. ffolliott, 'The Furnishings of a Palladian House in 1742–3: Barbaravilla, county Westmeath', *The Irish Ancestor*, XI, No. 2 (1979), 87.

17 Pronunciation of 'furrums' described in a letter to the author from John Ryan of Piltown, county Kilkenny, describing traditional furniture from the county Wexford house where his father was reared (19 June 1991).

18 For areas of distribution throughout Ireland of this type of house plan read C. Ó Danachair [or K. Danaher] 'Some distribution patterns in Irish Folklife', *Bealoideas*, The Journal of the Folklore Society of Ireland, XXV (Dublin, 1957). Such houses most commonly occurred to the east of a line drawn through Youghal, Limerick, Lough Neagh and Belfast. Gailey, *Rural Houses of the North of Ireland*, 164–71.

19 U.F.M. Quest (1964) Q1b/95; Templepatrick, county Antrim; The illustrated plan of the kitchen given here shows a 'bench seat' placed against the jamb wall, with a 'small window about 2' square called "bole"'.

20 P. Kennedy, *The Banks of the Boro* (Dublin, 1875), 185.

21 P. Kennedy, *Evenings in the Duffrey* (Dublin, 1869), 66.

22 H.C. Parliamentary Papers: Report of the Commissioners (II) 1836. Supplement to Appendix E. XXXII, county Donegal, 304.

23 The most comprehensive article about bog wood is A.T. Lucas, 'Bog Wood A Study in Rural Economy' in *Bealoideas*, The Journal of the Folklore Society of Ireland, XXIII (1954), 71–134. Bog wood was also used to make ropes for bed cords and resinous 'splits' for lighting fires. Traditional houses in county Donegal often had their roofs built from this contorted material, which was then thatched. Where turf is still cut by hand piles of bogwood are still to be seen stacked up to dry, for firewood.

Open Frame Settles

24 J. Wright, *The English Dialect Dictionary*, R-S, V (London, 1904), 337.

25 R. Edwards, *The Dictionary of English Furniture*, III (Woodbridge, 1924, 1983), 108.

26 F.H. Aalen, 'Furnishings of Traditional Houses in the Wicklow Hills' in *Ulster Folklife*, XIII (Belfast, 1967), 63. Dr Aalen mentions 'the seat called 'the rack' in old houses in county Kerry'.

27 H.C. Parliamentary Papers: Report of the Commissioners (II) 1836. Supplement to Appendix E. XXXII. Iveragh, county Kerry, 90.

28 C. Gilbert, *English Vernacualr Furniture 1750–1900* (London, 1991), contains several interesting accounts and illustrations of 'long settles' in England.

29 J. Ayres, *The Shell book of the Home in Britain, Decoration, Design and Construction of Vernacular Interiors, 1500–1850* (London, Boston, 1981), 200, fig. 178. The example illustrated here dates from the late 18th/early 19th century and is part of the furniture collection of the Highland Folk Museum, Kingussie, Scotland.

30 U.F.M. Quest. (1964) Q1b/58.

The 'Carbery Settle'

31 C. Kinmonth, 'Country Seats' in *Country Life* CLXXXIII No. 33 (17 August 1989), 56–9. Also C. Kinmonth, 'Practical Styling' in *Crafts, the Decorative and Applied Arts Magazine* (London, January 1989), 48–51, fig. 2.

32 E. Cross, *The Tailor and Ansty* (Cork and Dublin, 1942, 1987), 28. I visited the house where this celebrated couple used to live, hoping to see the settle still in place. However, unfortunately, it had (like many other similar traditional houses), already been gutted of old furniture and modernised.

33 D.I.F. Ms. Vol. 462 (1937), M.C., farmer born 1850, Carrigroe, Innis Cein, barony of Kinalmeaky, county Cork. 211–12.

34 U.F.M. colour slides refs; CM: 213, 217, 218, 228, 230 and 232. Unless more similar examples turn up in county Derry it is difficult to ascertain whether this amounts to a local style.

35 J.C. Loudon, *Encyclopaedia of Cottage, Farm and Villa Architecture* (London, 1833, 1842 edn.), 317. Quoted in Ayres, *The Home in Britain*, 200, 209.

36 Edwards, *Dictionary of English Furniture*, III, 113, fig. 11.

37 L. Oliver, *Reconnaître les Styles Régionaux* (Paris, n.d. 1980?), 83, fig. 145. This illustration is of a settle with attached one-legged falling table which folds upwards to be held in palce by a pair of wooden turnbuckles at the top of the settle's high back. It is more similar to the Carbery settle than any other examples which I have found outside Ireland. J. Stany Gauthier, *La Connaissance des meubles régionaux français* (Paris, 1976), 148, fig. 96; Here another version is illustrated, with a smaller table, which when lowered rests on the front of the settle's seat rather than on the floor. It is also from the Basque area.

The Settle Bed

38 S. Heaney, 'The Settle Bed' from *Seeing Things* (London, Boston, 1991), 28.

39 Evidence from the D.I.F. questionnaires on furniture, Mss. vols. 1663–4 (1950s) and the U.F.M. (1964) Q1b questionnaire for counties Donegal, Derry, Antrim, Tyrone, Armagh, Down, Fermanagh, Monaghan and Cavan, backed up fieldwork by the author which shows that the settle bed was well known in every county of Ireland.

40 J.C. Walton, 'The Household Effects of a Waterford Merchant Family in 1640', *Journal of the Cork Historical and Archaeological Society*, LXXXIII, No. 238 (July–December, 1978), 102.

41 Ormond Inventories 1673–1745; National Library of Ireland Ms. 2553 (1675); 'An Inventory taken of the goods now standing in his graces house at Clonmell this 2nd day of April 1673', Document No. 1, 15. Also N.L.I. Ms. 2554, His Grace the Duke of Ormond, Dublin Castle, 1 September 1684, 48.

42 R. ffolliott, B. de Breffny, 'The contents of Burton Hall, co. Cork in 1686' in *The Irish Ancestor*, V, No. 2 (Dublin, 1973), 109.

43 O.C. Goodbody, 'Inventories of Five Dublin Quaker Merchants in the late Seventeenth century' in *The Irish Ancestor*, X, No. 1 (Dublin, 1978), 42, 46; 'In the kitching of John Johnston, weaver, co. Dublin, *c.*1694'; '(a settle bed for – *erased*) servants & beding [sic]' and Joseph Deane of Meath Street, a Dublin Shearman, had in 1695 in his kitchen 'A settle bedstead [and] flock bed' the latter presumably kept inside it.

44 A. Gailey, 'Kitchen Furniture' in *Ulster Folklife*, XII (Belfast, 1966), 29.

45 A list of six inventory entries for settle beds between 1695 and 1758 was drawn up by F. Carragher in her article 'Settle Beds in the Ulster Folk and Transport Museum' in *Ulster Folklife*, XXXI, (Belfast, 1985), 36–40. The following list of eighteenth-century descriptions enlarges on hers:

1709 '1 oak settell bed'. Thomas Weston, miller from Athy, county Kildare.
From O.C. Goodbody, 'Quaker Inventories' in *The Irish Ancestor*, 3, No. 1 (Dublin, 1971), 58.

1731 'A settle bed & close . . . 10s'. Bernard Brett (bankrupt) 'minor gentry' of Ballynewport, Lecale, county Down.
From J. Stevenson, *Two Centuries of Life in county Down* (Belfast, 1931), 324.

1735–6 'The Servants Hall; 1 Settle Bed with bed and bolster in ye little Hall'. Rt. Hon. Earl of Fingall, Killeen Castle, county Meath.
From R. ffolliott, 'An Inventory of Killeen Castle in 1735–6' in *The Irish Ancestor*, IX, No. 2 (Dublin, 1977), 105.

1742 'The Yellow Roome, one settle Bed of yellow.' Account book of Barbavilla House, St Feighan's, county Westmeath.
From ffolliott, 'The Furnishings of a Palladian House in 1742–3: Barbavilla, co. Westmeath', 92.

1755 'in the Kitchen . . . 2 settle beds for servants', Advertised to let, furnished, Seamount House, county Dublin.
From A.K. Longfield, 'Up For Sale' in *The Irish Ancestor* XVII, No. 1 (Dublin, 1985), 32. Reprinted from the *Universal Advertiser*, 29 July 1755.

1758 'In deary [sic] 1 Dresser and Settle bed under it £1'. Robert Fayle, farmer of Killone, north county Offaly.
From O.C. Goodbody, 'Quaker Inventories' in *The Irish Ancestor*, III, No. 1 (Dublin, 1971), 61.

1767 'Settle Beds', Auction of furniture of Revd. Mr Grange, Sallymount, near Wicklow.
From A.K. Longfield, 'Up For Sale' in *The Irish Ancestor*, XVII, No. 1 (Dublin, 1985), 33. Reprinted from *Sleater's Public Gazateer*, 4 April 1767.

1769 'One New Settle bed.' James Upington, Mallow, county Cork.
From M.D. Jephson, *An Anglo-Irish Miscellany* (Dublin, 1964), Appendix VI, 383.

1780 'a settle bed...in the servts Hall', George Ryan, Inch, county Tipperary.
From J. Condon, 'Don Jorge Rian of Inch, co. Tipperary (1748–1805)' in *The Irish Ancestor*, XVIII, No. 1 (Dublin, 1986), 10.

1797 '1 settle with bed etc. Kitchen'. Mrs Burgess, innkeeper, Mallow, co. Cork.
From R. ffolliott, 'The Furnishings of An 18th Century Inn' in *The Irish Ancestor*, II, No. 1 (Dublin, 1970), 44.

46 To avoid possible confusion I have not listed the further half-dozen or so references to 'settee beds' or the many references to 'servant's beds', some of which must have been settle beds, for example:

P.R.O.N.I. T1062/29; 'An Inventory of...Joseph Williamson & debts and cridditt of Creanagh in the parish of Kilmore and co. of Armagh...died 27th of 9th mo. 1729; a servants bed ordanery at £0.3.0.' Also P.R.O.N.I. T1062/24; 'An inventory of the goods and chattles of John Reed of Ballyberoan in the parish of Loughgall and co. of Armagh. Died 1728; In the room the other end of the house 2 servants beds etc. all £1.0.6.' [the latter document courtesy of The Religious Society of Friends].

The term settle bed is also commonly shortened to settle, but descriptions like 'sleeping *in* the settle' or the 'settle *containing* flock bed etc.' clearly indicate settle beds rather than open frame, bench type settles.

47 The press bed is a folding bed which can be disguised as a cupboard by day (see later, pp. 168–72). Only one out of the 120 respondents to the Ulster Folk and Transport Museum furniture questionnaire, definitely called their settle bed a 'press bed', along with one other writer from county Tyrone. However, these two descriptions are exceptional and for the purposes of this book the two terms are used in their most popular sense.
U.F.M. Quest. (1964) Q1b: Dr Gailey quotes questionnaire respondents who use the term 'press bed' for the settle bed. He presumably refers to responses 41, 48 and 28, in his article 'Kitchen Furniture' in *Ulster Folklife*, XII (Belfast, 1966), 28. However, the only reliable responses indicating that the settle bed was called the press bed are U.F.M. Quest. (1964), Q1b/151, E.M. county Monaghan; 'This settle bed was called a 'press-bed'. It opened out like a deep box and could hold two adults comfortably.' Also possibly respondent number 173 from county Fermanagh indicated this.
Another writer from county Tyrone backs this up by describing how 'A pressbed is a wooden article used for a person to sleep in at night and is used during the day for a seat...The person who slept in the pressbed always lay in the kitchen and could never go to bed until all the other members of the family retired. He had to be first up too, unless he didn't mind the others using the kitchen while he slept.' from K.M. Harris, 'Extracts from the Committee's Collection' in *Ulster Folklife*, VI (Belfast, 1960), 20.

48 P.R.O.N.I., D288/174 (3 September 1817); 'Inventory and Valuation of the effects of the [late] Joshua McGeough esq. Drumsill, county Armagh.' [The latter document courtesy of The late Sir Walter MacGeoughBond].

49 U.F.M. Questionnaire 'Certain Articles of Furniture'; U.F.M. Quest. (1964) Q1b. and D.I.F. Questionnaire 'Furniture', (1957) Mss. Vols. 1663–4: together all these respondents demonstrate that the settle bed was known throughout Ireland. This is backed up by the author's fieldwork.

Settle Beds and Servants

50 Extracts from the Ordnance Survey Memoirs are published and discussed in R.L. Harris, 'The Ordnance Survey Memoirs' in *Ulster Folklife*, I (Belfast, 1955), 43–52. Harris explains that the government grant for the written records was cut early in the proceedings, so unfortunately detailed memoirs were only written for counties Antrim and Derry. Memoirs are also being published by region, by A. Day and P. Williams eds., *O.S. Memoir of Ireland* (Institute of Irish Studies, Queen's University, Belfast, in conjunction with the Royal Irish Academy, Dublin).

51 O.S. Memoir, Box 16, IV, 22 (1840), 1–97 (with additions from Section 15, (1834–5?) 1–17; Parish of Templecorran, county Antrim.

52 O.S. Memoir, Box 15, VI, 1 (June, 1840), 1–111; Parish of Raloo, county Antrim.

53 P. Kennedy, *Legends of Mount Leinster* (Dublin, 1855), 57, 7.

54 H.C. Parliamentary Papers: Report of the Commissioners (II) 1836. Supplement to Appendix E. XXXII. Barony of Conello Upper, Ballingarry, Castletown and Kilmeedy, county Limerick. 225.

55 T. Ó Criomhthain, quoted in P. O'Sullivan, *Field and Shore* (Dublin, 1977), 125.

56 See D.I.F. and U.F.M. questionnaires for examples of this.

57 D.I.F. Ms. Vol. 462 (1937) M.C. Innis Cein, Kinalmeaky, county Cork 211–12.

58 Kennedy, *The Banks of the Boro*, 50.

59 M. Harkin and S. McCarroll, *Carndonagh* (Dublin, 1984), 173.

60 Carleton *Traits and Stories of the Irish Peasantry* (Dublin, 1835), 192.

61 Harkin, and McCarroll, *Carndonagh*, 173.

62 D.I.F. Ms. Vol. 1664 (1957), 52, county Limerick.

63 U.F.M. Quest. (1964) Q1b/73.

64 C.M. Arensberg and S.T. Kimball, *Farm and Community in Ireland* (Harvard 1940), 38.

65 R. Flower, 'The Dance' from *The Western Isle or the Great Blasket* (Oxford, 1944), 48.

66 D.I.F. Schools Book 750 (1937), Ballymahon, county Longford. 424.

67 Only 4 descriptions, out of over 240 questionnaires sent out, state that the settle bed was used sometimes at mealtimes as a table. D.I.F. Ms. Vol. 1664 (1957) Tipperary, 60. D.I.F. Ms. Vol. 1663, Kilkenny, 48, 55; 'sometimes used as a table' and 'sometimes ate dinner off it'. U.F.M. Quest. (1964) Q1b/134 and 156, county Down; 'when folded up it served as a seat, bench, and was used sometimes as a table.' and 'in some cases a table'.
Also see K.M. Harris, 'Extracts from the Committee's Collection' in *Ulster Folklife*, V (Belfast, 1959), 37.

68 D.I.F. Ms. Vol. 1664, J.D. county Cork, 36.

69 D.I.F. Ms. Vol. 1664 (1957) county Limerick, 52.

70 U.F.M. Quest. (1964) Q1b/70, F.E.H. Castleblayney, county Monaghan. D.I.F. Ms. Vol. 1664 (1958), county Armagh, 79. Also M.J. Murphy, *At Slieve Gullion's Foot* (Dundalgan Press, 1942), 25. A photograph from the Poulaphouca Reservoir Survey in county Wicklow of the 1930s also depicts this use.

71 D.I.F. Ms. Vol. 1663, county Wexford, 89.

Settle Bed Construction and Variation in Design

72　U.F.M. Quest. (1964) Q1b/166. Dr P.Q., Mourne and South Down.

73　P. Warner, *A Visitor's Guide to the Comeragh Mountains* (Belfast, 1978), 67.

Settle Beds Abroad

74　L. Sammallahti, 'Sofa, Bed or Bed-Sofa?' in *Ethnologia Fennica*, XI (Helsinki, 1981), 6–12, Sammallahti describes and illustrates various types of laterally extendable beds or pull-out sofas common in Finland and Scandanavia. See also P. Thornton, *Seventeenth Century Interior Decoration in England, France and Holland* (Yale, 1978), 169, 368. 'Settle bedstead' at Tart Hall.

75　J. Mannion, *Irish Settlements in Eastern Canada* (Toronto, 1974), 152–8.

76　H. Pain, *The Heritage of Upper Canadian Furniture A Study in the Survival of Formal and Vernacular Styles from Britain, America and Europe, 1780–1900* (Toronto, 1978), 159–62, 498.

77　R.H. Kettell, *The Pine Furniture of Early New England* (New York, 1929, 1956), fig. 69.

78　G. Cornall, *Memories, A Survey of Early Australian Furniture in the Collection of The Lord McAlpine of West Green* (Perth, 1990), 174–5. T and J. Hooper, *Australian Country Furniture* (Victoria, 1988), 55–60.

79　Cornall, *Memories*, 130, fig. 4. See also fig. 63.1.

Settle Tables

80　The fact that settle tables had not been written about helps explain why the museum and folklife questionnaires did not include them in their surveys.
　　Settle tables and single-seater settle tables are described and illustrated in C. Kinmonth, *Country Seats* in *Country Life*, CLXXXIII, No. 33 (17 August 1989), 56–9.

81　See G. Sturt, *The Wheelwright's Shop* (Cambridge, 1923, 1984 reprint), 79–80, 159–61. On the subject of chamfering, Sturt tells us: 'Usefulness, not beauty, was wanted . . . For this "shaving" was one of the ways by which a wheelwright reduced the weight of his always too cumbersome product . . . with the drawshave'. Similarly much of the blacksmith's labour was spent on 'drawing down' the ironwork, making it lighter. The decorative effect of chamfering, so common on Irish vernacular furniture, served a different, ornamental purpose compared to its use on carts. It was second nature to the wheelwright.

82　F.S. Robinson, *English Furniture* (New York, London, 1905), 115, plate LVII, 2–3.

83　F. Gordon Roe, *English Cottage Furniture* (London, 1949, 1961), 105.

84　Edwards, *Dictionary of English Furniture*, III, 111, fig. 7. The same Victoria and Albert Museum example is illustrated in H. Cescinski and E. Gribble, *Early English Furniture and Woodwork*, II (London, 1922) fig. 253, while figs. 230, 231 and 254 also illustrate two different examples of chair tables.

85　V. Chinnery, *Oak Furniture the British Tradition* (Woodbridge, 1979), 258–60.

86　These have been studied (but not yet published) by Gabriel Olive, an antique dealer with a keen local interest, and although his examples are different in style to the 'open frame' Irish settle tables, the location and proximity to the south-east of Ireland suggests a link. The 'slab ends' of these Somerset settle tables (or Monks' Benches, as they are tagged by dealers) are reminiscent of board-ended settle beds from the north of Ireland. Olive states that 'the notable feature of West Country settles' is these slab ends, in his article 'West Country Settles' in *Furniture History*, XVII (London, 1981), 20. The author is grateful to Gabriel Olive and Christopher Gilbert for entering into correspondence on this subject.

87　Examples of settle tables and chair tables have been mentioned as originating in Lancashire, Gloucestershire, Cheshire and Cardiff. An example of a chair table is on show in the castle at the Welsh Folk Museum, St Fagans. Perhaps fieldwork combined with documentary research might reveal more about the distribution of such settle tables in the British Isles, in order to draw conclusions as to the origins of the design. From the few examples published so far, it is impossible to conclude that settle tables were a common part of vernacular furniture in England, as they were in south-east Ireland.

88　Oliver, *Reconnaître les styles régionaux*, 85–6, figs. 148 and 152. He also illustrates a form of late 19th-century settle table with a back which hinges down in two separate parts, from Auvergne, southern France.

89　Kettell, *Pine Furniture*, figs. 70–3, 95. It is surprising that no settle tables and chair tables have been found in Australia.

90　R. and T. Kovel, *American Country Furniture* (New York, 1979), figs. 530–2. One of these has a table top hinged onto the arms of a distinctly Irish style hedge chair. The 'hutch table' here has a round top and double-ended sledge feet.

Chapter 3　THE DRESSER

Introducing The Dresser

1　Anon, 'Thady O'Brady, Favourite Irish Comic Song' (n.d. but *c*.1800) from an unreferenced book in the National Library of Ireland.

2　Antique dealers often resort to sawing dressers in half to extract them from the kitchens in which they were originally built. Occasionally the dressers built after the 1930s with glazed doors on the upper section were made in two separate pieces, making them less cumbersome to move.

3　D.I.F., Ms. Vol. 1664 (1957), 70.

Stone Shelves

4　V.G. Childe and D.V. Clarke, *Skara Brae* (Edinburgh, 1983), 7–12. These semi-recessed three-tier 'dressers' are always positioned in the wall opposite the front doorway, they are 'generally two-storied, and supported by three legs in the front'. There are also recessed stone cupboards let into the considerable thickness of the walls.

5　E.E. Evans, *Irish Folk Ways* (London, 1st edn, 1957, 1979), 91.

6　O. Goodbody, 'Inventories of five Dublin Quaker merchants in the late seventeenth century' in *The Irish Ancestor*, X, No. 1 (Limerick, 1978), 40; In 1693 John Inglefield, a Dublin chandler had in his kitchen a 'dresser and shelves'; Isachar Wilcocks, a grocer from Dublin had 'dressers' presumably for the display of his twenty-five pewter dishes, in his kitchen.

7　N.L.I. Ms. 29, 709 (9) Harvey Papers; An Inventory of Killiane Castle. 2 August 1760. Listed in the 'Kitching . . . 1 coop, 2 tables . . . a meatrack, 4 feather tubs & some old lumber on the loft, the dresser', etc.

8 H.C. Parliamentary Papers: Report of Commissioners (II) 1836. Supplement to Appendix E. XXXII. County Longford and Leitrim. 92.

9 W. Carleton, 'The Courtship of Phelim O'Toole' in *Six Irish Tales* (Dublin, 1833), 26.

10 H.C. Parliamentary Papers: Report of Commissioners (II) 1836. Supplement to Appendix E. XXXII. County Kerry. 216. Also G. de Beaumont quoted in R.B. McDowell, *Social Life in Ireland 1800–45* (Dublin, 1957), 49; 'Some had small dressers of two or three shelves but usually the shelves were built into a recess in the wall.'

Ware

11 P. Colum, 'The old woman of the road' from *The Poet's Circuits* (Portlaoise, 1985), 110.

12 D.I.F. Ms. Vol. 1664, R.E. from the Glens of Antrim, 70.

13 C. Elizabeth, *Letters from Ireland* (London, 1838), 41; When describing the poverty of some households in county Wexford, she lists meagre furnishings and writes: 'Plates, knives, and such appendages are unthought of. Whatever surplus may remain after satisfying the priest, must go towards treating the friends of the family.' Also see T. O'Neill, *Life and Tradition in Rural Ireland* (London, 1977), 26. Also, G. Stokes, ed. *Pococke's Tour in Ireland in 1752* (Dublin, 1891), 87; 'The poor here use scollop shells for all uses they can . . . I saw him give a dram about in the eggshell'.

14 W. Moore, 'A County Down Farm Kitchen' in *The Irish Monthly*, 58 (1930), 455.

15 A. Young, *A Tour in Ireland, 1776–9*, II (London and New York, 1980), 124; 'In England a man's cottage will be filled with superfluities before he possesses a cow. I think the comparison much in favour of the Irishman; a hog is a much more valuable piece of goods than a set of tea things.'

16 H.C. Parliamentary Papers: Report of the Commissioners (II) 1836. Supplement to Appendix E. XXXII. County Cork, Barony of Carbery West. 181.

17 R. ffolliott, 'Household Stuff' in I, No. 1 *The Irish Ancestor* (1969), 'Inventory of the worldly substance of Jonathon Kent late of Ballyhagh, county Tipperary, gent, deceased.' 45–9.

18 Ibid., 46–7. 'Inventory of ye goods and Chattels of John McNamara of Killaloe in ye county Clare, Broguemaker, deceased . . . 20 February 1741' (originally from Brit. Mus. Add. Ms. 31, 882).

19 D. Thomson and M. McGusty, *The Irish journals of Elizabeth Smith, 1840–1850* (Oxford, 1980), 12. This diary contains an account of two sisters 'throwing pewter pots at some men's heads in a publick house' in county Wicklow. See also, W. Carleton, *Traits and Stories of the Irish Peasantry* 2 vols, II (London, 4th edn 1835), 160; 'and the dresser with noggins, wooden trenchers, and pewter dishes perfectly clean, and as well polished as a French courtier'.

20 Ibid. I, 16.

21 S.O. Suilleabhain, Mmlle. F. Henry and F.E. Stephens, *Poulaphouca Survey*: Michael Twyford's House (May, 1939), D.I.F. Ms. Vol. 654, 111; 'In this house there are twelve old pewter dishes and plates.'

22 G. Griffiths, *Chronicles of the County Wexford* (Enniscorthy, 1877), 242.

23 I have rarely found marked spongeware; the only marks found corresponding to Arklow or Belleek. It was also made in Scotland and other parts of the British Isles and imported into Ireland. The study of Irish spongeware has been sadly neglected, although Mrs E. Mosse's museum of spongeware at Bennettsbridge,

county Kilkenny is well worth visiting. Read B. Arnold, 'Irish Objects' in B. Share ed., *Irish Craftsmanship* (Irish Section, World Crafts Council, 1970), 13–14, for more information on Belleek and transferware and its manufacture in Dublin since the first half of the 18th century.

24 H. Glassie, *Passing The Time, Folklore and History of an Ulster Community* (Dublin, 1982), 363, 761.

25 W. Hanbidge, *The Memories of William Hanbidge. Aged 93. 1906. An Autobiography* (St Albans, 1939), 26.

26 S. Gmelch, *Tinkers and Travellers* (Dublin, 1975), 28–30 The tinkers got their name from the sound made when mending metal pots. They made and sold all sorts of kitchen ware; teakettles, ponnies (pint mugs), buckets, lanterns and milk pails as well as equipment for distilling illicit poteen, they also swept chimneys and repaired metal ware. A woman to whom I spoke in west county Cork recalled being told not to touch the brass candlestick that the tinkers repaired for her 'for two days', by which time of course they were long gone, should the repair fail.

27 O'Neill, *Life and Tradition in Rural Ireland*, 28.

28 H.C. Parliamentary Papers: Report of the Commissioners (II) 1836. Supplement to Appendix E. XXXII. County Cork, Barony Carbery [sic] West. 181; 'a miserable dresser, under which the pig lies, on its top the hens roost, the middle is occupied by a few broken plates and basins'. It is possible that the use in the south of the term basin originated via the old trade links with neighbouring France, the French for bowl is *bassin*.

29 B. O Madagain, 'Gaelic Work-songs' in *Ireland of the Welcomes*, XL, No. 2 (March/April 1991), 32.

30 W. Moore, *A County Down Farm Kitchen* in The Irish Monthly, LVIII, (1930), 455.

Display Shelves

31 P. Macquoid and R. Edwards, *The Dictionary of English Furniture*, II (Suffolk, 1983), 218; 'On the Continent dressers were built up of many stages (their number serving to indicate the degree of the owner), and to such towering proportions did they attain in France that steps were sometimes provided to enable servitors to reach articles placed at the top.'

32 A. Taylor, *To School through the Fields* (Dingle, 1988), 15.

33 D.I.F. Ms. Vol. 1664, county Cavan, 73.

34 C. Kinmonth, 'Pride of An Irish kitchen' in *Country Life*, CLXXXIV No. 41 (London, 11 October 1990), 80–3, figs. 1, 4 and 9.

35 A. Gailey, 'Kitchen Furniture' in *Ulster Folklife*, XII (Belfast, 1966), 22.

Spoon Display

36 H.C. Parliamentary Papers: Report of the Commissioners (II) 1836. Supplement to Appendix E. XXXII. County Westmeath, Baronies Clonlonan, Kilkenny, Corkaree. 126.

37 Hanbidge, *Memories*, 27.

38 P. Kennedy, *The Banks of the Boro, A Chronicle of County Wexford* (London, 1867), 345.

40 T. O'Neill, *Merchants and Mariners in Medieval Ireland* (Dublin, 1987), 44–8. R. Dudley Edwards, *An Atlas of Irish History* (New York, 1981), chapter 10.
The following references all illustrate spoons displayed on dressers;
L. Oliver, *Mobilier Normand* (Paris, n.d.), 19, 63; J. Gauthier, *Le Mobilier Auvergnat* (Paris, 1932), plates

8, 13, 37; L. Oliver, *Reconnaitre les styles régionaux* (Paris, n.d.), pl. 92, 64 and pl. 99, 66; from the Auvergne and Normandy areas. J.S. Gauthier, *La Connaissance des meubles régionaux Français* (Paris, 1976), fig. 174, 247; shows a dresser from Picardy region, with 42 spoons and forks hung along the entire length of upper shelf. H. Pain, *The Heritage of Upper Canadian Furniture; A study in the survival of formal and vernacular styles from Britain, America and Europe, 1780–1900* (Toronto, 1984), plate 957. 359. This plate shows a typically Irish style of dresser, under the heading 'the Germanic tradition'. The shelf has a row of fourteen centrally placed spoons.

41 I. Pickford, *Silver Flatware, English, Irish, and Scottish 1660–1980* (Woodbridge, 1983), 56–7. Pickford illustrates a 'turned-over or hook-end' spoon *c.*1761, Dublin: 'A variation which appears to be peculiar to Ireland . . . found principally with eighteenth century serving pieces. As the name implies, the end of the stem is literally turned back for hanging the piece up.' Douglas Bennett, author of *Irish Georgian Silver* (Cassell, 1972), *Collecting Irish Silver* (Souvenir Press, 1984), and *The Silver Collection of Trinity College Dublin* (Trinity College Dublin Press, 1988), knows of examples of 'crook-ended' spoons dating from the 1720s onwards, with adapted versions from the 1920s. The National Museum of Ireland (Dublin) have about half a dozen examples amongst their flatware collection.

Hanging Dressers

42 Hanbidge, *Memories*, 20.
43 O'Neill, *Life and Tradition in Rural Ireland*, 26. O'Neill also mentions the term 'ware rack', the possible varieties could be endless.
44 The term 'rack' crops up fairly frequently in Irish material culture, so its use and interpretation should be treated with caution, particularly when deciphering inventories. In county Kerry 'rack' is the word used to describe a local type of fireside settle. In county Wexford, the rack was also another word for the fire crane; a hinged system for suspending pots over the open hearth; O Suilleabhain, Henry and Stephens, *Poulaphouca Survey*: D.I.F. Ms. Vol. 654, 51. Several inventories from big houses during the 18th century also refer to wooden or iron racks.
45 D.I.F. Ms. Vol. 1664 (1950s), 79.
46 O Suilleabhain, Henry and Stephens, *Poulaphouca Survey*: Butler's House, Humphreystown, (May, 1939), D.I.F. Ms. Vol. 654, 45–179.

Sledge Feet

47 For examples of English furniture with sledge feet see H. Cescinsky and E. Gribble, *Early English Furniture and Woodwork* (London, 1922), II, 99–100, 131–2, 175, 191. The latter two page references show illustrations of a settle table and a chair table which both have sledge feet (although surviving Irish examples do not). English examples of these made in the early 19th century, and of Cornish settles do however sometimes retain this medieval feature.
48 My close examination of the many dressers in store in the Ulster Folk and Transport Museum revealed pronounced differences in the colour and thickness of accumulated layers of paint between these feet and the rest of the dresser base, bearing out my theory.
49 C. Kinmonth, 'Beside an Irish Hearth' in *Country Life*, CLXXXV No. 21 (London, May 23 1991), 110–11.

Built-in Dressers

50 H.C. Parliamentary Papers: Report of the Commissioners (II) 1836. Supplement to Appendix E. XXXII. Corbally, county Tipperary. 241. Similar descriptions are given from counties Cork, Kerry, Clare, Kilkenny, Longford, Meath, Offaly, Wicklow, Limerick, Donegal and Down.
51 Such an arrangement can be seen in a single-storey thatched house painted by James Brenan RHA (1837–1904), *Committee of Inspection*, (fig. 171).
52 D.I.F. Ms. Vol. 1664 (1950s) county Limerick, 55. There are houses in Bunratty Folk Park with sleeping lofts reached by ladders and dressers as integral parts of the parlour wall. I have seen a surviving loft supported by a dresser in Killybegs townland, near Baltinglass, county Wicklow in 1988 (subsequently 'modernised'). The dresser's use as a loft support was most commonly acknowledged as having been widespread in parts of Connaught and Munster according to the D.I.F. Mss. Vols 1663–4 (1950s).
53 D.I.F. Ms. 1664 (1950s) 49.
54 T. Ó Criomhthain, *The Islandman* (1937, reprinted Oxford, 1987), 26.
55 D.I.F. Ms. 1664 (1950s) county Donegal. 98.
56 Gailey, 'Kitchen Furniture', 22.
57 Ibid., 19–22.

Coops and Coop Dressers

58 Goodbody, 'Inventories of Five Dublin Quaker Merchants', 39.
59 N.L.I. Ms. 29, 709(9) Harvey Papers. An Inventory of Killiane Castle, county Wexford. 2 August 1760. P.R.O.N.I. D288/174: Inventory . . . of the late Joshua McGeough esq., 3 September 1817, Drumsill, county Armagh. In the 'New Kitchen . . . Chicken Coop . . . £2.5s.6d.' Courtesy of The late Sir Walter MacGeough-Bond. R. ffolliott, 'The furnishings of a Palladian house in 1742–3: Barbavilla, co.Westmeath' in *The Irish Ancestor*, XI, No. 2 (Limerick, 1979), 87–8.
60 C. Kinmonth, 'The role of oral history in researching Irish vernacular furniture' in *Oral History*, Journal of the Oral History Society, XVIII No. 2 (London, 1990), 64–5, 32–3, 'Coom' is a term used in the Skibbereen district of county Cork.
61 Goodbody, 'Inventories of Five Dublin Quaker Merchants', 39.
62 D.I.F., Ms. Vol. 1664 (1950)s, 30; Respondent J.E.D. from Union Hall, county Cork, describes the dresser 'the lower part had a slatted front. It was called the "coob" (coop) and was used to house the hens.' Also in county Kerry (D.I.F., Ms. Vol. 782, 394), respondent P.D. describes how the pigs used to sleep under the bed by night and 'the hen coob was in the kitchen too'. The term 'coob' rather than coop, seems to have been used most frequently in Munster.
63 C. Kinmonth and John O'Sullivan, transcript of recorded discussions. Ms. No. 8804; 9/1/1988. Skibbereen, county Cork, 20. I have found that traditional furniture makers' memories of furniture are often the most accurate: as tradesmen, they have a thorough professional interest for details of design and construction. Such descriptions can then be compared with surviving objects, my sketches and documentary evidence, for accuracy.
64 Young, *A Tour in Ireland*, 25. Referring at this point to the south-east of Ireland.
65 M. Doyle, *Hints to Small Holders, on Planting, Cattle, Poultry, Agricultural Implements, Flax, etc.*

(Dublin, 1832), Ch. XIX Fowls and Chickens, 54–7. The fact that the gentry did not always keep their fowl indoors is borne out by '1 Chicken coope 3*s*.4*d*.' listed in the Yard of a Captains house in 1741–2. See R. ffolliott, 'Captain Balfour's Auction 15th March, 1741–2' in XVI, No. 1 of *The Irish Ancestor* (Kilkenny, 1984), 24.

66 Doyle, *Hints to Small Holders*, 56–7.

67 R. ffolliott, 'Household Stuff', 47.

68 R. ffolliott, 'An Inventory of Killeen Castle in 1735–6,' (county Meath) in *The Irish Ancestor*, IX, No. 2 (Limerick, 1977), 102–7.

69 ffolliott, 'The furnishings of a Palladian house in 1742–3', 87–8.

70 E. MacLysaght, *Irish Life in the Seventeenth Century: After Cromwell* (Dublin and Cork, 1939), 111.

71 Ibid., 138–41.

72 M. Harkin and S. McCarroll, *Carndonagh* (Dublin, 1984), 170. This was apparently said by a local person while Maura Harkin gathered material for this book.

73 T.H. Mason, *The Islands of Ireland* (London, 1938), 78. Also E.E. Evans, *Irish Folk Ways* (London, 1st edn, 1957, 1979), 60–1, describes 'the sitting hen warmly ensconsed in a stone-box alongside the fire' in county Down.

74 E.E. Evans, *Irish Heritage* (Dundalk, 1945), 72. Evans, *Irish Folk Ways*, 61. Olga Pyne Clarke, writing of her childhood in county Cork in the 1930s, writes of a single-roomed house where hens 'hatched under the dresser in specially made nesting places' in *She Came of Decent People* (London, 1986), 75. The author is grateful to Dr Austin O'Sullivan for pointing out this text to her.

75 C. Ó Danachair, 'The combined byre and dwelling in Ireland' in *Folk Life*, II (Cardiff, 1964), 60, 74.

76 Ibid., 61. Evans, *Irish Folk Ways*, 61.

77 Ó Criomhthain, *The Islandman*, 27–9. R. Flower, *The Western Island or The Great Blasket* (Oxford 1st ed. 1944, 1985), 42; 'a dresser boarded in below to serve as a hen-coop'.

78 D.I.F., Ms. Vol. 1663–4. Many respondents to the 1950s D.I.F. furniture questionnaire described coops beneath dressers or hatching places. One reply (from Vol. 1664, 5) mentioned that in county Clare some of these 'old type' of dressers still remained, during the 1950s. Coop dressers are now all but gone from traditional houses; with very few exceptions, they are solely museum objects.

79 Ó Criomhthain, *The Islandman*, 26.

80 Ibid., 186.

81 Ó Danachair, 'The combined byre and dwelling in Ireland', 60.

82 Mr and Mrs S.C. Hall, *Ireland its Scenery, Character, etc.* I, (London, 1841), 102; observed in a 'neat and well ordered' cabin near Kilcrea, county Cork.

83 M. Garbery, *The Farm by Lough Gur, The Story of Many Fogarty (Sissy O'Brien)* (1st edn 1937, Cork and Dublin 1986), 21, 51.

84 Ibid., 21.

85 C.C. Ellison, 'Setting up house-1825 Style' in *The Irish Ancestor*, VIII, No. 2 (Limerick, 1976), 80; Listed among carpenter's work done for a wealthy curate by John Fox at Kilgeffin (county Roscommon) is a 'dresser and drainer'. The large plate-draining racks found accommodating the entire base of such dressers would not have been appropriate to the needs of the small Irish farmhouses. Such examples, which often are offered for sale as 'cottage' furniture, usually originate from the kitchen of a 'big house'.

86 ffolliott, 'An Inventory of Killeen Castle in 1735–6', 105.

Small-sized Dressers

87 K. Tynan, 'Irish Types and Traits' in *The Magazine of Art* (London, Paris, New York, 1888), *Matchmaking*, 128.

Chapter 4 STORAGE OF FOOD & CLOTHES

The Keeping Hole

1 S.C. and A.M. Hall, *Ireland: Its Scenery, Character etc.*, III (London, 1841), 297.

2 M. Bourke, *Painting In Focus: 'The Aran Fisherman's Drowned Child' by F.W. Burton* (Dublin, 1987), 29.

3 N. Webster, *Webster's New Twentieth Century Dictionary* (New York, 1983, 2nd edn), 204; *Bole* is defined as 'a small recess in a wall. [Scot.]' County Antrim's close proximity to Scotland geographically and culturally, explains the local use of this Scots term.

4 E.E. Evans, *Irish Folk Ways* (London, 1979), 65–6.

5 P. O'Sullivan, *Field and Shore* (Dublin, 1977), 124.

6 K. O'Neill, *Family and Farm in Pre-famine Ireland* (Wisconsin, 1984), 118; O'Neill discusses labourers' habits and customs, mentioning particularly the use of tobacco. Traditional houses in county Clare sometimes have a pair of triangular keep holes.

7 W. Hanbidge, *The Memories of William Hanbidge. Aged 93. 1906. An Autobiography* (St Albans, 1939), 20, 169. Also see K.M. Harris, 'Extracts from the Committee's Collection' in *Ulster Folklife*, V (Belfast, 1959), 38.

8 E.E. Evans, *Mourne Country* (Dundalk, 1st edn 1951, reprinted 1989), 198.

9 D.I.F. Ms. 1664 (1957), county Donegal, 102. These spills are resinous splinters of inflammable bog-wood, which when applied to glowing turf flare up dramatically.

10 M.J. Murphy, *At Slieve Gullion's Foot* (Dundalk, 1942), 26.

Salt Boxes

11 Anon, 'Thady O'Brady; Favourite Irish Comic Song' (n.d: Probably early 19th century), N.L.I.

12 A. M'Kenzie, *Poems and Songs on Different Subjects* (Belfast, 1810), 117–21; 'Cabin-comfortless, near Ballywalter, 18 December 1807.' From A. Gailey 'The Housing of the rural poor in Nineteenth-century Ulster', *Ulster Folklife*, XXII (1976), 50.

13 O.C. Goodbody, 'Inventories of five Dublin Quaker Merchants in the late Seventeenth Century', *The Irish Ancestor*, X, No. 1 (1978), 44.

14 R. ffolliott, 'An Inventory of Killeen Castle in 1735–6', *The Irish Ancestor*, No. 2 (1977), 105; 1 small salt box. Also An Inventory of Killiane Castle [county Wexford], 2 August 1760, N.L.I. Ms. 29, 709 (9) Harvey Papers; mentions a 'Salt-Box' in the 'Kitching' and in the In-cellar is 'One Salt tub half full of Beef' and 'half a barrel of Salt'.

British Museum Add. Mss 31,882, 74; Inventory of Widow Ballard of Toryglass, died 1736, includes 'one Salt box'.

P.R.O.N.I. D288/174; Inventory of [late] Joshua McGeough esq. Drumsill, county armagh, died 3 sept. 1817; Salt box etc £1.0.0. – Courtesy of the late Sir Walter MacGeough-Bond.

Further 18th and 19th century inventories published in *The Irish Ancestor* (No. 2, 1979 and No. 1, 1984) provide ample evidence of salt boxes having been a familiar aspect of the kitchen furnishings.

15 Harris, 'Extracts from the Committee's Collection', 37–8.

Ceiling Racks and Hanging Shelves

16 R. ffolliott, 'An Inventory of Killeen Castle in 1735–6', *The Irish Ancestor*, IX, No. 2 (1977), 102–7. The word 'rack' has several meanings and where quoted here is distinct from the 'iron rack' which is another term for the crane, from which pots were hung over the open hearth. It should not be confused with the county Kerry 'rack' which in that area is a form of open framed settle.

17 An Inventory of Killiane Castle [county Wexford], 2 August 1760, N.L.I. Ms. 29, 709 (9) Harvey Papers.

18 Such purpose-built ceiling racks made between joists have also been recorded in Wales where they were used for drying grain. See F. Thompson, *Lark Rise to Candleford* (1973), 77. 'The apple crop was stored on racks suspended beneath the ceiling and bunches of herbs dangled below', quoted in C. Gilbert, *English Vernacular Furniture, 1750–1900* (New Haven, London, 1991), 52.

19 K. Danaher, *In Ireland Long Ago* (Cork/Dublin, 1st edn 1962, 1986), 32.

20 P. Kennedy, *The Banks of the Boro, A Chronicle of County Wexford* (London, 1867), 100.

21 R. ffolliott, 'Captain Balfour's Auction 15th March, 1741–2', *The Irish Ancestor*, XVI, No. 1 (1984), 31.

22 L. Doyle, *An Ulster Childhood* (1921, reprinted Belfast, 1985), 116–17. The author recalls, like so many others, his childhood horror of this annual event and the lopsided football that he used to be given, made from the pig's bladder. See F. Crowley, *In West Cork Long Ago* (Dublin and Cork, 1980), 100–3; Crowley explains in full detail the entire pig-killing process, as well as how it was salted, pickled and hung.

23 People often recall this major annual event vividly. Processes varied from place to place, and the pork was often the main form of meat eaten on the farm. On at least one Kilkenny farm the pig was hung up out of doors from the apex of a pair of ladders. It was then carried into the kitchen and laid on the falling table to be cut up. My questions about the deeply scored and rutted table top gave rise to this story. Oral account, May 1991, Miss N. Leahy and Mr N. Leahy.

Meal Chests

24 L.M. Cullen, *The Hidden Ireland, Reassessment of a Concept*, (Lilliput Press, 1988), 30, 45. (Originally appeared in *Studio Hibernica*, 1969.) Poem extract from *Caismirt an photaire leis an uisge-beatha* by the blind poet Raftery of Connacht. Thankyou Professor Cullen for drawing my attention to this piece of poetry.

25 Kennedy, *The Banks of the Boro*, 110, ch. XIX; 'The Harvest Home'. For another description, with an illustration, see *The Illustrated London News* (15 September 1849), 188. Some 19th-century descriptions of such gatherings and dances are quoted in K. Danaher, *The Year in Ireland* (Dublin, 1972), 193–6.

26 'Yalla meal' is a reference to the Indian corn or maize that Sir Robert Peel introduced into Ireland from the U.S.A. It was intended to help to feed the starving during the appalling famines of the 1840s, and to keep down the soaring prices of other foodstuffs. Relief commissions were set up to provide employment (although many were too weak to finish a day's work), because it was decided to sell rather than to give the food to the starving populace. See T.W. Moody, F.

Martin, *The Course of Irish History* (Cork, 1967), 263–74.

27 Danaher, *In Ireland Long Ago*, 30. Also E.E. Evans, in *Irish Heritage The landscape, the people and their work* (Dundalk, 1945), 70, records such 'tramping' of meal by barefooted children, adding that it was an ancient custom, 'now almost gone'. According to I.F. Grant, *Highland Folk Ways* (London, 1961, 1975), 173, There were similar items of furniture and customs In Scotland; 'Even the most primitive would have one for meal . . . To ensure the keeping of the meal in such a kist it had to be packed very tightly and was generally tramped with the bare feet.' I have examined one of these chests at the Folk museum at Auchindrain (west coast of Scotland) which was identical to many of the Irish ones.

28 R. ffolliott, and B. De Breffny, 'The contents of Burton Hall, co. Cork in 1686', *The Irish Ancestor*, V, No. 2 (1973), 111.

29 John Dunton's Letters (originally from the Rawlinson Mss. in the Bodleian Library: Rawl. D. 71) published as Appendix B, in E. MacLysaght, *Irish life in the Seventeenth century: After Cromwell* (Dublin and Cork, 1939), 371, 382. 'Two hooches' are listed during the 16th century in the household of an English noble, settled in Ireland; W. Pinkerton, 'Inventory of the Household Effects of Lord deputy Lord Leonard Grey, in 1540' in *The Ulster Journal of Archeology*, 1st ser. 7 (1859), 211. Also D.I.F. Ms. Vol. 448. 69–70. No meal chests with such arched lids emerged during this survey, but in Wales (quite close to county Kildare) that design is common.

30 R. ffolliott, 'Captain Balfour's Auction 15th March, 1741–2', 31. or a 'Flour bin' in R. ffolliott, 'An Inventory of Reynella, co. Westmeath in 1827', *The Irish Ancestor*, XII, Nos. 1 and 2 (1980), 111.

31 H.C. Parliamentary Papers: 1st Report of Commissioners (II) 1836 Supplement to Appendix E. XXXII. 95.

32 W. Carleton, 'The Courtship of Phelim O'Toole', in *Six Irish Tales* (Dublin, 1833), 26.

33 E. Cross, *The Tailor and Ansty* (Cork and Dublin, 1942, reprinted 1987), 20–2.

34 W.B. Yeats (editor and selector), *Fairy and Folk Tales of the Irish Peasantry* (London, 1888), 59–60, 321. Extract from 'The Stolen Child' by W.B. Yeats, 'The places mentioned are in the vicinity of Sligo.'

35 H. Piers, *A Chorographical description of the county of West-meath, A.D. 1682*, quoted in Vallencey, *Collectanea de Rebus Hibernicis* (Dublin, 1770).

36 Danaher, *The Year in Ireland*, 87; 'to have hay still left in the haggard at Mayday was a sign of good husbandry . . . The housewife . . . should, if she had managed thriftily . . . still have meal for bread baking and for porridge.'

37 Maure Roche, of Screen, Enniscorthy. Extract from a letter to the author describing traditional local furniture, 1989.

38 W. Carleton, *Traits and Stories of the Irish Peasantry*, II (Dublin, 1830), 231.

39 T. Ó Criomhthain, *The Islandman* (Dublin, 1937, reprinted Oxford, 1987), 27.

40 Carleton, *Six Irish Tales*, 26.

The Stillion

41 R. ffolliott and B. de Breffny, 'The Contents of Burton Hall, Co. Cork, in 1686', 111. N.L.I. Ms. 2553 (Ormonde Inventories, 1673–1745), 2–3, c.1673.

42 R. ffolliott, 'Household Stuff', in *The Irish Ancestor*, I, No. 1 (1969), 47–9; Inventory of Dr McKeogh of

Nenagh, Tipperary, 1751; '5 Beer Barrels, 2 small stillions, 2 milk peeks'. Also Richard Ryan of Nenagh, 1756; '1 sullion'.
British Museum Add. Mss: 31,882 (Court Book from the Diocese of Killaloe), 209; 'Invenory . . . of Francis Carroll late of Arraghbeg in the county of Tipperary . . . 27th Feb 1752 . . . a Stillion £0.0.6 [from a total of £45.10.7].' and Ibid, Mss 31,882, 159; 'Inventory . . . of Wm. Newstead of Derrynaslin in the county of Tipperary . . . deceas'd 22 April 1749 . . . 1 old sillion £0.2.0.' Also see An Inventory of Killiane Castle (county Wexford), 2 August 1760. N.L.I. Ms. 29, 709. (9) Harvey Papers; In the Brew House were '6 stillions' in the Out-cellar 'Two Stillions' and in the In-cellar '6 stillions'. Where stillions are mentioned in inventories they are usually listed amongst barrels and containers for liquid.

43 Other derivations of the word include stellion, stelling, steillean, sullion and steilan.

44 For Instance K. Danaher, *The Hearth and Stool and all!* (Cork and Dublin, 1985) 42. Also D. McCourt, 'The Outshot House-type' in *Ulster Folklife*, II (Belfast, 1956), 29.

45 Hanbidge, *The Memories of William Hanbidge*, 20.

46 A. M'Kenzie, *Poems and Songs on Different Subjects* (Belfast, 1810), 117–21; Philip McClabber, 'Cabin-comfortless, near Ballywalter, 18 December 1807'; quoted in Gailey, 'The Housing of the Rural poor' 50.

The Ware Press

47 T.C. Irwin, *Versicles* (Dublin, 1883), 45.

48 A. Taylor, *To School through the fields, an Irish Country Childhood* (Dingle, 1988), 9.

49 W.M. Thackeray, *The Irish Sketchbook* (London, 1843), 87.

Food Presses

50 House of Commons Parliamentary Papers: 1st Report of Commissioners (II). 1836 Supplement to Appendix (E). XXXII, 241.

51 Ibid., 246.

52 Ibid., 38–48.

Places for Clothes

53 P.R.O.N.I. Mss. T1062/17; Inventory of . . . Wm. Richardson of Agrelougher, Parish of Loughgall and county of Armagh, 3 May 1716. Courtesy of the Religious Society of Friends.

54 H.W. French, *Our Boys In Ireland* (New York, 1891), 134–5.

55 Murphy, *At Slieve Gullion's Foot*, 25–6.

56 The painting by H. O'Neill of a Lauga Law kitchen interior, in the Folklife dept. of The National Museum of Ireland: CF719.

57 E.E. Evans, *Irish Heritage, The Landscape, the People and their Work* (Dundalk, 1945), 70.

58 I am grateful to Brendan Kellegher (a 'Clare man'), of the Edmund Rice Centre, county Kilkenny, (where one can see such a row of pegs) for this information.

59 Danaher, *In Ireland Long Ago*, 31.

60 E.O. Somerville and V.M. Ross, *Through Connemara in a Governess Cart* (1st published 1893, London, 1990), 99.

The Clothes Chest

61 A.K. Longfield, 'Up For Sale', *The Irish Ancestor*, XVII, No. 1 (1985), 34.

62 Ibid., 32–4.

63 J.C, Walton, 'The Household Effects of a Waterford Merchant Family in 1640' *Journal of the Cork Historical and Archaeological Society*, LXXXIII, No. 238 (July-December, 1978), 99–105; This inventory mentions numerous 'greate Cheasts and Trunckes'.

64 H.C. Parliamentary Papers: 1st Report of the Commissioners (II) (1836). Supplement to Appendix E, XXXII, County Antrim, 276. Further such reference occur for county Antrim; 259, Armagh; 283, Donegal; 306, Fermanagh; 354, Tyrone; 281, Limerick; 225, Cavan; 296, Westmeath; 'a large box for locking up things' 126. Clare; 'a box to hold their clothes', 160.

65 H.C. Parliamentary Papers: Reports of the Commissioners, 9 (1836), XXX. Appendix C, parts I and II, 163.

66 W. Carleton, *Tales of Ireland* (Dublin and London, 1834), 149.

67 Mr and Mrs S.C. Hall, *Ireland: Its Scenery Character, etc.* III vols (London, 1841), III, 300.

68 D. Thomson and M. McGusty, eds., *The Irish Journals of Elizabeth Smith, 1840–1940* (Oxford, 1980), 8 April 1847.

69 D.I.F. Ms. Vol. 750 (1937), 426.

70 H.C. Parliamentary Papers: Reports of the Comissioners (II) 1836. XXXII, 69 and 91.

71 Revd J. Hall *Tour Through Ireland, particularly the interior and lesser known parts etc.* 2 Vols. (London, 1813), I, 187.

72 Anon, 'Thady O'Brady' N.L.I. unreferenced Ms.

73 Ó Criomhthain, *The Islandman*, 26.

74 Danaher, *Hearth and Stool and All!* 42.

75 Somerville and Ross, *Through Connemara*, 99.

76 D.I.F. Ms. Vol. 485, 218.

Dowry Chests

77 Museum collections contain examples from counties Kilkenny, Limerick, Kerry and Roscommon.

78 D.I.F. Ms. Vol. 1663 (1957), Castle Plunkett, Castlerea, county Roscommon. 39.

79 M. Carbery, *The Farm by Lough Gur* (First published Dublin and Cork 1937, reprinted 1986), 22.

80 *Bealoideas*, IX, 293. Quoted in O'Neill, *Life and Tradition*, 24–5. He also mentions that furniture was traditionally given at weddings, except for the bed and the table.

81 D.I.F. Ms. Vol. 1663, Castle Plunkett, Castlerea, county Roscommon, 39.

82 Ibid.

83 Ibid.

84 Cullen, *The Hidden Ireland*, 30–2.

85 Kennedy, *The Banks of the Boro*, 157.

86 Ibid., 158.

87 Ibid.

88 These prices are quoted in M. McGrath editor and translator of 'The Diary of Humphrey O'Sullivan' in *The Irish Texts Society*, XXX (1928–31), 16. April 1832, 135 and 19 August 1829, 191. Humphrey O'Sullivan was a schoolteacher and schoolkeeper whose meticulous diary is mainly concerned with the area of county Kilkenny, he frequently mentions prices of pigs as he is often buying and selling them at markets. These prices for food given at around the time that Patrick Kennedy was describing, provide a rough idea of the veritable fortunes which were often given as dowry.

89 Mr and Mrs Hall, *Hall's Ireland, Mr and Mrs Hall's*

Tour of 1840, II (London, 1984), II, 422. Examination of surviving dowry chests shows that their design has altered little since the eighteenth century. The existence of closely similar examples, dating from the first quarter of the nineteenth century, made by Irish settlers in Upper Canada, supports the theory that their design stemmed from an already well established eighteenth century Irish tradition. For examples see H. Pain, *The Heritage of Upper Canadian Furniture, A study in the Survival of Formal and Vernacular Styles from Britain, America and Europe, 1780–1900* (Toronto, 1984), fig. *606*, 235. Pain calls his example a chest on chest, saying that it is similar to an example illustrated in Jean Palardy's, *The Early Furniture of French Canada*, Plate 22.

Chapter 5 BEDS

Thorough Beds and Shake-downs

1 Philip McClabber, 'Cabin-comfortless, near Bally-walter, December 18, 1807', quoted from 'The Meenagarragh Cottier's House', An Ulster Folk and Transport Museum Information Leaflet (Belfast, *c*.1985), 2.
2 Don Francisco de Cuellar (1588–9), quoted in C. Maxwell, *The Stranger In Ireland* (London, 1954), 49.
3 For examples see H.C. Parliamentary Papers: Report of the Commissioners (II) 1836. Supplement to Appendix E. XXXII; County Mayo, Baronies Clanmorris to Costello, 21.
    County Wicklow, Kiltegan, Rathvilly, 48. 'A straw bed on the ground'.
    Counties Longford and Leitrim, Cashel, 92, 94.
    County Meath, Baronies of Navan, lower and upper, 111, 113.
    County Clare, 158. 'very often without bedsteads'.
    County Cork, Barony of Carbery (west), 179, 181, 186. 'no pillow but a piece of fir, seats and cupboards are the only furniture'.
    County Limerick, 225.
    County Tipperary, 245.
    County Waterford, 252, Barony Decies, 254–5, 257.
    County Antrim, Barony Toom Upper, 279. 'bedsteads little used'.
    County Armagh, 280. 'a standing bed is a rare article . . . straw on the ground'.
    County Cavan, Barony Castleraghan, 294. 'the family sleep on some dried rushes or straw thrown on the floor in the chimney corner, as the warmest place in the house . . . their clothes thrown over them to assist the scanty bed clothes'.
    County Donegal, 318. 'the best of these cabins may have a small kitchen, with a room capable of holding two beds, about five feet high in the side walls . . . There may be, in some instances, a fixture to raise the bed off the ground, but most commonly they are straw beds, laid on the floor.'
    County Derry, Monaghan, 370. 'six persons may perhaps sleep in one bed, with little covering, three at each end, the feet meeting in the centre.'
4 P. Dineen, *Irish-English Dictionary* (Dublin, 1927), 1109. Also T. de Bhaldraithe, *English-Irish Dictionary* (Dublin, 1959), 651; Shake-down = Irish *Sraideog*.
5 Quoted in J.C. Walker, *An Historical Essay on the Dress of the Ancient & Modern Irish* (London, 1788), 47.
6 J. Stevens, *Journal* (1689–91), quoted in F. Murphy, *The Bog Irish* (Australia, 1987), 51. The word 'flock' in this context is more likely to have meant pieces of cloth, old rags etc. rather than simply wool, which would have been of value for spinning (but it is another, valid definition). N. Webster, *Webster's New Twentieth Century Dictionary* (New York, 1983), 703.
7 'John Dunton's Letters', Appendix B of E. MacLysaght, *Irish Life In The Seventeenth century: After Cromwell* (Dublin, 1939), 336–40.
8 A. Young, *Autobiography*, IV (1898), 72. Quoted in J. A. Simpson and E. S. C. Weiner, *The Oxford English Dictionary*, XV (Oxford, 2nd edn 1989), 146. See also A. Young, *A Tour in Ireland, made in the years 1776, 1777 and 1778* (Cambridge, 1925), 188: 'beds are not found universally, the family lying on straw, equally partook of by cows, calves and pigs, though the luxury of styes is coming to Ireland, which excludes the poor pigs from the warmth of the bodies of their master and mistress.'
9 Walker, *Historical Essay*, 145–6.
10 C. Otway, *Sketches in Erris & Tyrawly* (Dublin, 1841), 32, 13.
11 J. Connery, *The Reformer* (Dublin? 1st edn 1832, 1837), 44.
12 A.P. Morton, translator of Baron E. de Mandat-Grancey, *Paddy at Home, 'Chez Paddy'* (London, 1887), 102. The author is grateful to F. Carragher for drawing her attention to this text.
13 D. Thomson and M. McGusty eds. *The Irish Journals of Elizabeth Smith, 1840–1850* (Oxford, 1980), 35, 52. Smith also describes the sleeping conditions of one of her tenants: 'A wad of straw in a corner, a little pile of chaff near it on which lay folded a ragged and single blanket – all, father mother and three babies slept *there*.
    T. O'Neill Lane, *Larger English-Irish Dictionary* (Dublin, Belfast, 1916), 1392: 'Shakedown; a temporary bed on a floor or on chairs'.
14 H.C. Parliamentary Papers: Report of the Commissioners (II) (1836) Supplement to Appendix E. XXXII. 294.
15 A. Day and P. Williams eds., O.S. Memoir of Ireland (I.I.S./R.I.A., Belfast, 1991), XI, county Londonderry; Parish of Magilligan [1835], 108.
    M. McGrath ed., 'The Diary of Humphrey O'Sullivan, 1827–1832,' in *Irish Texts Society*, XXX (London, 1936), 28 June 1832, 163; O'Sullivan, A schoolteacher, describes the 'Stingingly Painful Livid Disease' [cholera], writing that 'There are many 'John's Wisps' aflame tonight throughout the country'. and that 'Straw for bedding is being distributed "gratis"'. in the Callan area of west co. Kilkenny.
    Mrs S. C. Hall, *Ireland: Its Scenery, Character, etc.*, III (London, 1841), 291. She describes how a 'truckle bed' is reserved for the 'old people' while the other members of the family 'rest upon straw or heather, laid on the floor, covered with a blanket' or clothes.
16 Lord George Hill, *Facts From Gweedore* (5th edn 1887, reprinted Belfast, I.I.S. 1971), 16–17. Mountain *bent* meant coarse stalks or reedy grasses, gathered like hay, from the mountain side, as opposed to bent gathered from sand dunes.
17 According to Webster, *Webster's*, 1907. A bed-tick is a closely-woven, strong often striped linen, cotton [or ticking] case, filled with cotton, feathers, hair, [wool, chaff] etc. In Ireland these were often made up by recycling the bags from animal fodder or Indian meal, which could then be filled with threshed straw (known as chaff), or goose feathers.
18 Hill, *Facts From Gweedore*, XXVI.
19 H.C. Parliamentary Papers: Report of the Commissioners (II) (1836) Supplement to Appendix E. XXXII. 60.

20 Recorded by the author from the memories of Mrs S. Connor, from west county Kerry.
   The term shake-down was still used to describe 'some straw thrown on the kitchen floor, plus bed-clothes' as recently as 1964, by a county Donegal writer in a response to a museum questionnaire: U.F.M. Quest. (1964), Q1b/78. In some regions, the practice survived up until this century particularly in the single-room byre dwellings, which have been described in detail by A. Gailey, *Rural Houses of the North of Ireland* (Edinburgh, 1984), 142–8.

21 I.F. Grant, *Highland Folk Ways* (London, 1989), 168.

22 Burt, *Burt's Letters from the North of Scotland*, 2 vols. (1754, reprinted Edinburgh, 1974), I, 116–17.

23 Letter from Capt. W. Barton to J. Dawson, Justices of the peace (Thomastown, 30 October 1712) quoted in Murphy, *The Bog Irish*, 144.

24 P. Kennedy, *Banks of The Boro* (London, 1867), 291.

25 The following entries are a representative sample, and not intended to be considered as comprehensive;
   W. Pinkerton, 'Inventory of the Household Effects of Lord Deputy Lord Leonard grey, in 1540' in *The Ulster Journal of Archaeology*, 1st ser., VII (1859), 206; 'Two trussing beds' which Pinkerton explains could be readily trussed up and transported on a horse.
   J. Walton, 'The Household Effects of a Waterford Merchant Family in 1640' in *The Cork Historical and Archaeological Society Journal*, LXXXIII, No. 238 (Cork, 1978), 103: 'One standinge Beddsteede a Truckle bedd'. British Museum Additional Manuscript 31,882, 158; The inventory of William Newstead of Derrynaslin, county Tipperary (deceased 22 April 1749); '1 old truckle' mentioned amongst furniture listed. H.C. Parliamentary Papers, Report of the Commissioners (II) (1836), Supplement to Appendix E. XXXII. 101, county Meath: 'a truckle bedstead'.
   Mrs S.C. Hall, *Hall's Ireland, Mr & Mrs Hall's Tour of 1840*, II (London, 1984), 421; 'There is generally a truckle bed in a corner for the owner'.
   H.W. French, *Our Boys In Ireland* (New York, 1891), 40; 'fighting on a truckle bed'.

26 R.B. McDowell (ed.) *Social Life in Ireland 1800–1845* (Dublin, 1957), 49. The section by T.P. O'Neill (Rural Life) quotes Gustave de Beaumont, a visitor to Ireland in the 1830s. A. Gailey, 'The Housing of the Rural Poor in Nineteenth Century Ulster' in *Ulster Folklife*, XXII (Belfast, 1976), 49. This description sounds similar to the way an outshot bed was built-in, see p. 153. Further similar descriptions appear amongst the H.C. Parliamentary Papers (1836).

The Outshot Bed

27 N.F. Brannon, 'Three Bed-outshot Houses in Castletown Townland, County Tyrone' in *Ulster Folklife*, XXIX (Belfast, 1983) 29–32.

28 Gailey, *Rural Houses of the North of Ireland*, 156. Also of valuable reference here, the following pioneering works: C. Ó Danachair, 'The Bed Out-shot in Ireland' in *Folk-Liv*, XIX-XX (Stockholm, 1955–6), 26–31; D. McCourt, 'The Outshot House Type' in *Ulster Folklife*, II (Belfast, 1956), 25–34.

29 Gailey, *Rural Houses in the North of Ireland*, 151. Ó Danachair, 'The Bed Out-shot', 29.

30 A. T. Lucas, 'Contributions to the History of the Irish House: A Possible Ancestry of the Bed-Outshot (Cuilteach)' in *Folk Life*, VIII (Cardiff, 1970), 81–98.

31 B. Walker, 'A Re-Appraisal of the Byre-Dwellings at Machaire Gathlan, Bunbeg, Co. Donegal' in *Ulster Folklife*, XXXVI (Belfast, 1990), 74–9. Ó Danachair, 'The Bed Out-shot', 28–31.

32 A. Gailey, 'Kitchen Furniture' in *Ulster Folklife*, XII (Belfast, 1966), 26. Also E. E. Evans, *Irish Heritage* (Dundalk, 1945), 60. H.M.S.O., *Inventory of Ancient Monuments in Glamorgan*, IV, Part 2, Farmhouses & Cottages (London, 1988), 153; Bed outshuts [sic] are said to be characteristic of the Gower area: beds here have been inside a double-door cupboard, beside a hall hearth. Some examples dating from as early as the 16th century, Built-in fireside benches are also a local feature, like those found in county Wexford. Brittany, Belgium, Holland, north-west Germany, Denmark, Norway, parts of southern and western Sweden, Scotland, northern England are other areas with outshot alcoves (known in Ireland as 'outshot' and in some other places as 'outshut').

Bedrooms

33 E.O. Somerville and V. M. Ross, *Through Connemara in a Governess Cart* (1893, reprinted 1990), 99.
   Gailey, *Rural Houses of the North of Ireland* 217. See also Gailey, 'Kitchen Furniture', 26, for mention of children sleeping on the 'thallage', a type of half-loft close to the chimney hood in particular houses, with jamb-walls. See also A. Gailey, 'The Ballyhagen Inventories, 1716–1740' in *Ulster Folklife*, XV, (Belfast, 1977), 47, for evidence from the early 18th century of parlours being used as bedrooms. During fieldstudies in county Cavan in 1989 I was shown into a traditional parlour in which was kept a large press bed for the use of visitors. Parlours still often double as spare bed rooms in many areas.

34 Kennedy, *The Banks of the Boro*, 170.

35 Ibid., 342.

Bed Cords and Bedding

36 R. ffolliott, 'Household Stuff' in *The Irish Ancestor*, I, No. 1 (1969), 45, 49. Provides a copy of the 'Goods and Chattels that Richard Ryan of Anamalle died possessed of – taken at Nenagh, 27 December 1756's. ffolliott also provides transcripts of several other inventories of people of different means, both rich and poor.

37 R. ffolliott and B. de Breffny, 'The Contents of Burton Hall, county Cork in 1686' in *The Irish Ancestor*, V, No. 2 (1973), 106–13; This substantial inventory mentions bedsteads, cordes and matts (mattresses), with curtains and hangings, about eighteen times; the very best beds were equipped with 'Rodds, cupps and spriggs' which presumably were a more luxurious form of support for the mattress.

38 R. ffolliott, 'An Inventory of Killeen Castle in 1735–6 [county Meath]' in *The Irish Ancestor*, IX, No. 2 (1977), 103.

39 U.F.M. Quest (1964) Q1b/13; Castledawson, county Antrim.

40 D.I.F. Ms. Vol. 1664 (1958), 56. County Limerick, 'Camp beds of bog deal'.

41 A. T. Lucas, 'Bog Wood, a study of Rural Economy' in *Bealoideas*, The Journal of the Folklore Society of Ireland, XXIII (Dublin, 1954), 103–5. Lucas describes how the hardened bog timber was beaten out into small filaments which were then twisted in the manner of *súgán* into ropes. This is documented as early as 1709 and was in general use by the mid 19th century. Areas of use are confined to areas of long standing bog timber extraction, particularly in the west and the north of Ireland. T. MacEvoy, *Statistical Survey of the County of Tyrone* (Dublin, 1801), 188;

'Bog-fir . . . when beaten out into small filaments, is found to answer for ropes, which are principally used for the cording of beds, and in damp places, will last considerably longer than hempen ropes. Twenty yards is the usual length for a bed-cord, which is commonly bought for 10d. The roots and fragments of the bog-fir are used for this purpose, and it is a kind of trade with many poor people in the vicinity of bogs.'

42 O. S. Memoirs, Box 5, II 13 (March-May 1837), 1–117.
Brit. Mus. Add. Mss. 31,882 (Court Book from the Diocese of Killaloe), includes 'Debts and creddits of Dan Darrane late of Nenagh, co. Tipperary. Merchant (27 January 1743)', 142, 146; '1 bed cord at 00.00.6d.'.

43 O.S. Memoirs, Box 34. Londonderry. XI. (20 November 1834) Dungiven Ph.II.

44 O.S. Memoirs, Box 5, II 13 (March-May 1837), 1–117.

45 U.F.M. Quest. (1962) Q1/159, J.J.P. Ballymena, county Antrim. D.I.F. Ms. Vol. 654 (Poulaphouca Resevoir Survey, 1939), 145; 'her grandmother made feather-beds from the *ceannabahn* (white bog-cotton).' Also some people could not afford 'ticks' but slept on straw mats 'about 1″ thick or 2″ thick' which they plaited themselves: D.I.F. Ms. Vol. 976 (Newton, Rostrevor, county Down), 66.

46 U.F.M. Quest. (1964) Q1b/186; East Donegal. Q1b/8; county Armagh. Q1b/130 county Antrim. U.F.M. Quest. (1962) Q1/159, J.J.P. Ballymena, county Antrim.

47 McGrath ed., c The Diary of Humphrey O'Sullivan, 193. 'Murphy the feather merchant' mentioned in 1833 in county Kilkenny.

48 An Inventory of Killiane Castle. 2 August 1760. N.L.I. Ms. 29, 709 (9) Harvey Papers.

49 A. Day and P. Williams eds., O.S. Memoir of Ireland (I.I.S./R.I.A., Belfast, 1991), X, Parishes of co. Antrim, Islandmagee (1840), 92; 'Feather beds are not as plenty as in other parishes, as there are very few geese kept in the island and those few are sold [in Carrick-fergus] . . . Chiefly chaff beds are used.' See also U.F.M. Quest. (1964) Q1b/130; county Antrim.

50 H.C. Parliamentary Papers: Report of the Commissioners (II) 1836. Supplement to Appendix E. XXXII, County Clare, Barony of Tulla, parish Kilseiley, Killuran and Kilnoe: The houses of the poor 'are generally furnished with 2 bedsteads, and always one feather bed, which invariably forms part of the marriage portion'. Also U.F.M. Quest. (1964) Q1b/160, county Antrim. P.R.O.N.I. 1062/14; An Inventory of the goods and chattels of William Morton, Crenagh, co. Armagh (9 May 1708). Beds and bedsteads were 'divided amongst the children and daughters', which is significant, because almost everything else was sold.

51 U.F.M. Quest. (1962) Q1/83, W.J. county Armagh.

52 H.C. Parliamentary Papers: Report of the Commissioners (II) 1836. Supplement to Appendix E. XXXII, county Clare, 161; 'bedsteads and always 1 feather bed which invariably forms part of the marriage portion.' Also information pertaining to the 1930s recorded from conversations between the author and Mrs S. Connor, who was raised on a small farm between Camp and Castlegregory, west county Kerry.

Plaited Straw Mattresses

53 There are straw mattresses in the collections of The Ulster Folk and Transport Museum, the Folk Museum in Carndonagh, county Donegal and The National Museum of Ireland, who have amassed many related objects made from plaited straw such as mats

and seats. The Irish Agricultural Museum have an example of a straw hen's nest.

54 For more about the range of uses for plaited straw read K.M. Harris, 'Plaited Straw-work' in *Ulster Folklife*, IX (Belfast, 1963), 54, 53–60.

55 D.I.F. Ms. Vol. 259, 652. quoted in T. O'Neill, *Life and Tradition in Rural Ireland* (London, 1977), 23, 107.

Low Bedsteads

56 For an illustration of such a simple bedstead, see T. O'Neill, *Life and Tradition*, fig. 36; 'Fireplace, co. Galway', Bord Failte, TY18/48.

57 D.I.F. Ms. Vol. 1664, county Clare, 4.

58 A. Taylor, *Quench The Lamp* (Dingle, 1990), 69–70.

Enclosed Beds

59 Only a small sample of inventories are cited in this section, as few refer specifically to vernacular furniture. Many of the terms used in the 16th to 18th centuries to describe the beds of the aristocracy were still being used in rural areas well into the 20th century. The regional use of more recent terminolgy can be examined by reading the two main sets of questionnaires enquiring about furniture (see pp. 208–9).

Tester Beds

60 The word 'tester' is defined by G.B. Adams in his 'Glossary of Household Terms' in *Ulster Folklife*, XII (Belfast, 1966), 32: 'Not a specifically dialect word but . . . the word and the object have gone out of general use. A canopy over a bed supported on bed-posts or from the ceiling; formerly also a bed's head-board and its fittings. The form *tester-bed* is recorded from 1622 (*Shorter Oxford English Dictionary*, 1964). An earlier meaning was: a piece of armour for the head (1484) (SOED). From Old French *testiere, a derivative of teste* (modern *tete*), head.'

61 For example (from county Wexford) see P. Kennedy, *Evenings in the Duffrey* (Dublin, 1869), 327; 'she made a shake down for herself' instead of 'sleeping in her own good high-standing bed'.

62 W. Pinkerton, 'Inventory of the Household Effects of Lord Deputy Lord Leonard Grey, in 1540' in *The Ulster Journal of Archaeology*, (1st ser. 7., 1859), 201–12, 204; 'Two standing bedis'. 207; 'A tester and curtyans of black saye'.

63 P.R.O.N.I. T 1062/15: An Inventory of Goods and chattels of David Kell, deceased of Coragh, Loughgall, county Armagh (28 February 1712). Several 'Standinge beedsteedes' are listed amongst J.C. Walton 'The household Effects of a Waterford Merchant Family in 1640' in *The Journal of the Cork Historical and Archaeoligal Society*, LXXXIII, No.̇ 238 (Cork, July-December, 1978), 99–105.

64 British Museum Add. Ms. 31,882: Court Book from the Diocese of Killaloe: Inventories of A. Buchanan (May 1745), 89; Mrs Matthew Dwyer of Birr, county Offaly (5 January 1753), 207.

65 D.I.F. Ms. Vol. 1663, 72. D.I.F. Ms. Vol. 1664, 84. D.I.F. Ms. Vol. 1663, county Mayo; Ballina, 18, Tyrawly 21, Newport 24. County Galway; 2, 15. The term tester/taster was also used in west county Cork, applied to a domed roofed bed; D.I.F. Ms. Vol. 1664; 26, also 18, 20.
Also see U.F.M. Quest (1964) Q1b, for numerous

descriptions of tester beds; having four posts rising to support a flat wooden tester, hung with curtains and with a valance surrounding the top. These are specific descriptions, which need sorting out from the simple 'yes' answers, as this questionnaire asks about 'box beds, tester beds etc.'

66 Anon, 'Thady O'Brady, Favourite Irish Comic Song' (c.1900), from an unreferenced book in the National Library of Ireland. The author is grateful to Dr Kevin Whelan for drawing her attention to this text.

67 W. Carleton, 'The Courtship of Phelim O'Toole' in *Six Irish Tales* (Dublin, 1833), 26.

68 H.C. Parliamentary Papers: Report of the Commissioners (II) 1836. Supplement to Appendix E, XXXII. County Meath, Barony of Skreen, Dunsany, Tara and Killeen. 113.

69 T. Ó Criomhthain, *The Islandman* (1st edn., 1937. Oxford, 1987), 26–7.

Canopy or Camp Beds

70 D.I.F. Ms. Vol. 1663, 49.

71 D.I.F. Ms. Vol. 1663, 63. Other respondents who mentioned that such beds used to be found particularly in thatched houses; D.I.F. Ms. Vol. 1664, county Limerick, 57. Gweedore, county Donegal, 102. County Monaghan, 121.

72 ffolliott and de Breffny, 'The Contents of Burton Hall, Co. Cork in 1686', 107.

73 ffolliott, 'An Inventory of Killeen Castle in 1735–6', 104.

74 C.C. Ellison, 'Setting up House – 1825 Style' [county Roscommon] in *The Irish Ancestor*, VIII, No. 2 (Dublin, 1976), 75. Also R. ffolliott 'An Inventory of Reynella, Co. Westmeath in 1827' in *The Irish Ancestor*, XII, Nos. 1 and 2 (Dublin, 1980), 10.

75 D.I.F. Ms. Vol. 1663; county Laois (canopy) 58, counties Kilkenny and Carlow (roof/ed bed and crib) 41, 51, 55. County Wexford (canopy bed with rounded top) 90.

76 D.I.F. Ms. Vol. 1664; county Clare (Camp) 11, 12. County Limerick (Camp) 52, 55, 56. County Kerry (Camp) 38, 45, (canopied) 43. West county Cork (camp) 27 (taster and domed roof taster) 18, 20, 26. County Tipperary (canopied) 64 (covered car) 68. Also, as exceptions regionally D.I.F. Ms. Vol. 1663, county Leitrim ('Canopy and curtained bed') 37. H.C. Parliamentary Papers, Report of the commissions (II) 1836. Supplement to Appendix E. XXXII. Brigoon, Carbery West division, 183, 184, 'a camp bedstead, boarded at one side and on the top, in which all the family generally sleep'. And in county Limerick, Barony Smallcounty, 231, 'a kind of wooden bedstead, with a roof, is used to shelter from the rain'.

77 D.I.F. Ms. Vol. 1664, 10.

78 D.I.F. Ms. Vol. 1663, 1, 22, 31. See I.G. Sparkes, *Four Poster and Tester Beds* (Shire Album 253, 1990), 30.

'Covered Car Beds'

79 P. Parley, *Tales about Ireland and the Irish* (London, 1845), 104. The wording of the D.I.F. Questionnaire, like that of the U.F.M., provides too much information on terminology, enquiring specifically about 'covered -car beds'. Only two replies repeat the term and therefore confirm its use; D.I.F. Ms. Vol. 1664, Bantry, county Cork, 22 ['the names were teastair and covered car'], and county Tipperary, 68. Only one respondent, from county Donegal specified that they were not called 'covered car beds', but 'tasters' (horse-drawn covered cars did not travel through county Donegal). The use of such specific terms, in both sets of otherwise useful questionnaires, is their main shortcoming.

80 An account confirming this link can be read in D.I.F. Ms. Vol. 107, 44.

81 French, *Our Boys in Ireland* 176.

82 M. Scott ed., *Hall's Ireland, Mrs and Mrs Hall's Tour of 1840*, I (London, 1984), 29.

83 S. F. Petit, *This City of Cork, 1700–1900* (Cork, 1977), 118–19. The author is grateful to Dr Austin O'Sullivan for locating this text.

Box Beds

84 The term 'box bed' was specifically stated by the following; U.F.M. Quest. (1964) Q1b/: County Fermanagh (out of 11 respondents); 66, 112, 170, 182. See P. Thornton, *Authentic Decor, The Domestic Interior, 1620–1920* (London, 1984), fig. 51, 46–7. This shows 'A more modest Dutch bedchamber' with a built in 'box type' bed with its opening near a fireplace.
County Derry (14 respondents); 3. County Donegal (17 respondents); 154. County Down; 27; 'Beds in the walls with shutters in the daytime'. 42 'Built in beds with doors that closed flush with the wall, concealing the bed in the daytime'.
County Monaghan (6 respondents); no responses mentioned box beds.
County Tyrone (18 responses); 16, 14, 187.
County Cavan (1 resondent, did not mention box beds).
County Armagh (7 respondents); 8, 54, 172.
County Antrim (30 respondents); 28, 36, 58, 73, 80, 95, 131, 142, 147, 160. Also used by county Antrim respondent from D.I.F. Ms. Vol. 1664, 69. Significantly, the term box bed was used specifically most often in county Antrim, closest in proximity to Scotland, where they were widely used and referred to in that way. Only one respondent amongst (over 100 in total) to the D.I.F. questionnaires provided that term (although some of the responses in Irish were not included in this survey). No references to 'box beds' has been discovered by the author in Irish inventories. See D. Jones, 'Box beds in Eastern Scotland' in *Regional Furniture*, V (Leeds, 1991), 79–85. also J. C. Loudon's *Encyclopaedia of Cottage, Farm and Villa Architecture* (London, 1846), 79. The Highland Folk Museum, in Kingussie in the Scottish Highlands, has a good example of a box bed, as does St Fagans, Welsh Folk Museum near Cardiff, Wales.

85 J. Morris, 'One and One Makes Four' in *The Ulster Folk and Transport Museum's Annual Reports Year-book* (Belfast, 1977/8), 12–14.

Alternative Forms of Enclosed Beds

86 Ibid., 13.

87 R. H. Buchanan, 'Box-Beds and Bannocks. The Living Past' in *Review of Scottish Culture* (November 1984), 66. See Dr J. Weyns, *Bokrijk, Tuin Van de Vlaamse Volskultuur* (Hasselt, 1961), 99–101. He explains that in some Kempischer farmhouses, beds made of planks were placed between the house and the cowshed and this enabled the farmer and his wife to listen for disturbances amongst their cattle. Beds with canopies were also used in Dutch farmhouses, but not as widely as beds in alcoves. Some beds had stripey curtains for privacy etc. The author is grateful to Shaunagh

Champion de Crespigny Grant for translating this text.

88 R. Shaw, *Carleton's Country* (Dublin, Cork, 1930), 36.

89 D.I.F. Ms. Vol. 1664 (*c*.1957), 4.

90 D.I.F. Ms. Vol. 1663 (1957), county Galway, 'Half canopy' 13. U.F.M. Quest (1964), Q1b/county Armagh, 172. County Monaghan, 'Half roofed', 168. The discovery of faked 'half testers' being made near Kinsale, county Cork, in 1990, suggested to the author the possibility of this design having once been locally known. For early versions of 'angel' and 'half tester' beds see P. Thornton, *The Italian Renaissance Interior 1400–1600* (London, 1991), fig. 178 [*c*.1602], 167, 359. Thornton, *Authentic Decor*, fig. 101, 82; fig. 357, 270, 226: Thornton quotes Cassell's *Household Guide* of the early 1860s, which illustrates a half-tester bed, as saying that 'Medical men considered it the more healthy plan to sleep on beds with as few draperies as possible'.

Wicker Beds

91 Revd. J. Hall, *Tour Through Ireland, particularly the Interior & lesser known parts etc.* 2 vols. (Dublin, 1813), I, 277.

Built-in Beds

92 U.F.M. Quest (1964) Q1b/68, Castle Dawson, county Antrim; 66, Garrison, county Fermanagh. Kennedy, *The Banks of the Boro*, Glossary: 'Natch – The side of a box bed farthest from the wall.' According to O Siochfradha, *Learner's Irish-English, English Irish Dictionary; Cnaiste* translates as 'Side-rail of bed.' A pair of enclosed beds made of bog fir and recently collected from a house in county Fermanagh by the Ulster American Folk Park, at Omagh, have their inner side-rails made of bog oak, rather than fir. The oak would have been more hard wearing and less likely to splinter than the fir, perhaps making a more suitable seat.

93 U.F.M. Quest (1964) Q1b/61.

94 Many people relined such enclosed beds habitually, it helped keep out dust as well as decorating the insides. This can be seen not only from surviving examples, but it is also described by questionnaire respondents: U.F.M. Quest (1964) /Q1b. 58, 95 and D.I.F. Ms. Vol. 1664, county Limerick, 57.

95 Gailey, *Rural Houses of the North of Ireland* 151, 153, figs. 159a-b. Also U.F.M. Quest (1964) Q1b/62.

96 D.I.F. Ms. Vol. 1664, Gweedore, county Donegal, 102.

97 Thomson and McGusty, *The Irish Journals of Elizabeth Smith*, 54; 26 August 1842.

98 U.F.M. Quest (1964) Q1b/county Donegal; 165, 185. County Antrim; 19, 43, 131.

99 D.I.F. Ms. Vol. 782 (1941), Parish Lack, county Kerry, 393. 'In a great many of the houses there wasn't any timber doors. The doors they had were made out of twigs and hung onto the doorframe by two gads also made of twigs... The bed room was divided from the kitchen by a wall made of pieces of branches of trees... briars or twigs woven between them... The beds that was used in the houses were called 'camp beds'. These beds had a covering over them. All the beds [were] made of timber. It is rushes, and long grass called shesk that was used on the bottom of them... a feather tick placed on top of that'. See also Gailey, *Rural Houses of the North of Ireland*, 133–4.

Bed Hangings

100 D.I.F. Ms. Vol. 1664 (1957), 120.

101 Thomson and McGusty, *The Irish Journals of Elizabeth Smith*, 72; 28 July 1845.

102 U.F.M. Quest (1964) /Q1b. 35.

103 K. Tynan, 'Irish Types and Traits' in *The Magazine of Art* (London, Paris, New York, 1888), 128.

104 J. M. Synge, 'In the Congested Districts. The Homes of the Harvestmen' in *The Manchester Guardian* (Saturday, 1 July 1905).

105 The greens in this watercolour have faded to a blue colour, as can be seen by the blue cabbages on the right in the foreground; so although the bed appears blue, it seems originally to have been painted in a fugitive green.

106 Tynan, 'Irish Types and Traits', 23 Coloured drapes are mentioned in U.F.M. Quest, (1964), Q1b/county Down; 134 (white), 169 (blue and white), 138 (red curtains). County Derry; 25, checked blue and white 'harn' coarse linen.

107 Cloth testers are mentioned specifically in U.F.M. Quest. (1964), Q1b/68, county Antrim. Also D.I.F. Ms. Vol. 1664 (1957), county Down, 113. Also Thomson and McGusty, *The Irish Journals of Elizabeth Smith*, (26 August 1842), 54.

108 D.I.F. Ms. Vol. 1664, county Cavan, 84. U.F.M. Quest. (1964), Q1b/81.

109 U.F.M. Quest. (1964), Q1b/70; Loughmourne, Castleblaney, county Monaghan. 68, county Antrim.

110 U.F.M. Quest. (1964), Q1b/43, 58.

111 U.F.M. Quest. (1964), Q1b/68, county Antrim.

Bed Folklore

112 O'Neill, *Life & Tradition*, 23. O'Neill describes some of these beliefs, mentioning that religious custom was followed when a new bed was introduced into a house and sometimes when straw bedding was changed.

113 McGrath ed., 'The Diary of Humphrey O'Sullivan,' 163.

114 Letters of J. Dunton, from the Bodleian Library: Rawl. D. 71. Reprinted as Appendix B in E. MacLysacht, *Irish Life in the Seventeenth Century: After Cromwell* (Dublin, Cork, 1939), 358.

115 O. S. Mem, Box 21, IX, 1 (1821), 42; quoted for S. Donegal by Gailey, *Rural Houses of the North of Ireland*, 64.

116 K. M. Harris, 'Extracts from the Committee's Collection' in *Ulster Folklife*, IV (1958), 45. Account from county Antrim.

117 P. Kennedy, *Evenings In the Duffrey* (Dublin, 1869), 78.

Chapter 6 PRESS BEDS & OTHER DISGUISED BEDS

1 N. Webster, *Webster's New Twentieth Century Dictionary* (2nd edn, New York, 1983), 1424: 'Press bed, a folding bed; a bed built in solid woodwork, resembling a cupboard.'

2 'A pressbed is a wooden article used for a person to sleep in at night and is used during the day for a seat along usually the back wall in country kitchens.' Quoted from K.M. Harris, 'Extracts from the Committee's Collection' in *Ulster Folklife*, VI (Belfast, 1960), 20. Also some respondents to the Ulster Folk Museum's Questionnaire on furniture indicated that when they used the term press bed they actually meant a settle bed: U.F.M. Quest. (1964) Q1b/41 and 28.

3 U.F.M. Quest. (1964) Q1b/166; 'Cupboard beds appear to have been common in Bright, Downpatrick, where as a very young child I was brought on a visit say 1908 or so. I did not see them again until I saw them in elegant New York apartments where I think they are called Press beds.' Also such beds are commonly referred to as 'Murphy Beds' in California: a link to their Irish origins.

4 Analysis of responses to questionnaires about furniture sent out between 1950 and 1964; D.I.F. Mss. 1663–4 (1950s) and U.F.M. Quest (1964) Q1b, together with other literary descriptions, inventories and surviving examples, results in the following patterns:

In Connaught the press bed is mentioned rarely; only in county Roscommon 2, and county Galway 1.

In Ulster there were 17 positive responses (from all of the old nine counties), county Down having 4, counties Tyrone, Fermanagh, Armagh, Monaghan and Cavan each with 2. Counties Donegal, Derry and Antrim each with 1.

Leinster had 13 positive responses from the following counties; Longford 5, Westmeath 1, Kildare 2, Dublin 1, Wexford 1 and Kilkenny 3.

Munster had the greatest number mentioned; none from county Waterford but of the following counties Kerry had 6, Cork 3, Limerick 4, Tipperary 4, Clare 4.

5 There are far more inventory entries for settle beds than for press beds, although many houses owned examples of both.

6 Gilbert mentions that in England some Edwardian examples of the similar 'dess beds' were fitted with wire spring mattresses. C. Gilbert, *English Vernacular Furniture, 1750–1900* (New Haven, London 1991), 140. .

7 Idid., 140.

8 R. Edwards and P. MacQuoid, *The Dictionary of English Furniture*, I (Woodbridge, 1983), 68.

9 C. Edwards, 'Press Bedsteads' in *Furniture History*, XXVI (1990), 42–52.

10 Gilbert, *Enghish Vernacular Furniture*, 139.

11 Where mentioned, I have listed the bedding which was kept hidden inside the press in the daytime. It provides important clues as to the quality of the press bed and therefore who might have slept in it. It is significant that feather bedding, which was considered a comparative luxury, is rarely listed.

1686 'a Press-bed and curtains, 2 ruggs and 3 blankets one bed and boulster'... in Mr Hyde's Roome ... 1 folding bedstead and bays curtains ... in the old Nursery'. Inventory of Sir John Percivale of Burton Hall, county Cork. From R. ffolliott and B. de Breffny, 'The Contents of Burton Hall, co. Cork in 1686' in *The Irish Ancestor*, V, No. 2 (1973), 109.

1709 'A Press Bed, one fether bed, one boulster and two pillows ... £2.0.0.'. Inventory of Thomas Weston, miller of Athy, county Kildare. From O.C. Goodbody, 'Quaker Inventories' in *The Irish Ancestor*, III, No. 1 (1971), 57.

1755 'there is a press bed in one of the parlours, glass-framed, resembling a book-case, and done in the neatest manner'. Described amongst contents of house to let near Skerries, county Dublin. From *The Universal Advertiser*, 29 July 1755, quoted in A.K. Longfield, 'Up For Sale' in *The Irish Ancestor*, XVII, No. 1 (1985), 32.

1786 'oak press bed, and a variety of servants bedding'. Sale of [wealthy] Robert Brooke's possessions, Prosperous, county Kildare. From *The Dublin Evening Post*, 9 November 1786. in A.K. Longfield, 'Two Eighteenth Century House Furnishing Auction

Lists' in *The Journal of The Royal Society of Antiquaries of Ireland*, Ser. 7 XIV (1944), 169–71.

c.1797 listed three times; '1 press bedstead with bed etc, [and] 1 press bed, bedstead and bedding,' amongst the late Mrs Burgess's Inn furnishings, Mallow, county work [4 out of 24 beds listed were press beds]. R. ffolliott, 'The Furnishings of an 18th century Inn' in *The Irish Ancestor*, II, No. 1 (1970), 44.

c.1806 'One Press bed, feather bed, blanketts and large Quilt £2.16s10½d., Servants Hall' Inventory of Luke Mahon, Strokestown, county Roscommon. From R. ffolliott, 'Luke Mahon's Inventory' in *The Irish Ancestor*, XIII, No. 2 (1981), 85.

1817 'Servants Hall-Press bedstead Furnished, £5.00. Housekeeper's Room-Press bedstead/ Furnished/extra bed, £10.00. From the inventory of J. McGeough, Drumsill, county Armagh, in P.R.O.N.I. D288/174.

The 'Press-bed and curtains' [1686] and the one described as 'glass-framed, resembling a book-case' [1755], may well have resembled the somewhat later English versions reproduced by Clive Edwards in 'Press Bedsteads', figs. 4 and 6. 49–50.

12 Longfield, 'Up for Sale', 32.

13 Gilbert, *English Vernacular Furniture*, 137–9, figs. 223–4 and 227.

14 T. Ó Criomhthain, quoted in P. O'Sullivan, *Field and Shore* (Dublin, 1977), 125.

15 O. Pyne Clarke, *She Came of Decent People* (London, 1986), 75.

16 U.F.M. Quest. (1964) Q1b/147.

17 D.I.F. Ms. Vol. 750 (1937), 423.

18 K. Tynan, 'Irish Types and Traits' in *The Magazine of Art* (New York, Vol. 1888), 128.

19 J. C. Loudon, *Encyclopaedia of Cottage, Farm and Villa Architecture* (London, 1833, 1846 edn), 329–30.

20 D.I.F. Ms. Vol. 1663 (*c.*1950), 92.

Other Disguised Beds

21 R. ffolliott, 'The Furnishings of a Palladian house in 1742–3: Barbavilla, county Westmeath' in *The Irish Ancestor*, XI No. 2 (1979), 94.

22 R. ffolliott, 'An Inventory of Killeen Castle in 1735–6' in *The Irish Ancestor*, IX, No. 2 (1977), 103–4.

23 Edwards, 'Press Bedsteads', fig. 8, 52. The Gillow design for a bureau bedstead in deal, of 1788, is reproduced in Gilbert, *English Vernacular Furniture*, 139.

Chapter 7 CRADLES

1 H.C. Parliamentary Papers: Report of the Commissioners (II) 1836 Supplement to Appendix E. XXXII, 17–245.

2 F. Carragher, 'Irish Cradles: An Introductory Look' in *Regional Furniture*, VI (due for publication at time of writing, 1992).

3 Anon. 'Thady O'Brady, Favourite Irish Comic Song'. N.L.I., unreferenced book (n.d. c.1800).

4 Mr and Mrs S.,C. Hall, *Ireland: Its Scenery, Character, etc.* III (London. 1841), 25.

5 An example of a straw mat from county Longford is described in a response to the Questionnaire: 'Certain articles of furniture'. D.I.F., Ms. Vol. 1663, 59. Carragher, 'Irish Cradles'.British Museum Additional Ms. 31,882 (Court Book from the Diocese of Killaloe): An account of the things belonging to Maud Dan McMahon (1 August 1747), 126.

6 R. ffolliott and B. de Breffny, 'The Contents of Burton Hall, co. Cork in 1686' in *The Irish Ancestor*, V, No. 2 (1973), 107. Listed in the nursery are '2 Twigg cradles'.

7 Revd J. Hall, *Tour Through Ireland, particularly the Interior and lesser known parts etc.*, 2 Vols, I (London, 1813), 88.

8 J.M. Synge, *The Aran Islands* (1907, reprinted Oxford, 1985), 14.

9 T.H. Mason, *The Islands of Ireland* (London, 1936), 78.

10 The term 'Moses basket' is still used in counties Cork, Limerick, Donegal and Antrim, and probably elsewhere.

11 See P. Smyth, *Osier Culture and Basket-making, A study of the basket-making craft in south west county Antrim* (Lurgan, 1991), 64. Shows a photograph of a 'Moses Basket' raised on a stand and made by James Mulholland of Moss road. Another wicker cradle made recently in county Galway by Joseph Hogan is illustrated in D. Shaw-Smith ed., *Ireland's Traditional Crafts* (London, 1986), 129.

12 P. Kennedy, *Legendary Fictions of the Irish Celts* (London, 1866), 100. For an illustration of a Welsh 'lip-work' straw cradle with oak rockers, see V. Chinnery, *Oak Furniture, The British Tradition* (Suffolk, 1986), 68, fig. 2, 32.

13 D. Hartley, *Made In England* (London, 1939), 72–7. Hartley provides a fascinating account of several different types of strawwork, illustrating coiled straw hooded chairs, tubs, baskets, a hive or *skelp* [skep] and an ingenious coiled straw bed.

14 Shaw-Smith, *Ireland's Traditional Crafts* 139–40. David Shaw-Smith's excellent television series, 'Hands' devoted one programme to the craft of bee skep making by the late Jack Carey of Clonakilty, recording his traditional technique in loving detail. Makers of bee skeps were also responsible for the manufacture of coiled straw bosses, chairs, seed lips etc. With the recent death of Jack Carey of Clonakilty, county Cork, the traditional practice of this craft appears to be approaching extinction in Ireland, although it is still practised in some parts of the British Isles.

15 D.I.F. Ms. Vol. 1664 (1957), The Glens of Antrim, 70: 'Baskets for babies were also made from plaited straw'.

16 E.E. Evans, *Irish Folk Ways* (London, 1979), 93.

17 J.G. Jenkins, *Traditional Country Craftsmen* (London, 1965), 142–4. 'lip-work' is discussed here in detail, 'the word *lip being a derivation of the Scandinavian lob*; coiled basketry'. Such a term is not commonly used in Ireland, which is why I have refrained from referring to the Irish craft in this way. However, techniques appear to be closely similar; in Wales holly bark is often used, rather than the favourite split bramble or brier. An example of a coiled straw basket can be seen on display at the birthplace of Edmund Ignatius Rice, Callan, county Kilkenny.

18 G. Sturt, *The Wheelwright's Shop* (Cambridge, 1984), 97.

Chapter 8 TABLES

The Variety of Tables

1 W. Moffet, *Hesperi Neso Graphia; The Western Isle Described, in eight Cantos* (Dublin, 1724), Canto 1, 10.

2 J. Derricke, *The Image of Irlande, with a Discoverie of Woodkarne* (1581).

3 T. O'Neill, *Life and Tradition In Rural Ireland* (London, 1977), 30.

4 E.E. Evans, *Irish Folk Ways* (London, 1957, 1979), 88–9.

5 G. Hill, *Facts From Gweedore* (London, 1887; republished Belfast 1971) 16, 25.

6 P. Kennedy, *The Banks of the Boro, a Chronicle of Co. Wexford* (London, 1867), 256.

7 Revd J. Hall, *Tour Through Ireland*, I (1813), 86, 199–200.

8 I.F. Grant, *Highland Folk Ways* (London, 1961, reprinted 1989), 177.

9 Mist's Weekly Journal (England, 27, July 1728).

10 Mrs S.C. Hall, *Hall's Ireland, Mr & Mrs Hall's Tour of 1840*, II (1841; republished in 2 vols London 1984), 422–3.

Improvised Tables and Potato Skibs

11 This poem (which in full amounts to a poor labourer's inventory), from Ballywalter, county Down, is published in A. Gailey 'The Housing of the Rural Poor in Ulster' in *Ulster Folklife*, XXII (Belfast, 1976), 50.

12 D.I.F. Ms. Vol. 463, 1.143; Account recorded from a woman born in 1863 from Ballymoe, county Galway. 'The one and only three-legged wooden stool in the house' serves as a table.

13 For several references to tables being used, and one to a 'stoole or table' in rural west Connaught homes, see Appendix B; 'John Dunton's Letters' [17th century] in E. MacLysaght, *Irish Life in the Seventeenth Century: After Cromwell* (Dublin/Cork, 1939), 338, 343, 345.

14 G. Stokes ed., *Pococke's Tour in Ireland in 1752* (Dublin/London, 1891), 86.

15 R. Shaw, *Carleton's Country* (Dublin, 1930), 20. The term *kitchen* was commonly used during the 19th and 20th centuries to describe additions to the basic meal of potatoes; sometimes this consisted of buttermilk, milk or salt, all of which helped improve the taste of the food. According to *Webster's New Twentieth Century Unabridged Dictionary* (U.S.A., 2nd edn 1983), one of the definitions is 'to feed, or supply with food from a kitchen.'

16 P. Knight, *Erris in the Irish Highlands* (1836), 104. Quoted by C. Otway, *Sketches in Erris and Tyrawly* (Dublin, 1841), 358–9.

17 A. O'Dowd, 'Folklife & Folk Traditions' in D. Gillmor (ed.) *The Irish Countryside* (Dublin, 1989), 154. Also for full description of skib making etc. see J. Delaney, 'Baskets and their uses in the Midlands' in A. Gailey and D. Ó hÓgáin eds., *Gold Under The Furze, Studies in Folk Tradition* (Dublin, c.1982), 215–27. Also D.I.F. Ms. Vol. 1663, 10, 11, 51 and Vol. 1664, 105–6.

18 D.I.F. Ms. Vol. 1663 (6 June 1957), 73.

The Baking Board

19 The following are inventory listings of lossets from different areas of Ireland since the 17th century: J.C. Walton, 'The Household Effects of a Waterford Merchant Family in 1640' in *The Journal of the Cork Historical and Archaeological Society*, LXXXIII, No. 238 (July–December, 1978), 104.

P.R.O.N.I. Ms. T1062/22: Inventory of John Williamson of Ballyhagen in parish of Killmore, county Armagh, died 31 January 1723: 'Tubbs barralls lossats etc. at 1.3.0.' (Courtesy of the Religious Society of Friends).

Also R. ffolliott, 'The Furnishings of a Palladian House in 1742–3: Barbaravilla, co. Westmeath' in *The Irish Ancestor*, XI, No. 2 (Dublin, 1979), 87: 'small losett for macking bread'.

British Museum Additional Ms. 31, 882; Court Book from the Diocese of Killaloe [Munster], 221: Inventory of goods of 'John Dubarry of Derrygowna' (21 Dec. 1755); includes '1 losset'.

An Inventory of Killiane Castle (2 August 1760), N.L.I. Ms. 29, 709 (9) Harvey Papers. 'Two bread-lossets' are mentioned as being found in the Out-Cellar, indicating that the term is an old established one in county Wexford.

20 T. Ó Criomhthain, *The Islandman* (Oxford, 1987), 30.
21 A. Gailey, *Rural Houses of the North of Ireland* (Edinburgh, 1984), 211, fig. 227, This photograph shows a woman kneading bread in a baking board on a kitchen table, for cooking on a griddle over her open fire.

The Falling Table

22 U.F.M. Quest. (1964) Q1b.
23 D.I.F., Mss Vols. 1663–4 (1950s) and Vol. 654 (1939), 179. and U.F.M. Quest. (1964) Q1b.
24 D.I.F., Mss Vols. 1663–4 (1950s) and Vol. 654 (1939), 179.
25 U.F.M. Quest. (1964) Q1b/53, county Down.
26 P.R.O.N.I. Ms. T1062/15: Inventory of David Kell, of Coragh, Loughgall, county Armagh, 1712. (Courtesy of the Religious Society of Friends).
27 P.R.O.N.I. T1062/19: William Allen's inventory of Coragh, Loughgall, county Armagh, died 1717. Also P.R.O.N.I. T1062/21: Inventory of George Wickliff of Coragh, Loughgall, county Armagh, 1719: 'A frame table and a little fall table at 16s.0.' [in the buttrey]. P.R.O.N.I. T1062/23: Inventory of John Brownloe of Tullymore, Killmore, county Armagh: 'A fall table and nine oack chaers in sd parlore all at 1.0.0'. (All courtesy of the Religious Society of Friends).

Interesting comparisons can be made between the terminology used by U.F.M. Questionnaire respondents in the 1960s, and furniture listed in inventories of the early 1700s. For instance a 'Cupboard Table' is listed in the inventory of, P.R.O.N.I. T1062/17: W. Richardson, Aghrelougher, Loughgall, county Armagh, 1716, and the same thing is mentioned by a respondent living within 30 miles at Randalstown in the 1960's: U.F.M. Quest. (1964) Q1b/132. A cupboard table was also described recently by a west county Cork woman as a falling table fixed to the front of a press, which when let down, revealed the ware inside.
28 H.C. Parliamentary Papers: 1st Report of the Commissioners (II) 1836. Supplement to Appendix E. XXXII, 216 and 246.
29 P. Kennedy, *Evenings In The Duffrey* (Dublin, 1869), 66, also 49.
30 P. Kennedy, *Legends of Mount Leinster* (Dublin, 1855), 47.
31 Evans mentions the 'falling leaf table' which he says *drops* when not in use (other recent authors have consequently also made this mistake, probably having never seen an example). This is somewhat misleading as the length and height of most falling tables would make it impossible to fold them away downwards. It seems that there may have been some confusion with the terminology of the entirely different and free-standing 'drop leaf table'. E. Evans, *Irish Folk Ways*, 88.

32 F.H.A. Aalen, 'Furnishings of Traditional Houses in the Wicklow Hills' in *Ulster Folklife*, XIII (Belfast, 1967), 63–4. Also D.I.F. Vol. 1663, 17–23 and Vol. 654, 45–179.
33 Gailey, *Rural Houses of the North of Ireland*, 216.
34 D.I.F., Ms. Vol. 1404, 501–2.
35 A. Symons, *Cities & Sea Coasts & Islands* (London, 1918), 307. Inishmore is one of the largest of the Aran Islands, off the Clare and Galway coasts, Symons described it as a very primitive hotel where the landlady slept in the kitchen, presumably in a fireside bed. The table he mentioned was in the upstairs dining-room.

The Kitchen Table

36 See for examples inventory entries for various 'boards' and tables listed in W. Pinkerton, 'Inventory of the Household effects of Lord Deputy Lord Leonard Grey, in 1540' in the *Ulster Journal of Archaeology*, VII (1859), 2018. and Walton, 'The Household Effects of a Waterford Merchant Family in 1640', 102–3.
37 An Inventory of Killiane Castle (2 August 1760). N.L.I. Ms. 29, 709 (9) Harvey Papers.
38 M.J. Murphy, *At Slieve Gullion's Foot* (Dundalgan Press, 1942), 25. F. Crowley, *In West Cork Long Ago* (Dublin/Cork, 1980), 102. P. Kennedy, 'The Wake at Pedher Mor's' ch.XIV of *The Banks of the Boro*, 56.
39 Ó Criomhthain, *The Islandman*, 28–9.
40 V. Chinnery, *Oak Furniture, The British Tradition* (Woodbridge, 1979), 288–95.
41 W. Hanbidge, *The Memories of William Hanbidge, aged 93, 1096* (St Albans, 1939), 20; 'They sit on four legged deal stools scrubbed like the table with white river sand.' Kennedy, *The Banks of the Boro*, 169–70; In preparation for the Stations '. . . everything so clean and formally arranged and the marks of shelly-sand here and there'.
42 M. Carbery, *The Farm by Lough Gur* (Cork, 1986), 21; refers to a long oak kitchen table, in the centre of the kitchen. Kennedy, *Evenings In The Duffrey*, 64; refers to the parlour being furnished with dark cupboards, dark oak tables, and dark oak chairs.
43 Gailey, *Rural Houses of The North of Ireland*, 213. H. Glassie, Passing The Time (Dublin, 1982), 396–7.
44 Kennedy, *Evenings In The Duffrey*, 8.
45 Ibid., 3.
46 A. Nicholson, *The Bible in Ireland* (1844–5) quoted from F. Murphy, *The Bog Irish, Who they were and How they Lived* (Australia, 1987), 195.
47 Gailey, *Rural Houses of The North of Ireland*, 217.
48 *Ordnance Survey Memoir*, Box 4, V, 1 (1838), 13, quoted from Gailey, *Rural Houses of the North of Ireland*, 217.
49 K. Danaher, *The Hearth & Stool and All!* (Cork/Dublin, 1985), 45–8.

Chapter 9 THE HEARTH AND THE SHRINE

The Use of Roasting Spits

1 The 18th-century Gaelic poet Egan O'Rahilly here praises the hospitality of the planter, Warner. Quoted in L.M. Cullen, *Life in Ireland* (London, 1968), 70.
2 E.E. Evans, *Irish Folk Ways* (London, 1979), 76. K. Danaher, *In Ireland Long Ago* (Cork, 1962, reprinted 1986), 21; 'In some farmhouses meat was roasted on spits; you can still see the slots which held the spits in the old dressers.' Also,

'Wines, newly opened, being drunk, and jollity, Viands on spits, and uisquebagh on tables' by Aodhagán Ó Rathaille (Egan O'Rahilly), translated from Irish, describing the O'Callaghans at Clonmeen, county Cork, *c.*1724. Also,

Loaves fresh kneaded for me,
Roast on the spits for me,
Beeves slaughtered for me,
The comfort of a fine bed for me,
Sleep in the down of fowl for me'

by Eibhlín Dubh, translated from the Irish, *c.*1774, both from D. Corkery, *The Hidden Ireland, A Study of Gaelic Munster in the Eighteenth Century* (Dublin, 1924, 1986), 50–2.

3 Patrick Kennedy, writing about county Wexford during the first quarter of the 19th century, describes 'the goose turning on the spit'. See P. Kennedy, *The Banks of the Boro, A Chronicle of County Wexford* (Dublin, 1875, reprinted Enniscorthy, 1989), 297.

4 A roasting spit and stand is illustrated in T. O'Neill, *Life and Tradition in Rural Ireland* (London, 1977), plate 23, 20–1. His example is part of the collection of the National Museum of Ireland (N.M.I. EF151), Dublin. The Ulster Folk Museum, Belfast, have a good collection of such iron spit holders which often double as bread-hardening or 'harnen stands'. The Irish Agricultural Museum at Johnstown Castle, county Wexford, have at least one spit in their collection.

5 Except in the baronies of Forth and Bargy, county Wexford, where many of the houses have retained features associated with medieval English settlement, according to Evans, *Irish Folk Ways*, 77.

6 M. McGrath editor and translator, 'The Diary of Humphrey O'Sullivan, 1827–32' in *Irish Texts Society*, XXX (1928–31), 13 April 1827, 19–21. See also W.S. Mason, *A Statistical Account or Parochial Study of Ireland*, 3 vols, I (Dublin, 1819), 94; Of Ardbraccan, county Meath; 'They seldom partake of animal food: the lower class of farmer not often, except, perhaps, at Christmas and other festivals, family feasts, and other solemn, occasions.'

7 McGrath, 'The Diary of Humphrey O'Sullivan', 14 February 1828, 229. It is interesting to compare these meat prices with contemporary wage rates. In county Derry at that time a [farm] labourer earned about 9*s.* per week, a tradesman earnt anything up to twice that amount. Food prices in both counties were comparable (the rates were lower in the west); Ordnance Survey of the County of Londonderry, vol. I (Dublin, 1837), 200. D.I.F. Ms. vol. 462 (20 January 1938), 78-year old labourer from East Carbery, county Cork, 215; 'we wouldn't see bit o' "mate" from Christmas till Christmas only praties an' a salty herring roasted in the greesuck [embers] that's why we used to go out "bird killin'". A good blackbird or a good thrush roasted on the coals would be a nice pickin' for us them times.'

8 H.C. Parliamentary Papers: Report of the Commissioners (9), 1836. Supplement to Appendix C, XXX, parts I and II, Maryborough, 23.

9 A. M'Kenzie, *Poems and Songs on Different Subjects* (Belfast, 1810), 117–21. Quoted in A. Gailey, 'The Housing of the Rural Poor in Nineteenth-Century Ulster' in *Ulster Folklife*, XXII (Belfast, 1976), 50.

The Clevy or Spit Rack

10 E. Cross, *The Tailor and Ansty* (Cork, 1942, reprinted 1987), 19. In E.E. Evans, 'The Fireside' in *The Louth Archaelogical Journal* (Journal of the county Louth Archaeological Society), X, No. 3 (1943), 198. Evans states 'the mantlepiece has no place in the traditional Irish kitchen'. The word mantlepiece may not occur. However, the clevy has incidentally created a mantle-piece in many traditional homes and even in its absence, a long shelf above the fireplace is commonly depicted in early illustrations and photographs, of hearths without hoods or canopies.

11 In many traditional houses, the massive width of the original chimney is usually the first element to be altered during 'improvements'; a narrower opening creates a more efficient fire and yet the clevy often remains above a recently installed stove. Fieldwork into the clevy was facilitated by the fact that in derelict houses they were often left in place, long after all the other furniture had been removed, being worthless to the antique trade.

Regional Variations in Clevy Design

12 P. Warner, *A Visitor's Guide to the Comeragh Mountains* (Belfast, 1978), 68.

13 The National Museum of Ireland, Dublin, has several examples of these clevy/coop dressers, all from Pallas Green, county Limerick in their collection (fig. 306). Their exact accession is unfortunately unknown, but they were probably all collected in the Limerick area.

14 D.I.F. Ms. Vol. 1663 (*c.*1957), J.D. North county Cork, Questions 8 and 9; 36.

15 One of this type can be seen displayed in the labourer's house from Athea, in Bunratty Folk Park. K. Danaher, *The Hearth and Stool and All! Irish Rural Households* (Cork, 1985), 19; 'the hanging dresser, locally called a 'clevvy'. Also another example from county Limerick is displayed amongst the collection of the Irish Country Furniture Society at The Irish Agricultural Museum, county Wexford.

16 For examples see W. Pinkerton, 'Inventory of the Household Effects of Lord Deputy Lord Leonard Grey, in 1540' in *The Ulster Journal of Archeology*, 1st Ser. VII (1859), 209–10; 'Eight spitts' and 'A paier of standing racks. A paier of small racks.' Pinkerton's footnote here states 'These racks were, probably, used for holding spits.', 'Iron rostynge racks,' and 'spitt racks' occur in several of the old inventories.

The author is grateful to Dr W. Vaughan for pointing out a 19th-century ballad called 'The Kitchen Furniture', containing the following verses:

The spit stood up like a naked man
And swore he'd fight the dripping pan
the dripping pan then without fail
Swore that the broom should go to gaol.

the tonge being by the fire side,
Stood up on his long legs and cried
I'll fight the spit that long beeked thief
Although his work is roasting beef

Trinity College Library ref. no. OLS 89.t.1, no. 86. (n.d. but 19th century). Also J.C. Walton, 'The Household Effects of a Waterford Merchant family in 1640' in *The Journal of the Cork Historical and Archaeological Society*, LXXXIII No. 238 (July–December 1978), 104; 'one drippinge pann . . . one spitt and fire fork valued 2*s.* . . . . two axes a Brasse ladle and a spitt valued at 4*s.*'. The author is grateful to Rosemary ffolliott for drawing her attention to the publication of this and many other invaluable inventories.

Also see R. ffolliott, 'An Inventory of Killeen Castle in 1735–6' in *The Irish Ancestor*, IX, 2 (Dublin, 1977), 104; In 'The Kitchen . . . 1 large and 1 small Iron Racks 1 Iron Spit . . . 2 Wooden Racks over ye Chimney' [county Meath]. Also British Museum Add.

Ms. 31,882, The Killaloe Court Book (25 May 1751), 187; From the goods and household furniture of Doctor John McKeogh deceased: '2 iron spits 1 pair of spit racks' (from Nenagh, county Tipperary); (27 December 1756) Goods and Chattles that Richard Ryan of Aghnameade died possessed of (Nenagh, county Tipperary): '1 cliever 1 spitt'.

Also An Inventory of Killane Castle (2 August 1760) N.L.I. Ms. 29,709 (9) Harvey Papers; In the Kitching 'Racks Fender Tongs, Poker and 2 Spits, Dog-wheel and chain' [for turning the spit by means of a running dog].

The Origin of the Word Clevy

17 In 1813 Rowlandson illustrated a four-tier spit rack above the fireplace of an alehouse. The latter is reproduced in C. Gilbert, *English Vernacular Furniture, 1750–1900* (London, 1991), fig. 127, 90: It is interesting that this one also holds and displays plates and potlids, as the hanging dresser-style clevies of county Limerick do. Rowlandson illustrates another spit rack (similar to the fixed county Cork types), *c*.1800, from an inn kitchen, Newcastle Emlyn, south Wales, in G. Jekyll, *Old English Household Life* (London, 1939), figs. 51, 52 and 77 shows a drawing of another three-tier spit rack over a hearth, incorporating a shelf. James Ayres illustrates a good example of an 18th-century spit rack which he found in a London house. See J. Ayres, *The Shell Book of the Home in Britain, Decoration, Design and Construction of Vernacular Interiors, 1500–1850* (London, 1981), fig. 17, 30. An example which is closely similar to the most common county Cork designs (fig. 302A) is in the collection of the Geffrye Museum, London, given to the museum by Stoke Newington Council in 1935, who no longer have accession records for that year.

18 J. Wright, *The English Dialect Dictionary* (London, 1898), 625, 638: Clevy see Clavel. Under Clavel ('The beam of wood serving as a lintel over an old fashioned fireplace; the shelf above the fireplace, the mantlepiece.) he provides 19th-century literary examples of the word being pronounced 'clavey, clavy-buoard, clavey-board and clavi-tack' from Wiltshire, Dorset and Somerset respectively. T. de Bhaldraithe and N.O. Donaill, *Focloir Gaeilge-Bearla* (Irish English Dictionary) and P. Dinneen, *Irish-English Dictionary* (Dublin, 1927, reprinted 1975), 203; The Irish word *cleibhí* is pronounced clevy and translates into English 'clevy' (also clavel, clevis). See Ó Siochfhradha, *Learner's Irish-English, English-Irish Dictionary* (Dublin, 1958), 24; *clabhar* means mantlepiece.

19 P. O'Sullivan, *Field and Shore, Daily Life and Traditions, Aran Islands 1900*, Book 2 (Dublin, 1977), 124.

20 Danaher, *The Hearth and Stool and All!*, 19.

The Crane

21 Revd J. Hall, *Tour Through Ireland, Particularly the interior and lesser known parts etc.*, 2 vols, I (London, 1813), 199–200.

22 McGrath, 'The Diary of Humphrey O'Sullivan,' entry for 26 August 1829, 193.

23 T.H. Mason, *The Islands of Ireland* (London, 1936), 80.

Holy Shelves and Shrines

24 C.M. Arensberg and S.T. Kimball, *Family and Community in Ireland* (1940), 133.

25 For examples see P. Baneat, *Le Mobilier Breton* (Paris, n.d., *c*.1930), 22–3.

Appendix: SMALL FURNISHINGS

Domestic Utensils

1 Anon, 'Thady O'Brady, Favourite Irish Comic Song' (n.d., but *c*.1800), from an unreferenced Ms. in the National Library of Ireland.

2 As such it is very similar to Andrew M'Kenzie's 'Poor Man's Petition' of 1807 from *Poems and Songs on Different Subject* (Belfast, 1810), 117–21 (and in The Ulster Folk Museum's pamphlet entitled *Meenagarragh Cottier's House*).

3 The county Wexford example is on display at the Irish Agricultural Museum, county Wexford. See E. Pinto, *Treen and other Wooden Bygones, An Encyclopeadia and Social History* (London, 1969), fig. 147, 134–5 for an example of a Welsh stepped spoon rack. See O. Sharkey, *Common Knowledge, the Irishness of Everyday Things* (Melbourne, 1988), 64 for an illustration of a similar three-tiered 'cutlery box'.

4 K. Danaher, *The Hearth and Stool and All! Irish Rural Households* (Cork, 1985), 75.

5 Court Book from the Diocese of Killaloe. British Museum Add. Ms: 31,882 [in first half of book]; '1 Knife Box' amongst the inventory of small farmer Richard Ryan, of Anamalle, Nenagh, county Tipperary (27 December 1756). Inventory listings of specific items such as knife boxes or wooden bowls are hard to find, perhaps because of their comparatively low value and frequent use they are more often listed simply amongst 'small boxes' or 'dishes' etc.

Tinsmiths' Work

6 M.J. Murphy, *At Slieve Gullion's Foot* (Dundalk, 1942), 26.

7 D. Thomson and M. McGusty eds., *The Irish Journals of Elizabeth Smith, 1840–50*, 13 January 1847 (Oxford, 1980), 120.

8 G.C. Bonthrone, 'Childhood Memories of county Antrim' in *Ulster Folklife*, VI (Belfast, 1960), 41–2.

Woodturners' Work

9 J. Small ed., *The Image of Ireland by John Derricke*, 1581 (Edinburgh, 1883), 54; quoted in T. O'Neill, *Life and Tradition in Rural Ireland* (London, 1977), 26.

10 R. ffolliott, 'The Furnishings of a Palladian House in 1742–3: Barbavilla, county Westmeath' in *The Irish Ancestor*, XI, No. 2 (Dublin, 1979), 87; In ye kitchen: 'two threnchers 3 new ones bought at Mullingar'. Ordnance Survey Memoir, Box 5, II (May 1837), Lisburn Market, Parish of Blaris, county Antrim, 1–117. These were said to be in abundant supply in the March (1837) market and were being sold at various prices: they were 'chiefly from Dromore, 7 miles [away].' Some of these memoirs are now published by A. Day and P. Williams eds., O.S. Memoir of Ireland (Institute of Irish Studies, Queens University, Belfast and Royal Irish Academy, Dublin), vols 1–18. Joseph Peacock (*c*.1783–1837) painted *The Patron [sic]*, or *Festival of St. Kevin at the Seven Churches, Glendalough* which shows in great detail stalls selling food, toys and cooper's ware, along with many other domestic utensils. It is in the Ulster Museum and is described in great detail in W. Craw-

ford, 'The Patron, or the Festival of St. Kevin at the Seven Churches, Glendalough, County Wicklow 1813' in *Ulster Folklife*, XXXII (Belfast, 1986), 37–47. Also reproduced in A. Crookshank and The Knight of Glin, *The Painters of Ireland c.1660–1920* (London, 1978), figs. 185–6, 196–7.

11 N. Webster, *Webster's New Twentieth Century Dictionary* (New York, 2nd edn, 1983), 166. Here beetle is defined as 'mallet, hammer', with several alternative precise uses. In Ireland its most appropriate definition is '2. a household mallet or pestle for mashing or beating.' C. Ó Síocháin, translated by R.P. Breatnach, *The Man from Cape Clear, the life of an Islandman, Seanchas Chléire* (Cork, 1975), 79: 'a beetle or pounder. When the "sugawns" were being put on the houses long ago the straw had to be pounded with a beetle first before they could be made.'

A. Gailey, 'Illustrations of the Irish linen Industry in 1783, by William Hincks' in *Ulster Folklife*, XXIII (Belfast, 1977), 6. Hincks illustrates amongst this important set of prints, 'A girl seated on the ground . . . with a beet of flax held in her left hand over a stone beats the flax with a cylindrical beetle held in her right hand.' H. Dutton, *Statistical Survey of County Clare* (Dublin, 1808), 180–1; 'In every part of this county [Clare] the clothes (I mean those of the lower rank) are washed by beating them in a river on a large smooth stone with a flat board, called a beetle'. For an illustration of such clothes washing using a beetle in Galway, see W.M. Thackeray, *The Irish Sketchbook* (London, 1843), 173.

12 G. Griffiths, *Chronicles of the County Wexford, being a record of memorable incidents, etc . . . brought down to the year 1877* (Enniscorthy, 1877), 242. The author is grateful to Dr Kevin Whelan for drawing attention to this and other useful texts.

13 M. McManus, 'Joseph Hughes: An Armagh Woodturner' in the journal *Tools and Trades*, I (Suffolk, 1983), 43–8. This article, based on the letter of a woodturner written in 1936 (now D.I.F. Ms. Vol. 302, 67–77) provides a detailed case study of one family's work, as well as describing techniques, materials, other turners' work etc. The author is grateful to Dr W. H. Crawford for drawing attention to this text and many others.

14 The following list is not exhaustive but is intended to provide a few examples of entries for woodenware. Valuable ware made of pewter, brass etc is more commonly delineated than that made of timber;

J.C. Walton, 'The Household Effects of a Waterford Merchant Family in 1640' in *The Journal of the Cork Historical and Archaeological Society*, LXXXIII, No. 238 (Cork, 1978), 104: '4 dozen trenchers'.

O.C. Goodbody, 'Inventories of five Dublin Quaker Merchants in the late Seventeenth century' in *The Irish Ancestor*, X, No. 1 (Dublin, 1978), 40, 44: Probate Inventory of John Inglefield of Dame street, Dublin, chandler, 1693; 'In the Kitchin . . . 2 doz Trenchers'. Probate Inventory of Isachar Wilcocks of Dublin, grocer, 1694; 'In the Kitchin . . . dressers, wooden ware'.

J. Stevenson, *Two Centuries of Life in county Down* (Belfast, 1920), 324; Bankrupt Michael Ward, landowner's possessions in 1731; '4 Wooden bowls . . . £0.2.6'.

Court Book from the Diocese of Killaloe, British Museum Add Ms: 31, 822, 47; Probate inventory of Mr Richard Dennis (12 December 1732); '2 plates a dozen trenchors [sic]'.

ffolliott, 'The Furnishings of a Palladian House in

1742–3': 87; In ye kitchen: 'two threnchers 3 new ones bought at Mullingar . . . One Wooding Dish, 3 Wooding Bowls, one trencher brock [broken], one Wooding Bowl'. etc.

N.L.I. Ms. 29, 709(9) Harvey Papers. An Inventory of Killiane Castle. August 2 1760; In the Kitchen; '2 wooden pot lids, 15 trenchers, 6 platters'. In the Vault; '6 small wooden Vessels, 5 Trenchers'.

W. Carleton, *Traits and Stories of the Irish Peasantry*, II (Dublin, 1835), 160; 'the dresser with noggins, wooden trenchers and pewter dishes perfectly clean, and as well polished as a french courtier.'

15 Mr and Mrs S.C. Hall, *Ireland: Its Scenery, Character, Etc*, 3 vols, I (London, 1841), 250.

16 D.I.F. Ms. Vol. 782 (1941), Parish Lack, county Kerry, 393. The scrubbing of milk-pails, tubs and dishes is also mentioned in P. Kennedy, *The Banks of the Boro* (Dublin, 1875, republished, 1989), 293. Also 'a wooden mug full of milk' is mentioned in T. Ó Criomhthain, *The Islandman* (Oxford, 1937, reprinted 1987), 28.

17 Anon, 'Thady O'Brady'.

Coopers' Ware

18 E.E. Evans, *Irish Folk Ways* (London, 1957, 1979), 96; shows a map of churn types throughout Ireland. This plus his other maps, can be a useful when identifying the origins of illustrated interiors.

19 P.R.O.N.I. Ms. D 288/174; Inventory and valuation of the effects of the [late] Joshua McGeough esq. Drumsill [died 3 September 1817] as taken by J. Jones, appraiser, 'In the Dairy; Meal Barrell . . . 6s. 8d.'

20 Griffiths, *Chronicles*, 242.

21 T.H. Mason, *The Islands of Ireland, Their Scenery, People, Life and Antiquities* (London, 1936, 1938), fig. 101, 66.

22 C. Otway, *Sketches in Erris and Tyrawly* (Dublin, 1841), 29.

23 J. Wright, *The English Dialect Dictionary*, IV, M-Q (London, 1903), 289.

24 'A Dialogue in the Ulster Dialect' in *The Ulster Journal of Archaeology*, VI (1858), 43.

25 Northern Irish quote in Wright, *English Dialect*, 289.

26 A noggin is 'a small mug or cup . . . as a noggin of milk, Irish *naigin*: W.A. Neilson, ed., *Webster's New International Dictionary of the English Language*, II (London, 1934, 2nd edn), 1860, 1658. See also E.E. Evans, *Irish Heritage The Landscape, The People and their work* (Dundalk, 1945), 122; 'a piggin or milking vessel . . . Two smaller stave-built noggins for holding water, milk or porridge.'

27 Evans, *Irish Heritage*, fig. 69, 123. T. O'Neill, *Life and Tradition in Rural Ireland*, fig. 19, 26.

28 C. Kickham, *Knocknagow, or The Homes of Tipperary* (Dublin, 25th edn, 1887), 372: ''Tis many a piggin uv milk she made me dhrink'. Also 'The Dublin Shopkeeper's address to the gentleman White boys' in *Cork Hibernian Chronicle* (2 March 1786), 1; 'they are obliged to drink sour milk out of wooden piggins, and eat stirabout with shells, or pewter, or horn spoons.' quoted by O'Neill, *Life and Tradition*, 26.

29 E.H. Pinto, *Treen and other Wooden Bygones* (London, 1969), fig. 46, 47. Pinto explains that the projecting stave/handle of the piggin was called a lug, hence the Scottish term 'luggie'. He illustrates a Scottish luggie which is similar to the Irish piggin but instead of having parallel sides it tapers inwards towards a narrower base and has a proportionately taller 'lug'. Wright, *English Dialect*, 497

30 Evans, *Irish Heritage*, 72.

31 For example P.R.O.N.I. Ms. 1062/20 Probate Inventory of John Anderson, Bellytrue, county Armagh, dd. 1718; 'In the kitchin ... Dish shelves and dressers with some noggins – 8s.O.' *Mist's Weekly Journal* (England, 1728); Between Dublin and Dundalk, in the house of a principal farmer [of very few possessions]; '3 noggins.' ffolliott, 'The Furnishings of a Palladian House', 87; In ye kitchen: 'two Nogen – Lost by Nancy Robison – paid, one nogen – lost by Nancy Murtagh ... Bought at Mullingar 4 Nogens June 25th 1749.' M. Denham Jephson, *An Anglo Irish Miscellany* (Dublin, 1964), 383; 'Household Possessions of James Upington.' dd. 1769, Mallow, county Cork, 'Six wooden platers. Eight wooden Trenchers, Three piggins.' R. ffolliott, 'An Inventory of Reynella, county Westmeath in 1827' in *The Irish Ancestor*, XII, Nos. 1 and 2 (Dublin, 1980), 12; 'In Laundry and Dairy ... 1 Milk piggin'. Carleton, *Traits and Stories of the Irish Peasantry*, II, 160; 'the dresser with noggins'. W. Hanbidge, *The Memories of William Hanbidge. Aged 93. 1906. An Autobiography* (St Albans, 1939), 26; [at Tinnahinch, county Wicklow] 'in my younger days we got potatoes and milk for breakfast. Our milk in wooden noggins, and other things used for plates were wooden trenchers.'

32 M. Carbery, *The Farm by Lough Gur, the story of Mary Fogarty* (Cork, 1937, 1986), 21. Mary Carbery here uses the term piggin, to describe the containers they used for their lunchtime milk, which held about 1¹⁄₂ pints. Evans, *Irish Folk Ways*, 74. Evans describes and illustrates a county Down noggin which is a mere 3 inches high, suggesting that such a craft had ancient origins and alluding to others from Scandinavia and throughout the Asiatic Arctic region.

33 'Peasant Art in Sweden, Lapland and Iceland' in *The Studio* (London, Autumn, 1910), figs. 103–6. Also G.J. Monson-Fitzjohn, *Drinking Vessels of Bygone Days* (London, 1927), 3. The author is grateful to James Ayres for drawing her attention to these two articles.

34 Heywood, *Philocothonistra or the Drunkard Opened, Dissected and Anatomized* (1635); quoted in Monson-Fitzjohn, *Drinking Vessels*, 27.

The Mether and Madder

35 Extract from a poem by Hugh McGauran, who gave an English translation to Jonathan Swift (1667–1745), 'who used it as a basis for this rendering'; quoted in Frank Murphy ed., *The Bog Irish, Who they were and How they Lived* (Australia, 1987), 16–19. Murphy reproduces five early illustrations of wooden drinking vessels, one described as a madder, 16, 68. Another four-handled square-topped madder is illustrated in the foreground of a 'Station' scene by Carleton, *Traits and Stories of the Irish Peasantry* (Dublin, 1864 edn), opp. 176; 'Paddy Entertaining the Priests'.

36 P. Dinneen, *An Irish-English Dictionary* (Dublin, 1904), 472: '*Meadar*, a churn; an Irish quadrangular drinking-cup of one piece, hollowed by a chisel, a "mether".'

'Mether; An old wooden drinking vessel of a square form with a handle or ear on each side, out of which all the family drank successively. [various spellings; from Ulster – meather, from Mayo – medha, from Wexford – medher]: Wright, *English Dialect*, 97.

A. MacBain, *An Etymological Dictionary of the Gaelic Language* (Sterling, 1911); 'Meader = a hollowed out drinking vessel or churn, from *metur* [middle Irish] and from latin metrum = a measure.'

37 National Museum of Ireland, accession number W.

64/WK 168 is an example of a mether from Killarney (fig. 319). It belonged to the Ó Donoghue family and shows hardly any signs of wear. Apparently made from yew, it has been thoroughly smoke-blackened, presumably from standing in a smoky room for decades. However, when inverted, the underneath is pale and new looking. It shows none of the signs of crystallisation associated with wood-dating from the early 1700s. Instead it appears to have been made during the nineteenth century, to a traditional pattern. Two more in the same collection have incised dates of 1590 and 1793. The fact that many of these drinking vessels are described as made of sycamore, is another indication of their comparatively late date, as this tree was not introduced into Ireland until the seventeenth century according to E. McCracken, *The Irish Woods Since Tudor Times* (Newton Abbot, 1971), 17–8, 20. A mether which apparently dates from the 16th century is illustrated and described in 'The Irish Mether' in *The Dublin Penny Journal* II No. 84 (8 Feb. 1834), 249. It is inscribed 'Dermot Tully 1590'.

38 See Archaeoligical Acquisitions in the Year 1965: 'Two handled Mether' in *The Journal of the Royal Society of Antiquaries of Ireland*, No. 98, pt. 2 (Dublin, 1968), 141–2. For full drawings and third angle projection with structural description, of a two-handled mether from county Monaghan. Two more double-handled examples are photographed in A. Deane, 'Irish "Methers" or Drinking Cups' in *Belfast Municipal Art Gallery and Museum Quarterly Notes*, No. 8 (December 1907), 12–13. The Ulster Museum also houses a sizable collection of methers.

39 A good example of an unusually tall, narrow mether, dug up in a bog in county Clare, and with a single decorated handle, is described and illustrated by G. Macnamara, 'Ancient Wooden Drinking Cup' in *Limerick Field Club Journal*, III, No. 12 (1905–8), 213–16.

40 For illustrations of four-handled methers and further discourse read Pinto, *Treen and Other Wooden Bygones*, pl. 44, 55–6.

41 John Dunton's Letters (originally from the Rawlinson Mss. in the Bodleian Library; Rawl.D. 71). Published as Appendix B in E. MacLysacht, *Irish Life in the Seventeenth Century: After Cromwell* (Dublin, Cork, 1939), 338–9.

42 G. Stokes ed., *Pococke's Tour in Ireland in 1752* (Dublin, 1891), 87.

43 Carleton, *Traits and Stories of the Irish Peasantry*, i, 97. See P. Knight, *Erris in the Irish Highlands* (1836), 104; 'In 1813, I slept at a man's house who had one hundred head of black cattle and two hundred sheep ... no bed but rushes, – no vessel for boiling their meals but one, nor any for drinking milk out of but one, (the *Madder*,) which was handed round indiscriminately to all who sat round the potato-basket ... placed upon the pot for a table'. Quoted in C. Otway, *Sketches in Erris and Tyrawly*, 359.

44 Otway, *Sketches in Erris and Tyrawly*, 28. It is not always clear whether staved or solid Vessels are being referred to; 'The tea was drawn in a broken pot, and drunk from wooden vessels', from M. Doheny, *The Felon's Track* (1848), quoted in D. Corkery, *The Hidden Ireland* (Dublin, 1924, 1986), 26.

45 'P', 'The Ancient Irish Mether' in *The Dublin Penny Journal*, I, No. 38, (16 March 1833), 300.

46 Mr Bell of the Dungannon Museum, quoted in 'Herenagh and Corbe – Meddars – Bracken Cloth' in *The Ulster Journal of Archaeology*, I (1853), 157. Mr Bell writes of the Scots meadars, saying that the 'Scoto-Irish' ones had no fixed relative proportions.

47 Pinto, *Treen and other Wooden Bygones*, 55–6. An-

other account refers to 'medhers of many forms and of every substance, -silver, pewter, and carved wood.' P. Kennedy, *Evenings in the Duffrey* (Dublin, 1869), 229.

    The Hebridean example, and other Scottish relatives of the Irish mether, are discussed by T.J. Tenison, 'On Methers and Other Ancient Drinking vessels' in *The Kilkenny and South-East Ireland Archaeological Society Journal*, Ser. 2, III, pt. 1 (1860), 54–61.

48 A. Deane, 'Irish "Methers" or Drinking Cups' 13; quoted from *The Dublin Penny Journal*. II, (July 1833), 25. The author is grateful for the advice of Dr Caroline Earwood, whose Phd. thesis should be consulted for further early historical information; C. Earwood, *Domestic Wooden Artifacts from prehistoric and Early Historic Periods in Britain and Ireland; Their Manufacture and use*, unpublished Phd. thesis for Exeter University (1990): now published as *Domestic Wooden Artifacts, In Britain and Ireland from Neolithic to Viking Times* (University of Exeter Press, 1993). Also see B. Estridge, *Wooden drinking vessels (Methers)* unpublished B.A. thesis for Dept. of Archaelogy, Queen's University (Belfast, 1983).

49 T. De Bhaldraithe, *English-Irish Dictionary* (Dublin, 1959), 208. M. McGrath ed., 'The Diary of Humphrey O'Sullivan,' *Irish Texts Society*, xxx (London, 1936), 16 April, 1832, 135. For illustrated example see 'P', *Ancient Irish Vessel* in I, No. 41, The Dublin Penny Journal, (16 April, 1833), 328.

50 Evans, *Irish Folk Ways*, 195–8. Evans discusses the issue of bog butter and why it was buried, as well as providing four contrasting drawings of turned or carved solid methers from county Derry and from the Aran Islands. See also 'C. Herenagh and Corbe – Meddars – Bracken Cloth' in *Ulster Journal of Archaeology*, I (1853), 157.

51 18th- to 20th-century examples of lossets/kneading troughs, are usually assembled from separate pieces to form a tray-like area to save flour in (described in ch. 8). However, 'dug-out' examples of lossets of shallow, oval form, were also known in Ireland and were still in use in the 19th century (and in rural France) and were made in the same way as the madders/methers. For, examples see O'Neill, *Life and Tradition*, fig. 20 shows a 'dug-out' kneading trough from county Limerick, from the National Museum of Ireland; Accession number N.M.I. EF103. Also L. Oliver, *Reconnaitre les styles régionaux* (Paris, n.d. c.1980), 79. Fig. 137 shows a solid oval *calebaste* (kneading trough) from Correze, south-west France.

52 P. Dinneen, *Focloir Gaedhilge Agus bearla* (Dublin, 1927); Lámóg = 'a water-pail.' See Pinto, *Treen and other Wooden Bygones*, 55; Pinto suggests that 'Lámhógs' were more common than methers, illustrating an example with *Cead mile fáilte* (A hundred thousand welcomes) engraved on it. He says surviving examples are often of willow, beech, elm and ash (made entirely from a single block, on a reciprocating pole-lathe). Some were apparently exported for use in inns in the west of England and Wales.

53 The term *lámhóg* probably came from the Irish; *lámh* [handle] is a term used by T. Bhaldraithe, *English-Irish Dictionary* (Dublin, 1959), 164. Three 'Irish lámhógs' are illustrated by Pinto, *Treen and other Wooden Bygones*, fig. 44.

Basketry

54 P. Colum *The Poet's Circuits, Collected poems of Ireland* (Portlaoise, 1985), 84–6.

55 See P. Smyth, *Osier Culture and Basket-making, A Study of the Basket-making Craft in South West county Antrim* (Belfast, 1991). Smyth combines descriptions of techniques, with early photographs and oral history, providing a fascinating insight into the commercial manufacture of baskets around the late 19th/early 20th centuries.

56 A. O'Dowd, 'Baskets' in D. Shaw-Smith, *Ireland's Traditional Crafts* (London, 1986), 118. Also see A. O'Dowd, 'Folklife and Folk Traditions' in D. Gillmor ed., *The Irish Countryside* (Dublin, 1989), 154.

57 A. Young, *A Tour in Ireland, with general observations on the state of that Kingdom, made in the years 1776–9*, II, 2nd edn. (London, 1892), 169.

58 Ibid., 41–2.

59 Revd J. Hall, *Tour Through Ireland, particularly the interior and lesser known parts etc.*, 2 vols. I (London, 1813), 277.

60 J. Delaney, 'Baskets and their Uses in the Midlands' in A. Gailey and D. Ó hÓgáin ed, *Gold Under the Furze, Studies in Folk Tradition* (Dublin, 1982), 215.

61 A. Gailey, *Rural Houses of the North of Ireland* (Edinburgh, 1984), 115–19.

62 W. Carleton, 'The Courtship of Phelim O'Toole' in *Six Irish Tales* (Dublin, 1833, 1962), 26.

63 D. Hartley, *Irish Holiday* (London, 1938), 245.

64 For example, see M. Gorman, *Ireland from old Photographs* (Batsford, 1971), fig. 22. The huge subject of wicker chair design and manufacture throughout Ireland is beyond the scope of this volume, but would repay study.

65 Carleton, 'The Courtship of Phelim O'Toole', 26. Straw examples of hen's 'nests are described in the section about straw chairs (pp. 63–8).

66 Hartley, *Irish Holiday*, 245.

67 Kickham, *Knocknagow*, 56–8, 221.

68 Mainly, J. Delaney, 'Baskets and their Uses in the Midlands' in A. Gailey and D Ó hÓgáin ed., *Gold Under the Furze*, 215–27; Evans, *Irish Folk Ways*, 52, 202–10, 231, 234–6, 251; O'Dowd, 'Baskets' in Shaw-Smith, *Ireland's Traditional Crafts*, 118–27; O'Neill, *Life and Tradition*, figs. 47, 49, 50. pp. 30, 41, 69, 74–81, 89; Smyth, *Osier Culture*.